THE TABERNACLE OF DAVID

THE TABERNACLE OF DAVID

Kevin J. Conner

Published by City Bible Publishing
9200 NE Fremont
Portland, Oregon 97220

Printed in U.S.A.

City Bible Publishing is a ministry of City Bible Church, and is dedicated to serving the local church and its leaders through the production and distribution of quality materials.

It is our prayer that these materials, proven in the context of the local church, will equip leaders in exalting the Lord and extending His kingdom.

For a free catalog of additional resources from City Bible Publishing please call 1-800-777-6057 or visit our web site at www.citybiblepublishing.com.

The Tabernacle of David

ISBN 0-914936-94-8
Australian ISBN 0-949829-00-5

THE TABERNACLE OF DAVID
INDEX

PREFACE
FOREWORD AND ACKNOWLEDGEMENTS
FOREWORD TO NEW, REVISED AND ENLARGED EDITION

CHAPTER — PAGE

PART ONE
THE DAVIDIC COVENANT

1. The Use of the Old Testament in the New Testament ... 1
2. The Tabernacle of David – A Word Study ... 7
3. The Historical Setting of Acts 15 ... 21
4. Significance of David's Life Story ... 29
5. The Three Anointings of David ... 33
6. The Davidic Covenant ... 41

PART TWO
THE DAVIDIC KINGDOM TABERNACLE

7. Two Tabernacles Of David? ... 49
8. Building Again The Tabernacle Of David ... 57
9. The Coming In Of The Gentiles ... 63
10. Two Tabernacles Combined In One ... 71

PART THREE
THE DAVIDIC WORSHIP TABERNACLE

11. As in the Days of Old ... 81
12. The Tabernacle of Moses – Sinai to Shiloh ... 83
13. The Ark of the Covenant ... 85
14. Go Back To Shiloh ... 91
15. Captivity and Journeyings of the Ark ... 99
16. The Preparation of David's Tabernacle ... 107
17. The Ark Taken Into the Tabernacle of David ... 115
18. Two Tabernacles – Moses' and David's ... 125
19. Walk About Zion ... 135
20. According to the Commandment of David ... 145
21. Divine Order of Worship ... 151
22. A Brief History of Music ... 159
23. The Order of Singers and Musicians ... 183
24. Psalm Titles and Inscriptions ... 187
25. Musical Instruments in Bible Times ... 195
26. Satan's Counterfeit Musicale ... 213
27. The Power and Evaluation of Music ... 221
28. Tabernacles in the Book of Hebrews ... 229
29. The Priesthood of Zadok ... 235
30. As the Mountains Round About Jerusalem ... 243
31. The Ark Into Solomon's Temple ... 247
32. Theological Truths in the Tabernacle of David ... 251

Conclusion ... 253
Appendix I. Interpretation of "Selah" ... 255
Appendix II. Dancing ... 259
Appendix III. Biblical History of the Ark of the Covenant ... 263
Bibliography ... 269

PREFACE

For nearly 500 years the Church has been coming out of the Dark Ages and has seen a continual unfolding of Truth being restored and new light shining on the Church's pathway.

With the Restoration of Truth and the Church walking in the light of that which has been revealed, it is not some strange thing that the Spirit of God would unfold this revelation of "The Tabernacle of David."

The purpose of God is to have a Church as truly perfected and glorified as Moses' Tabernacle and Solomon's Temple -- yes, even more so.

Therefore, it was essential that God should begin to open up the Scriptures of the Prophets and give a true pattern for the Church to relate to and by which to be fashioned.

Reverend Kevin Conner's grasp of the truth and his masterful portrayal of the pattern brings true balance unto the Church and aids in revealing the final details as the Holy Spirit restores the Church.

Reverend David E. Schoch
Bethany Chapel
6th & Dawson Avenue
Long Beach,
California 90814
U.S.A.

FOREWORD

IN THESE CLOSING DAYS of grace, to those who have eyes to see and ears to hear and hearts to perceive, there is evidently a tremendous move of the Holy Spirit in the world and in the Church as a whole.

The Lord Jesus Christ as Head of the Church is bringing a number of particular emphases to the Church as he seeks, by the Spirit, to complete the preparation of His Church in order "That He might present it to Himself a glorious Church, not having spot, wrinkle, or any such thing; but that it should be holy and without blemish" (Ephesians 5:27).

Various truths are being emphasized in order to mature God's people and lead and guide them into all truth as it is in Jesus. Emphasis is being laid upon the Lordship of Christ, the Ministry of the Holy Spirit, the Church as the Body of Christ, Discipleship, Divine Righteousness, the Fruit and Gifts of the Spirit, Restoration of the Local Church, the Ascension Gift Ministries, as well as other related truths.

Truth must be seen in all of its glorious facets as one related whole.

One of the hardest things to maintain in all these various facets of truth that God is bringing to the Church is BALANCE! It is a point worthy of recognition that heresy in its many forms originated in truth. In fact, it is impossible to have heresy apart from truth. There can never be the counterfeit without the genuine article first. The counterfeit is never the original. The original comes first; the imitation follows. So it is with truth and error. Truth existed before error. Error uses truth to launch out upon, to build upon. What is heresy? Heresy is simply an aspect of truth taken to extreme and pushed out of proportion with the whole body of truth. It creates party-spirit in those that respond to it.

It is because TRUTH is not seen as one related whole that this happens. No one facet of truth can be used to contradict or distort another facet of truth, otherwise heresy begins. Taking one facet of truth and majoring on it alone to the neglect or violation of other truths brings discord; hence, the need for balance in every emphasis that is being brought to the Church today. Balance is harmony, and harmony is having all parts combined in an orderly and pleasing arrangement.

It is in the light of this that we say that another of the great emphasis being brought to the Church in our day is that which pertains to DIVINE ORDER OF WORSHIP.

Man was made to worship. How hard it is for the human heart to accept the fact that it really does not know how to worship God acceptably. Hence, we develop various forms of worship and people congregate to a particular form which appeals to their spiritual, emotional, and mental level. Because of man's ignorance and inability to know of himself how to worship God, as God desires, God has laid down in His Word how, when, where, and why we are to worship Him. The Lord Jesus expressed it clearly by saying that the Father God seeks those who are true worshippers who would "worship Him in SPIRIT and in TRUTH" (John 4:24).

How much there is to be comprehended in that "worship Him in Spirit and in Truth" will be seen in measure in this textbook.

For many years, as the writer has moved around in ministry in conventions, minister's conferences and teaching seminars, as well as many local churches, he has considered the various forms and expressions of worship and longed for some solid foundation in Scripture upon which such could be founded. This desire has found a measure of fulfillment in the study of THE TABERNACLE OF DAVID. A word of explanation as to how this book came to be written would be appropriate here.

It was in the year 1965 that Reverend David Schoch of Bethany Chapel, Long Beach, California, U.S.A. was invited to speak at a Convention in New Zealand. In the course of one of the preaching and teaching sessions he had cause to refer to the Scripture in Amos 9:11 where God said, "In that day will I raise up the Tabernacle of David that is fallen, and close up the breaches thereof; and I will raise up his ruins, and I will build it as in the days of old."

He mentioned in a passing moment that it was not "The Tabernacle of Moses" that God said He would build again as in the days of old, but "The Tabernacle of David." The writer in talking since to Brother Schoch feels that even he did not understand the full significance of that Scripture or his own statement and what would become of it. However, as a prophet of God, he had dropped a Divine "seed." Several of the brethren in New Zealand caught this "seed," the Spirit of God began to water it, and the Scriptures opened up a whole new area of truth pertaining to worship under this title, "The Tabernacle of David."

The writer had the privilege of fellowshipping with these brethren and saw that there was something there. However, there were many questions unanswered and much uncertainty on the subject. This caused many hours of research in the Word of God to be done and thus this book is the result.

For many years the glorious truths of "The Tabernacle of Moses" had been taught and majored upon. But, "The Tabernacle of David," what was this? Why was there need for the "Tabernacle of David?" Did it contradict that which was set forth in the "Tabernacle of Moses?" Can both of them be reconciled? What did it all mean? I did not even know that David had a Tabernacle.

This textbook is the answer to these questions. It is written mainly from a theological point of view, though it also is devotional in many areas. My acknowledgement must go to Brother David Schoch for that "seed" as well as to several unnamed brethren in New Zealand for their contribution to my understanding of this theme. As the Scripture says: "Who then is Paul, and who is Apollos, but ministers by whom ye believed, even as the Lord gave to every man? I have planted, Apollos watered; but God gave the increase. So then neither is he that planteth any thing, neither he that watereth; but GOD that giveth the increase. Now he that planteth and he that watereth are one; and every man shall receive his own reward according to his own labour" (1 Corinthians 3:5-8).

As research was done on this subject, the writer found that this became a most suitable and appropriate title on which to found these things. Such a vast reservoir of truth relative to true worship was found. Numerous Scripture verses and passages opened up by the discovery and use of this "Key of David" (Revelation 3:7).

Since that time the writer has taught many times on "The Tabernacle of David." The response of many of God's people has been enthusiastic and enlightening. It has answered so many questions pertaining to expressions of worship in the Church. Above all, it has given so many a Scriptural foundation for the things which may be done in a New Testament local church order of worship.

In the writer's measure of understanding, one of the richest and greatest avenues of approach to Divine order of worship, whether for Old Testament or New Testament saints, is to be found in a presentation of "The Tabernacle of David."

Let it be reiterated that that which is presented in this book is only a facet of truth. It is not the whole body of truth, but it is another portion of truth upon which the Spirit of God is laying emphasis. It must not be abused, distorted, or overemphasized out of proportion with the whole body of truth. Otherwise, extremism, confusion and disorder results instead of that which it is designed to bring; that is, Divine order of worship. Well may Hebrews 1:1,2 (Amp. N.T.) apply here. "In many separate revelations - each of which set forth a portion of the Truth - and in different ways God spoke of old to (our) forefathers in and by the prophets. (But) in the last of these days He has spoken to us in (the person of a) Son, . . ." "The Tabernacle of David" is one of many of these separate and distinct revelations, setting forth in the Old Testament a portion, a fragment of the truth. It is not the complete body of truth but simply a facet or part to be related to the whole.

Perhaps this presentation under this title may be a whole new area of truth to the reader. It is recommended that the book be read through carefully, along with the Scriptures given, meditating on the thoughts expressed. Read and ponder this subject. Pray that the Spirit of Truth will illuminate the mind and heart to the glories of God as set forth in "The Tabernacle of David."

Paul himself testified before Felix and the Council saying, "But this I confess unto thee, that after the way which they call heresy, so worship I the God of my fathers, believing all things which are written in the LAW and the PROPHETS" (Acts 24:14). Search the Law, the Psalms, and the Prophets, for all that is written therein find their fullest expression in the New Testament through the Gospels, the Acts, and the Epistles in Christ and His Church. Be as the noble Bereans, who, when the Apostle Paul presented the New Covenant Gospel of Christ to them "searched the Scriptures daily, whether those things were so" (Acts 17:11).

The book is primarily meant to be used as a textbook for teaching, and is separated to aid in such a series of studies.

May the Spirit of Truth lead, guide, and direct the reader into this aspect of "Present Truth," (i.e., "The truth that is presently coming to you" 2 Peter 1:12 as pertaining to

"THE TABERNACLE OF DAVID"

Kevin John Conner

Note - Special capitalization and underlining are used throughout by the author for emphasis. All Scripture quotations are taken from the Authorized King James Version of the Bible unless otherwise stated.

FOREWORD TO NEW, REVISED AND ENLARGED EDITION

The author is grateful for the many people who have expressed their thanks and appreciation for the blessings through the truths received in the previous publications of "The Tabernacle of David".

However, over the same time, the author has also received some correspondence having very important and challenging questions regarding the use of the Acts 15 and Amos 9 passages of Scripture as being a valid application of the David order of worship.

Following we note the major questions that have been raised, all of which has caused the author to research more thoroughly certain passages of Scripture used as a base in this text.

The questions run after this manner. Is it right, Scripturally, to even use the expression "The Tabernacle of David"? It is argued that the expressions "The Tabernacle of Moses" and "The Temple of Solomon" are never ever used in Scripture as such. And it is upon this kind of reasoning it is said that "The Tabernacle of David" should not be used either. Is this true?

And again the question is asked, Does the use of "The Tabernacle of David" in Amos 9:8-12 refer to the rebuilding of the lineage, family or house of David. Does the use of the Hebrew word "Sukkah" (hut, or booth) refer to the lowly state of the Davidic kingdom, David's house and throne, or does it refer to the Davidic order of worship established in "The Tabernacle of David", the "ohel" on Mt. Zion?

And yet again, Does the Acts 15 passage along with the Amos 9 passage, quoted by the apostle James, refer to the Gentiles coming into the Davidic order of worship? Or does it refer to the family line of David, his throne and kingdom, as fulfilled in the Lord Jesus Christ? Which is a valid and Scriptural interpretation? Can the "restoration of Davidic worship" be founded on Acts 15 seeing "worship" is not expressly the topic there? Is the Acts 15 passage wrongly used as a "proof text" upon which to build the Tabernacle of David teaching?

And finally, Is "The Tabernacle of David" mentioned by Amos and quoted by James in Acts 15 the same "Tabernacle of David" as mentioned in 2 Samuel 6:17 and 1 Chronicles 16:1? The argument is put forth that there are two different Hebrew words used (ie., "Sukkah" and "Ohel") and therefore they cannot refer to the one and same "tabernacle".

In summary, these questions bring us to the real issue. Does the expression "The Tabernacle of David" refer to THE DAVIDIC KINGDOM or does it refer to THE DAVIDIC ORDER OF WORSHIP? Into what are the Gentiles, along with the Jews, being brought? This is the real issue. How do we interpret the Amos 9 and Acts 15 passages in the light of the 2 Samuel 6 and 1 Chronicles 16 passages? The answers to these questions are certainly vital to a proper interpretation of the Scriptures under consideration.

Commentaries differ on these things. Some emphasize the Gentiles coming into the Davidic Kingdom and thus interpret "The Tabernacle of David" in that way. Others emphasize the Davidic Order of Worship and thus interpret the Scripture as the Gentiles coming into the "The Tabernacle of David" in that way. Some see that BOTH could be involved.

After much more research on the matter and a desire to honestly consider these questions, the author believes that BOTH the Davidic Kingdom and the Davidic Worship is involved.

Some would only emphasize the Davidic Kingdom and totally miss, or reject or neglect the Davidic Worship. Others would only emphasize the Davidic Worship and miss, neglect or reject the Davidic Kingdom. The danger then is overemphasis of expressions of praise and worship; thus the neglect of the basic issue of the Gentiles coming into the Kingdom of the Son of David, Jesus Christ, is missed. Balance is always needed. The author believes that one should not be used at the expense of the other.

In previous editions, the author has clearly shown the coming in of the Gentiles, along with the Jews, into the Kingdom of David. However, the emphasis in the text was more on the Davidic order of worship.

Because of the correspondence received, and the valid questions raised, and after further research, it was felt that further amplification and clarification of these questions be given in this new, enlarged and revised edition.

Chapter Two has been completely re-written dealing very fully with a word study on "tabernacle" in both Old and New Testaments.

A complete new chapter has been written dealing with the dual use of the expression "The Tabernacle of David". In this chapter the distinction between the Davidic Kingdom and the Davidic Order of Worship is seen.

Other material has been added in other portions of the text concerning the relationship of the Davidic kings and the Davidic worship. However, the major part of the book still deals with the Davidic Order of Worship in the tent he raised in Mt. Zion.

For those who have had these genuine questions, the author trusts that this edition will provide the further clarification needed.

Kevin J. Conner
16 O'Brien Crescent
Blackburn South
Victoria 3130
AUSTRALIA

1986

PART ONE
THE DAVIDIC COVENANT

CHAPTERS **PAGE**

1. The Use of the Old Testament in the New Testament 1

2. The Tabernacle of David – A Word Study 7

3. The Historical Setting of Acts 15 21

4. Significance of David's Life Story 29

5. The Three Anointings of David 33

6. The Davidic Covenant 41

Chapter 1

THE USE OF THE OLD TESTAMENT IN THE NEW TESTAMENT

Before launching into a detailed study of the Tabernacle of David, it would be profitable to refer to important principles used in interpreting Scripture, for it is through the discovery and use of these that the truth is to be found. "It is the glory of God to conceal a thing, but the honour of kings is to search out a matter" (Proverbs 25:2).

It should be remembered that the Early Church had no New Testament. Their "New Testament" was to be found in the "Old Testament." Concerning the Old and the New Testaments it has been aptly said:

"The New is in the Old contained,
The Old is in the New explained,
The New is in the Old concealed,
The Old is in the New revealed,
The New is in the Old enfolded,
The Old is in the New unfolded."

Hence, because the New Testament Canon of Scripture had not been written or completed in Early Church history, the Apostles continually appealed to the Old Testament writings for everything that God was doing in their midst.

A. Christ's Opening of the three-fold division of the Old Testament.

Luke 24:26-45. In this passage of Luke's Gospel we find two of the disciples on the road to Emmaeus, sad at heart because of the sufferings and death of the Lord Jesus. Various reports had come to their ears that He had risen and had appeared to certain of the women disciples.

As they discussed the tragic events of the last several days, Jesus Himself drew near and walked with them. They did not recognize Him. Jesus asked them what sad things they were discussing and upon being told, He began to upbraid them for their slowness of spiritual perception. As He continued to walk with them, He expounded unto them the Old Testament Scriptures. Beginning at Moses and continuing on through the Prophets, He expounded, explained, and interpreted the Scriptures to them, teaching them those things concerning Himself. He shewed them that "In the volume of the Book" it was indeed written of Him (Hebrews 10:5-9. Psalm 40:6-8). He had come to do the Father's will and fulfill in Himself the Old Testament Scriptures.

Note the three-fold "opening" that the risen Lord gave to these two disciples.

1. They experienced opened eyes. vs 31.
2. They heard the opened Scriptures. vs 32.
3. They had opened understanding. vs 45.

   The word "opened" means "to open up completely" and is used literally and metaphorically in Scripture.

In verse 44 we have Christ's own three-fold division of the Old Testament . . .

1. The Law.
2. The Psalms.
3. The Prophets.

The Law, the Psalms, and the Prophets are as a "sealed book" until the risen Lord unlocks and breaks the seals. He must open the spiritual eyes. He must break open the Scriptures. He must open the closed understanding. Unless He does, truth in the Old or New Testament will never break forth upon the heart.

The opening of the eyes speaks of the release from religious blindness and spiritual darkness.

The opening of the Scriptures signified the unlocking of the truth therein, which the natural or carnal man can never see.

The opening of the understanding speaks of that light and illumination that comes to the heart in connection with these previous two openings. Paul reasoned with the Jews out of the Scriptures and showed to them how that Jesus of Nazareth was the prophetical and historical fulfillment of them (Acts 17:1-3). The correspondences between these two were evident.

It is the Lamb of God, Jesus Christ, who only can take the Seven Sealed Book (Greek Biblion) as in Revelation and open the seals thereof, giving understanding, not only to John, but also to the Churches (Revelation 5:1-9).

The Apostle Paul, in contrasting and comparing the glories of the Old Covenant and the New Covenant in II Corinthians 3, explained the blindness that settled upon the heart of Jewry as a whole in regard to their Messiah. Their Old Testament Scriptures had foretold the coming of Messiah, His sufferings, and the glory which was to follow, yet blind unbelief settled upon the nation. They could not discover Christ in their own Scriptures because of this blind unbelief. Paul writes:

> "But their minds were blinded; for until this day remaineth the same vail untaken away in the reading of the Old Testament; which vail is done away in Christ. But to this day, when Moses is read, the vail is upon their heart. Nevertheless when it (the heart) shall turn to the Lord, the vail shall be taken away" (II Corinthians 3:14-16).

The tragedy of all this is evident even amongst many of God's people in the Church today. There seems to be a veil upon the heart, a state of spiritual blindness in the reading of the Old Testament.

How many times have believers said, "That is from the Old Testament; there is nothing in the Old Testament for us today, that was all done away in Christ, we only need the New Testament." The Old Testament is looked upon as an historical book only. The writings of the prophets are relegated to natural Israel and thus the Church is robbed of much truth that belongs to it by this type of reasoning.

A genuine turning to the Lord would rend this veil on the heart, and the eyes of our understanding would be enlightened. Then we would see Christ and His Church in the reading of the Old Testament; in the Law, the Psalms, and the Prophets. The Lord, by His Holy Spirit, is opening these books to the Church in a greater way than ever before.

B. Why Study the Old Testament?

Because much of this study of the Tabernacle of David causes us to go to that which is shadowed forth in the Old Testament, it is necessary to understand why we need to study these writings.

Following are a number of reasons why the believer may use the Old Testament Scriptures in searching out that which pertains to this subject.

1. The Tabernacle of David is part of the Scripture that was given by inspiration of God and is profitable for doctrine, reproof, correction, and instruction in righteousness (2 Timothy 3:16).

2. Christ Himself expounded the things in the Old Testament Scriptures concerning Himself in the Law, the Psalms, and the Prophets (Luke 24:26, 27, 44, 45).

3. The things that were written aforetime in the Old Testament were written for our learning that we through patience and comfort of the Scriptures might have hope (Romans 15:4).

4. Jesus Himself came to fulfill the Law and the Prophets (Matthew 5:17, 18).

5. Jesus said that the Law and the Prophets prophesied (Matthew 11:13).

6. The Old Testament prophets spoke of the sufferings of Christ and the glory that should follow. It was revealed to them that their utterances did not just concern their own generation but another (1 Peter 1:10-12).

7. The things which happened in Old Testament history in Israel were for types and ensamples and these things are written for our admonition upon whom the ends of the ages are come (1 Corinthians 10:6, 11).

8. The writer to the Hebrews said, "In the volume of the book it is written of Me," that is, of Christ (Hebrews 10:7. Psalms 40:6-8).

9. The Scripture speaks of "first the natural and afterwards that which is spiritual" (1 Corinthians 15:46, 47), and this is a principle which may well be applied in this study.

10. The Tabernacle of Moses was given as a shadow, a type, a pattern of the eternal, spiritual, and heavenly realities (Hebrews 8:5; 9:23, 24). This is surely applicable also to the Tabernacle of David.

The Tabernacle of David sets forth Divine knowledge and truth in a material tent, in external form. We go back and look at the external form to discover the knowledge and truth hidden therein. The external forms of the Old Covenant may pass away but the knowledge and truth therein, and that which is retained by the New Testament, remains (Romans 2:20. Amp. N.T.).

C. The Use of the Old Testament in the Early Church.

The Book of Acts, as also the whole of the New Testament, reveals what an "opening" the Apostles did receive concerning Christ and His Church as foreshadowed and prophesied of in the Old Testament. Many believers see Christ in the Old Testament, but fail to see the Church in the Old Testament. These cannot be separated. Christ the Head and the Church which is His Body are one. God foretold not only the things concerning Christ but also the things which concern His Body, the Church.

Thus, the Apostles continually appealed to the Law, the Psalms, and the Prophets for all that the Lord, by the Holy Spirit, was doing in their midst.

Following are a number of references taken from the Book of Acts. Each of these show clearly the use the Early Church made of the Old Testament and also how they interpreted many passages therefrom. A close consideration of these passages will show that the New Testament writers became the infallible interpreters of the Old Testament Prophets. They therefore give us safe guidelines to follow as we interpret Old Testament Scriptures in the light of Christ and His Church.

The passages are briefly listed here, with the emphasis being on those persons who wrote the Law, the Psalms, and the Prophets.

1. Acts 1:18-20. The Psalms. David spoke by the Spirit concerning Judas.

2. Acts 2:14-21. The Prophets. Joel foretold the outpouring of the Holy Spirit in the Last Days.

3. Acts 2:22-36. The Psalms. David spoke of Messiah's resurrection, and exaltation to the Father's throne.

4. Acts 3:19-22. The Law. Moses as a Prophet foretold the coming of Christ.

5. Acts 3:23-25. The Prophets. Samuel and all the Prophets that followed him spoke of these days.

6. Acts 4:23-30. The Psalms. David spoke of Messiah in the Psalms.

7. Acts 8: 30-35. The Prophets. Isaiah prophesied of Messiah's sufferings on the Cross.

8. Acts 13:15, 38-41. The Law and the Prophets. The Prophet Habakkuk spoke of God's work in Messiah's times.

9. Acts 10:43. The Prophets. All the Prophets who spoke foretold the sufferings of Christ and the glory to follow.

10. Acts 17:2-3. The Prophets. The Old Testament Scriptures. Paul opened and alledged that Jesus of Nazareth was the fulfillment of the Scriptures (At 2 Corinthians 3:13-16).

11. Acts 28:23-31. The Law and the Prophets. Moses and Isaiah spoke of Christ.

12. Acts 15:15-18. The Prophets. It was the Prophet Amos who prophesied of the Tabernacle of David and the coming in of the Gentiles.

A cursory glance over this brief list of references shows how much insight the early Apostles received and how much they used the Law, the Psalms, and the Prophets. They used these as being prophetic and interpretive of God's movement in their times.

The diagram illustrates the truth of these things and shows how the Old Testament prophets pointed to New Testament times.

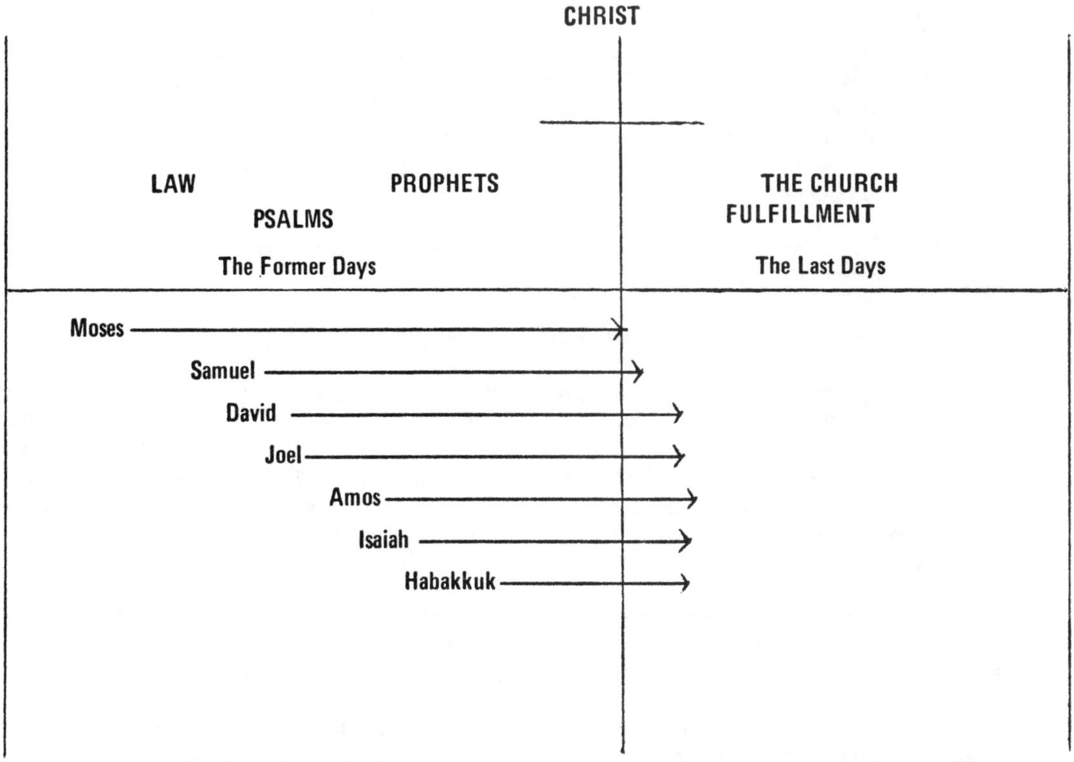

Thus, the whole of the New Testament is a revelation of that which was in the "seed" of the Old Testament. The Gospels, the Book of Acts, the Apostles, the Book of Revelation, abound in quotations, allusions, and interpretive revelation of that which was hidden in the Law, the Psalms, and the Prophets.

There are rivers and streams of truth in the Law, Psalms and Prophets relative to the Tabernacle of David, all of which are confirmed by the New Testament and that "opening" given to the writers thereof.

D. Old Testament Divine Cameos.

Webster's Dictionary defines the word "cameo" as "a gem having two layers with a figure carved in one layer so that it is raised on a background of the other."

The Old Testament provides us with many "cameos." Many things in Old Testament history were actually designed by God to be such. God often asked men to do typically what He Himself would fulfill actually. Please note, this is not to say that these things did not actually take place in the Old Testament. It is simply to say that the historical event was also a typical foreshadowing of that which God would fulfill in Christ and His Church in the New Testament era.

1. Abraham offering Isaac. Genesis 22.

In this chapter we have the account of Abraham being called by God to offer up his only begotten son, Isaac, as a burnt offering on Mt. Moriah. The Father Abraham took his only begotten Son, Isaac, and after three days journey offered him typically on this chosen Mount. Here the redemptive name of Jehovah Jireh – "The Lord will provide" -- was revealed. A ram was offered in the stead of this only begotten son. Hebrews 11:17-19 tells us that Abraham offered up Isaac the son of promise and received him back from the dead in a figure.

Who can fail to recognize this as a Divine cameo? The gem of truth on one layer raised on the background of another is evident. God the Father would in due time offer His Only Begotten Son, Jesus, (John 3:16) on Mt. Calvary in connection with sign of thee days and three nights (Matthew 12:39-40). The Son of Promise would be raised from the dead after that. However, instead of an animal being offered in His stead, as it was for Isaac, He would be offered in the stead of animals, thus abolishing Old Testament animal sacrifices by His sinless, perfect and once-for-all sacrifice.

Thus, God got Abraham to do typically in the Old Testament what He Himself would do actually in the New Testament. This was indeed a Divine cameo!

2. The High Priest Aaron. Exodus 28, 29. Leviticus 8, 9, 16.

Another cameo is that which is represented in the High Priestly ministry of Aaron. Aaron is taken from among men, and ordained for men to offer both gifts and sacrifices for the nation of Israel (Hebrews 5:1-5). In his priestly ministrations, as officiating Sanctuary Priest and Offerer of sacrifice, he shadows forth the ministry of the Lord Jesus Christ. Aaron represented in himself the whole nation of Israel before Jehovah. There was but one High Priest, one Mediator between God and man and all in Israel who would come to God must come to God by Aaron.

Who can fail to appreciate the Divine cameo set forth here? The writer to the Hebrews sets this gem of truth forth on its layer as it is raised on the background of Israel's history, as the other layer. Aaron's ministry pointed to Christ's ministry.

The greater exceeds the lesser in that in the Old Testament, Priest and sacrifice were two separated things, while in the New Testament Christ is both Priest and sacrifice in one Person (Hebrews 7, 8, 9, 10). Christ ministers in the Heavenly Sanctuary, and all who would come to God universally must come to God through Him.

Thus, God got Aaron the High Priest to do typically what His Son as High Priest after the order of Melchisedek would do actually. Another Divine cameo indeed! There are numerous Divine cameos in the Old Testament. Once the principle of Divine cameos is seen, then it opens up the Scriptures in a remarkable way. We have these Divine pictures, "snapshots" within their particular framework, setting forth the truths typically in the Old Testament as they would be fulfilled actually in the New Testament.

3. The Tabernacle of David.

The same is true when it comes to the Tabernacle of David. God took King David and got him to demonstrate actually and typically what He would do actually and spiritually in Christ and the Church.

The Tabernacle of David is another of these Divine cameos. Upon the historical background of David's times there is raised this gem of truth. It has its limited framework, as all Old Testament types do, but within this framework God sets forth much spiritual truth which is carried over into the New Testament Church through the Cross of our Lord Jesus Christ.

Upon these foundation principles of interpretation of Scripture we will now proceed to the exposition of David's Tabernacle.

Chapter 2

THE TABERNACLE OF DAVID
(A Word Study)

There are a number of Scriptures which directly or indirectly speak of or allude to the Tabernacle of David.

The Scriptures presently before us specifically refer to this title. These verses, along with many other directly or indirectly related Scriptures will be considered in our research and word study together.

A. What the Prophet Samuel said.

2 Samuel 6:17, "And they brought in the Ark of the Lord, and set it in His place, in the midst of the Tabernacle that David had pitched for it; and David offered burnt offerings and peace offerings before the Lord." (Also, 1 Chronicles 16:1)

B. What the Prophet Isaiah said.

Isaiah 16:5, "And in mercy shall the Throne be established; and He shall sit upon it in truth in the Tabernacle of David judging, and seeking judgement, and hasting righteousness."

C. What the Prophet Amos said.

Amos 9:11,12, "In that day will I raise up the Tabernacle of David that is fallen, and close up the breaches thereof; and I will raise up his ruins, and I will build it as in the days of old; That they may possess the remnant of Edom, and of all the heathen, which are called by My Name, saith the Lord that doeth this."

D. What Stephen said.

Acts 7:45-47, "...The days of David, who found favour before God, and desired to find a Tabernacle for the God of Jacob. But Solomon built Him a house..."

E. What the Apostle James said.

Acts 15:16,17, "After this I will return, and will build again the Tabernacle of David, which is fallen down; and I will build again the ruins thereof, and I will set it up; That the residue of men might seek the Lord, and all the Gentiles, upon whom My Name is called, saith the Lord, who doeth all these things."

In the FOREWORD to this new, revised and enlarged edition, we noted some of the questions which have been raised concerning this subject. Questions have been raised as to the validity of the use of the expression, "The Tabernacle of David". One of the points raised concerned the use of the preposition "of" in "The Tabernacle OF David". Does "The Tabernacle of David" mean the Tabernacle built by David or indwelt by David? Some say it simply means that David dwelt there, not that he built the place.

Isaiah's prophecy would be applicable, in principle, for those who "make a man an offender for a word" (Isaiah 28:21). In this case it is making a man "an offender for a preposition!"

Webster's Dictionary under "OF" (#7) says it means, "having to do with; relating to; according to; pertaining to; with reference to; concerning, about..." Sometimes the use of the preposition "of" may involve the meaning of "by" or "built by" and other times it may involve the thought of "in which one dwells." Both thoughts are applicable. One example is seen in Ruth 4:11, "...which two did BUILT the house OF Israel."

Thus "Tabernacle of David" can involve that which pertains to, or relates to David, that built by David, or it could also involve the tabernacle in which David dwelt.

While expressions like "Tabernacle of Moses", or "The Temple of Solomon" are not specifically used in Scripture, nevertheless, "Tabernacle of David" is. However, by "The Tabernacle of Moses" is to be understood the Tabernacle that was built by Moses. To use exact Scriptural language we would quote 1 Chronicles 21:29, "The Tabernacle of the Lord, which Moses the servant of the Lord had made in the wilderness..."

"OF the Lord" tells us who dwelt there, while "HAD MADE" tells us who built it.

"The Tabernacle OF the Congregation" refers to the congregation of Israel gathered together to meet the Lord. It was also built by certain of them, yet all gathered together to meet the Lord God, though they did not dwell therein (Exodus 33:7-11).

"The Tabernacle OF the Lord" was built by Moses and other builders, yet "He that built all things is God", for every house is builded by some man (Hebrews 3:1-6). The Lord dwelt in this tabernacle.

The same is true of "The Temple OF Solomon". 2 Chronicles 3:1 says, "Then Solomon began to build the house of the Lord at Jerusalem..." It was not that Solomon dwelt there, but it was the house of the Lord that Solomon built.

Solomon built "the house of the Lord, in which the Lord dwelt". Solomon also built his own house in which he dwelt. The house OF Solomon was both the house he built and the house in which he dwelt (1 Kings 6:1; 7:1; 2 Chronicles 2:1; 8:1).

Hence, on the one hand, when we speak of Tabernacle OF David" we may mean the Tabernacle pitched by David, especially the tent for the Ark of God on Mt.Zion and the accompanying order of priestly ministrations. Then, on the other hand, it may also mean "The Tabernacle OF David" where his throne was, involving his house and his kingdom. Only the context shows which is being referred to, as the following references indicate.

> "...for he had pitched a Tent (ohel) for it at Jerusalem" (2 Chronicles 1:4).
>
> "...set the Ark in the midst of the Tent (ohel) that David had pitched for it" (1 Chronicles 16:1).
>
> "And they brought in the Ark of the Lord, and set it in his place, in the midst of the Tabernacle (ohel) that David had pitched for it" (2 Samuel 6:17).
>
> "The Ark and Israel and Judah abide in tents (sookah)..." (2 Samuel 11:11).

These Scriptures specifically refer to the Ark of God in the Tabernacle of (pitched by) David.

On the other hand, when the Scriptures speak of "Tabernacle of David" it also includes the house that he built and in which he dwelt. BOTH thoughts are consistent with Biblical revelation.

The Lord promised to build David an house (2 Samuel 7). How was the house of David actually built? By David himself and his seed. The house of David was both built by him and indwelt by him, or else, by his successors to his throne (Isaiah 7:13).

"Tabernacle of David", the "ohel" of David in Isaiah 16:5 and the "sookah" of Amos 9:11 along with the "skene" of Acts 15:15-17 speak of the house which David built, in which he dwelt, in which his seed dwelt, thus establishing his kingdom.

When we speak of "The House OF Israel" and "The House OF Judah", we speak of the house that Jacob built, which was the nation of Israel, especially the ten tribes of the northern kingdom and the house of Judah which was the southern kingdom with its three tribes. These houses were built by him and therefore became the houses, nations or kingdoms in which the Israelites lived.

Thus "Tabernacle OF David" involves that which pertains to, or relates to David, that built by David, or that in which David dwelt. David cannot be separated from that which he built for the Lord or that which the Lord built for him.

Further questions have been raised concerning the Hebrew and Greek words translated "tabernacle" in the Authorized Version of the Scriptures.

Can the truth of the Tabernacle of David be fully discovered or limited in its meaning by the use of different Hebrew (or Greek) words?

Does the expression "Tabernacle of David" refer to the tent that David pitched in Zion for a new order of worship around the ark of God? Or, does it speak of the royal house of David and his throne in Mt. Zion? What do the Hebrew words mean when using this this expression? Is it Scriptural and Biblical Hermeneutics to build the concept of a Davidic order of worship on this foundational title, "Tabernacle of David?"

A study of the various Hebrew and Greek words will show that the inter-relatedness of thought as to the word "tabernacle" being "a dwelling place" is consistent. It can refer either to the sacred or secular dwelling places of God or man or creatures.

We consider, first of all, several Old Testament Hebrew words, noting definitions from Strong's Concordance, and other Hebrew/Chaldee Lexicons and Dictionaries.

A. Old Testament Hebrew/Chaldee - Word Definitions

1. OHEL

(a) Strong's Concordance - SC168. OHEL; a tent (as clearly conspicuous from a distance): - Translated as covering, dwelling, dwelling place, home, tabernacle, tent.

(b) Theological Wordbook of the Old Testament - Harris/Archer/Waltke
OHEL; dwelling, home, tabernacle, tent. Ohel, a masculine noun, occurs 340 times and is used for the animal skin or goat's hair (Cant 1:5); dwelling place of nomadic people (Genesis 4:20; 13:5; 18:16; 25:27; etc), shepherds (Jeremiah 6:3), women (Genesis 31:33; Judges 4:17, cf. Isaiah 54:2, warriors (1 Samuel 17:54; Jeremiah 37:10; etc), and cattle (2 Chronicles 14:14)). It is also used for the bridal tent (2 Samuel 16:22).

The word 'ohel' continued to be used for a habitation or home (1 Kings 8:66; 12:16; Psalm 91:10; Judges 19:9), including David's palace (Isaiah 16:5) long after the Israelites had adopted more permanent dwellings.

'Ohel' is figuratively used for the people of Edom (Psalm 83:7), Qedar (Psalm 120:5; Canticles 1:5), Judah (Jeremiah 30:8), Cushan (Habakkuk 3:7) and others.

The "tent of the daughter of Zion" (Lamentations 2:4) is a figure for Jerusalem.

The tabernacle was essentially a tent, composed of two layers of cloth and two layers of skins stretched over a wooden framework (Exodus 27:7,14,15). It is designated as "tent of meeting" (Exodus 33:7-11), as well as "tent of testimony" (Numbers 9:15; 17:22-23, etc).

(c) William Gesenius - A Hebrew and English Lexicon of the Old Testament
Ohel; a tent, fellow-dwellers, family.
Gesenius says of this Hebrew word:

(1) Tent of Nomad - Jeremiah 6:3; 49:29; Song 1:5
- Dweller in tents - Genesis 4:20; 25:27
- Tents of cattle - 2 Chronicles 14:14
- Tent of soldiers - 1 Samuel 17:54
- Tent of pleasure on housetop - 2 Samuel 16:22. Bridal tent, bridal pavilion

(2) Dwelling, habitation - Psalm 91:10
- Habitation of my house - Psalm 132:3; Daniel 11:45
- Habitation or palace of David where throne erected - Isaiah 16:5
- House of wicked - Job 8:22

(3) The Sacred Tent in Worship of God
Referring to the Tabernacle of the Lord which Moses had made. It is called:
- The Tent
- The Tent of meeting of God with His people
- The Tent of the congregation or assembly - Exodus 33:7-11; Numbers 12:5, 10; Deuteronomy 31:14,15
- The Tent of the Testimony - Numbers 9:15; 17:22,23; 18:2 (as contain ing the Ark and Tables of Testimony).
- David erected a tent for the Ark of God in Mt. Zion - 2 Samuel 6:17; 1Chronicles 15:1; 16:1; 2 Chronicles 1:4.
  God went from one tent to another tent - 1 Chronicles 17:5 with 2 Samuel 6:17.

Generally speaking, the OHEL was the exterior cover or coverings of skins which were placed over the proper dwelling or tabernacle framework which Moses made in the wilderness at Mt. Sinai.

(d) Secular Use of OHEL
The following references show how the word OHEL is used in a secular way for a covering, dwelling place or home of man or creatures, or a family, a household.

- The Tents of Shem - Genesis 9:27.
- Abraham, Isaac and Jacob dwelt in tents - Genesis 12:8; 13:3,5; 24:67; 25:27; 31:25,33.

- Israel lived in tents (Exodus 16:16; Numbers 24:6; Deuteronomy 1:27; Joshua 3:14; Judges 7:8; Psalm 78:55; Jeremiah 30:18).
- Tents were also shelters for cattle at times - 2 Chronicles 14:15.
- The heavens are a tabernacle for the sun - Psalm 19:4.
- The Tents of Cushan - Habakkuk 3:7.
- The Tents of Judah - Zechariah 12:7.
- The Tabernacles of Jacob - Malachi 2:12.
- The Tents of Kedar - Psalm 120:5; Song 1:5.
- The Tabernacles of Edom - Psalm 83:6.
- The Tabernacle of Joseph - Psalm 78:67.
- The Tabernacles of Ham - Psalm 78:51.
- The Tents of wickedness - Psalm 84:10.
- The Shepherd's Tent - Isaiah 38:12.
- The Tabernacles of robbers - Job 12:6.
- The Tabernacles of bribery - Job 15:34.

(e) Sacred Use of OHEL

Of the several hundred uses of this Hebrew word,over 150 references pertain to the Tabernacle of the Lord, the Tabernacle which Moses built. It was called:

(1) The Tabernacle of the Lord - 1 Kings 1:39; 2:28-30; 2 Chronicles 1:5. This "tabernacle" was the TENT over the STRUCTURE of boards.

- A covering (ohel) upon the tabernacle (mishkan) - Exodus 26:7.
- The Tabernacle - Exodus 26:9.
- The tent (ie., covering) - Exodus 26:11,12,13,14,36.
- The tabernacle of the congregation - Exodus 27:21; Leviticus 1:7; 24:3; Numbers 2:17,28; 4:25; 8:19.
- The tabernacle of witness - 2 Chronicles 24:6; Numbers 17:7,8; 18:2.
- The tent of meeting, which Moses the servant of the Lord had made in the wilderness - 2 Chronicles 1:3.

(2) The Tabernacle of the Congregation

It seems also that there was A TENT (Ohel) of the Congregation where Moses met the Lord before the Tabernacle proper was set up - Exodus 33:7,8,9,10,11.

(3) The Tabernacle of David

The tent or tabernacle that David pitched for the Ark of the Lord was 'ohel' and was God's dwelling place by reason of the Ark.

- The Tabernacle of David - 2 Samuel 6:17.
- The Tent that David had pitched for the Art - 1 Chronicles 15:1; 16:1.
- The Lord had moved from tent (ohel) to tent (ohel) - 1 Chronicles 17:5.
- The Lord had walked in a tent (ohel) and a tabernacle (mishkan) - 2 Samuel 7:6.
- David pitched a tent at Jerusalem for the Ark - 2 Chronicles 1:4.
- David will have someone sit in his throne in the Tabernacle of David - Isaiah 16:5.

SUMMARY:

OHEL then is used of a covering, a dwelling place, a home, a tabernacle or tent for cattle, for man, for families or for God Himself. It has both secular and sacred uses as a dwelling place for either man or for God.

The very fact that the ARK of the Covenant, where the Lord dwelt between the cherubims (2 Samuel 6:2), was placed in the Tabernacle of David (2 Samuel 6:17) shows that the "ohel of David" was God's house, God's dwelling place, God's home. The Ark was not placed in David's house, as it had been in Obed-edom's house for three months. It was placed in a tent (ohel) that had been pitched in Mt. Zion. Here the Davidic order of worship was inaugurated, and Zion took on a more sacred meaning from here on, both ecclesiastically and politically.

2. MISH-KAN

(a) Strong's Concordance - SC4908
Another Hebrew word generally translated as "tabernacle" is "mish-kan". Strong's says "MISH-KAN; a residence (including a shepherd's hut, the lair of animals, figuratively, the grave; also the Temple); specifically the Tabernacle (properly, its wooden walls): - Translated, dwelleth, dwelling, habitation, tabernacle, tent.

(b) William Gesenius - Hebrew-Chaldee Lexicon to the Old Testament
Gesenius says of this word "Mish-kan" the following:

(1) Habitation, dwelling-place, as of men (Job 18:21; Psalm 87:2), of animals (ie., den, Job 39:6), of God (ie., Temple, Psalm 46:5; 84:2; 132:5).

(2) Specially a tent, a tabernacle - Song 1:8; especially the holy tabernacle of the Israelites - Exodus 25:9; 26:1; the Tabernacle of the testimony - Exodus 38:21; Numbers 1:50,53; 10:11.

(c) Secular use of MISH-KAN
As with OHEL, so with MISH-KAN. Mish-kan has both secular and sacred uses as a tent or tabernacle. Examples of secular use of the word are seen in:

- The Tabernacle of Korah - Numbers 16:24,27.
- The Tabernacles of Israel - Numbers 24:27.
- The Shepherd's Tents - Song 1:8.
- Dwelling-places - Jeremiah 30:18; 51:30; Habakkuk 1:6; Job 21:28.
- Habitations - Isaiah 54:2; 22:16; Psalm 78:28.

(d) Sacred Use of MISH-KAN
Of the approximately 136 uses of this word, over 113 uses speak of the Tabernacle of the Lord which Moses had built to Divine instructions. Exodus 25:9—40 chapters use this word numerous times. Also note Leviticus 8:10; 15:31; 26:11; Numbers 1:50-53; 3:23-38. It is translated as:

- The Lord's Tabernacle - Joshua 22:19.
- The Tabernacle of Shiloh - Psalm 78:60.
- The Tabernacle of the Lord - 1 Chronicles 21:29.
- Thy Tabernacles - Psalm 43:3; 84:1; 132:7.
- The Habitation of the Lord - 2 Chronicles 29:6.
- The place where Thine honour dwelleth - Psalm 26:8.
- The Tabernacles of the Most High - Psalm 46:4.
- The Dwelling place of Thy Name - Psalm 74:7.
- An Habitation of the mighty God - Psalm 132:5.

Note - The Tabernacle of David is never called "Mishkan" because it was only a tent and not a wooden structure.

(e) OHEL and MISH-KAN

It is worthy of note to see the connection between "ohel" and "mish-kan" in a number of passages. In relation to the Tabernacle of the Lord which Moses built, BOTH words are used and translated either as "tent" or "tabernacle" generally. However, the tent (ohel) was the covering over the tabernacle (mishkan), or the wooden structure, but both connected as the Lord's Tabernacle.

- The Lord had walked in a tent (ohel) and a tabernacle (mishkan) - 2 Samuel 7:6.
- The Tabernacle (mish-kan) and his Tent (ohel) - Exodus 35:11.
- For the Tent (ohel), over the Tabernacle (mish-kan) - Exodus 36:14.
- Spread the Tent (ohel) over the Tabernacle (mish-kan) - Exodus 40:19.
- He forsook the Tabernacle (mish-kan) of Shiloh, the Tent (ohel) which He placed among men - Psalm 78:60.

Thus the OHEL was the covering Tent over the MISH-KAN, or the wooden structure called 'Tabernacle'. One was a tabernacle over the tabernacle.

SUMMARY: -

MISH-KAN then is also used for a dwelling, a habitation, whether for animals, for man, or for God Himself. It also has natural and spiritual or secular and sacred uses. However, the predominant use is of the Lord's Tabernacle, especially that which Moses built to Divine pattern at Mt. Sinai. Mishkan is the place where God resided in Old Testament times.

3. SOOK-KAH (Or Sukkah)

Another Hebrew word translated "Tabernacles" is SOOK-KAH. We note definitions of the word.

(a) Strong's Concordance - SC 5521

Strong says "SOOK-KAW"; feminine of SC 5520(SOKE; a hut, as of entwined boughs; also a lair:- Translated covert, den, pavilion, tabernacle); a hut or lair:- Translated booth, cottage, covert, pavillion, tabernacle, tent.

(b) William Gesenius - Hebrew-Chaldee Lexicon to the Old Testament

Gesenius says of this word "Sook-kah" the following:

(1) A booth, a cot, made of leaves and branches interwoven - Jonah 4:5; Job 27:18; Isaiah 4:6.
The Feast of Tabernacles, the Feast of Booths of branches - Leviticus 23:34; Deuteronomy 16:13.
    - The Tabernacle (or Booth) of David - Amos 9:11.
    - Tents of curtains - Leviticus 23:43; 2 Samuel 11:11; 22:12.
    - Habitation of God - Psalm 18:11; Job 36:29.

(2) A booth for cattle - Genesis 33:17.

(3) The lair of lions - Job 38:40.

(c) Secular Use of SOOK-KAH

As with OHEL and MISH-KAN, so with SOOK-KAH. This Hebrew word also has natural and spiritual application. It is used of secular and sacred, for both man and God.

- Booths for men cattle and man - Genesis 33:17; Job 27:18;Jonah 4:5.
- Booths for a lion in his lair - Job 38:40.

• Tents for Israel and Judah - 2 Samuel 11:11.
• Pavilions for the Kings of Israel - 2 Samuel 22:12; 1 Kings 20:12,16; Psalm 31:20.
• A Cottage - Isaiah 1:8.

(d) Sacred Use of SOOK-KAH
Sook-kah was also used in relation to sacred things for God and His people.

• The Feast of Tabernacles in the seventh month was the Feast of Booths, most joyful of all the Festivals of the Lord - Leviticus 23:34; Deuteronomy 16:13,16; 31:10; 2 Chronicles 8:13; Ezra 3:4.
Booths - Leviticus 23:42,43; Nehemiah 8:15-17; Zechariah 14:16,18,19. Tabernacles month was the most sacred month in Israel.

• The heavenly habitation of God is also SOOK-KAH, His booth - Job 36:29; Psalm 18:11.

• God will place his cloudy pillar of fire fand glory on the tabernacle (booth) in Mt. Zion - Isaiah 4:6. Note - The glory-cloud of fire was once on Mt. Sinai and the Tabernacle of the Lord that Moses built. Now it is on Mt. Zion. This signifies a transfer of glory and presence to this tabernacle (Sook-kah).

• Uriah said that "The ARK, as well as Israel and Judah were in tents (booths)" and so reasoned he would not go to his tent that night - 2 Samuel 11:11. Note - The Ark was placed in OHEL (2 Samuel 7:1,2; 6:17), yet this same tent is here called SOOK-KAH. The Tent was a Booth!

• God promised that He would build again the Tabernacle (Sook-kah, Booth) of David that was fallen down - Amos 9:11. Most expositors see in this a Messianic prophecy which was taken up by James in Acts 15:15-18 with the coming in of the Gentiles in Christ's Kingdom. It therefore has spiritual import.

• A counterfeit religious Tabernacle is the Tabernacle of Moloch, which, Strong defines (SC5522, SIK-KOOTH), as, Siccuth your king, an idolatrous booth; translated, Tabernacle - Amos 5:26.

SUMMARY: -
SOOK-KAH therefore also has both natural and spiritual applications. As a temporary dwelling place, a booth or tabernacle, it is used for animals, for man, and for God's dwelling place in the heavens which are to pass away before the eternal new heavens and earth are brought in.

It will be seen then that these three Hebrew words have both secular and sacred applications. These dwellings, dwelling-places, habitations, tents or tabernacles could be used by animals, by man or by the Lord Himself. It is WHO lives in such that determines whether it is sacred or secular in thought.

In relation to "Tabernacle of David" we have the following thoughts.

1. The TENT or TABERNACLE that David pitched in Zion for the sacred Ark of the Lord was OHEL, or a covering, a dwelling place, or home for the Ark until the Temple was built by Solomon (1 Chronicles 15:1; 16:1; 2 Chronicles 1:4; 2 Samuel 6:17). Here the priests ministered before the Lord.

2. The TENT or TABERNACLE of David would have someone to sit upon the throne judging righteous judgment in due time. This tent was OHEL (Isaiah 16:5).

3. The TABERNACLE of David that had fallen down and was in ruins would be built again and the heathen would come to the Lord in relation to this Tabernacle. This Tabernacle was the SOOK-KAH or BOOTH of David (Amos 9:11).

The Tabernacle of David is never referred to as MISH-KAN, because it was simply a tent, not a wooden structure as was the Tabernacle of the Lord built by Moses. However, although the Tent or Tabernacle pitched by David in Mt. Zion is ohel and not mish-kan, yet there was a new order of worship established there. In due time this was incorporated into the Temple order and this house of the Lord as built by Solomon. The pattern for the Temple order given by the Spirit to King David and the Tent or Tabernacle of David was prepatory to this Temple order.

The Tabernacle of David was but a temporary dwellingplace for the Ark of the Covenant of the Lord until the Temple, the more permanent house was built.

B. New Testament Greek - Word Definitions

We come now to a consideration of the New Testament Greek words. The New Testament spoke of these Old Testament Hebrew dwelling places. It will be seen that there are several related Greek words, interpreting these Old Testament words, yet the basic thought is that of a dwelling place, a habitation, a place of residence. These words are also applied to God and to man.

1. SKENE

(a) Strong's Concordance - SC4633
SKENE; apparently akin to SC 4632 and 4639; a tent or cloth hut (lit. or fig.):- Translated habitation, tabernacle.

(b) Vine's Expository Dictionary
SKENE; akin to SKENOO, to dwell in a tent or tabernacle, and is rendered "habitations" in Luke 16:9, AV., (RV, "tabernacles"), of the eternal dwelling places of the redeemed. Means "a tent, booth, tabernacle." It is used of: Tents or dwellings - Matthew 17:4; Mark 9:5; Luke 9:23; Hebrews 11:9. Let us make three tabernacles. Abraham, Isaac and Jacob lived in tabernacles.

(1) The Mosaic Tabernacle - The Tabernacle of Witness - Acts 7:44; Hebrews 8:5; 9:1,8,21, tent of meeting, tabernacle of the congregation; the outer court, Hebrews 9:2,6; the inner sanctuary, Hebrews 9:3.

(2) The heavenly prototype, the true Tabernacle - Hebrews 8:2; 9:2,3,6,8,11, 21; Revelation 13:6; 15:5; 21:3 (of its future counterpart).

(3) The eternal abode of the saints, eternal habitations - Luke 16:9.

(4) The Temple at Jerusalem, as continuing the service of the Tabernacle - Hebrews 13:10.

(5) The house of David, ie., metaphorically of his people. Build again the Tabernacle of David that is fallen - Acts 15:16.

(6) The portable shrine of the god of Moloch. The Tabernacle of Moloch - Acts 7:43 with Amos 5:26.

2. SKENOPEGIA

Strong's defines this word as follows in SC 4634: SKENOPEGIA; from SC4636 (from SKEOS, from SC4633, a hut or temporary residence. ie., (fig.) the human body (as the abode of the spirit),:- tabernacle, and, from SC4078, PEGNUMI, a probable form of a primitive verb (which in its simplest form occurs only as an alternative in certain tenses), to fix("peg"), ie., (spec.) to set up (a tent):- pitch), the Festival of Tabernacles (so called from the custom of erecting booths for temporary homes):- tabernacles.

The Jews Feast of Tabernacles was nigh at hand - John 7:2.
Called the Feast of Ingathering in Exodus 23:16; 34:22.
Called the Feast of Tabernacles or Booths in Leviticus 23:34; Deuteronomy 16:13,16; 31:10; 2 Chronicles 8:13; Ezra 3:4 with Nehemiah 8:14-18. It was a reminder to them that their fathers dwelt in these in the wilderness journey.

Thus the Hebrew SOOK-KAH becomes SKENOPEGIA in Greek. The dominant thought is a temporary dwelling place, a temporary home.

3. SKENOPOIOS

Strong's defines SKENOPOIOS, SC4635, from SC4633 and 4160, a manufacturer of tents:- tentmaker. Used in Acts 18:3. Paul was a tentmaker with Aquilla and Priscilla.

4. SKEENOS

Strong's defines SKEENOS, from SC4633; a hut or temporary residence, ie., (fig) the human body (as the abode of the spirit):- tabernacle. 2 Corinthians 5:1,4.

5. SKEENOO

(a) Strong's (SC4637) defines SKEENOO, from SC4636; to tent or encamp, ie. (fig.), to occupy (as a mansion) or(spec.) to reside (as God did in the Tabernacle of old, a symbol of protection and communion:- dwell.

The WORD was made flesh and dwelt (lit. tabernacled) among us - John 1:14.
The Lamb shall dwell (lit. tabernacle) with them - Revelation 7:15.
Those that dwell in heaven - Revelation 12:12; 13:6.
God will dwell (tabernacle) with His people - Revelation 21:3.

(b) Vine's says this means "to spread a tabernacle over", "to pitch a tent".

6. SKEENOMA

(a) Strong's, SKENOMA, from SC 4637; an encampment, ie. (fig.), the Temple (as God's residence), the body as the tenement for the soul: – tabernacle.

(b) Vine's – (SC 4638) defines SKEENOMA, as a booth, or tent pitched (akin to SKENE), is used of the Temple as God's dwelling, as that which David desired to build, Acts 7:46 (RV, "habitation", AV, "tabernacle"); metaphorically of the body as a temporary tabernacle (2 Peter 1:13,14).

Tabernacle for God – Acts 7:46.
Tabernacle for man – 2 Peter 1:13,14.

(c) The New International Dictionary of New Testament Theology, Colin Brown (Vol. 3, pp. 811-812). In dealing with the Greek word translated Tent or Tabernacle, Brown has this to write:

In the LXX skene and skenoma are used synonymously, although the former word is found five times more frequently than the latter. Generally they render 'ohel (a pointed tent), sometimes miskan (dwelling), and on occasion sukkah (a matted booth, shed or hut).

The tabernacle (LXX, skene, skenoma) is never called sukkah but 'ohel or 'ohel mo'ed ("tent of meeting", the appointed place where God meets His people, cf. Exod. 36:26; Josh. 6:24) or sometimes miskan (the place where God resides).

Colin Brown in commenting on The Lucan writings, in Acts 15 says: "As he summarized the findings of the Jerusalem council (Acts 15:13-21), James appealed to Amos 9:11-12 (LXX). He recognized the rebuilding of David's fallen dwelling (skene, possibly alluding to a matted hut in which he lived or held audience when on military expeditions) in the resurrection and exaltation of Christ and the rise of the church as the new Israel. Precisely because of this restoration, Gentiles were seeking the Lord (Acts 15:17-18); the Gentile mission was therefore not illegitimate (Acts 15:19). (Emphasis author's)

Colin Brown emphasizes the thought of the Gentiles coming into the church which is the new Israel on the basis of Christ's resurrection and exaltation. He interprets David's tabernacle as David's fallen dwelling place used in his military battles.

IN SUMMARY:

These Greek words are all rooted in the idea of a dwelling place, either for God or man, either temporary or eternal, either earthly or heavenly.

The truth of the Hebrew words as also these Greek words is certainly, first of all, fulfilled in the Lord Jesus Christ. He is God's TENT (Ohel). He is God's TABERNACLE (Mish-kan). He is God's BOOTH (Sook-kah). He is God's HABITATION, the Word tabernacled among us (Skene). He is the fulfilment of the Tabernacle that Moses built. He is the fulfilment of the Tabernacle that David pitched. He is God's dwelling place. The fulness of the Godhead bodily dwells in Him (Colossians 1:19; 2:9; John 1:1-3, 14-18). He took upon Himself a human body, a human tabernacle, and "pitched His tent amongst us". This body never saw corruption and now He lives in the power of an endless life since His resurrection, eternally God's dwelling place.

In bringing our chapter to its conclusion we note the hermeneutical principles involved in our word study. The suitability of "The Tabernacle of David" to express both the concept of the Davidic order of Worship as well as the concept of the Davidic Kingdom has to do with hermeneutics.

Does the phrase "The Tabernacle of David" adequately express the intended meanings of the Hebrew and Greek words? The answer is in the positive.

Two basic hermeneutical principles have been used here. i.e.,

1. The New Testament interprets the Old Testament

If the New Testament interprets the Old Testament, then correct interpretation of the Old Testament must be based on the New Testament. If this is so, then we commence with the New Testament and consider its language. It is a recognized fact that the New Testament writers are the infallible interpreters of the Old Testament prophets. Though written in Greek, the New Testament writers were Hebrew in thought and concept and, under the inspiration of the Holy Spirit, would use the correct words to convey to us what was in the mind of the Lord.

2. The Context Principle

In our word study we have used the Context Principle. The Context Principle not only involves verse but also passage context, Testament context and includes in its use the whole-Bible-context.

The great gap to be bridged is the linguistic gap. Because Bible believing Christians accept the "plenary-verbal" inspiration of the Scriptures, we accept the fact that the very words and thoughts of Scripture in the original languages were inspired by the Holy Spirit.

Of the Greek words that are used to expressed the concept of "tabernacle" in the New Testament (as translated primarily from the Septuagint translation of the Hebrew Scriptures), only one word is used to speak of both the Tabernacle of Moses and the Tabernacle of David. This word, as noted, is "Skene".

The New Testament writers, though writing in Greek, were mainly Hebrew believers. They did not make any distinction between the sacred or the secular. They used the same word to express both making no distinction. Only the gramatical use of the word tells us which tabernacle is being referred to.

Whether speaking of "The Tabernacle of Moses", or "The Tabernacle of David", or the heavenly Tabernacle, or even "The Feast of Tabernacles", the same root Greek word is used for all without distinction. This in itself is significant. Had there been cause to distinguish them then distinction certainly would have been made.

If the New Testament writers made no distinction by the use of different Greek words from the different Hebrew words, then that is sufficient reason for us to accept. For, it has been clearly proven that even all the different Hebrew words basically have the same meaning, ie., a dwelling place, whether secular or sacred!

In the light of this, Acts 15 and Amos 9 passages must be considered in the light of verse, passage, book, Testament and, most importantly, the whole-Bible-context. Only by an examination of the concept of "The Tabernacle of David" through the total Bible will we come to a proper interpretation of the passages under consideration.

Hermeneutically speaking, we do not use the Old Testament to interpret the New Testament, but we New Covenant believers use the New Testament to interpret the Old Testament, passing all to and through the cross. The cross is the key! Why then is there need to make distinction of the use of different Old Testament Hebrew words on "tabernacle" when the New Testament writers themselves did not do so?

Old Testament Hebrew	New Testament Greek
1. Ohel	1. Skene
2. Mishkan	2. Skene
3. Sookah	3. Skenopegia

"The Tabernacle of David" is clearly a Scriptural expression. It pertains to all that David was and all that he did. It will be seen that it truly involves BOTH the Davidic KINGDOM as well as the Davidic WORSHIP order he established in Mt. Zion.

There have been many great books and expositions written concerning "The Tabernacle of Moses" and this area of Scripture is much more familiar to God's people in general. But the Scriptures concerning that which relates to "The Tabernacle of David" brings a whole area of truth before the believer. It opens up so many, many verses and passages in the Bible that seemed to have had no real significance until this expression was brought to our attention. Therefore, "What saith the Scriptures" about this Tabernacle?

We present a summary diagram of the major facts of our word study on "Tabernacle".

SUMMARY DIAGRAM OF WORD STUDY

OLD TESTAMENT	OLD TESTAMENT	OLD TESTAMENT	OLD TESTAMENT
TABERNACLE OF THE LORD MISH-KAN	TABERNACLE PITCHED BY DAVID – OHEL	TABERNACLE OF DAVID OHEL	TABERNACLE OF DAVID SOOKAH
Tabernacle of the Lord built by Moses at the high place in Gibeon (1 Chron. 16:39; 2 Chron: 3-6,13; 1 Kings 3:4,5) Zadok & priests offered offerings morning and evening at this tabernacle (1 Chron. 16:40) Some singers & musicians placed here by David (1 Chron. 16:41,42)	David prepared a place for the Ark of God. David pitched a Tent for the Ark of God at Mt. Zion at Jerusalem. (2 Sam. 6:17-19; 1 Chron. 15-16). David placed certain Priests and Levites there as singers and musicians to minister before the Ark of God daily. Davidic order of worship was established in Mt. Zion. The Ark of God was in this Tent. God's Throne in earth. Priestly Ministry.	David would have some one of his seed to sit in the throne, in the Tent, judging just and righteous judgment in mercy and truth. The throne of David was in this Tent (Isaiah 16:5). Kingly Ministry.	The Lord will build again the Booth of David that was fallen down, and in ruins. He would raise it up as in the days of old. The remnant of Edom and heathen would be possessed. The name of the Lord would be called upon them. <u>Note</u> – Amos 9:11, 12. <u>Note</u> – 2 Samuel 11:11. The Ark of God is spoken of also as being in "sookah" (a booth).

NEW TESTAMENT
TABERNACLE OF DAVID SKENE
The Lord will build again the Tabernacle of David (Skene) that is fallen down. He will raise it up from its ruins. The Gentiles will come into it. His Name would be called on them. They would call on the Name of the Lord (Acts 15:15-18). James said this was the fulfilment of what Amos prophesied. Jews & Gentiles together in Messiah's Tent are Kings and Priests unto God. The Order of Melchisedek

Chapter 3

THE HISTORICAL SETTING
(ACTS CHAPTER 15)

A brief analysis of Acts 15 is necessary at this time, because it is under this occasion that that which pertains to The Tabernacle of David is specifically introduced for us by the New Testament writer, Luke, and more particularly by the Apostle James.

It was about the year A.D. 50-51 in Early Church history when the events in the historical setting as seen in Acts Chapter 15 took place. The Lord Jesus Christ, according to His promise, was building His Church. Of course, the full revelation of the truth of the Church as the Body of Christ had not yet been seen by the Apostles or the believers as a whole.

About 18 years earlier (A.D. 33) the Lord Jesus had poured out His Spirit upon the Jew, baptizing them into the Church which is His Body (Acts 2:1-4). Then again about 8 to 10 years later (A.D. 41) the Lord had poured out His Spirit upon the Gentiles in the house of Cornelius, baptizing them into the same Body (Acts 10-11). Peter had been the instrument in both accounts to use the Keys of the Kingdom of Heaven to let both Jew and Gentile into the Kingdom by the Door of Faith, as the Lord had promised (Matthew 16:15-19).

However, the revelation that the Jew and the Gentile were in the one Church, the one Body of Christ, had not yet fully dawned upon the early Apostles. It remained for the Apostle Paul to declare this fact. Thus in 1 Corinthians 12:13, he wrote saying, "For by one Spirit are we all baptized into one body, whether we be Jews or Gentiles, whether we be bond or free; and have been all made to drink into one Spirit." The Apostle Paul had stepped into the Door of Faith which had been opened unto the Gentiles (Acts 14:27) and became the great Apostle to the Gentiles.

As was Paul's consistent pattern of approach, he went always to the Jewish Synagogues first, or, "to the Jew first" (Romans 1:16) taking the Gospel of Christ. A study of these Scriptures in Acts confirms this fact. Read Acts 13:5, 15; 14:1; 17:1; 18:5; 19:8; Romans 1:13-16; 2:9-10; 10:12.

After going to the Jew first, Paul turned then to the Gentiles, as this was his distinctive ministry. Especially after the Jews rejected the Gospel of Christ, and judged themselves unworthy of eternal life. Read Acts 13:46; 28:25-29; Romans 15:9-18, 27; 16:4. Acts 9:15.

With the increase in opposition from the Jews, Paul was driven more and more to the Gentiles with the Gospel. The Gentiles responded to the Gospel of the Grace of God. This provoked the Jew to jealousy, which was God's intention as foretold by their own prophets (Romans 10:19-21; Isaiah 65:1,2).

The problem at the time of the account in Acts 15 was the conflict over the thousands of Jewish believers and the thousands of Gentile believers coming into the Church of the Lord Jesus Christ.

It must be remembered that the Early Church was in the great transitional period, emerging out of the Old Covenant with its Laws, Ceremonials, and all that gendered to bondage, into the New Covenant with its liberties in Christ. It looked as if the whole of the Early Church would be rent into two factions, two Churches -- a Jewish Church and a Gentile Church, thus dividing the Body of Christ.

A. THE PROBLEM - verses 1-5.

In this section of the chapter under consideration we find that certain men had come out of Judea and had been travelling around the Churches of the Gentiles. Their contention was basically over two main things.

1. The Gentiles should be circumcised.

This was the Seal of the Abrahamic Covenant (Genesis 17) and had been confirmed under the Mosaic Covenant (Exodus 12:43-50). Generally, Gentile strangers or proselytes to the Jewish faith only were able to enter into Covenant relationship with God by the rite of or the Covenant of Circumcision (Acts 7:8).

2. The Gentiles should keep the Law of Moses.

This involved Moral, Civil and Ceremonial Laws pertaining to the Mosaic Covenant.

Their contention was that the Gentiles must do these things along with believing in Christ in order to be saved. It was Moses on the one hand and Christ on the other hand. It was a mixture of faith and works, Law and Grace, Moses and Jesus, the Old Covenant and the New Covenant.

Paul and Barnabas, who had been especially sent to the Gentiles by the Church at Antioch (Acts 13:1-4) had much dissension and disputation with these Judaizing teachers.

It was finally decided upon by the brethren that the parties involved should go up to Jerusalem, back to the Local Church from whence these brethren had come troubling the Churches of the Gentiles.

Jerusalem was the first Church and had the original Apostolic government of the Twelve Apostles there, hence this was the only place where they could gather in order that the issue might be settled.

Passing through the various cities enroute, they declared to the Churches the conversion of the Gentiles and there was great joy to all the brethren.

On their arrival in Jerusalem, they were received by the Apostles, the Elders, and the Church as a whole. Paul and Barnabas declared to the Church in general what God had wrought amongst the Gentiles. The points of contention raised by the Sect of the Pharisees were then brought before the Apostles, the Elders, the Church.

B. THE COUNCIL - verses 6-21.

A temporary Council convened, consisting of the Apostles and the Elders to consider this matter. There was much disputation. Undoubtedly, the arguments for and against were presented. The question was a great doctrinal issue. It really involved the conflict between the Old Covenant Church and the New Covenant Church, or, Law and Grace. How could the Circumcised and Uncircumcised be reconciled in one Body? The problem between flesh and spirit, ritual law and spiritual law was evident. Was salvation with circumcision, or without circumcision? Could one be saved without Law or only with Law?

Paul and Barnabas, circumcised Hebrews, disputed with the Judaizing teachers, legalists, mixtures of Law and Grace, having Christ in one hand and Moses in the other hand. The Apostles stood against this "leaven of legality" which was being implanted in the Churches of the Gentiles.

There was strong dissension, or, "standing up against" and much disputation as the matter was debated. The dissension and disputation eventually settled itself down into four main authorities, Apostolic authorities, these being Peter, Barnabas and Paul and finally James.

Let us consider what their verdict is as given in the Jerusalem Council.

1. The Apostle Peter - Apostle of the Circumcision (Acts 15:7-11, Galatians 2:7-8).

The Apostle Peter is the first main speaker here. He recounted to all how the Lord Jesus chose him to go first to the Gentiles that they should hear the Gospel by his mouth and believe unto salvation. This was in fulfillment of the prophetic word of Christ to him as in Matthew 16:15-19, where he was given the "Keys of the Kingdom of Heaven."

In the book of Acts we find Peter using these keys. First to the Jew on the Day of Pentecost under the first sovereign outpouring of the Spirit (Acts 2). Then secondly, to the Gentiles in the house of Cornelius under the next sovereign outpouring of the Spirit (Acts 10-11).

A perusal of Acts 10-11 show how reluctant Peter had been to go to the Gentiles. It was the Lord Jesus who had given Peter the vision of the unclean beasts and creeping things on the sheet let down from heaven. This vision had been repeated three times, so that "in the mouth of two or three witnesses" every word would be established (Deuteronomy 19:15).

The Holy Spirit told Peter to go with the men that HE had sent. It was the Spirit who bade Peter go. Peter, as yet, had no idea what was going on, or what God's intention was for the Gentiles.

Thus, Peter and six other brethren accompanying him went down to the house of Cornelius, or to the Gentiles. He confessed to them that it was beginning to dawn upon him that God was no respector of persons; that in every nation God honoured them that feared Him.

As Peter ministered the Word of the Gospel, the Lord sovereignly poured out His Spirit upon the Gentiles, attesting to the same by the same evidence given under the sovereign outpouring of the Spirit upon the Jews at Pentecost, that is, speaking in other languages (Acts 10:44-46; 11:15-17; 2:1-4).

Peter had no intention of baptizing the Gentiles in water, it would seem. However, when he saw that the Lord Jesus had baptized them in the Holy Spirit he commanded the Gentiles to be baptized in water in the Name of the Lord. The one baptism pointed to and was the completion of the other.

When Peter returned to Jerusalem, the circumcision contended with him over this matter of going to the Gentiles. Before the cross, Jesus had forbidden the Twelve to go to the Samaritans or the cities of the Gentiles (Matthew 10:5). Since the cross, He commanded them to go into all the world, to all nations, and preach the Gospel (Matthew 28:19-20; Mark 16:15-20). They had not fully received the implications in this commission as yet.

Upon Peter's testimony, they of the circumcision were willing to accept the fact of Divine visitation and they rejoiced that God was indeed granting the Gentiles repentance unto life (Acts 11:18).

Summarizing Peter's remarks at the Council, we note.

a. God used Peter to take the Gospel to the Gentiles.

b. The Gentiles believed the Gospel, apart from circumcision, and apart from Law.

c. God bore witness to their hearts, their believing hearts, by pouring out the Holy Spirit on them, giving them the same evidence as to the Jews.

d. The Gentiles had their hearts purified by faith.

e. Circumcision and the Law was spoken of as a "yoke on the neck" that neither Jews then nor their forefathers could bear.

f. Peter summarized his word by saying that the Gentiles would be saved by GRACE even as would the Jews.

Thus, Circumcision or Uncircumcision, Jew or Gentile, were saved by grace through faith, apart from circumcision or works of the Law. God saw the heart. This was Peter's testimony and evidence.

2. The Apostles Barnabas and Paul (Acts 15:12).

The Book of Acts shows that Barnabas and Paul had been sent together to work amongst the Gentiles (Acts 13:1-4).

In Acts 11:19-22, the disciples had been scattering the Seed of the Word under a time of persecution. The result was that many of the Gentiles believed.

The Church at Jerusalem sent Barnabas down to Antioch, who, after seeing the grace of God on the Gentiles, went to Tarsus to seek for Saul. Finding him, he brought him to Antioch where together they taught the Gentile believers (Acts 11:22-26).

After several years there the Holy Spirit indicated expressly that Barnabas and Saul were to be separated unto special work. After fasting and prayer with the laying on of hands of the prophets and teachers, both Barnabas and Saul were recommended to this work (Acts 13:1-3).

Acts 13:4–14:28, records for us the events of this first Apostolic journey and the great response of the Gentiles in various cities, as well as the response of some Jews in the Synagogues, and much opposition from others.

God confirmed His Word amongst the Gentiles in signs and wonders. Many churches were established amongst them.

In due time Barnabas and Paul returned to their Local Church at Antioch and reported that which God had done with and through them.

Barnabas and Paul would be well qualified to testify before the Jerusalem Council how God had saved the Gentiles apart from circumcision and apart from works and ceremonials of the Law. God had saved both Jews and Gentiles by grace through faith.

In the minds of Barnabas and Paul, it was the heart that God saw and not that which pertained to the flesh.

Paul was particularly the Apostle of the Uncircumcision, the Apostle of the Gentiles

(Galatians 2:7-9). Paul's Gospel of justification by faith is set forth in Romans and abundantly witnesses to the true Gospel of Christ for both Jew and Gentile (Romans 2:24-29; 3:29, 30; 4:9-12). God made no difference in salvation of the Jew or Gentile. Both were saved on the same ground, the ground of God's grace.

3. The Apostle James (Acts 15:13-18).

After Peter's testimony of the sovereign outpouring of the Spirit on the Gentiles under his ministry, and then the evidence of God's saving grace on the Gentiles under the ministries of Barnabas and Paul, the Apostle James rises to speak.

James, along with Peter and John, were pillars in the Church at Jerusalem (Galatians 2:9).

A study of Galatians, Chapters 1 and 2 reveals to us the extent of the problem in the Early Church over the Gentile situation. The transition period from the Old Covenant Dispensation into the New Covenant Dispensation certainly had its labour pains and travail.

Peter obeyed the revelation at the first concerning God's grace on the Gentiles but later on backed out, fearing the brethren of the circumcision who had come down from James.

Even Barnabas seemed to vacillate also and was carried away with the dissimulation, although he had seen the power of God's grace among the Gentiles (Galatians 2:13).

The case for circumcision would be pleaded on the grounds that it was the Seal of the Covenant made with Abraham, before the Law (Genesis 17; Romans 4:11). Anyone who refused this rite was cut off. Only as a person was circumcised were they in Covenant relationship with God and entitled to the blessings, privileges and promises in this Covenant (Acts 7:8).

Again, they would contend, circumcision was confirmed under the Law. So serious was this rite that God sought to kill Moses when his own sons were not circumcised, or in Covenant relationship with God (Exodus 4:24-26).

In the Nation of Israel, none could keep the Passover, whether Jew, Israelite or Gentile, unless they were circumcised (Exodus 12:43-50; Joshua 5:1-10).

Such, undoubtedly, would be the arguments in favour of this rite. Circumcision was given under the Abrahamic Covenant and confirmed under the Mosaic Covenant. If this was so, then it must continue under the New Covenant.

However, as already noticed, Peter, Barnabas and Paul, all witness that God saved the Gentiles apart from circumcision. They presented the case against circumcision, and apart from the works of the Law.

It was the Apostle Paul who had to withstand Peter over this matter when Peter backed out of his earlier testimony. If Peter, a Jew, went down and ate with the Gentiles and saw God's grace upon the Gentiles as Gentiles, then why expect the Gentiles to live as Jews?

The Jew could not expect the Gentile to become a Jew in order to be saved, when God Himself did not expect it, and when God Himself had saved the Jew as a Jew and the Gentile as a Gentile by faith in Christ's redemptive work.

In Christ neither Jew nor Gentile counted, but the New Creation only. Jew and Gentile spoke of the natural and national birth. In Christ God accepted the new and spiritual birth. All were one "in Christ" (Galatians 3:28; 6:15). This was the true Israel of God.

National distinctions cease to exist in Christ, in the Church, the Body of Christ. This is the true Commonwealth of Israel, the Israel of God (Galatians 6:16; Ephesians 2:11-22; 3:5-6).

We return to Acts 15 and consider what James the Apostle had to say concerning the Gentiles and their coming into Christ.

After Barnabas and Paul had finished their testimony, James closed the Council with an appeal to the Scriptures. He confirmed Peter's witness that God was indeed taking out of the Gentiles a people for His Name.

The Scripture reference is quoted here in full. Acts 15:15-18.

> "And to this agree the words of the prophets; as it is written, After this I will return and will build again the Tabernacle of David which is fallen down; and I will build again the ruins thereof, and I will set it up; That the residue of men might seek after the Lord, and all the Gentiles, upon whom My Name is called, saith the Lord, who doeth all these things. Known unto God are all His works from the beginning of the world."

Here we see James quoting from one of the Old Testament Prophets. He appeals to their own Scriptures as the final court of appeal. However, before this passage is considered more fully, we will note the final sentence of the Jerusalem Council.

4. The Final Sentence (Acts 15:19-21).

The end result was that James gave sentence that the Gentile Churches did not have to be circumcised or come under the Law of Moses, or be troubled by the Judaizing teachers of the Law.

Four things were prohibited to the Gentiles, even as to the Jews.

a. Abstinence from pollution of idols.
b. Abstinence from fornication.
c. Abstinence from things strangled.
d. Abstinence from blood.

Read in connection with these things 1 Corinthians 8:1-13; Genesis 9:4; Leviticus 17:10-14; 22:8; 1 Corinthians 5:1-13; 6:13-20; 7:2.

These briefly were forbidden; idolatry and immorality, which things were also forbidden to anyone in true Covenant relationship with God.

5. The Letters to the Gentile Churches (Acts 15:22-35).

Letters were written to the Gentile Churches and sent by the Apostolic team which included the Prophets Judas and Silas with Barnabas and Paul.

On the return to Antioch there was great joy among the Gentile believers over the epistle.

Thus, the great schism that threatened the Early Church, the one Body of Christ, was prevented under Apostolic leadership and revelation.

We return now to a fuller consideration of the passage of Scripture that James quoted. This passage provokes a number of questions.

Let the reader note that it was not Peter's vision of ministry to the Gentiles, Barnabas' and Paul's ministry to the Gentiles, but the Old Testament Scriptures became the final court of appeal to the Council convened at Jerusalem.

James, by a Word of Wisdom quotes this unusual passage of Scripture concerning the Gentiles, even as Peter on the Day of Pentecost had quoted from the Prophet Joel concerning the outpouring of the Spirit of the Jew. The quotation is taken from Amos 9:11-12. It is interesting to note the slight differences or rather the Apostolic interpretation, by the Spirit, of the word of the Prophet.

Perhaps a contrastive and comparative look may lift these differences more distinctly to our view:

The Prophet Amos (Amos 9:11-12)		The Apostle James (Acts 15:14-17)
• In that day	---	• After this I will return
• Will I raise up the Tabernacle of David that is fallen	---	• And will build again the Tabernacle of David which is fallen down
• And close up the breaches thereof	---	
• And I will raise up his ruins	---	• And I will build again the ruins thereof
• And I will build it as in the days of old	---	• And I will set it up
• That they may possess the remnant of Edom	---	• That the residue of men might seek the Lord
• And of all the heathen	---	• And all the Gentiles
• Which are called by My Name	---	• Upon whom My Name is called
• Saith the Lord that doeth this.	---	• Saith the Lord who doeth all these things.

The main points are brought more sharply into focus here.

- God is visiting the Gentiles to take out of them a people for His Name.
- The words of the Old Testament Prophets agree with this.
- Though speaking of the Prophets, in the plural, James quotes but one Prophet, Amos.
- The burden of the prophecy states that:

> After this <u>I will</u> return
> <u>I will</u> build again the Tabernacle of David
> The Tabernacle of David had fallen down
> <u>I will</u> raise again the ruins thereof
> <u>I will</u> set it up

- The purpose is that the remnant of Edom (residue of men) might seek the Lord, and that the heathen (Gentiles) might have the Name of the Lord called upon them.

- It is God who is doing these things.

- These works were known to God from the beginning of the world.

Remember, the Early Church as yet did not have the New Testament Scriptures. All that God was doing in their midst had to find its roots and foundation in the Old Testament Scriptures. This is their only infallible court of appeal. They have to discover the New Testament in the Old Testament. Thus James is given, by the Spirit, a Word of Wisdom, which Old Testament Scripture would appropriately settle the issue concerning the Gentiles.

These passages of Scripture from the Old and the New Testaments immediately provoke for us today a number of questions that desire answers.

Why did the Apostle James quote this passage of Scripture from the Prophet Amos? It seems to have absolutely nothing to do with the immediate context, either before or after. It seems that James takes it right out of context altogether in his use and application of it.

Then, what has the rebuilding of the Tabernacle of David got to do with the Gentiles coming into the Gospel Dispensation? What is the Tabernacle of David? Why not have the Gentiles come into the Tabernacle of Moses? Did David have a Tabernacle? What was it? What was it all about? Did Gentiles get into David's Tabernacle?

Again, where was David's Tabernacle at this time? If it is to be built again and its ruins raised up, and if it is to be built again as in the days of old, then what does this building again mean? Exactly what did happen in the days of old?

When James quoted this Scripture and applied it here in the settling of the Jewish and Gentile contention, did he mean it to be accepted in a literal or spiritual way? Do we look for a restoration of a literal Tabernacle of David, or is there some spiritual significance and application to be sought for?

And the Gentiles coming in? What has this got to do with the Gentiles, the heathen, and the residue of men, or the remnant of Edom?

If this Tabernacle of David is literal, then where is it today? Was it ever rebuilt in the Early Church, or Church History? Or is it some future building to be built?

Just what is the significance and proper interpretation of this Scripture? Or is this to do with the Jews or the Jewish Nation? Did this Nation rebuild or enter into the Tabernacle of David? How can this be reconciled with the Tabernacle of Moses in the Nation of Israel?

The whole passage is thought provoking indeed. Questions arise out of such a passage and these questions seek an answer from God's word.

SUMMARY

Thus we have considered the historical setting in Acts 15 in the Early Church and the Jerusalem Council's decision concerning the Jewish and Gentile problem. The Word of God became the final court of appeal. The Gentiles as well as the Jews would be welcomed into the Tabernacle of David which God was building - whatever the significance of that was!

Having proposed these questions, let us seek some answers.

Chapter 4

SIGNIFICANCE OF DAVID'S LIFE STORY

There are numerous persons in the Bible who present great character studies. Recognizing this as one of the chief reasons why God caused things to be written concerning various persons, some more, some less, depending upon their character clues as they relate to the purposes of God, helps us to understand the Word of God.

Certain persons are types of Christ or believers, either in character, office, or function. Either in what they are or what they do. Adam, Noah, Isaac, Joseph, Moses, Aaron, Samuel, Isaiah, Jeremiah, Ezekiel, Daniel, and many others amongst the Judges, Prophets, Priests and Kings may all be set forth as types of Christ in His character, offices, and functions.

Certain other persons are types of Antichrist or unbelievers in character, office, and function. Cain, Ham, Absalom, Saul, and Judas, as well as others, portray certain character clues which relate them to Satan and the Spirit of Antichrist. Or else it relates them to the characters of the ungodly and unregenerate.

Generally, both groups have individuals who manifest some distinctive characteristic of those which they typify.

- ADAM shadows forth Christ as the Last Adam, the Second Man, the Lord from heaven (1 Corinthians 15:45-47; Romans 5:14).

- ISAAC, the Only Begotten Son of the Old Testament, manifests certain characteristics shadowing forth Jesus, the Only Begotten Son of the New Testament (Hebrews 11:17-19; John 3:16).

- JOSEPH, the beloved and rejected and exalted son of Jacob, manifests certain unique characteristics typifying Jesus, the New Testament beloved, rejected, and then exalted Son of God (Philippians 2:1-12; Acts 2:34-36).

- AARON, as already noted in Divine cameos, in this office and ministry as Israel's High Priest and Mediator of the New Covenant (Hebrews 7:1-12).

    And so may these things be seen throughout the various persons mentioned above, each typifying some distinctive truth concerning the person of Christ.

    The same is true on the negative side of the other godless persons mentioned.

- CAIN manifests characteristics of Satan, as the murderer, liar and blood-of-the-lamb rejector (Genesis 4:1-16; John 3:12).

- KORAH and his company manifest the characteristics of Satan's rebellion against Divine government (Numbers 16).

One of the greatest types of Messiah in the Bible is David the King, the sweet singer and Psalmist of Israel. His name is mentioned hundreds of times in Scripture. Abraham is outstanding because of who he was before God. Moses is marked out because of his distinctive ministry. David also is a marked man because of that which is outworked in his life relative to the purposes of God.

At the outset it should be recognized that there is no such thing as a "perfect" or complete type. The very nature of the persons God Himself used as types were all stamped with imperfection and infirmity. God had to use the imperfect to shadow forth His Son until He Himself came. This is abundantly seen in many persons. Moses, the Prophet; Aaron, the High Priest; and others of the

Judges, Prophets, Priests and Kings. All were marked with frailty, imperfection, and infirmity, but God did use them to typify and shadow forth facets of His Only Begotten Son's ministry.

This is true also of King David. David, though stamped with imperfection and infirmity of sinful nature, is used by the Lord God to shadow forth Messiah, the True Son of David.

The life of David, within this framework of interpretation, may be divided basically into two periods, shadowing the life story of Messiah, David's greater Son.

1. The Period of Rejection.
2. The Period of Exaltation.

1. <u>The Period of David's Rejection.</u>

David is first seen in the role of a Shepherd of Bethlehem-Judah. With the collapse of King Saul's obedience into rebellion, God called the Prophet Samuel to go and anoint the Shepherd boy, David, to be King in God's appointed time. His name interpreted means "Beloved."

Samuel called all of Jesse's sons and all passed before him unaccepted of the Lord for Kingship. Finally David is brought in from keeping the sheep. The Lord commanded Samuel to anoint him for high and holy office. The Spirit of the Lord sealed this anointing by coming upon David from that day forward. However, the Spirit of the Lord departed from King Saul and an evil spirit troubled him (1 Samuel 16:1-15). Little did David realize then that the way to the throne would be by way of the valley of humiliation and rejection.

David is brought before the King to play his harp and cause the troubling spirit to depart from Saul for a season (1 Samuel 16:16-18). In due time David became Saul's armourbearer as well as providing the ministry of music to refresh the King when troubled by this evil spirit (1 Samuel 16:19-23).

The Lord used David to conquer the Giant Goliath (1 Samuel 17). King Saul asked Jesse the father of David that David be allowed to stay in the King's residence. David was set over the men of war. David behaved himself very wisely and was accepted and loved by all in the palace.

With the praise given to David over the conquering of Goliath, King Saul became exceedingly jealous of him. When the evil spirit troubled him and David began to play the harp, Saul threw the javelin at him and David escaped with his life on several occasions. Saul feared the wise behaviour of this young man. He did not then realize that this same man would in due time replace him in the throne over Israel as a nation (1 Samuel 18).

Saul's envy and jealousy caused him to seek to murder David. David fled to the wilderness and caves of Judea where those in distress, in debt, and discontented gathered themselves unto him and he became a Captain over them (1 Samuel 22:1-2). This was David's army!

David became a fugitive, hunted by King Saul and his men. He experienced a period of humilitation and rejection. Hunted by King Saul, David escaped with his life on several occasions by the mercy and mind of God through Abiathar, the Priest with the Ephod.

Throughout this period, though David twice had the opportunity to slay King Saul, he manifested a right spirit that would not touch the Lord's Anointed even though King Saul had lost that anointing!

"Touch not the Lord's Anointed" was a lesson that David had deeply written on his heart, even though the Lord's Anointed was wrong (1 Samuel 24:1-15; 26:5-25; Psalms 105:15).

In due time Saul died for his transgression in seeking to a witch for Divine counsel (1 Samuel 28; 1 Samuel 31; I Chronicles 10:13, 14). Thus ended David's period of humilitation and rejection at the hands of Saul.

2. The Period of David's Exaltation.

The second stage was the period of exaltation. With the death of Saul after 40 years reigning as the first King of Israel, the people seek David to be their King. They recognize that the anointing of God is upon him for this office. Thus, David comes to the throne to begin a glorious reign over the whole nation. Those who had suffered with him in the wilderness experiences now reign with him in the glory of the Davidic Kingdom.

The first 20 years of David's reign is one of victory over enemies, and unification of the 12 Tribes of Israel as a great united Kingdom.

It is after this exaltation to the throne of Israel that David set up the Tabernacle of David and all that is involved therein (2 Samuel 2:1-4; 5:1-12).

The pattern is clear. First, David is anointed as Shepherd to be King. Then the period of humiliation and rejection comes under the system of Saul. After this there is the time of exaltation to the throne of David, after which he builds the Tabernacle of David and establishes the order of worship therein. First the anointed Shepherd, then follows the suffering; after that the King is enthroned and exalted and becomes the builder of the Tabernacle which is called by his name.

As a foreshadowing of the life of Christ, the greater Son of David, the correspondences and application should be evident.

1. <u>The Period of Rejection for Christ.</u>

Jesus, like David, was born in Bethlehem of Judah. He was anointed with the Holy Spirit in Jordan. The Spirit of the Lord came upon Him in the midst of His brethren. He was accepted and loved by the common people who recognized that anointing upon Him (Luke 4:18-22). He was the Good Shepherd willing to lay down His life for the sheep (John 10:11).

However, the religious leaders of His day, the Priests, Scribes, Pharisees, and Sadducees, became envious and jealous of Him, thus turning the people against Him. They represented the "Saul-system" of His time. They had lost the anointing though standing as the Lord's Anointed. They soon began to throw the "javelins" of false accusations, hate, envy, and murder at Him (Matthew 12:14; Mark 15:10).

In this period Jesus gathered to Himself disciples who were counted as the "riff-raff" of His day. These would be willing to suffer with Him in His rejection. In due time Christ was rejected and crucified at Calvary. This closed off His period of humiliation (Isaiah 53).

2. <u>The Period of Exaltation for Christ.</u>

The second period of Messiah's ministry is one of exaltation and enthronement. After His humiliation and death, God raised Him from the dead to His own right hand, highly exalting Him and giving Him a name above every name (Ephesians 1:21-23; Acts 2:29-36; Philippians 2:1-12).

He is now seated in the Father's throne in glory. The prophets foretold the sufferings of Christ and the glory that would follow (1 Peter 1:10-12; Revelation 3:21).

Those who suffer with Him shall reign with Him (2 Timothy 2:12). It is after His exaltation to the throne that He also begins to build His Tabernacle -- The Church -- that is called by His Name. This is the True Tabernacle of David (Matthew 16:18-19; Acts 15:15-18).

Thus Christ Jesus is first the Shepherd, who, after His anointing, experiences the sufferings of the Cross, and then becomes the King enthroned in glory. He is the greater Son of David, for He is the Root and Offspring of David (Matthew 1:1; Revelation 22:16).

The diagram illustrates these periods.

OLD TESTAMENT TYPE

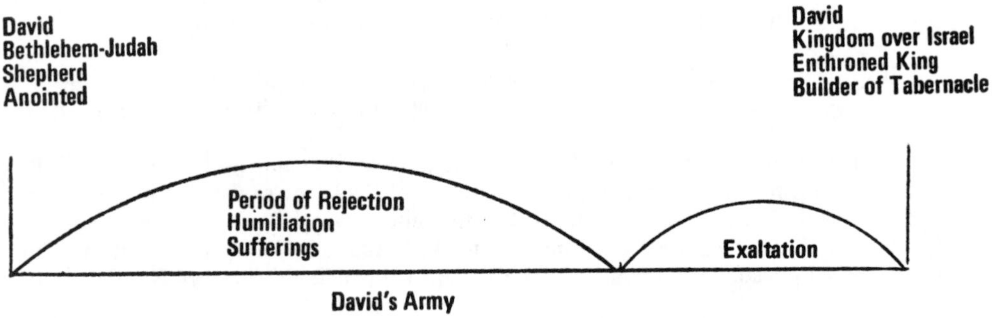

NEW TESTAMENT ANTITYPE

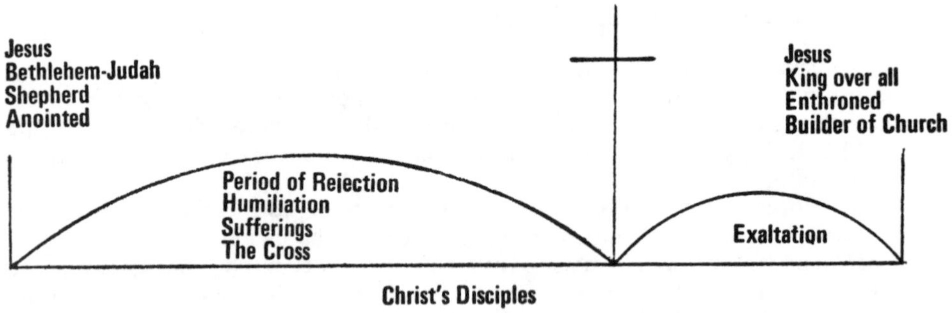

NOTE: There is a similar pattern in the life of three men in Scripture to that above.

1. Moses -- First a Shepherd, then a King, then a Builder of a Tabernacle, the Tabernacle of Moses. Rejected, then exalted.
2. David -- First a Shepherd, then a King, then a Builder of a Tabernacle, the Tabernacle of David. Rejected, then exalted.
3. Jesus -- First a Shepherd, then a King, then a Builder of the True Tabernacle, The New Testament Church. Rejected, then exalted.

Chapter 5

THE THREE ANOINTINGS OF DAVID

One of the most remarkable things in the life story of David is seen in the fact that he received three distinct anointings. He is the only person in the Scripture specifically said to have received such. Undoubtedly the Spirit of God has recorded this with some significance in mind. Before looking at the spiritual significance of these anointings, we list the passages in which these are to be found. The significance of the custom of anointing will be considered also.

1. David's first anointing - in the midst of his brethren (1 Samuel 16:1, 12, 13).

2. David's second anointing - as King over the house of Judah (2 Samuel 2:4, 7, 11).

3. David's third anointing - as King over all Israel (2 Samuel 5:1-5).

A. The Revelation of the Holy Anointing Oil.

In the Book of Exodus, under the instructions given by the Lord to Moses concerning the Tabernacle of Moses and its whole economy, we have the specific instructions concerning the holy anointing oil. Read Exodus 30:22-33.

The most prominent points are noted in the following:

1. It was to be made of principal spices.

Pure myrrh	500 shekels
Sweet cinnamon	250 shekels
Sweet calamus	250 shekels
Cassia	500 shekels
	1500 shekels, after the standard of the Sanctuary.

One hin of olive oil blended all together.

Thus we have 5 ingredients blended together to constitute the holy anointing oil. The number 5 is significant of the grace of God, of life, of the atonement. It is only through the grace of God and the atonement that the anointing oil can be provided.

These spices were a blending of the sweet and bitter, and the olive oil bound all together. Note these Scriptures which refer to these spices: Song of Solomon 1:13; 3:6; 4:6; Psalms 45:5-8.

The olive oil binding all together spoke of that unity involved in the holy anointing of the Lord upon His ministers (Psalms 133; Exodus 30:22-33).

The holy anointing oil was indeed very costly. "Gethsemane" means "Oil press," and it was through the costly sufferings of Christ that the holy anointing oil of the Spirit was provided for the Church.

2. It was to be compounded together.

This compounding together spoke of that unity and blending of these sweet and bitter spices from various trees by reason of the olive oil (Psalms 133:1-2). True anointing is manifest in the unity of the Church.

3. It was to be a holy anointing oil before the Lord.

It was significant of the Holy Spirit of God. Nothing unholy was to be upon the people of the Lord anointed to office and ministry in the Sanctuary.

4. It was to continue throughout all generations.

Each generation must experience that holy anointing of the Lord. There must be that fresh anointing of the Spirit for service. One generation cannot live on the anointing that was upon the previous generation (cf., Judges 2:10).

5. It was not to be poured upon man's flesh.

This speaks of the Adamic nature, unregenerate human nature. Man is "flesh" and God does not require ministry of the flesh in its fallen and corrupt state. Much activity in the House of the Lord is simply religious flesh in God's mind, and the anointing oil was not to be poured on such.

6. It was not to be poured upon strangers.

One is a "stranger" if not born into the True Israel of God. It is only by regeneration that one is no longer a stranger or foreigner but a citizen of the Household of God (Ephesians 2:12-22). The holy oil of God is not for strangers (John 14:17; Acts 8:14-24).

7. It was not to be imitated by man.

God absolutely forbad imitations or similar compositions of this holy anointing oil. Substitutes or counterfeits of this anointing would come under Divine judgement. This speaks of the imitation of that which is Divine. Many today have substitutes for this anointing of the Spirit. The last days reveal that there will be false Christs, false anointed ones, and upon them will be a false anointing.

8. Any who violated the commandment would be cut off.

Those who presumed to imitate or substitute the holy anointing oil in Israel were to be cut off from the people of God. Many today are "cut off" because of religious counterfeits of this anointing.

Thus the Lord was very exacting in the revelation for the making of this holy oil. It was different from all other perfumes. It was not to be counterfeited in any way or the person would come under the Divine penalty.

B. The Divine Use of the Holy Anointing Oil.

God also gave very definite instructions concerning the use of this holy anointing oil. Listed below are a number of things or persons which came under the Divine anointing. These show us God's specified use for this holy oil. The anointing sanctified all, setting all apart for holy use.

1. The Tabernacle was anointed (Exodus 30:26-28; 40:1-11).
The Ark of the Testimony, the Table of Shewbread, the Golden Candlestick, the Altar of Incense, the Altar of Burnt offerings, the Laver and his foot, and all vessels pertaining to these articles, were anointed with oil.

2. The Patriarchs are spoken of as the Lord's anointed (Psalms 105:15).

3. Aaron and his priestly sons were anointed (Exodus 30:30; 40:12-16).

4. Lepers in their cleansing ceremony were anointed (Leviticus 13:15-18).

5. Kings in Israel were anointed (1 Samuel 9:16, 10:1, 15:17; 1 Kings 19:15-16).

6. At times Prophets were anointed (1 Kings 19:16; Revelation 11:3,4).

The significance of the anointing of these things or persons is summed up in that which speaks of "The Lord's Anointed."

Most Bible expositors see that the holy anointing oil is symbolic of the ministry of the Holy Spirit, in quickening and illuminating power upon the one who is anointed or that which is anointed (Luke 4:18). This is confirmed by a consideration of the Hebrew word used to express this.

C. The Lord's Anointed.

The Hebrew word for "Anointed" is "Mashiyach," and it speaks of an anointed one, usually a consecrated person, as a King, Priest or Saint. It pointed expressly to the Messiah, Jesus Christ.

The expression "His anointed" is first used by Hannah in her song unto the Lord concerning the birth of Samuel (1 Samuel 2:10).

1. King Saul is spoken of as "The Lord's Anointed," by reason of this holy anointing oil poured upon him by Samuel the prophet (1 Samuel 24:6, 10; 26:9-16; 2 Samuel 1:14).

2. King David is spoken of as "The Lord's Anointed" by reason of that same anointing oil poured upon him (2 Samuel 19-21; 2 Chronicles 6:42; Psalms 20:6).

3. Messiah, the Son of David, is spoken of in prophecy and in the Messianic Psalms as "The Lord's Anointed" (Psalms 2:2; Daniel 9:25, 26; John 1:41, margin).

The significance of the anointing in the Old Testament, as well as the New Testament, is that one is set aside as the Lord's Anointed to function in a particular sphere or office. In the light of this we consider David's three anointings.

D. David's First Anointing (1Samuel 16:1, 12-13).

David's first anointing was in the midst of his brethren. King Saul had forfeited the anointing through his willful rebellion and disobedience to the Word of the Lord. The Prophet Samuel mourned over the Lord's rejection of King Saul. The Lord challenged Samuel to quit mourning over that which the Lord Himself had set aside. God told Samuel to fill his horn with holy oil and go to Bethlehem to the house of Jesse where he was to anoint a young man to be the new King in Israel in God's appointed time. Samuel obeyed.

After the appointed sacrificial feast, Samuel called all of Jesse's sons to pass before him. The Lord clearly told Samuel that none of them were chosen as king, "for the Lord seeth not as man seeth; for man looketh on the outward appearance, but the Lord looketh upon the heart" (vs 7).

Samuel enquired of Jesse if all of his sons were present. Jesse told Samuel that his youngest son, David, was out minding the sheep. David was called before the prophet of the Lord. As soon as he arrived, the Lord witnessed to Samuel, "Arise, anoint him; for this is he" (vs 12).

Then Samuel took the horn of oil, that horn which had been provided upon the basis of sacrificial blood (no blood, no oil!), and poured it on the head of David in the midst of his brethren. The Holy Spirit came upon David from that day forward. It is noteworthy that the Holy Spirit worked in connection with the symbol of His own being; for, when the holy anointing oil came upon David, so did the Holy Spirit! In other words, THE Anointing Oil Himself came upon David when the symbolic anointing oil came on him. This was David's first anointing. However, years would elapse before David actually became king.

E. David's Second Anointing (2 Samuel 2:4).

The second anointing came after the death of King Saul; a number of years after that first anointing. He was 30 years of age (2 Samuel 5:4). David was a young man when first anointed. He was young and immature and not as yet qualified to rule the people of God. As noted in the panoramic view of David's life story, David, after his original anointing as the shepherd boy had to wait God's time. He learned by the things that he suffered. The lion, the bear and the giant Goliath had to be conquered by the might of the Lord. David also served in Saul's Court as court musician. David was also Saul's armourbearer for a while. If David did not learn what to do under Saul's reign he certainly learned what not to do! God had His king in preparation for the throne. David had to experience rejection, suffering and humiliation under the hands of Saul. Between anointing, promise, and fulfillment were the wilderness experiences. All were part of the dealings of God to take David to the throne. Even though at times David had opportunity to kill Saul, he would not touch the Lord's Anointed, even though Saul had lost that true anointing. The details of these years are accounted for in 1 Samuel 16-30.

In due time, Saul and his sons died (1 Samuel 31; 2 Samuel 1). David revealed his true attitude and the Spirit of Christ as he wept and mourned over the death of Saul and his sons. Though David had been through bitter experiences he did not allow himself to become bitter in spirit. Truly the grace of God manifested in the life of the shepherd-king.

Upon the death of Saul, David enquired of the Lord as to His will. The Lord told David to go up to Hebron ("Fellowship") and there the men of Judah came and anointed David as King over the House of Judah.

The House of Judah recognized that David had been established under God to be the king to replace Saul. David reigned in Hebron 7 ½ years. This took place under David's second anointing (2 Samuel 2:7-11).

F. David's Third Anointing (2 Samuel 5:1-3).

The third anointing came after 7 ½ years of David's reigning in Hebron. Israel, as a whole, did not accept David as King. The House of Judah did. The Sceptre had been promised to the Tribe of Judah in the prophetic word of Jacob over his 12 sons (Genesis 49:8-12). David was of the Tribe of Judah. However, Israel endeavoured to maintain the Sceptre of the House of Saul who was of the Tribe of Benjamin.

There was long war between the House of David and the House of Saul but the House of Saul waxed weaker and weaker and the House of David waxed stronger and stronger (2 Samuel 3:1).

With the death of Ishbosheth, Saul's son whom Abner had set on the throne (2 Samuel 2:8-10; 4:1-12), the 12 Tribes came to David desiring him to be king over the whole of the united nation. They acknowledged the prophetic word that had gone on before David years before and now they enter into a league with David before the Lord. Here David is anointed as King over all Israel. This was his third anointing (2 Samuel 5:3). David was 30 years old when he began to reign and he reigned for 40 years as King, as the Lord's anointed (2 Samuel 5:4,5).

G. Spiritual Significance of the Three Anointings.

It should be evident that beyond the actual anointings of David in their historical settings, there is some richer spiritual significance. There is no doubt that David touched something in his experiences before God in these anointings, as the Lord's Anointed. In these anointings he shadows forth the Lord Jesus Christ, who is David's greater Son.

In these three anointings there seems to be an allusion to the three main offices to which persons were anointed in the Old Testament. These three offices are shadowed forth in David and find their fulfillment in the Lord Jesus Christ and His threefold office. These offices were prophet, king, and priest.

1. Prophets – The Ministry of the Word (1 Kings 19:16).
Prophets at times were anointed. All true prophets were anointed by the Spirit of God for the Word of God.

2. Kings – The Ministry of Reigning and ruling (1 Samuel 10:1; 15:1,17; 16:1-3; 1 Kings 1:34-39).
The Kings of Israel and Judah were anointed to rule.

3. Priests – The ministry of Reconciliation (Leviticus 8:1-13; Exodus 30:20; Leviticus 21:12).
The Priests were anointed for Sanctuary ministry.

A consideration of David's life-story shows him to have touched these three offices of Prophet, King, and Priest.

1. David as Prophet - The First Anointing.

David's first anointing shadowed forth this office of the prophet. The Scripture expressly states that David was a prophet (Acts 2:29,30). In the Old Testament the evidence of a person receiving the Spirit was generally manifested in prophecy (Numbers 11:24-30; 1 Samuel 10:1-13; 19:18-24). Many of the Psalms were written by David. Many of these are Messianic revelations and the New Testament abounds with quotations from these Psalms. This confirms the fact that after David's first anointing, when the Spirit of the Lord came upon him, that the prophetic Spirit was indeed upon him. Thus, as a prophet he foretold the sufferings of Christ and the glory that should follow (1 Peter 1:10-12).

2. David as King - The Second Anointing.

This second anointing indeed confirmed David as King. It shadowed forth the Lord Jesus as King. The dominant office to which David was anointed was that of a king. The first anointing did not make him a king. He was anointed as a shepherd to become king in God's appointed time. After the word of the Lord tried him, he came to the throne of Judah and was anointed as king. After 7 ½ years he was anointed as king over all Israel. Again, many of the kingly Psalms of David are prophetic of Messiah King Jesus, the King of Kings and Lord of Lords. David, as king, shadowed forth Christ the King (Psalm 2; Psalm 72; Psalm 110; Psalm 133; Psalm 89).

3. David as Priest -- The Third Anointing.

The Scripture also sets forth in David's experience that which pertains to the ministry of a priest. This is not seen until David's third anointing as King over all Israel. In measure, David shadows forth the Order of Melchisedek as King-Priest. This is seen in the fact that after David is anointed the third time, he captures Zion and sets up the Tabernacle of David there, exercising priestly functions. It should be recognized that it was in this experience that David touched priestly ministrations.

In the Old Testament, the offices of Prophet, King and Priest were not united, except by two distinct persons. Anyone who dared to presume from one office into another, or presume to unite these offices in one person were Divinely judged.

King Saul, after his anointing, tried to be a King-Priest and presumed to offer sacrifices instead of waiting for Samuel the Prophet-Priest to do it. For this he forfeited the kingdom (1 Samuel 13:5-15).

King Uzziah dared to presume into the Temple of the Lord and usurp Priestly ministry in burning incense. The priests withstood him. God stepped in and judged him by smiting him with leprosy in the forehead until the day of his death (2 Chronicles 26:15-21; Isaiah 6:1).

If David as a King was presuming to be a Priest, or a King-Priest, God would surely have judged him. Such was not the case. David acted as King-Priest in the institution of the Tabernacle of David.

- David wore a linen ephod, as a Priest (2 Samuel 6:14).
- David set the Ark of the Covenant in the Tabernacle that he had pitched for it (2 Samuel 6:17).
- David offered burnt and peace offerings before the Lord -- Priestly sacrifices (2 Samuel 6:17).
- David blessed the people in the Name of the Lord of Hosts. This was Priestly blessing (2 Samuel 6:18 with Numbers 6:24-27).
- David thus officiated as King-Priest, the Order of Melchisedek (1 Chronicles 15:27; 16:1-3).

The significance of David's three anointings indeed points to the threefold offices in one person of Prophet, King and Priest. David thus foreshadowed his Son, Jesus Christ, who would unite in His one person these same three offices, as the Lord's Anointed.

The Scripture reveals three persons who united these three offices in themselves, each of them builders of a Tabernacle.

1. Moses -- Builder of Tabernacle of Moses - The Mosaic Covenant.

   a. Prophet -- Deuteronomy 18:15-18.
   b. King -- Deuteronomy 33:5.
   c. Priest -- Leviticus 2:1-3, 10. Of Priestly Tribe of Levi.

2. David -- Builder of Tabernacle of David - The Davidic Covenant.

   a. Prophet -- Acts 2:29,30.
   b. King -- 2 Samuel 2:4; 5:1-3. King out of Tribe of Judah.
   c. Priest -- 2 Samuel 6:14-18.

3. Jesus – Builder of True Tabernacle - The New Covenant.

a.	Prophet	--	Acts 3:22-26	God's Word.
b.	King	–	Revelation 19:16. King of Tribe of Judah.	God's Rule.
c.	Priest	–	Hebrews 7:1-14. Order of Melchisedek.	God's Mediator.

All places, things or persons anointed in the Old Testament pointed to or prophesied of the Lord Jesus Christ, who is THE MESSIAH, THE Lord's Anointed. Jesus is indeed Prophet, King and Priest. He is the Tabernacle of God and all its furnishings personified (John 1:14). He was anointed of the Father with the Holy Spirit. He did not receive the Spirit by measure (John 3:33,34; 1:17-18; Colossians 1:19; 2:9). It was reason of the Divine anointing upon Him that He could function in the threefold office of Prophet, King and Priest.

Though known as Jesus of Nazareth for 30 years, He publicly and officially became Jesus CHRIST, or Jesus ANOINTED at the River Jordan after His water baptism and the coming of the Holy Spirit upon Him without measure. It was after this He was able to say, "The Spirit of Jehovah is upon Me because He hath anointed Me . . . ." (Isaiah 62:1-2; Luke 3:21-23; 4:1, 14-19).

The Greek word for "Anointed" is "CHRISTOS" from which we have the word CHRIST translated. It is the Greek equivalent to the Hebrew word "Messiah" (John 1:41, margin).

The three interrelated words pertaining to the anointing are as follow:

1. Chrio – The Greek verb meaning "To Anoint." The Father God is the Anointer (Acts 4:27; 10:38; 2 Corinthians 1:21; Hebrews 1:9).

2. Christos – The Greek noun meaning "The Anointed." The Son of God is the Anointed (John 1:41).

3. Chrisma – The Greek noun meaning "The Anointing." The Holy Spirit is the Anointing (1 John 2:20,27).

The Lord Jesus is THE Christ, Jehovah's Anointed. And the believers, which constitute the Church which is His Body are also the Lord's Anointed. Head and Body are both partakers of the same anointing, constituting "The Christ" (1 Corinthians 12:12, 27).

Christ is "The Anointed One." He is the Head. Christians are "Anointed ones" and are Members of the Body of Christ, the Body of the Anointed, by reason of that same anointing of the Holy Spirit within and upon them.

The Greek word "Chrisma" is the Greek word for "Oil, anointing." The Holy Spirit is that Divine anointing oil (Isaiah 10:27 with 1 John 2:20,27).

In the Old Testament the anointing always involved a triunity in its inauguration.

1. The Anointer – i.e., Samuel, Elijah, etc.
2. The Anointed – i.e., Saul, or David, etc.
3. The Anointing – i.e., The Holy Oil.

The New Testament shows the fulfillment of that triunity involved in Old Testament anointing in the Godhead: Father, Son, and Holy Spirit.

1. The Anointer – The Father.
2. The Anointed – The Son.
3. The Anointing – The Holy Spirit.

The Church, the Body of Christ, partakes of the same anointing of the Spirit. This is why the Church is called the Body of CHRIST (2 Corinthians 1:21-22; 1 Corinthians 12:27; Isaiah 10:27; 1 John 2:20,27).

Joined to the risen Head, the Church is to bear upon it the Prophetical, Kingly and Priestly anointings.

1. Prophetic Anointing – Ministry of the Word, Ministry Gifts and Gifts of the Spirit (Revelation 10:10; Ephesians 4:9-11; 1 Corinthians 14:1).

2. Kingly Anointing – Ministry of Authority, Ruling, Reigning and power over all the enemy (Revelation 1:6; 5:10; 1 Peter 2:5-9; Matthew 16:16-18).

3. Priestly Anointing – Ministry of Reconciliation, Intercession, Prayer, Worship and Praise unto God (1 Peter 2:5-9; Revelation 1:6; 5:10).

The three anointings of David therefore shadow forth that fullness of the Prophetic, Kingly, and Priestly offices in Christ and His Church. It is after this third anointing that David captures Mt. Zion, which then becomes the City of David and it is here that the Tabernacle is set up which is called by his own Name. The importance of Zion will be considered in a subsequent section.

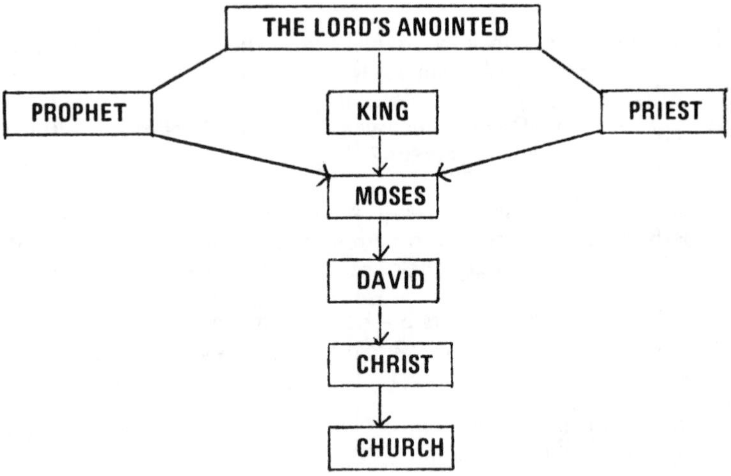

Chapter 6

THE DAVIDIC COVENANT

The Bible reveals that God is a Covenant-making and Covenant-keeping God. Before David's time, the great Covenants in existence were:

the Edenic Covenant	-	Genesis 1,
the Adamic Covenant	-	Genesis 3,
the Noahic Covenant	-	Genesis 8-9,
the Abrahamic Covenant	-	Genesis 15, 17, 22,
the Mosaic Covenant	-	Exodus 24, Deuteronomy 4-5,
the Palestinian Covenant	-	Deuteronomy 29-30.

The last of the great Covenants of God made in the Old Testament was that which God made with David. It is spoken of as the Davidic Covenant. David is set forth as:

1. A Witness,
2. A Leader, and
3. A Commander (Isaiah 55:4).

The details of the Covenant are mainly to be found in 2 Samuel 7, 1 Chronicles 17, and Psalms 89, 132. Most Bible expositors accept the fact that the ultimate fulfillment and realization of the Davidic Covenant is to be found in the Lord Jesus Christ, David's greater Son. He is the One who established the New Covenant. The Davidic Covenant involved Jesus Christ as the ultimate Ruler of the universe; King of Kings and Lord of Lords.

Undoubtedly there is the earthly, natural and national fulfillment of the Covenant in Israel. However, above and beyond this is the heavenly, spiritual, and eternal fulfillment of the Covenant in Christ and the Church. It is this latter aspect that comes under consideration in this chapter. One cannot understand or appreciate that which is spiritual and eternal unless one first sees the natural and temporal (2 Corinthians 4:18). It is first the natural and afterward that which is spiritual (1 Corinthians 15:46).

One of the basic principles of interpretation in relation to the Old and New Testaments is to see that which is set out in the following two columns. This will be seen in the Davidic Covenant and the New Covenant.

	The Old Testament	---	The New Testament
1.	The Type	---	The Antitype
2.	The Shadow	---	The Substance
3.	The Earthly	---	The Heavenly
4.	The Natural	---	The Spiritual
5.	The Temporal	---	The Eternal
6.	The Promise	---	The Reception
7.	The Prophecy	---	The Fulfillment
8.	The Anticipation	---	The Realization
9.	The National Israel	---	The Spiritual Israel, The Church
10.	The Davidic Covenant	---	The New Covenant

The student should read carefully the chapters pertaining to the Davidic Covenant as well as the other Scriptures given in relation to the things in this Covenant.

After David had been anointed King over all Israel, he captured Zion and there set up the Tabernacle by which his name is known. As he was sitting in his own house one day, after the Lord had given him a victory over his enemies, David became greatly concerned about a house for God.

He said to the prophet Nathan that he had a beautiful house as a King in Israel, but the Ark of God, the King of Kings was in a tent, within curtains. Nathan encouraged David to do what was in his heart. David's desire was to build God an house and put the Ark therein.

However, the Word of the Lord came to the prophet Nathan telling him to tell David that he would not build God an house, but his son, Solomon, would.

The Lord reminded David that ever since the time of Israel's exodus from Egypt, He had not asked anyone to build Him an house. The Lord plainly stated, "For I have not dwelt in an house since the day that I brought up Israel unto this day; but have gone from tent to tent, and from one tabernacle to another" (1 Chronicles 17:5 with 2 Samuel 7:6).

Moreover, the Lord told David that He would build him an house. God gave the contents of the Covenant to Nathan by the vision in the night and he communicated it to David. There are a number of Scriptures scattered throughout the Psalms and the Prophets pertaining to the Davidic Covenant. It is impossible to read these without seeing that they point to Jesus Christ, David's Son, in ultimate fulfillment.

It has already been noted that there is that which pertains to the natural house of David, but underlying all is that which is Messianic. This is abundantly confirmed by the New Testament writers and their use and application of the things in the Davidic Covenant to Jesus Christ, the Root and Offspring of David. The New Testament writers are the infallible interpreters of the Old Testament writings.

Because of the great amount of material concerning the Davidic Covenant, we will choose 9 prominent things involved in the Covenant. We will briefly look first at the natural, then at the spiritual. We will consider that which is given to David and then that which is fulfilled in David's greater Son, Christ Jesus. The student should read and correspond the given Scriptures.

1. The Covenant with David.

The Natural - (Psalms 89:3, 34-37; Jeremiah 33:17-26).

God entered into Covenant with David. This Covenant was an everlasting Covenant involving David's seed, house, kingdom and throne. It was an unbreakable Covenant. Though it did involve punishment on David's sinful seed, yet God would never break that Covenant. The Lord gave this Covenant to the prophet Nathan in vision, and he communicated it to David. The Bible reveals that God is a Covenant-keeping God. God confirmed this Covenant by an oath (Psalms 89:3, 49).

The Spiritual - (Matthew 26:26-28; Hebrews 13:20).

Jesus Christ is the fulfillment of the Davidic Covenant, as the Son of David. He established the New Covenant which is an everlasting Covenant. In reality, the New Covenant was in the Davidic Covenant, and both of these were in the Abrahamic Covenant. Each was the extension of the other. God has confirmed the New Covenant personified in Jesus Christ with an oath (Psalms 110:4; Hebrews 7:20-22, 28).

2. The Seed of David.

The Natural - (Psalms 89:4, 29-36; 2 Samuel 7:12-15; 1 Chronicles 17:11-13; Jeremiah 33:17-26; Psalms 89:26).

David was always to have his seed remain. Although the seed of David may be guilty of iniquity, God would punish that seed but He would always preserve it. God would treat them on the basis of a Father-Son relationship. Who can fail to see that a number of the Kings of the Davidic line came under Divine chastisement? God, however, did preserve that seed according to His Covenant.

The Spiritual - (Isaiah 7:13-14; Matthew 1:1; Romans 1:3-4; Revelation 5:5; 22:16; Jeremiah 33:15-16).

There is no doubt about the fact that David's natural seed line continued on through the centuries. But THE seed of David finds its true expression in Jesus Christ, who is the seed of David after the flesh. Christ is David's Lord and Root as to His Deity. Christ is David's Son and Offspring, as to His Humanity. The same truth is here as in the fact that Christ is Abraham's seed also according to the flesh (Galatians 3:16). The writer to the Hebrews applies this "Father-Son" relationship clause of the Davidic Covenant to Jesus Christ. Compare 2 Samuel 7:14 with Hebrews 1:5.

3. The House of David.

The Natural -- (1 Chronicles 17:10, 16-27; 2 Samuel 7:4-7, 12-29).

David desired to build God a material house. The Lord said that He would build David a natural house. The fulfillment of this was in the continued household of David over the centuries in David's lineage.

The Spiritual -- (Hebrews 3:1-6; 1 Timothy 3:15; Ephesians 2:21-22; 2 Timothy 2:20; Galatians 6:10; 1 Peter 2:4-5).

Jesus Christ, being the seed of David, must also have a house. The Scriptures listed clearly show that the Church is His house. It is not a material or natural house. It is a spiritual house. Christ is a Son over His House, whose House we are. Both Jew and Gentile are brought into the household of faith through Jesus Christ.

4. The Kingdom of David.

The Natural -- (2 Samuel 7:12-17; 1 Chronicles 17:11,14).

David was always to have a kingdom, a dominion, a people over which to rule and reign. Bible history attested to this fact. The contrast with the Kings of the House of Israel, the Northern Kingdom, which had a changing dynasty was seen in the unchanging dynasty of the Kings of the House of Judah, of the line of David. The Kingdom of David continued its dominion in Palestine from David to Zedekiah. At this time the dominion was broken. It is this apparent violation of the Davidic Covenant that the Psalmist seems to allude to in Psalm 89:38-52. The prophet Jeremiah confirms the fact that God's Covenant with David will never be broken or disannulled (Jeremiah 33:17-26). The natural Kingdom of David pointed to the unending Kingdom of Christ.

The Spiritual -- (Isaiah 9:6,7; Jeremiah 23:5-6; 33:15-16; Luke 1:30-33; Revelation 5:5; Hebrews 1:8; Daniel 2:44).

The New Testament writers, as well as the Old, expressly show that the Kingdom of David continues in and through Christ. Jesus showed that His kingdom was not of this world system. His kingdom is an HEAVENLY and spiritual kingdom (John 18:36-37). It is entered by new birth (John 3:1-5). The Angel Gabriel announced to Mary that her Son Jesus would reign over the house of Jacob forever, and of His kingdom there would be no end. Christ certainly did not speak of a nationalistic or materialistic kingdom in His ministry. The Gospel of Matthew which is the Gospel of the King and the Kingdom reveals that this kingdom is a heavenly, spiritual, and eternal kingdom.

5. The Throne of David.

The Natural -- (2 Samuel 7:13,16; 1 Chronicles 17:11-15; Psalms 89:29-36; 122:5; 132:11).

David was always to have a throne. A throne is significant of kingship and rulership. It is vitally connected with the Kingdom. A kingdom needs a throne. A dominion needs a ruler, a sceptre. The throne of David continued in one unbroken dynasty from David through to Zedekiah, who was the last of the Judo-Davidic kings to rule over the House of Judah in Palestine. However, the same Scriptures given concerning the kingdom of David are also applicable to the throne of David (Psalms 89:38-52; Jeremiah 33:17-26). God's Covenant is everlasting and unbreakable. He is a Covenant-keeping God. The throne of David is eternal.

The Spiritual -- (Isaiah 9:6,7; Luke 1:30-33; Acts 2:22-36; Romans 1:3).

Again, the New Testament writers speak of the fact that Jesus Christ was to receive the throne of David. Not a materialistic, nationalistic throne -- it was a heavenly throne of rulership. When David foresaw that God would raise up Christ to sit on his throne, he spoke of the resurrection of Christ and His exaltation to the Father's right hand. Christ is to sit in the Father's throne, at God's right hand, now and until all His enemies become His footstool (Psalms 110:1-4; Matthew 22:44; Hebrews 1:3; 10:11-13; Revelation 3:21; Ephesians 1:20; 1 Corinthians 15:25,26). The earthly throne of David pointed to the heavenly throne of the Son of David.

6. The Sure Mercies of David.

The Natural -- (2 Samuel 7:12-17,15; 1 Chronicles 17:13; Isaiah 55:3-4; Psalms 89:1,2, 14, 28-34).

The Covenant that God made with David is a Covenant of mercy. If David's seed became iniquitous, then God would chastise them, but He would not take away His mercy utterly from them as He did from Saul. God judged King Saul and brought him into judgment down to the grave. He took away His mercy from him. No mercy meant death. However, God promised to David His sure mercies even though He would punish the sins of his seed. It was a Covenant of mercy, the sure mercies of God. No wonder many of the Psalms of David speak of the mercy of the Lord, of His mercy and truth (Psalms 85:10).

The Spiritual -- (Acts 13:27-37, 34; 2 Timothy 2:8; Romans 1:3-4).

Paul, in the Book of Acts, interprets the sure mercies of David to involve the resurrection of Christ from the dead. Christ, as the Son of David, was wounded for our transgressions, and bruised for our iniquities. He was brought to the grave on our account. The sure mercies, or the just and holy things (Acts 13:34, margin) of David involved Christ's resurrection from the dead, even as it involves the resurrection of the saints. Because of Christ's death and resurrection, the sure mercies of David, via the New Covenant, are extended to all who believe in Christ. God's mercy is extended to all who believe, but the resurrection to immortality is the greatest of the sure mercies of God (Revelation 20:6; Ephesians 1:3). The sure mercies involve the resurrection, and the throne involves His exaltation to God's right hand.

7. The Key of David.

The Natural -- (Isaiah 22:20-25,22).

This is the only specific Scripture which mentions the key of David in the Old Testament. The prophecy was spoken to Eliakim ("The Resurrection of God" or "God the Avenger"). To him was promised the key of the house of David. A key is simply an opener. It lets people in or locks them out. It is an instrument used to lock or unlock doors. David as King was able to give "the key" of his house, his throne, his kingdom to whomsoever he willed. The one using the key would be the true successor to David's house, and all his store of wealth, He would be the governor. The Old Testament shadowed forth the handing on of this key.

The Spiritual -- (Revelation 3:7).

There is no mistaking the New Testament spiritual significance of the Key of David. Jesus Himself, in the letter to the Church in Philadelphia, states that He is the One who is holy, just and true, and He has the key of David. He shuts doors, and opens doors, and no one can reverse His decision. He is the True Eliakim, "The Resurrection" and "The Avenger."

The New Testament reveals that He holds all the keys.

He has the Keys of the Kingdom of God (Matthew 16:19).
He has the Key of Knowledge (Luke 11:52).
He has the Keys of Death and Hades (Revelation 1:18).
He has the Key of the Bottomless Pit (Revelation 9:1; 20:1).
He has the Key of David (Revelation 3:7).

He has the key to every situation. He lets people in, and keeps them out. Unless he uses the key to open the door, then none can enter. This is the real significance of its use in Acts 15:15-18. The key of David is that which opens the door of faith and lets both Jew and Gentile into New Covenant relationship with God through Christ.

8. The Horn of David.

The Natural -- (Psalms 132:17; 92:10; 89:20,24; 18:2; 1 Kings 1:39).

The Horn in Scripture speaks of power and anointing to rule (Psalms 75:4,5,10). Horns speak of kings and kingdoms. For David, the horn was symbolic of anointing to office. David valued the anointing of the Spirit of God. The horn had been provided through the death of a sacrifice. Blood had been shed to provide the horn for the oil. This pointed to the atonement by blood, before the anointing with oil. When the Lord said that He would make the horn of David to bud, it implied the union in him of the dual offices of King-Priest. God had attested to Aaron's priesthood by causing Aaron's rod to bud. The budding rod testified that Aaron was God's anointed and appointed High Priest. So the budding horn would attest that David was God's anointed King-Priest.

The Spiritual -- (Luke 1:67-70; Revelation 5:6).

Zacharias the Priest of the Tribe of Levi, who was the father of Messiah's forerunner, John the Baptist, prophesied of the fulfillment of the horn of David. He said that the Lord God of Israel had visited and redeemed His people and had raised up a horn of salvation to the house of David. The Lamb of God, who is the Root of David, is seen to have 7 horns. These are symbolic of completeness and fullness of power unto salvation. He, as the supreme sacifice, shed His blood. Through His sacrificial death He has provided the horn of oil, the anointing of the Holy Spirit. No blood, no oil! The Holy Spirit becomes that anointing oil in the Church because of the body and blood of the Lamb of God, who was the substitute ram of sacrifice (Genesis 22:13).

9. The Tabernacle of David.

The Natural - (Isaiah 16:5; Amos 9: 11-13; 2 Samuel 7:17-19; 1 Chronicles 17:1-3).

In the historical account we see how David pitched a tent or tabernacle for the Ark of God's presence. It was a material tent housing a material Ark. Here David set a company of priests and established a new order of worship and praise to the Lord God of Israel. It was pitched in Mt. Zion, the City of King David. Here many of the Psalms were given concerning Messiah. The purpose of this book is to explore this area more fully. It should be noticed that the Tabernacle of David and the Davidic Covenant are related even as the Tabernacle of Moses and Mosaic Covenant were related.

The Spiritual -- (Acts 15:13-18; Hebrews 12:22-24).

When the New Testament writers quote the prophetic reference to the building of the Tabernacle of David, it is evident that they were not looking for the literal restoration of a material tent or tabernacle, nor were they looking for a restoration of the material Ark of the Covenant. The natural pointed to the spiritual. The New Testament writers received the revelation of the spiritual significance of David's Tabernacle and that order established therein. Again, we repeat, the purpose of this book is to set forth that significance.

The Tabernacle of David involves Christ in His Church. The Church is His Tabernacle and is related in the New Covenant. One cannot have a Covenant without a Sanctuary and Priesthood (Hebrews 8:1-13).

SUMMARY:

The glory of the Davidic Covenant becomes apparent when we realize that it finds its true fulfillment in David's Son, Messiah Jesus, and in the New Covenant. It is the New Testament writers who take these 9 things in the Davidic Covenant and apply them to Christ and His Church. Hence, that which was natural, national, and material in the Davidic Covenant is found to be everlasting only in and through the spiritual, the heavenly and eternal in the New Covenant in Christ and the Church.

In fact, the very nature of those things involved in the Davidic Covenant confirm this. For, those things were material, fleshly, earthly, and temporal, which in themselves are not and could not be everlasting. The only way these things could be everlasting is in and through the New Covenant, in that which is spiritual and eternal (2 Corinthians 4:18).

PART TWO
THE DAVIDIC KINGDOM TABERNACLE

CHAPTERS PAGE

7. Two Tabernacles Of David? 49

8. Building Again The Tabernacle Of David 57

9. The Coming In Of The Gentiles 63

10. Two Tabernacles Combined In One 71

Chapter 7

TWO TABERNACLES OF DAVID

"O send out Thy light and truth; let them lead me; let them bring me unto Thy holy hill, and to Thy TABERNACLES" (Psalm 43:3).

"How amiable are Thy TABERNACLES, O Lord of Hosts!" (Psalm 84:1).

A consideration of the Scriptures pertaining to the Tabernacle of David indicate that there are two aspects of the same. One group of Scriptures point to the truth of the Tabernacle of David and speak of the aspect of the Davidic KINGDOM, involving David's house, family, lineage and throne. Another group of Scriptures point to the truth of the Tabernacle of David and speak of the order of Davidic WORSHIP, involving the Ark of God which was God's throne in the earth.

For the purpose of our text, when we speak of the Tabernacle of David as pertaining to David's house and throne it will generally be spoken of as the DAVIDIC KINGDOM TABERNACLE. When speaking of the Tabernacle of David as pertaining to the order of praise and worship David set up it will be referred to as the DAVIDIC WORSHIP TABERNACLE.

A. The Tabernacle of David – The Davidic Kingdom

As noted previously under the comments on the Davidic Covenant, God promised to build David a house and a kingdom. David desired to build God a house. David himself had moved from a tent into a royal house built of cedar. In this house was the throne of David. Here he ruled and reigned over the kingdom of Israel. Here he sat in counsel, surrounded by his council of men on the set thrones of judgment, the thrones of the house of David (Psalm 122:5).

The prophet Isaiah prophesied of the throne of David being established. Undoubtedly the prophecy is Messianic. "In mercy the throne will be established, and he will sit on it in truth, in the tabernacle of David, judging and seeking justice and hastening righteousness" (Isaiah 16:5. NKJV).

The Amplified Old Testament says, "Then in mercy and loving-kindness shall a throne be established and One shall sit upon it in truth and faithfulness in the tent of David, judging and seeking justice and begins swift to do righteousness."

The immediate context of Isaiah 16:1-5 mentions Zion, a throne, a judge and thus kingship is inferred in which justice will be manifest resulting in righteousness. The person alluded to is the Messiah who will sit in David's tent as ruler, Messiah being of the line or house of David. Isaiah 9:6-9 is very similar and speaks of government, a throne, justice and judgment on David's throne. All of this is Messianic indeed.

Jamieson, Fausset & Brown Commentary write: "Isaiah apparently puts these words in the mouths of the Moabite ambassadors to the king of Judah, but in "language so Divinely framed as to apply to 'the latter days' under King Messiah, when the Lord shall bring again (reverse) the captivity of Moab."

Here the TABERNACLE OF DAVID is associated with THE THRONE of David. The things associated with the throne of David are seed, house and kingdom, all of which belong to the Davidic Covenant, the Davidic kingdom. In other words, all find their ultimate fulfillment in messiah's kingdom, for, Jesus Christ is the greater Son of David.

The royal house of David, or "the tabernacle of David" with the throne of David was in the city of David, which was Zion.

Zion was the city of the king. Zion was the ruling city over Israel and was a city within a city. Zion was the ruling city in the city of Jerusalem.

The kingly Psalms of David speak of Zion as the city of the great king. It speaks of the Davidic kingdom, ultimately Messiah's kingdom.

"Yet have I set My KING on My holy hill of Zion" (Psalm 2:6). "Great is the Lord and greatly to be praised in the city of our God, in His holy mountain. Beautiful for situation, the joy of the whole earth is mount Zion on the sides of the north, the city of the great king" (Psalm 48:1-2).

The emphasis in these references is on KINGSHIP and that which pertains to the Davidic kingdom.

B. Quotes from Commentaries

We confirm these things concerning the two schools of interpretation as to which tabernacle is referred to by some rather full quotations. Following are two quotations which emphasize the kingdom of Messiah as prophesied in "the tabernacle of David".

1. Commentary on the Whole Bible, Matthew Henry

Matthew Henry in Commentary on the Whole Bible (p. 1268), comments on this passage in Amos, from which we quote rather fully, saying:

"To him to whom all the prophets bear witness this prophet, here in the close, bears his testimony, and speaks of that day, those days shall come, in which God will do great things for His Church, by the setting up of the kingdom of Messiah, for the rejecting of which the rejection of the Jews was foretold in the foregoing verses. The promise here is said to agree to the planting of the Christian Church, and in that to be fulfilled, Acts 15:15-18. It is promised, I. That in the Messiah the Kingdom of David shall be restored (vs. 11); the Tabernacle of David it is called, that is, his house and family, which, though great and fixed, yet, in comparison with the kingdom of heaven, was mean and movable as a tabernacle. The Church militant, in its present state, dwelling as in shepherds' tents to feed, as in soldiers' tents to fight, is the Tabernacle of David. God's Tabernacle is called the Tabernacle of David because David desired and chose to dwell in God's Tabernacle for ever Psalms 61:4.

Now, these Tabernacles had fallen and gone to decay, the royal family was so impoverished, its power abridged, its honour stained, and laid in the dust; for many of that race degenerated, and in the captivity it lost the imperial dignity. Sore breaches were made upon it, and at length it was laid in ruins. So it was with the church of the Jews; in the latter days of it, its glory departed; it was like a tabernacle broken down and brought to ruin, in respect both of purity and prosperity. By Jesus Christ these tabernacles were rasied and rebuilt. In Him God's covenant with David had its accomplishment; and the glory of that house, which was not only sullied, but quite sunk, revived again; the breaches of it were closed and its ruins raised up, as in the days of old; nay, the spiritual glory of the family of Christ far exceeded the temporal glory of the family of David when it was at its height. In him also God's covenant with Israel had its accomplishment, and in the Gospel Church the Tabernacle of God was set up among men again, and raised up out of the ruins of the Jewish state. This is quoted in the first council at Jerusalem as referring to the calling in of the Gentiles and God's taking out of them a people for His name. Note, While the world stands God will have a Church in it, and, if it be fallen down in one place and among one people, it shall be raised up elsewhere. II. That the kingdom shall be enlarged, and the territories of it shall extend far, by the accession of many countries to it (vs. 12), that the house of David may possess the remnant of Edom, and of all the heathen, that is, that Christ may have them given him for His inheritance, even the uttermost parts of the earth for His possession, Psalms 2:8. Those that had been strangers and enemies shall become willing faithful subjects to the Son of David, shall be added to the Church, or those of them that are called by My name, saith the Lord, that is, that belong to the election of grace and are ordained to eternal life (Acts 13:48), for it is true of the Gentiles as well as of the Jews that the election hath obtained and the rest were blinded, Romans 11:7. Christ died to gather together in one the children of God that were scattered abroad, here said to be those called by His name. The promise is to all that are afar off, even as many as the Lord our God shall call, Acts 2:39. St. James expounds this as a promise that the residue of men should seek after the Lord, even all the Gentiles upon whom my name is called." (Emphasis his)

2. The Pulpit Commentary

The Pulpit Commentary (pp. 177, 178) comments on this passage in Amos by saying:

"The passage is quoted by St. James (Acts 15:16, 17), mostly from the Greek, in confirmation of the doctrine that the Church of God is open to all, whether Jew or Gentile. The Tabernacle (sukkah); hut or tent (as Jonah 4:5); no palace now, but fallen to low estate, a 'little house' (ch. 6:11). The prophet refers probably to the fall of the kingdom of David in the ruin wrought by the Chaldeans. Interpreted spiritually, the passage shadows forth the universal Church of Christ, raised from that of the Jews . . . The Septuagint gives 'That the remnant of man may earnestly seek the Lord,' regarding Edom as a representative of aliens from God, and altering the text to make the sense more generally intelligible. This version, which reads 'Adam,' men, instead of 'Edom,' is endorsed by St. James. Which are called by My Name; 'over whom My Name has been called (Septuagint). This is closer to the Hebrew; but the meaning is much the same, viz. all those who are dedicated to God and belong to Him being by faith incorporated into the true Israel."

B. The Tabernacle of David – The Davidic Worship

The next aspect of the Tabernacle of David is that which pertains to the Ark of God, the Ark of the Covenant which was God's throne in the earth.

A study of these Scriptures, 2 Samuel 6:17; 1 Chronicles 15:1; 16:1 with their chapter contexts, along with 2 Chronicles 1:4 provide these historical facts about the Tabernacle of David, the tent pitched by David.

With the return of the Ark to Judah from the land of the Philistines, and the judgment of God on Uzza for his presumptuous act, the Ark of God was placed in the house of Obed-edom for 3 months. David, after consulting with the leaders, pitched a tent, or tabernacle (ohel) for the Ark in Mt. Zion at Jerusalem in the place he had prepared for it. David then placed certain Priests and Levities to minister as singers and musicians before the Ark of God daily. A Davidic order of worship was established in Mt. Zion. The Ark of God, which was His throne in Israel, was in the tabernacle pitched by King David. Mt. Zion took on greater significance from this time on in the mind of God and His prophets. The emphasis in this mount was PRIESTLY ministry. As will be seen, many expositors see in this a type, a prophetic foreshadowing, of the Gospel dispensation. History becomes prophecy; prophecy will become history.

Here "the tabernacle of David" is associated with the Ark of God, God's throne and presence amongst His redeemed people, Israel. The burden of this text concerns this aspect.

Again we note some other notable writers and quotes from Commentaries. The weight of opinion here is on the Tabernacle of David in Davidic worship, though not excluding the Davidic kingdom aspect.

1. The Hope of Israel, Philip Mauro

Philip Mauro, in The Hope of Israel (p. 213, 214) comments on Acts 15:14-18:

"According to the writer's understanding of the passage, the era contemplated by the words, 'After this I will return,' is this present Gospel dispensation, whereof the conversion of Gentiles is the conspicuous feature (the 'mystery'. (Ephesians 3:3-6); and that 'the Tabernacle of David' is a prophetic symbol of that 'spiritual house,' into which converted Gentiles, along with converted Jews, 'as living stones,' are being builded together, upon Christ, the 'sure Foundation,' 'for an habitation of God through the Spirit' (Matthew 16:18; Ephesians 2:20-22; 1 Peter 2:5, 6; Isaiah 28:16)."

"From James' words alone it is clear that God's promise through the prophet Amos, that He would 'build again the Tabernacle of David,' was related to what He was just then beginning to do, namely, visit the Gentiles, to take out from among them a people for His Name".

"This connects the promise concerning the building again of the Tabernacle of David directly with God's work, then just commenced, of converting sinners from among the Gentiles." (Emphasis his)

And continuing on pages 217, 218 & 222, Philip Mauro says:

"To begin with, let us note that it is not the temple of Solomon. The two structures were quite distinct; and typically they differ widely in significance. Amos prophesied concerning a "tabernacle," definitely associated with David, a tabernacle which, at the time of his prophecy, had "fallen," and was in "ruins." Amos prophesied "in the days of Uzziah, King of Judah" (1:1), at which time the temple of Solomon was standing in all its glory, and its services and sacrifices were being carried out in due order. There is doubtless something very significant in the fact that, while the temple of Solomon was yet standing, God declared His purpose to "raise up the Tabernacle of David that is fallen," and to "raise up its ruins."

"In the prophecy of Amos we have the words of God, "And I will build it, as in the days of old." The days when David pitched a tabernacle in Zion for the Ark were days of joy and gladness, of shouting and dancing, of victory and prosperity, the days when David reigned over a united and a happy people." (Emphasis his)

2. Commentary on the Whole Bible, Jamieson, Fausett & Brown

Jamieson, Fausett and Brown, in "Commentary on the Whole Bible" (p. 679) comment on Amos 9:11-12, saying:

"In that day – quoted by St. James (Acts 15:16,17), 'After this.' i.e., in the dispensation of Messiah (Genesis 49:10; Hosea 3:4,5; Joel 2:28; 3:1). Tabernacle of David – not "the house of David" 'which is used of his affairs when prospering (2 Samuel 3:1), but the tent or booth, expressing the low condition to which his kingdom and family had fallen in Amos' time, and subsequently at the Babylonian captivity before the restoration; and secondarily, in the last days preceding Israel's restoration under Messiah, the antitype to David (Psalm 102: 13,14; Isaiah 12:1; Jeremiah 30:9; Ezekiel 23:24; 37:24) . . .

'Tabernacle' is appropriate to Him, as His human nature is the tabernacle which He assumed in becoming Immanuel, 'God with us' (John 1:14). 'Dwelt,' lit., tabernacled 'among us' (cf., Revelation 21:3). Some understand 'the tabernacle of David' as that which David pitched for the ark in Zion, after bringing it from Obededom's house. It remained there all his reign for thirty years, till the temple of Solomon was built; whereas the 'tabernacle of the congregation' remained at Gibeon (2 Chronicles 1:3), where the priests ministered in sacrifices (I Chronicles 16:39).

Song and praise was the service of David's attendants before the ark (Asaph, etc.); a type of the Gospel separation between the sacrificial service (Messiah's priesthood now in heaven) and the access of believers on earth to the presence of God, apart from the former (cf., 2 Samuel 6:12-17; I Chronicles 16:37-39; 2 Chronicles 1:3)."

3. Harmony of the Divine Dispensations, George Smith, 1856

Philip Mauro (p. 224-225) in commenting on George Smith's "Harmony of the Divine Dispensations" says,

"Thus, the Tabernacle of David is evidently replete with typical meaning, concerning which it will suffice for our present purpose to remark, that, to David, the man after God's own heart, who was himself a conspicuous type of Christ, and who is more closely associated with the Gospel than any other of the patriarchs (Matthew 1:1; Acts 13:22, 34; Romans 1:3; 2 Timothy 2:8; Revelation 22:16) it was given to know the mind of God concerning real spiritual worship; and that he," being a prophet, and knowing that God had sworn with an oath to him, that of the fruit of his loins according to the flesh, He would raise up Christ to sit on His throne" (Acts 2:30) was permitted to give in the tabernacle pitched by him on Mt. Zion, a wonderful foreshadowing of the worship, by prayer, preaching and song, which characterizes the gatherings of God's people in this Gospel dispensation." (Emphasis his)

And again, on pages 226-228, Mauro says:

"The decision of that question, so vitally important to the rising Church, was formally referred to the apostles and elders at Jerusalem. Paul, Barnabas, and others went from Antioch to the Hebrew capital to take part in this important discussion. Peter, Barnabas and Paul recited the wonders wrought among the Gentiles by the preaching of the Gospel. But still there was wanting some clear, pointed, powerful, Scriptural authority to effect the permanent settlement of a question of such magnitude. And it was supplied by James, who quoted the words of the text (Amos 9:10, 11) as incontrovertable evidence on the case. The question was, Must the ritual law of Moses be obeyed by Christian converts? To this the apostle replied, 'Certainly not; for inspired prophecy declares that the kingdom of Christ is not to be a revival and extension of Mosaicism, but on the contrary a restoration of the Tabernacle of David. And since in that sanctuary the Mosaic ritual had no place, so it can have no claims in the Christian Church'."

"And there in Jerusalem itself, within sight of the temple, where the ritual of the law was still performed in all its extent and minuteness, the whole body of the Church repudiate its claims, and adopt the Tabernacle of David as the Divinely appointed model for all Christian practice and institutions."

"Circumcision fell and perished from the Christian Church before the Divinely inspired quotation of the prophecy of Amos by the Apostle James. Sacrifice was abolished with circumcision. For that institution formed no part of the worship offered to God on Mount Zion.

"With circumcision and sacrifices the priesthood was also abolished. Indeed an unsacrificial priesthood is a contradiction of terms; for every priest is 'ordained to offer gifts and sacrifices' (Hebrews 8:3). But there was nothing of that kind in the tabernacle of David, whose sacred services therefore vividly represented the worship proper to that Church which is redeemed by the blood of the Lamb, Whose 'one sacrifice for sins' is universally and everlastingly efficacious – 'once for all' (Hebrews 10:10). Nor must it be forgotten that, with those elements of the Mosaic economy, every existing typical and symbolical thing was swept away" (That is to say all the "shadows" of the law were abolished and replaced by the corresponding spiritual realities). (Emphasis his.)

4. Fundamental Revelation in Dramatic Symbol, Rev. J.T. Horger

Rev. J. T. Horger, in Fundamental Revelation in Dramatic Symbol (pp. 195-197, 204-207) speaks of the Tabernacle and the Temple. He writes:

"It was about 1491 B.C. when Moses built a temporary Tabernacle at Mt. Sinai, which served until he built the Tabernacle, the same year, according to the specific pattern given him by Jehovah, on Mt. Sinai, where the Israelites were then camped. This Tabernacle was carried by the Israelites, through the 40 years of wilderness life, and maintained as a Holy Sanctuary wherever they worshiped, for over 350 years in the land of Canaan. And then, about 1045 B.C., David built a new Tabernacle, and pitched it on Mt. Zion in Jerusalem; and went and got the Ark, which had been out of the Tabernacle which Moses built, for about 100 years, and put it in the new Tabernacle which he had built on Mt. Zion. (Read together I Sam. chapter 4 with I Chronicles, chapters 15 and 16). And then it was about 40 years after David installed the Ark in his new Tabernacle, that Solomon built the magnificent world-wonder Temple on Mt. Moriah, also located in Jerusalem. . . . As such, St. James refers to the Tabernacle built by David, and set up on Mt. Zion, in the southwestern corner of Jerusalem, as a type of the Church composed of the discples of Jesus Christ — quoting the prophet he says, "After this I will return, and will build again the Tabernacle of David" (Acts 15:16, 17).

Although the present writer does not follow fully the analogy of Horger in Fundamental Revelation in Dramatic Symbol, he does note these two Tabernacles as being significant of the two Covenants and that David's Tabernacle typified the Church of New Testament times.

Horger (pp. 204-207) says, "However, another most significant constitutional trait that characterizes this typical city is the fact that it was built upon two small elevations, called Mt. Zion and Mt. Moriah. To the mind of the writer, this is suggestive of the two covenants on which the plan of salvation is built, and, therefore, indicative of the two works of grace; namely, the new birth and the baptism of the Spirit . . . As already stated, the heart, life, and glory of the Tabernacle was the Ark of the Covenant in the Holy of Holies; and when the Ark was captured by the Philistines, as recorded in 1 Samuel 5th chapter, it is said that the Glory departed from the Tabernacle, to return no more, for the Ark never returned to the Tabernacle built by Moses. However, when David had taken Jerusalem from the Jebusites and God had designated it as the chosen city, in which He would dwell and bless His people, then David built a new Tabernacle of Mt. Zion. This new Tabernacle built by David was a type of the new Church built by Jesus Christ, for David was ever a type of Christ; and, in keeping with the same line of typology, David built the new Tabernacle and placed it on Mt. Zion, not on Mt. Moriah, for it was reserved for the location of the Temple built by Solomon as a type of the sanctified, Spirit-filled soul under the Holy Ghost dispensation."

The student will pardon such lengthy quotations (Used by Permission), but because this subject has been such a neglected subject, such quotations were felt to be beneficial and necessary.

Enough quotations have been given to confirm the fact that expositors have recognized that the Tabernacle of David may refer to the Davidic Kingdom Tabernacle or the Davidic Worship Tabernacle, or to both. Both were on Mt. Zion. Both are referred to as Tabernacles. One is royalty, the other is priestly.

Chapter 8

BUILDING AGAIN THE TABERNACLE OF DAVID

The Prophet Amos says: "IN THAT DAY will I raise up the tabernacle of David that is fallen, and close up the breaches thereof; and I will raise up his ruins, and I will build it as in the days of old" (Amos 9:11)

James, in quoting this verse, says: "After this I will return and will build again the tabernacle of David, which is fallen down; and I will build again the ruins thereof, and I will set it up. That the residue of men might seek after the Lord, and all the Gentiles, upon whom my name is called, saith the Lord, who doeth all these things" (Acts 15:16, 17).

In this chapter we come to the matter of "time element" as pertaining to the rebuilding of the Tabernacle of David. WHEN is the Tabernacle of David to be raised up again? WHEN will the Lord build again the Tabernacle of David that is fallen down? The "time element" needs to be considered.

The expositors in the Commentaries fall basically into two streams of thought as to the "time element" and the interpretation of these passages.

One group – the Dispensational School – interpret these passages as being fulfilled in a future Jewish Millenniel Kingdom, under Christ and the Gentiles being blessed in that period. They see the passages particularly speaking of the Davidic kingdom.

The other group, which we speak of the Realized Prophetic School, see these same passages being fulfilled here and now, having their beginning in the Book of Acts. However, even within this group there is difference of opinion as to WHICH Tabernacle is to be rebuilt. Some believe these passages refer only to the Davidic Kingdom Tabernacle, and others believe they refer to the Davidic Worship Tabernacle. Some believe that both could be involved.

Let us consider these two major interpretative views; Dispensationalism and Realized Prophecy in relation to the "time element" and WHEN the Tabernacle of David is to be rebuilt.

A. The Prophecy of Amos

1. The Dispensational View

The Dispensational view holds that the prophecy of Amos is yet to find fulfilment in the Millennial Kingdom, after the second coming of Christ. An example of this view is seen in Finnis Jennings Dake's annotated Bible and his comments on the Amos passage, which we quote here.

Amos 9:11, 12, is the reference in Amos under consideration:

In that day – the Millennium, when the Messiah comes to restore the kingdom and throne of David, and to reign over the house of Jacob forever (vs. 11; Isa. 9:6-7; Lk 1:32-33; Rev. 11:15; 20:1-10). The expression in that day is used particularly in Isaiah, where it is found 50 times as compared to only 5 in the book of Amos (2:16; 8:3, 9, 13; 9:11).

This passage is quoted in Acts 15:14-18 where it is clear that it was to be fulfilled after the church age. It reads, "Simeon hath declared how God at the first did visit the Gentiles, to take out of them a people for His name. And to this agree the

words of the prophets, After this (after taking a people from the Gentiles for the church) I will return, and will build again the tabernacle of David, which is fallen down; and I will build again the ruins thereof, and I will set it up."

The prophets agree that the tabernacle of David will be set up again; and in Acts 15 it is clear that it will not be until after the rapture of the church – after the taking out of the Gentiles a people for His name. It is also clear that this has never been fulfilled as yet, for Simeon made these statements about the time of the destruction of Jerusalem and the dispersion of Israel among the nations (Lk. 21:20-24). Since A.D. 70 the Jews have not had a kingdom with a king ruling in Jerusalem on the throne of David, so the reference must be to the future when Messiah will set up this kingdom and establish the throne of David again (v. 11; Isa. 9:6-7; Lk. 1:32-33; Rev. 11:15; 20:1-10).

David's tabernacle refers to his throne and kingdom, which are now fallen. They were overthrown in 616 B.C. and have been fallen down ever since; they will not be raised up again until after the church age – at the second advent of Christ.

As in the days of old – when David was King. David will become the future king of Israel under the Messiah (Isa. 9:6-7; 16:5; Jer. 30:9; Ezek. 34:23-24; 37:24-25; Hos. 3:4-5).

Cp. v. 12 with Acts 15:17. Here it is stated that Israel will possess the remnant of Edom and all the heathen, while in Acts 15:17 the purpose given is, that all men might seek the Lord. Both will be literally true. Israel will possess their enemies and when David's kingdom is set up again and he and Messiah reign, men will seek the Lord in a greater way than ever before. Cp. Isa. 11:9.

Thus the Dispensational view is that this prophecy of the Tabernacle of David concerns his house, throne and kingdom, and that this restoration will take place in the Millennium under David and Christ.

2. The Realized Prophetic View

By this is meant that the New Testament apostles realized that what God was doing in their midst was the fulfilment, at least the beginning of that which the Old Testament prophets spoke about of Messiah's times.

"In that day" – ie., Messiah's times, especially from His exaltation and onwards.

"I will raise up the Tabernacle of David that is fallen, and close up the breaches thereof; and I will raise up his ruins, and I will build it as in the days of old" — ie., The Booth (Sookah) of David to be raised up. It speaks of the house of David and his royal line that was to endure forever. The Booth refers to the lowly state David's throne would come to during its history. Uzziah was the king of the royal house of David at this time (BC787). He was a godly king until his presumptuous act, that of burning incense in the temple of the Lord (2 Chronicles 26). Thus the royal house of David was not "fallen down" or in "ruins" at that time.

"The breaches" — prophetically anticipatory of those years when there was no Davidic king on the throne of David from Zedekiah to Messiah, BC 606-BC 4. Also the Davidic worship order that generally fell into decay when there was no godly king over Judah.

Messiah's incarnation and exaltation fulfills this promise of the throne (Luke 1:30-33). He is David's Lord as well as David's son.

"To build it as in the days of old" – spoke of a restoration of the early glory of David's kingdom and house.

"That they may possess the remnant of Edom, and of the heathen, which are called by My name, saith the Lord that doeth this" — ie., David's kingdom would inherit the remnant of Edom and the heathen upon whom the name of the Lord would be called as they also would call upon the name of the Lord unto salvation (Acts 15:15-18; Acts 2:33-37; Joel 2:28-32; Romans 10:11-13).

Allusion may also be seen in Amos to the Tabernacle of David as to the Davidic order of worship that had fallen down and experienced breaches over the years because of ungodly kings of the line of David. This is seen in the references to Zion and David in Amos. "The Lord will roar from Zion and utter His voice from Jerusalem . . ." (Amos 1:2) "Woe to them that are ease in Zion . . . that chant to the sound of the viol, and invent to themselves instruments of musick, like David . . ." (Amos 6:1, 5).

"I will build again the Tabernacle of David that is fallen down . . ." (Amos 9:11)

The Realized Prophetic view sees the Amos passage as being fulfilled, or, the beginning of its fulfilment, in the outpouring of the Holy Spirit upon the Gentiles and their coming into the New Testament Church, the people of God. Or, in other words, the coming of the Gentiles would be into the Booth or house and kingdom of David's Son, Messiah Jesus. Hence it was not to be fulfilled in a coming Millennial kingdom but in this present Messianic Dispensation. Jew and Gentile would be one in this Tent, this Church!

B. The Prophecy of Isaiah

Another prophecy which mentions "the Tabernacle of David" is found in Isaiah 16:5. Both Isaiah and Amos prophesied during the reign of Uzziah, the king of Judah of the house of David. The two views are noted here.

1. Dispensational View

This is basically the same in the interpretation of the Amos passage. Read Isaiah 16:5. Someone will sit on the throne in David's Tent. It is said that this prophecy concerns Messiah and it will come to pass in the Millennium when Christ reigns over Israel on the throne of David.

2. Realized Prophetic View

The Realized Prophetic view sees this Scripture as being fulfilled now in this present era. Isaiah 16:5 is a Messianic prophecy. It finds its ultimate fulfilment in Christ, the Son of David, who was promised the throne of David (Luke 1:30-33).

Isaiah 16:1 speaks of the daughter of Zion. Mt. Zion was the city of David, the city where David's throne was as well as David's tabernacle. In verse 5 it particularly points to the throne of David, his house, his kingdom, his rule and reign.

"And in mercy shall the throne be established (prepared): and he (undoubtedly Messiah) shall sit upon it in truth in the tabernacle (ie., tent, ohel) of David, judging and seeking judgment, and hasting righteousness."

Thus Messiah would be the "he" of Isaiah 16:5 who would SIT enthroned in the tent of David. His rule would be just judgment and righteous.

In a time when the kings of Judah would be ungodly and unrighteous, the Lord God would have a righteous King sitting on David's throne (Jeremiah 23:1-5). This throne was in the TENT (ohel) of David. David's tabernacle was simply a tent. It was not called MISH-KAN, as this was the word most generally used of the Tabernacle of the Lord built by Moses, especially the wooden structure.

The TENT Over the Tabernacle of the Lord was ohel. The TENT of David was also ohel. The Throne of David was in the ohel. The Ark of God was also in ohel. This Isaiah passage has it emphasis on David's throne – his kingdom.

C. The Fulfilment according to James

James, the apostle, by a word of wisdom, quotes from the Amos passage and applies it to the coming in of the Gentiles. We note briefly the two views as to what James meant.

1. Dispensational View

There is no need to enlarge upon that which has been noted under the Dispensation View of the Amos passage. The same school of thought says that James is speaking of the Gentiles coming into the Church, then comes the rapture, and "after this" the Lord returns again and builds again the tent or house and kingdom of David. This will take place in the Millennium (Acts 15:15-18). The student is referred to the Dispensational View on The Prophecy of Amos.

2. Realized Prophetic View

The Realized Prophetic view believes that Acts 15:15-18 is finding its fulfilment in this present era.

James, given a word of wisdom by the risen head of the Church, Jesus Christ, quotes the Amos passage and applies it to the coming in of the Gentiles into the Messianic Kingdom and the movement of God among the Gentiles at that time.

The Church would be composed of Jew and Gentile. It should be remembered that the New Testament Apostles are the infallible interpreters of the Old Testament Prophets. The Old Testament prophets foretold the coming of the Gentiles into Messiah's Kingdom. Messiah was the Son of David and would sit on David's throne, in David's tent.

"After this" – ie., The "in that day" of Amos becomes "after this" of Acts by James. After the Old Testament, when Messiah is come, is what is understood by this time element.

"I will return" – ie., not the second coming or Christ, but His first coming, as the Lord returned to His people when they returned to Him (Hosea 5:15; 6:1-3; Jeremiah 4:1; 24:7; Joel 2:14; Malachi 3:7).

"And will build again the Tabernacle of David which is fallen down; and I will build again the ruins thereof, and I will set it up . . . " — ie., the "sookah" of Amos becomes the "skene" of James, speaking of David's lineage, house and kingdom. It is

David's dwelling place. This finds fulfilment in the exaltation of Messiah, the Son of David, to the throne of God, to the right hand of the Majesty on High, forever (Acts 2:33-37 with Acts 13:26-37).

"That the residue of men might seek after the Lord, and all the Gentiles, upon whom My name is called, saith the Lord who doeth all these things" – ie., the coming in of the Gentiles under the Gospel era and the outpouring of the Holy Spirit on the Gentiles as already seen under the witness of Peter, Paul and Barnabas in Acts 10-11, 13, 14, chapters. Amos and James together equate the restoration of the Tabernacle of David and his house with the ingathering of the Gentiles, both then, and on through this era.

We return to the issue raised in a previous chapter. Is "The Tabernacle of David" referring to the HOUSE or KINGDOM of David, or is it referring to the TENT that David pitched for the new order of worship around the Ark of God in Zion?

The difference of opinion arises out of how the verses in Isaiah 16:5 with Amos 9:11 in connection with 2 Samuel 6:17; 1 Chronicles 15:1; 16:1 are to be interpreted. Do they speak of David's house, involving his throne and kingdom (ohel, or sook-kah), or do they speak of the Tent for the Ark of God and the Davidic worship therein?

If they speak of David's house or kingdom, then the Acts passage must be interpreted as saying that the Gentiles are to come into David's house, David's kingdom, through Christ, the Son of David.

If they speak of David's tent in Zion, pitched for the Ark of God and priestly ministrations, then it means that the Gentiles are to come into David's order of worship, through Christ, the Son of God.

One is Kingly; the other is Priestly!

The author believes that both truths are there. This is seen in the totality of Scripture concerning David's House and David's Tabernacle. Both find their fulfilment in the Church, composed of Jew and Gentile, and now becoming through Christ, the order of King-Priests, the order of Melchisedek, as Christ Himself is.

Both are brought together in Christ who is KING and PRIEST, combining both offices in Himself.

Chapter 9

THE COMING IN OF THE GENTILES

We come now to consider some of the other issues raised in Acts 15 use of the Amos passage with reference to the building again of the Tabernacle of David and the coming in of the Gentiles into Christ. Into which Tabernacle of David are the Gentiles coming? Is it the Davidic Kingdom Tabernacle or the Davidic Worship Tabernacle?

We endeavour to answer these questions in this and the following chapter.

A. THE COMING IN OF THE GENTILES

In Chapter Three we considered the historical setting in the Book of Acts in which the Apostle James used the prophecy of Amos to be significant of the coming in of the Gentiles. There we asked ourselves a number of questions, the dominant question being: "What has the Tabernacle of David got to do with the Gentiles?" It is here that we bring our long quest to its conclusion regarding the Gentiles coming into blessing in the Tabernacle of David. Our considerations of this topic have shown that the Tabernacle of David becomes a prophecy of Christ and His Church.

The Judaizing teachers of the Law who had come down from Jerusalem were seeking to bring the believing Gentiles under the bondage of Law, under bondage to Moses. The purpose of the gathering of the apostles and elders at Jerusalem was to discuss this matter. The Gentiles were being brought into salvation through faith in Christ. What was to be their relationship to the Old Covenant and to the Mosaic ritual therein? As evident, vital issues were involved here because the decision of the apostles and elders would affect the whole future of the New Testament Church and the relationship of Jews and Gentiles for centuries. In the language of our study, the Judaizers were actually endeavouring to bring the Gentiles into the Tabernacle of Moses -- that Tabernacle which meant Law and bondage of works; that Tabernacle which involved circumcision, carnal ordinances, the Aaronic priesthood, and the sacrificial system. The question, asked again, really was, "What is the relationship of the Gentiles to the Mosaic Covenant and Mosaic ritual as demonstrated in the Tabernacle of Moses?"

As already noted in Acts 15:7 Peter related his experience first. He told how the Lord had poured out His Spirit on the Gentiles exactly as He had done on the Jews at Pentecost. And this apart from circumcision and apart from any Mosaic ritual or law. Peter's experience was of great value in the testimony concerning the coming in of the Gentiles. However experience is not enough. Is it Scriptural? Is it according to the Word of the Lord?

Paul and Barnabas (Acts 15:12) also gave their report of the signs and wonders wrought among the Gentiles, those who were called "The Uncircumcision," those who were "without law" (Ephesians 2:11-12; Romans 2:12-15). God had raised up Churches amongst the Gentiles apart from any of the Mosaic economy.

However, it was the Apostle James, who, by a word of wisdom quoted the Old Testament prophecy of Amos concerning the restoration of the Tabernacle of David and showed that the purpose of this was that "the residue of men and all the Gentiles might seek after the Lord" (Acts 15:15-17).

God did visit the Gentiles in the house of Cornelius to take out of them a people for His Name, as Peter had already testified. The words of the prophets agree to this. And although James quotes but one prophet, the prophet Amos, he does say that it was the prophets who spoke of the Gentiles coming into the blessing of the New Covenant.

Oftentimes verse 16 of Acts 15 has been misinterpreted to say that the Jews are going to come in after the Gentiles have been gathered out, or after the Church has been removed from the earth. The passage is sometimes used to support a future restoration of the Jewish nation to the Mosaic economy. But this is not so. It is verse 15 of the same chapter and the context of this chapter which makes all the difference.

What Peter, Paul, and Barnabas had seen God do among the Gentiles under their ministry was exactly what God had said He would do. Namely, to build again the Tabernacle of David. What for? That the residue of men and all the Gentiles upon whom His Name is called might seek after the Lord.

The prophets had clearly foretold a period of time when the Gentiles would come into blessing. These prophecies are generally placed into some future age, but it is in this present age that the Gentiles are to come in. This present age was ushered in by the death, burial, resurrection, ascension, and glorification of the Lord Jesus Christ. It was confirmed by the Lord Himself in the outpouring of the Holy Spirit on both Jews (Acts 2) and Gentiles (Acts 10-11).

It is this which becomes "the key of David" (Revelation 3:7). The key of David must not and cannot be limited to worship and praise although it involves that. The key of David is related to the keys of the kingdom. The Apostle Peter was specifically given the "keys of the kingdom" (Matthew 16:16-18). Did he really use these keys? What are these keys? What are keys used for? The Book of Acts unmistakably shows that Peter did use these keys. The purpose of a key is to open or lock a door; to let people in or to keep them out. The very word "key" means "an opener." Peter used these keys in the Book of Acts. It was Peter who the Lord used to be an opener of the door of faith to both Jews and Gentiles. The great missionary Church at Antioch rejoiced when they heard that God "had opened the door of faith to the Gentiles" (Acts 14:27).

It is to the Church of Philadelphia that the Lord addressed Himself as the One having the key of David. He told this Church that He had set before them a door that no man could shut once it was opened, and none could open once it was shut (Revelation 3:7). The Church of Philadelphia had a great door of evangelization of the Gentiles opened to it by this key of David. What would the key of David let the Gentiles into? The order of the Tabernacle of David or the Tabernacle of Moses? The answer should be evident. The key of David would let the Gentiles into the order of the Tabernacle of David.

The problem of what to do with the Gentiles is solved. They do not have to come under circumcision, or under the Law, that is, the Tabernacle of Moses. They come into the Tabernacle of David which has no Mosaic ritualism. The cross has ushered in a new order where both Jew and Gentile can come, apart form the Mosaic economy, into the Church, the New Testament Tabernacle of David. The Gentiles are coming into David's Tabernacle and should not be under bondage to Moses.

With this decision being reached, the apostles, elders, and the whole Church at Jerusalem under the witness of the Spirit rejoiced that no Mosaic burden was to be laid on the Gentiles.

The early Church was in the great transition period from the Old Covenant and Tabernacle of Moses order to the New Covenant and the New Testament Church order. It was the transition from one chosen nation receiving the Gospel to all nations receiving the Gospel. The Tabernacle of David was a prophetic symbol of the Church, "the habitation of God by the Spirit" in which Jews and Gentiles would gather together for worship (Ephesians 2:20-22).

B. Coming Out Of Covenantal Confusion

Undoubtedly the heart of Acts 15 has to do with COVENANTAL relationships. Though the word "covenant" is not specifically used in the chapter, covenants are implied. These covenants, by implication, are the Abrahamic, Mosaic, Davidic and New Covenants. The problem in this period of time was covenantal confusion.

- **The Abrahamic Covenant is implied by the rite of circumcision, circumcision being the sign and seal of covenantal relationship with God (Genesis 17; Acts 15:1-7; 7:8).**

- **The Mosaic or Old Covenant is implicit also. This is seen in the specific mention of Moses in this chapter. The Mosaic law confirmed the rite of circumcision as well as additional laws and ceremonies belonging to that covenant. The sect of the Pharisees said that it was needful to circumcise the Gentiles and to keep the law of Moses (Acts 15:5). Moses of old time has in every city them that preach him, being read in the synagogues every Sabbath day (Acts 15:21).**

- **The New Covenant is implicit also. Peter, Paul and Barnabas all testify of salvation by grace through faith in the Lord Jesus Christ, apart from circumcision and apart from the ceremonials of the Mosaic law (Acts 15:7-12).**

- **The Davidic Covenant is also implied by the very mention of the Tabernacle of David which had fallen down and was to be rebuilt again and established so that the Gentiles could come into it (Acts 15:13-17).**

The heart of the matter therefore is COVENANT! The chief promises of the Abrahamic Covenant and the chief promise of the Davidic Covenant concerns Christ Jesus. Jesus Christ was the Son of Abraham and the Son of David (Matthew 1:1). When the Gentiles come into Christ they became the seed of Abraham and come into the kingdom of David through the Messiah (Galatians 3:16, 29; Isaiah 55:3, 4).

C. Old Testament Prophecies

The Old Testament prophetic Scriptures concerning the Gentiles coming under the Gospel of Christ had to be opened to the early Church. We note some of these Old Testament prophecies as well as some New Testament portions which were opened to the early apostles, and more especially to Paul, the Apostle to the Gentiles.

1. Genesis 22:18, "In thy seed (Christ) shall all nations be blessed" (Galatians 3:8, 14-16, 29).

2. Isaiah 11:10, "In that day there shall be a root of Jesse, which shall stand for an ensign of the people; to it shall the Gentiles seek . . . . " (Isaiah 11:1-10).

3. Isaiah 42:1, "Behold My servant . . . he shall bring forth judgment to the Gentiles," (Isaiah 42:1-4; Matthew 12:17-20).

4. Isaiah 49:6, " . . . I will also give thee for a light to the Gentiles, that thou mayest be my salvation unto the end of the earth," (Isaiah 49:1-6; Acts 13:46-48).

5. Jeremiah 16:19, " . . . the Gentiles shall come unto thee from the ends of the earth . . . "

6. Malachi 1:11, " . . . My Name shall be great among the heathen."

7. Zechariah 2:11, "And many nations shall be joined to the Lord in that day, and shall be My people . . . " (Acts 10:45).

8. Luke 2:32, " . . . a light to lighten the Gentiles . . . "

9. Matthew 12:21, "And in His Name shall the Gentiles trust."

10. Matthew 28:18-19, "Go ye therefore and teach (disciple) all nations . . . "

11. Mark 16:17-20, preach the Gospel to every creature.

12. Acts 1:8, "Ye shall be witnesses unto Me in Jerusalem, Judea, Samaria and unto the uttermost parts of the earth."

13. Acts 11:18, " . . . God also to the Gentiles granted repentance unto life."

14. Acts 15:14, " . . . God at the first did visit the Gentiles . . . "

15. Romans 15:9-12, note the emphasis on the Gentiles in these verses.

    "And that the Gentiles might glorify God for His mercy . . . . as it is written, For this cause I will confess to thee among the Gentiles and sing unto thy name" (vs. 9).

    "Rejoice, ye Gentiles, with His people" (vs. 10).

    " . . . Praise the Lord, all ye Gentiles . . . " (vs. 11).

    " . . . in Him shall the Gentiles trust . . . " (vs. 12).

16. Romans 11, this chapter especially deals with the grafting in of the Gentiles into the good olive tree, the true Israel of God.

17. 1 Corinthians 12:13, "For by one Spirit are we all baptized into one body, whether we be Jew or Gentile . . . "

    (See also Ephesians 2:11-22).

Numerous other references could be quoted. All point to the coming in of the Gentiles into the New Testament Church, the one Body of Christ which is composed of Jews and Gentiles. The Jews who accept Christ are no longer under the Old Covenant or the law of Moses. They have to come out from the Mosaic economy. The Gentiles who accept Christ do not have to go into the Tabernacle of Moses or come under the Mosaic economy out of which the Jew had to come. Where do both go? Together, as one in Christ they go into the Tabernacle of David and its attendant worship, apart from the Mosaic ritualism.

In this Tabernacle Christ is sitting on the throne of David. "And in mercy shall the throne be established; and He shall sit upon it in truth in the Tabernacle of David, judging and seeking judgment, and hasting righteousness" (Isaiah 16:5).

Christ Jesus was promised the throne of His Father David (Luke 1:31-33). In Acts 2:29-36 Peter interprets the raising up of Christ to sit on David's throne to be prophetic of Christ's resurrection, ascension, and enthronement at the throne of God, sitting on the right hand of the Majesty on High. The resurrection was involved in "the sure mercies of David" (Acts 13:33-34).

Christ is sitting in the Tabernacle of David (Hebrew 1:3). He is enthroned as the Son of David. This Man indeed sat down expecting all His enemies to be made His footstool. He ministers in the true Sanctuary, the heavenly Sanctuary and He ministers in His Church in the midst of the worshipping congregation (Hebrew 10:11-13). He ministers after the order of Melchisedek (Psalms 110), to both Jew and Gentile.

The difference between the two Tabernacles is the key to the understanding of Acts 15. These Tabernacles were not identical. God was not duplicating the Mosaic order in both Tabernacles. He was giving us a prophetic foreshadowing even under Old Testament times of what He would do in New Testament times.

If James had said that God was "building again the Tabernacles of MOSES which is fallen down, that the Gentiles might seek the Lord" then it would have been clear that the Gentiles should come in under the Law Covenant. But He did not say that! The difference between the two Tabernacles is the difference between the two Covenants. The Jews knew the difference between the two orders, the Tabernacle at Gibeon and Zion, even if they did not fully understand it. It was the Spirit of God who directed James to bring this Scripture before the council at Jerusalem.

The fact of the Gentiles coming in may be seen possibly in the significant use of the name of Edom in the prophecy of Amos. "In that day will I raise up the Tabernacle of David that is fallen, and close up the breaches thereof; and I will raise up his ruins, and I will build it as in the days of old. That they may possess the remnant of Edom, and of all the heathen which are called by My Name, saith the Lord who doeth this." James in Acts 15:16-17 interprets "the remnant of Edom and the heathen" to be "the residue of men and all the Gentiles."

The name "Edom" being linked with the heathen seems to be a representative name for the Gentiles; all those of Abraham's line after the flesh, as well as all nations outside of the chosen nation through Isaac. Edom comes from Esau, Jacob's twin brother. Esau's name means "hairy, rough, rugged" while Edom means "red."

There are tremendous prophecies of judgment declared against Esau/Edom by the prophets of old. The following Scriptures speak of these judgments: Isaiah 11:14; 34:5-6; 63:1-4; Jeremiah 9:26; 25:21; 27:1-11; 49:7-11; Ezekiel 25:12-14; 32:28-29; Joel 3:19; Amos 1:6, 11-12; Psalms 60:8-9; 108:9-10; 83:6; Malachi 1:1-5.

Yet the prophet Amos (9:11, 12) shows that out of Edom as well as the rest of the heathen there would be a people upon whom the Name of the Lord would be called. This can only be through the Gospel and the reception of the Name of the Lord Jesus Christ in redeeming grace. The Book of Acts records for us the fact of the Gentiles accepting Christ and being called by His Name. The disciples were first called Christians at Antioch (Acts 11:26). This Church at Antioch was the great missionary Church to the Gentiles.

A possible example of this is found in the Tabernacle of David in the person and family of Obed-edom the Gittite (2 Samuel 6:6-12; 1 Chronicles 13:13-14; 15:25). His name means "Serving Edom" or "Servant of Edom." He was willing to receive the Ark of God into his house as a Levitical priest. In due time he came into the order of David's Tabernacle. The association is seen in the fact that this Gittite bears the name "edom" as part of his name, and it is concerning Edom that God promises blessing.

There seems to have been several Obed-edoms' associated with the service of the Tabernacle of David. According to Herbert Lockyer in All the Men of the Bible (p. 263) there were at least four Obed-edoms connected with David's Tabernacle.

1. A Levite, one of David's body guards, in whose house the Ark was hid for three months. Its presence brought blessing to Obed-edom and all of his family (2 Samuel 6:10-12; 1 Chronicles 13:13, 14; 15:25).

2. A Levite, gatekeeper of the Tabernacle, who marched before the Ark during its removal to Jerusalem (1 Chronicles 15:18-24; 26:4, 8, 15).

3. A Levite, a Merarite, of the second degree who did regular duty at the tent erected for the Ark (1 Chonicles 16:5, 38). He ministered before the Ark.

4. A son of Jeduthan, who also served at the Sanctuary. Perhaps Obed-edom the Korathite (1 Chronicles 16:38; 2 Chronicles 25:24). He apparently was a gatekeeper.

Thus the name "Edom" is connected with David's Tabernacle in its historical setting in these families by the name of Obed-edom, and also in its prophetical setting in Amos' prophecy. The author cannot help but think that these families identified with this name of the flesh-seed (Esau) become a foreshadowing of the coming in of "the remnant of Edom" as priests unto God in the New Testament Church.

Whatever may be the full significance of the prophecy the Book of Acts clearly shows that the apostles understood it to be a foretelling of the Gentiles coming into New Covenant relationship with God through Christ and this apart from Mosaic ceremonials.

Throughout the earth today, out of every kindred, tongue, tribe and nation God is taking a people out of the Gentiles for His Name. They are coming into His Church, the antitypical fulfillment of David's Tabernacle. They are not being placed under the Law or the Tabernacle of Moses, but under grace in the Tabernacle of David, there to be worshipping priests in song and praise to God through Christ.

The prophet Amos spoke of the days that would come when "the plowman shall overtake the reaper, and the treader of grapes him that soweth seed; and the mountains shall drop sweet wine, and all the hills shall melt" (Amos 9:13). This pointed to a time of great harvest and ingathering. The ploughman, the sower, and the reaper shall see the Lord doing a quick work. The Apostle Paul said in Romans 9:28 "For He will finish the work and cut it short in righteousness; because a short work will the Lord make upon the earth."

The fulness of the Gentiles (Romans 11:25) is upon the Church as the Lord takes out a people for His Name from all nations. They shall stand before His throne singing a new song, the song of redemption, and playing harps as they worship the Lamb after the order of David's Tabernacle forever (Revelation 5:9-10).

Matthew Henry in Commentary on the Whole Bible (p. 1268), comments on:

"The plowman overtaking the reaper" by saying "... that is, there shall be such a plentiful harvest every year, and so much corn to be gathered in, that it shall last all summer, even till autumn, when it is time to begin to plough again; and in like manner the vintage shall continue till seed-time, and there shall be such abundance of grapes that even the mountains shall drop new wine into the vessels of the grape-gatherers, and the hills that were dry and barren shall be moistened and shall melt with the fatness or mellowness (as we call it) of the soil. Compare this with Joel ii. 24, and iii, 18. This must certainly be understood of the abundance of spiritual blessings in heavenly things, which all those are, and shall be, blessed with, who are in sincerity added to Christ and His church; they shall be abundantly replenished with the goodness of God's house, with the graces and comforts of His Spirit; they shall have bread, the bread of life, to strengthen their hearts, and the wine of divine consolations to make them glad - meat indeed and drink indeed - all the benefit that comes to the souls of men from the word and Spirit of God. These had been long confined to the vineyard of the Jewish church; divine revelation, and the power that attended it, were to be found only within that enclosure; but in gospel-times the mountains and hills of the Gentile world shall be enriched with these privileges by the gospel of Christ preached, and professed, and received in the power of it. When great multitudes were converted to the faith of Christ, and nations were born at once, when the preachers of the gospel were always caused to triumph in the success of their preaching, then the ploughman overtook the reaper; and, when the Gentile churches were enriched in all utterance, and in all knowledge, and all manner of spiritual gifts (1 Corinthians i. 5), then the mountains dropped sweet wine.

Chapter 10

TWO TABERNACLES COMBINED IN ONE

Our previous several chapters have particularly dealt with the two Tabernacles of David; the Davidic Kingdom Tabernacle and the Davidic Worship Tabernacle. Enough evidence has been given showing the various thoughts of other writers.

There seems to be no doubt that, in Old Testament times, there were TWO TABERNACLES OF DAVID. The one was for David's throne, speaking of David's kingdom. The other was for the throne of God, the Ark of the Lord, speaking of the Davidic order of worship.

It is the failure to see these two tabernacles that has brought about the differences of opinion and the confusing of one tabernacle with the other. Some expositors lean heavily on the Tabernacle of David as Messiah's kingdom and the Gentiles coming into that. Others lean heavily on the Tabernacle of David as Messiah's worship order and the Gentiles coming into that.

David was involved historically in the two tabernacles and also involved prophetically with both as both pointed historically and prophetically to David's greater Son, the Lord Jesus Christ.

Now if the Gentiles come into David's Tabernacle, which Tabernacle will they come into? The Davidic Kingdom Tabernacle or the Davidic Worship Tabernacle? Some say one, some say the other. We would ask: "Can they come into the Tabernacle of David on Zion, David's house and kingdom, and NOT come into the Tabernacle of David, the Davidic order of worship which is also on Mt. Zion? How can we have one without the other? How can we accept one and reject the other? One should not be accepted or rejected at the expense of the other or overemphasized. Of course, Divine order is to come FIRST into the kingdom (John 3:1-5), then into Divine worship (John 4:20-24). BOTH aspects of the Tabernacle are of the Lord.

To say that the Gentiles were to come into the kingdom or house of David (ie., the Son of David, Messiah's kingdom), and not into the Tabernacle of David (ie., the Davidic order of priestly worship) is inconsistent with the New Testament revelation.

R.C.H. Linski, in "The Interpretation of the Acts of the Apostles" (pp. 609, 610) says: "'Tabernacle' refers to the Tabernacle of David's time before Solomon was permitted to build the Temple. In that Tabernacle David worshipped with Israel. It thus stood for the Church. And it was the Church that had fallen. The Church of Israel was, indeed, in a sad state, and had been so for years. God would restore it." (Augsburg Publishing House, Minneapolis, 1934).

The author believes BOTH Tabernacles are implicit. In the Old Testament there were two Tabernacles of David, both on Mt. Zion, the one being KINGLY, the other being PRIESTLY. One cannot separate the house("sookah") of David from the Tabernacle ("ohel") of David, for both were on Zion.

Passing all these things to and through the cross they become ONE TABERNACLE in the New Testament, in the person of the Lord Jesus Christ. He unites in Himself both offices of KING and PRIEST, thus uniting in Himself the TWO TABERNACLES and what they emphasized. This is evident in the fact that He is KING-PRIEST after the order of Melchisedek (Psalm 110; Hebrews 7).

Not only is this so concerning Christ the head, it is also true of the Church, His Body. Jews and Gentiles do not come into David's Tabernacle under Christ's KINGSHIP and kingdom and not come also to David's Tabernacle under Christ's PRIESTHOOD! New Covenant believers are members of the order of Melchisedek and are also kings and priests unto God and His Christ (Revelation 1:6; 5:9,10; 20:4,5; 1 Peter 2:5-9).

It has also been mentioned that the subject of "worship" is not the issue at hand in the Acts 15 passage. However, this again is implicit in the very language of the context.

The very purpose of God in building again the Tabernacle of David is "that the residue of men might SEEK AFTER THE LORD, and all the Gentiles, upon whom MY NAME is called, saith the Lord, who doeth all these things" (Acts 15:17). Can anyone really and truly SEEK THE LORD and not end up WORSHIPPING the Lord? If God takes out a people for His name and His name is called upon the people, how can this people not worship Him in spirit and in truth?

Attention has been drawn to the fact, also, that the expression "Tabernacle of David" is not mentioned anywhere else in the New Testament. However, this kind of argument does not prove anything. The words "born again" are never specifically mentioned in the Book of Acts or in any of the Pauline Epistles. What does this prove or disprove? Absolutely nothing! Other language is used in Acts to describe "born again" believers. Further to the point, although "Tabernacle of David" is not mentioned elsewhere in the New Testament, the language pertaining to it, both as to Davidic kingdom and Davidic worship is used in the New Testament quite often.

For instance, Mt. Zion, Jerusalem is mentioned in these references (Hebrews 12:22-24; Revelation 14:1-4; Matthew 21:4, 5; Romans 9:33; 11:26; Revelation 5:5-14; Hebrews 7, etc). One cannot speak of Mt. Zion without alluding to the Tabernacles of David as both were on Mt. Zion and gave Zion its significance in the days of David and onwards.

Here Christ is spoken of as both KING and PRIEST ruling His people in the heavenly Mt. Zion, the heavenly Jerusalem. All of this, by implication, is the language pertaining to the Tabernacle of David. Christ is the Root and Offspring of David. He is both David's Lord and David's Son (Revelation 22:16).

The Gentiles, with the Jews, come into DAVID'S HOUSE which is Messiah's Kingdom and also into DAVID'S TABERNACLE, which is Messiah's worship. How can these be separated in Christ, the Son of David? Jews and Gentiles come into New Covenant Zion and heavenly Jerusalem, into the Tent and House of David, into both Kingly and Priestly ministry, as typified in the Royal House of David on Zion and the Priestly Tabernacle pitched by David in Zion.

The importance of David cannot be overlooked. Jew and Gentile coming into David's booth, his house, his kingdom, will automatically come into all the blessings of David as to his house, and his order of worship. Jew and Gentile alike will enter into:

- The Covenant of David – Psalm 89:3, 34-37; Jeremiah 33:17-26; Hebrews 13:20.
- The Booth or Tent of David – Amos 9:11,12; Acts 15:15-17.
- The Kingdom of David – 2 Samuel 7:12-17; 1 Chronicles 17:11,14; Isaiah 9:6-9; Luke 1:30-33.
- The Throne of David – Isaiah 9:6-9; Acts 2:22-36; Romans 1:3; Psalm 122:5.
- The Seed of David – Jeremiah 33:17-26; Galatians 3:16,29.
- The House of David – 2 Samuel 7:4-7, 12-29; Hebrews 3:1-6; 1 Peter 2:5-9.
- The Sure Mercies of David – Isaiah 55:3,4; Psalm 89:1,2; Acts 13:27-37; 2 Timothy 2:8.
- The Key of David – Isaiah 22:20-25; Revelation 3:7.
- The Horn of David – Psalm 132:17; 92:10; 1 Kings 1:39; Luke 1:67-70; Revelation 5:6.
- The Songs and Psalms of David – Book of Psalms.
- The Instruments of Music ordained by King David – 2 Chronicles 29:25-28; 35:4,10,15; Ezra 3:10,11; Nehemiah 12:24, 44-47.
- The Tabernacle of David – 2 Samuel 6:17; 1 Chronicles 15:1; 16:1; 2 Chronicles 1:4.

David has been given as a Leader, Commander and a Witness of the Lord (Isaiah 55:3, 4).

The following comparison shows Zion involved both offices of KING and PRIEST and that the expression "Tabernacle of David" involve both thoughts without any contradiction of the total Biblical revelation.

OLD TESTAMENT

ZION
THE CITY OF DAVID

THE HOUSE OF DAVID THE ROYAL HOUSE FOR THE THRONE OF DAVID KINGLY – GOVERNMENTAL IN ZION	THE TABERNACLE OF DAVID THE PRIESTLY MINISTRY FOR THE ARK OF GOD PRIESTLY – ECCLESIASTICAL IN ZION
1. David built him a house and houses of cedars in the city of David (1 Chronicles 14:1; 15:1; 16:43). The Tabernacle (ohel) of David's house Psalm 132:3)	1. David prepared a place for the Ark of God and pitched a tent (ohel) for it (1 Chronicles 15:1; 2 Chronicles 1:4)
2. The strong hold of Zion is the city of David (2 Samuel 5:7; 1 Kings 8:1)	2. The Ark of God set in the midst of the tent David had pitched for it. Ark set in his place tabernacle that David had pitched for it (2 Samuel 16:17-19; 1 Chronicles 16:1-3)
3. David ruled and reigned as king on his throne in Zion. Type of Messiah, his Son reigning in heavenly Zion (1 Chronicles 11:4-9; Psalm 2:6-7; 146:10; Acts 4:23-26; 13:33; Hebrews 12:22-24)	3. David appointed certain Priests & Levites to minister before Ark of the Lord, to record, thank and praise the Lord God of Israel. (1 Chronicles 16:4-38)
4. David sitting in his house of cedars expresses concern for the Ark of God in curtains (1 Chron. 17:1-2; 2 Sam. 7:1-2; Psa. 132:1-18)	4. The Ark of God was under curtains in a tent or booth (ohel or sookah) (1 Chron. 17:1; 2 Sam. 7:1; 11:11)
5. The Lord forbids David to build Him a house but promised He would build him a house, and Solomon would build the Temple (1 Chron. 17:3-15; 2 Sam. 7:3-17)	5. The Lord David He had gone from tent to tent (ohel-ohel), and from one tabernacle (mish-kan -mishkan) (1 Chron. 17:5; 2 Sam. 7:6)
6. Zion & Jerusalem was the city where all kings of David, of the tribe of Judah reigned until the last king, Zedekiah. BC.606.	6. Zion has been chosen of God for His habitation. Sing praises to God who dwells in Zion, the city of the great king (Psa. 9:11, 14; 147:2; 48:1-3). Out of Zion, God shines (Psa. 50:1-2). Zion is loved more than all the dwellings (mish-kans) of Jacob (Psa. 87:2).
7. In mercy the throne of David would be established the Messiah ("He") would sit on it in truth, justice, judgment and in righteousness (Isaiah 16:5)	7. Christ would be a King-Priest in His Father's throne (Zechariah 6:12-13; Psalm 110; Hebrews 7).

NEW TESTAMENT

LORD JESUS CHRIST

CHRIST – THE SON OF DAVID
OF THE HOUSE OF DAVID
OF THE TRIBE OF JUDAH

TO ESTABLISH THE KINGDOM OF DAVID
THE KING FOREVER
THE DAVID COVENANT

(GOSPEL OF MATTHEW)

CHRIST – THE GREAT HIGH PRIEST
OF THE HEAVENLY TABERNACLE & TEMPLE
OF THE THRONE (ARK) OF HIS FATHER

TO ESTABLISH THE PRIESTHOOD
THE PRIEST FOREVER
THE NEW COVENANT

(BOOK OF HEBREWS)

THE CHURCH

(Amos 9:11, 12 with Acts 15:15-17)
THE TABERNACLE OF DAVID
BUILD AGAIN/RAISED OUT OF RUINS

THE JEWS — **JEWS & GENTILES INTO HIS TENT** — **THE GENTILES**

ORDER OF MELCHISEDEK
KINGS & PRIESTS

HEAVENLY ZION
HEAVENLY JERUSALEM

THE ROYAL PRIESTHOOD

Revelation 1:5, 6; 5:9, 10; 1 Peter 2:5-9

The New Testament shows that CHRIST and THE CHURCH together constitute the Royal Priesthood, Kings and Priests, after the order of Melchisedek. This brings together that which pertained to David and the revelation on the Tabernacle of David as pertaining to his Kingdom (Kingship), and to his order of Priesthood (Priest) which he established in the Tent for the Ark in Zion. Zion is a King-Priest city, and it shadowed forth the Gospel dispensation. In this era, Jews and Gentiles come together as ONE, as King-Priests, into the Tabernacle of David and worship the Lord.

Even as the TWO OFFICES of king and priest were separated in the Old Testament and brought together in the one person of Christ in the New Testament, so the TWO TABERNACLES of Zion were brought together in the one Tabernacle of the New Testament. This is in Christ and His church. The throne of David's Tabernacle and the throne of God's Ark in the other Tabernacle were combined in Christ.

It is with this understanding we move now into PART THREE of the text, especially as it pertains to Davidic worship, and this, without excluding the Davidic kingdom. Jews and Gentiles together come into Messiah's kingdom and Messiah's worship. Jew and Gentile become one in Christ. The two tabernacles becomes one in Christ. The two offices of king and priest become one in Christ. This is New Testament revelation.

The following diagram sets out the two Tabernacles as in the Old Testament times, with the two offices of kingly and priestly ministrations, and how both are brought together into one Tabernacle in the New Testament, in Christ, who is both king and priest upon His throne.

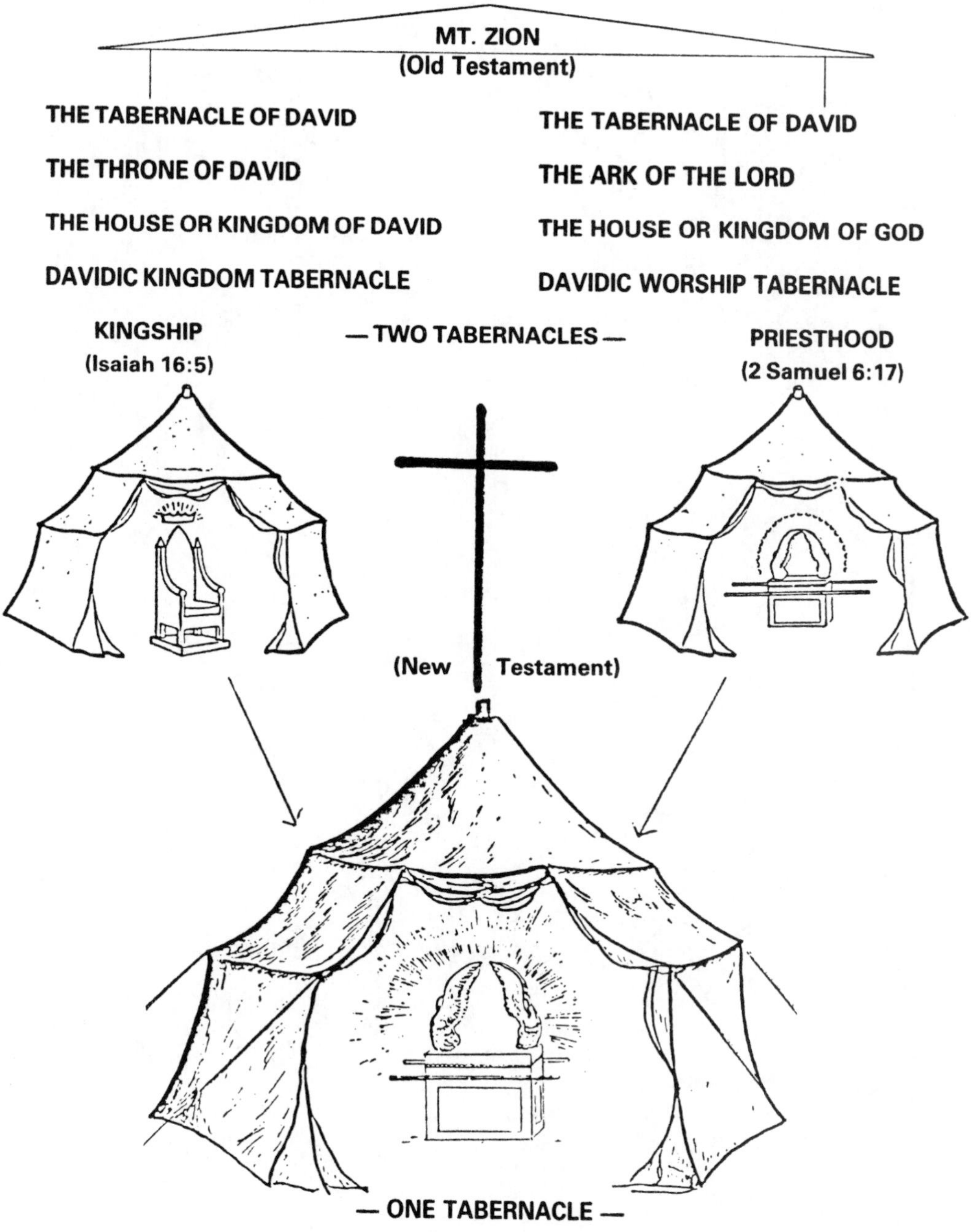

PART THREE
INTRODUCTORY – THE DAVIDIC WORSHIP TABERNACLE

CHAPTER		PAGE
11.	As in the Days of Old	81
12.	The Tabernacle of Moses – Sinai to Shiloh	83
13.	The Ark of the Covenant	85
14.	Go Back To Shiloh	91
15.	Captivity and Journeyings of the Ark	99
16.	The Preparation of David's Tabernacle	107
17.	The Ark Taken Into the Tabernacle of David	115
18.	Two Tabernacles – Moses' and David's	125
19.	Walk About Zion	135
20.	According to the Commandment of David	145
21.	Divine Order of Worship	151
22.	A Brief History of Music	159
23.	The Order of Singers and Musicians	183
24.	Psalm Titles and Inscriptions	187
25.	Musical Instruments in Bible Times	195
26.	Satan's Counterfeit Musicale	213
27.	The Power and Evaluation of Music	221
28.	Tabernacles in the Book of Hebrews	229
29.	The Priesthood of Zadok	235
30.	As the Mountains Round About Jerusalem	243
31.	The Ark Into Solomon's Temple	247
32.	Theological Truths in the Tabernacle of David	251
	Conclusion	253
	Appendix I. Interpretation of "Selah"	255
	Appendix II. Dancing	259
	Appendix III. Biblical History of the Ark of the Covenant	263
	Bibliography	269

INTRODUCTORY

THE DAVIDIC WORSHIP TABERNACLE

The author trusts that the truth of the Tabernacle of David as to its kingdom aspect and the coming in of both Jew and Gentile into it has been clearly established.

And again, the author trusts, that, though there were TWO Tabernacles of David in the Old Testament – one for the throne of David, the other for the throne of the Lord – it is seen that both are brought together through the cross into the ONE Tabernacle in the New Testament.

It is worthy to remember that Jesus Himself said He would BUILD HIS CHURCH (Matthew 16:15-19). He also said He would BUILD THE TABERNACLE OF DAVID (Acts 15:16, 17). The truth of the matter is that Christ is NOT building two different things in the New Testament. He is building but one thing and that is His CHURCH. Therefore, if the Tabernacle of David is to be built again, it will – it must – be that which is being built into the church.

The Tabernacle of David, as to both kingdom and worship, finds fulfilment in Christ and the church. It is a kingdom people who become a worshipping people. The kingdom aspect of David's Tabernacle and the worship aspect of David's Tabernacle, though both separated on Zion in the Old Testament, cannot be separated in the New Testament. As the offices of king and priest were separated in the Old Testament yet brought together in the New Testament, in Christ, so the two tabernacles are brought together in Christ. The throne of David and the Ark of the Lord actually point to one and the same thing. There are not two different thrones for Christ to sit on. There is only one throne in the New Testament. Jesus Christ sits on the throne of David (Acts 2:22-36; 13:22-37). Jesus Christ sits on the throne of God, symbolized in the mercy seat of the Ark of the Covenant. These are brought together in one since the cross and under New Covenant times.

The distinctive difference between the Old Testament and the New Testament is seen in the matter of the offices of king and priest. Kings came of the tribe of Judah. Priests came of the tribe of Levi. At the cross the Aaronic priesthood and the Levitical order were abolished. But the priestly office continues on through the cross into the order of Melchisedek who is both king and priest. Christ is Melchisedek. He is the king and priest of the tribe of Judah. This is the difference between the Old and New Covenant offices.

Also, the earthly throne of David has gone from the scene, even as the earthly Ark of the Covenant, but the heavenly Ark of God, the heavenly throne of God, remains (Revelation 11:19; 3:21; 5:1-10; 22:1-2). It is now the throne of God and the Lamb. He is a seated priest. He is a seated king. He is a king-priest on His throne and the counsel of peace is between both of these offices (Zechariah 6:12-14).

He is KING over His KINGDOM. He is PRIEST over His PRIESTHOOD. Kingship speaks of government, rule, dominion and authority over His subjects and domain. Priesthood speaks of reconciliation, intercession and worship.

Part three of our text deals more especially with the Davidic Worship Tabernacle. Although David was a king on his throne, he was a worshipper at the Ark of the Lord. With all that is written of David in his kingdom, over and above all David is a worshipper, the sweet singer and Psalmist of Israel (2 Samuel 23:1, 2). The word was in his tongue and the Spirit upon him in worship and praise.

Among the Old Testament characters David stands out uniquely. There are about fourteen chapters given over the Abraham's life story. There are about eleven chapters given over to the

life of Jacob and about fourteen chapters to his favoured son, Joseph. Ten chapters cover the life of the prophet Elijah. But when it comes to David we have approximately sixtysix chapters of the Bible given to his life story. There are about 1200 references to David's name in the Bible, 59 of these references in the New Testament.

If we think of a character who speaks of faith, we think of Abraham, the father of all who believe. If we think of a man of meekness, we speak of Moses or of Jesus. If we look for a man of miracles, we think of Elijah, or Elisha. But when we look for the Bible character for praise and worship, we speak of king David.

He is the man after God's heart. The Psalms of David are primarily worship Psalms.

David establishes Zion as his city and it is through David Zion comes into such prominence. Zion is the city of the great king, the Lord Himself, not just David.

While other ceremonials and ritualisms of the Old Testament pass to the cross and are abolished there, expressions of worship pass to the cross and through the cross into the New Covenant. Through the cross they become purified. Worship and praise will never be abolished. Worship and praise are eternal.

Of course, it is possible to have all the various expressions of praise and worship, to despise other groups of believers who may not exercise such and yet be "a hypocrite in Zion" (Isaiah 33:14). God looks at the heart. He accepts only that worship which is purified through Calvary's cross and is in spirit and in truth, not merely external form or lack of it.

The author asks the reader to keep these things in proper focus as we consider in the greater portion of this text that order of worship related to the Tabernacle pitched by David in Zion for the Ark of the Lord. This is the burden of the rest of this text, not the Tabernacle of David as pertaining to his kingdom. However, it must constantly be remembered that these two cannot be separated for they are now one in Christ. He is king. He is priest. He rules and reigns over His kingdom. We worship Him as King of kings, and Lord of lords, and Priest of the Most High God.

Chapter 11

AS IN THE DAYS OF OLD

The prophet Amos prophesied in the days of Uzziah the King of Judah, and the days of Jeroboam 11, the King of Israel (Amos 1:1; Amos 9:11-12).

It was about the year B.C. 787. Though his prophecy involves several of the surrounding Gentile nations, and the Southern Kingdom of the House of Judah, his ministry mainly concerns the Northern Kingdom of the House of Israel.

The House of Israel was in a backslidden and apostate condition. Each King of the House of Israel had perpetuated the Golden Calf system of worship established by Jeroboam I in 1 Kings 12:25-33, about B.C. 975, or nearly 200 years previously. In about 60 years time the House of Israel would be taken into Captivity to Assyria and from there dispersed among the nations (Amos 9:8; Hosea 1:4; Isaiah 7:8).

Amos and Hosea were contemporary prophets, both pronouncing the coming Assyrian Captivity of the House of Israel. The prophet Isaiah, though specifically ministering to the House of Judah, also speaks of the coming Assyrian Captivity of Israel.

Hence, it is against this historical background that Amos prophesies, "In that day will I raise up the Tabernacle of David that is fallen, and close up the breaches thereof; and I will raise up his ruins, and I will build it as in the days of old."

In the mind of the Nation of Israel and the prophet's generation, what did they understand this to mean? The Temple of Solomon was still standing in Jerusalem. The idolatrous Golden Calf system of worship was still in full function at Bethel and Dan, in the House of Israel, whose capital was Samaria.

Did the prophet mean that God would leave the Temple of Solomon and go back to an actual tent or tabernacle that David had pitched for the Ark before the Temple was built? Did any generation understand the prophet to mean that God would rebuild a literal material tent as in David's time and return to it? One would hardly think so.

Undoubtedly, in the minds of that generation, they would understand this utterance to speak of a restoration or revival of true and proper worship as was established in the days of King David.

The nation was backslidden, idolatrous, and immoral, far from the true worship of Jehovah. The worship was corrupted and polluted and far removed from the worship established in David's Tabernacle. The Tabernacle of David worship had indeed fallen. It was filled with breaches or gaps. It was indeed in ruins.

Hence, when the prophet spoke of the restoration of David's Tabernacle, he was not referring to a literal material tent being rebuilt or set up again. If this is what the prophet meant, then over 2800 years have gone by and never in this time has God ever had a material tent built, as David's Tabernacle was, for Him to inhabit. Neither shall it be ever in the future or in eternity. God will never go back to a material tent or tabernacle or temple.

When the prophet speaks of the fact that the Lord will build the Tabernacle as in the days of old, he is speaking of a restoration, an awakening, a revival of true worship that David established in his times at the pinnacle of the nation's response to the Lord.

Philip Mauro, in The Hope of Israel (pp. 217, 218, 222) says concerning The Tabernacle of David:

> "To begin with, let us note that it is not the temple of Solomon. The two structures were quite distinct; and typically they differ widely in significance. Amos prophesied concerning a "tabernacle." definitely associated with David, a tabernacle which, at the time of his prophecy, had "fallen," and was in "ruins." Amos prophesied " in the days of Uzziah, King of Judah" (1:1), at which time the temple of Solomon was standing in all its glory, and its services and sacrifices were being carried out in due order. There is doubtless something very significant in the fact that, while the temple of Solomon was yet standing, God declared His purpose to "raise up the Tabernacle of David that is fallen." and to "raise up its ruins."
>
> "In the prophecy of Amos we have the words of God, "And I will build it, as in the days of old." The days when David pitched a tabernacle in Zion for the Ark were days of joy and gladness, of shouting and dancing, of victory and prosperity, the days when David reigned over a united and a happy people." (Emphasis his)

In due time it will be seen that every awakening in Israel or Judah under godly kings was a return to the order of the Tabernacle of David - NOT to a material tent - but to that proper worship established under David's glorious reign. In other words, a return to the Tabernacle of David!

In order to understand what the Lord meant, both in the prophet's time and also in the time of the Book of Acts, we need to go back and look at "the days of old" when the Tabernacle of David was set up and the symbolical and typical significances thereof.

Chapter 12

THE TABERNACLE OF MOSES -- SINAI TO SHILOH

Because the central feature of the Tabernacle of David was the order of worship established around the Ark of the Covenant, which was taken out of the Tabernacle of Moses, it is necessary to have a brief understanding of Moses' Tabernacle.

One cannot appreciate the Temple of Solomon without an understanding of the Tabernacle of David, and one cannot appreciate the Tabernacle of David without an understanding of the Tabernacle of Moses. Each of these have their distinctive portions of truth.

The revelation of the details and construction of the Tabernacle of Moses is recorded in Exodus 25-40. (For a fuller exposition of the Tabernacle of Moses and its furnishings, the writer refers the reader to his companion book, "The Tabernacle of Moses," by the same Publishers).

The Tabernacle of Moses was the habitation of God with the children of Israel during the Wilderness wanderings from Mt. Sinai to Shiloh in the Promised Land. It consisted of a board structure, overlaid with various curtains and coverings. This structure had two places, spoken of as the Most Holy Place and the Holy Place. These two places were as one Tabernacle divided simply by a veil hung upon 4 pillars of acacia wood overlaid with gold.

The whole of this structure was 30 cubits long by 10 cubits high and 10 cubits broad. At the east end there was an embroidered linen hanging called "The Door of the Tabernacle." It was hung upon 5 pillars of wood overlaid with gold. This board structure and its pillars were all founded in silver sockets in the desert.

The Tabernacle structure was surrounded by a court, consisting of linen fence hung upon 60 pillars, in sockets of brass. The court was 100 cubits in length, 50 cubits in width, and the height of the curtain was 5 cubits. At the east end there was another entrance called "The Gate of the Court." It was of embroidered linen also.

The Tabernacle of Moses consisted of three places: the Holiest of All, the Holy Place, and the Outer Court.

In each of these respective places, God commanded certain furnishings to be set. All had to be built according to the Divine standard, to the pattern of the Lord given to Moses in the mount. All were built by the enabling of the wisdom and Spirit of God.

In the Outer Court there were two articles of brass. There was the Brazen Altar, made of acacia wood, overlaid with brass. It was the only place of blood sacrifice. All the sacrificial offerings were dealt with there. It was the place of blood atonement.

The second article of furniture in the court was the Brazen Laver, made of the looking glasses of the women of Israel. It was a bath filled with water and designed for the priests to wash their hands and feet before going into the Sanctuary of the Lord to minister. It was the place of cleansing by water.

In the Holy Place there were three articles of furniture. On the north side there was the Table of Shewbread bearing 12 loaves of bread. This Table was wood overlaid with gold, having a double crown on it. The bread upon it was the food of the priests. It was called "The Presence Bread."

Opposite the Table was the Golden Candlestick, on the south side of the Tabernacle. It was made of pure gold according to the Divine design. It had 7 branches and 7 lamps on the branches. The lamps were filled with oil and burned continually before the Lord. It was the only light in the

Holy Place. The priests ministered in the light of the Candlestick.

The third article of furniture was the Golden Altar of Incense. It was made of acacia wood overlaid with gold. It was also made according to the Divine pattern. It stood immediately before the curtain called "The veil," which divided the Holy Place from the Most Holy Place. Incense, compounded of fragrant spices, was burned on it before the Lord. The Sanctuary was filled with the fragrance thereof. It symbolized the prayers, worship, and intercessions of the people before the Lord. This altar had a crown also.

The Most Holy Place only had one article of furniture. This was called The Ark of the Covenant. It was the most important piece of furniture of all in the Tabernacle and its three places. All other pieces of furniture were meaningful only if the Ark of the Covenant was in the Most Holy Place.

The Ark was an oblong box made of acacia wood, overlaid within and without with gold. It had a crown of gold around the top of it. Acting as a lid was the Mercy Seat made of pure gold, having the figures of the Cherubim on each end of it. The contents of the Ark were threefold: the Golden Pot of Manna, the Tables of Law, and the Rod of Aaron that budded (Hebrew 9:1-5; Exodus 20; Exodus 16; Numbers 17).

It was upon this article of furniture that the visible Glory-Presence of God dwelt. Once a year it was sprinkled with blood, on the great Day of Atonement.

Thus, the Tabernacle was God's House, God's habitation among His people. The Glory-Presence of the Lord was evidenced by a Cloudy and Fiery Pillar all through Israel's wanderings in the Wilderness.

Once the Tabernacle had been erected at Mt. Sinai, the Lord travelled with His people through the 40 years wanderings. In transit, the articles were covered with appointed cloths and coverings. In function, all were set up in their proper places.

In due time, when the second generation entered Canaan under Joshua, the Scriptures tell us that the Tabernacle of Moses was set up at a place called Shiloh.

> "And the whole congregation of the children of Israel assembled together at Shiloh, and set up the Tabernacle of the Congregation there" (Joshua 18:1).
> Read also Joshua 18:8-10; 19:51; 21:2; 22:9, 12, 19. Judges 18:31.

Shiloh became the central meeting place for the religious life of Israel in Canaan for a number of years.

The Tabernacle of the Lord, with the Ark of God's Presence, travelled with Israel from Mt. Sinai through the Wilderness wanderings and now it finds its place in the land of promise, in the land of rest, in "Shiloh" which means "Rest, peace, sent."

Chapter 13

THE ARK OF THE COVENANT

Of all the furniture in the Tabernacle of Moses, the Ark of the Covenant was indeed the most important. This was because of the spiritual significance set forth in its wonderful symbolism. There are more references to this piece of furniture than all others. This shows us the importance of this in the mind of God.

The Ark of the Covenant, in all of its history and symbolism was the richest of all symbols pointing to the Lord Jesus Christ. All that the Ark was to Israel in the Old Testament, Jesus Christ is to His Church in the New Testament. The history of the Ark is the history of Christ. As the Ark was preeminent in the Tabernacle and Israel, so is Christ in His Church (Colossians 1:17-19).

There was only ever ONE ARK! From the Tabernacle of Moses, into the Tabernacle of David and from thence into the Temple of Solomon the Ark journeyed.

Before covering a brief history of the Ark we note the main truths represented thereby.

- The Ark represented the Throne of God in earth.
- The Ark represented the Presence of God amongst His redeemed people, Israel.
- The Ark represented the Glory of God revealed in Divine order in the camp of the saints.
- The Ark represented the Fullness of the Godhead Bodily revealed in the Lord Jesus Christ. Colossians 1:19; 2:9. All that the Ark was to and in Israel, Christ is to and in His Church.

A. The Ark at Mt. Sinai.

It was at Mt. Sinai that the Lord gave directions to Moses for the construction of the Ark of the Covenant (Exodus 25:10-22).

The Ark was a small oblong box, the measurements being 2½ cubits in length, by 1½ cubits in width, and 1½ cubits in height. This speaks of the fact that God's throne has a Divine standard about it.

It was made of shittim wood, or, as the Septuagint Version translates it "incorruptible wood." The shittim (or sometimes it is called acacia) wood is symbolic of Christ's perfect, sinless and incorruptible humanity (Psalms 16:10; Luke 1:35; 1 Peter 1:23; 1 John 3:5; Jeremiah 23:5; Zechariah 3:8, 6:12).

The Ark was overlaid within and without with gold. Gold is generally significant of Deity, or the Divine nature. In the wood and the gold construction we have symbolized the two natures in the one Person of Christ. It is significant of Deity and Humanity coming together in the new creation. The Fullness of the Godhead Bodily was in Him (1 Timothy 3:15-16; Isaiah 7:14; Isaiah 9:6; John 1:14; Colossians 1:19; 2:9).

Around the top of the Ark was a crown of gold. A crown is significant of kingship and this pointed to the truth of Christ's kingship. He is crowned with glory and honour (Hebrews 2:9; Revelation 19:11-21).

In the sides of the Ark there were rings, and staves were placed in these for the Ark when in transit. The truth symbolized here is that the Lord Jesus Christ, who is our Ark, has a worldwide ministry to His people. He journeys with the Church in her pilgrimage. The staves would help to keep the Ark balanced. The Church must have a balanced presentation of the Gospel of Christ (Acts 1:8;

Mark 16:15-20; Psalms 85:10).

Upon the top of the Ark, acting as a lid, was the Mercy Seat and the Cherubim (Hebrews 9:1-5; Romans 3:20-27). The Scriptures clearly identify the fact that the Mercy Seat is symbolic of Christ Jesus as our propitiation. The blood-stained Mercy Seat points to the sacrificial work of Jesus. The two Cherubim in absolute union with the Mercy Seat are symbolic of that union in the eternal Godhead, as Father, Son, and Holy Spirit. One piece of gold was fashioned into a triunity.

Within the Ark there were three articles: the Tables of Law, the Golden Pot of Manna, and the Rod of Aaron which budded. These were symbolic of the Father's Law, the Son as our heavenly manna, and the fruitfulness of the Holy Spirit. They also symbolize the Fullness of the Godhead Bodily in the Lord Jesus Christ (Hebrews 9:l-5; Exodus l6; Numbers l7; Exodus l9-20).

This Ark was made according to the Divine pattern given to Moses. It was made by the wisdom and Spirit of God upon Bezaleel (Exodus 35:12, 37:1-9; Hebrews 10:5-7; Galatians 4:4).

After being brought to Moses for inspection when finished, it was placed in the Holiest of All or the Most Holy Place (Exodus 39:35; 26:34; 40:3). It was first anointed with the holy anointing oil and then the Glory of the Lord filled the Tabernacle so that no man could minister by reason of that Glory (Exodus 30:26; 40:9; Acts 10:38; Isaiah 61:1-3). Jesus, our Ark, was indeed the Anointed One (Leviticus 8:10 with Luke 4:18).

It was here within the veil that the High Priest would come and sprinkle blood upon the Mercy Seat once a year, on the great Day of Atonement, and make atonement for the sins of the whole nation (Leviticus 16:1-2, 14 with Hebrews 6:18-20; 10:19-20; John 14:1-6). Christ Jesus was once and for all offered for our sins and now we have boldness to enter into the Holiest of All by His precious blood.

In transit the Ark was always covered. First, with the covering veil, symbolic of the flesh body of the Son of God; then, it was covered with a cloth of badger's skins, symbolic of the Father God, who is over all; and finally, it was covered with a cloth of blue, symbolic of the Holy Spirit from heaven (Numbers 4:5-6). Thus no human eye saw the Ark when in transit according to this Divine instruction. The Ark in transit had to be carried on the shoulders of the Kohathites (Numbers 3:27-32).

The position of the Ark was "in the midst" of the Camp of Israel when they were encamped (Numbers 4:13-28; 10:14-28, 21). The Lord Jesus Christ, our Ark, is always in the midst of His people (Matthew 18:20).

B. The Ark in the Wilderness Journeyings.

The Ark took the central position in the march of Israel. When the Cloud of Glory moved, then the trumpets blew for the journeys of the camp of the Lord (Numbers 4:13-28; 10:21; 14-28).

The Ark's first journey from Mt. Sinai leading the way to the promised land and seeking rest for Israel was three days journey (Numbers 10:33-36; Psalms 68:1-19). The Lord Jesus Christ brings His people into true rest on the basis of His three days and three nights redemptive work at Calvary (Matthew 11:28-30; 12:38-40).

Without the presence of the Ark of the Lord Israel was defeated in any battle (Numbers 14:44). The Church needs the presence of the Lord always in battles against the enemy. There will only be defeat without his presence.

When Israel murmured against Aaron as the Lord's anointed priest, God caused the rod of Aaron to bud in His presence. It was the seal of God upon that fact that Aaron was His chosen, appointed, and anointed High Priest and Mediator. This budding rod was placed in the Ark of God as a witness and attestation of Aaron's priesthood before God and Israel (Hebrews 9:4). Christ is God's anointed and appointed High Priest today. God sealed this fact by raising Him from the dead (Hebrews 4:14; Psalms 110:1-4).

The Book of the Covenant was placed in the side of the Ark (Deuteronomy 31:9-26). This shadowed forth the Lord Jesus who alone kept the Covenant and Laws of God perfectly for that Law was in His heart (Hebrews 10:5-7).

C. The Ark in the Promised Land.

The Ark of the Lord was used in the opening up of the river Jordan for the new generation to enter into Canaan land, even as the rod of God had opened up the Red Sea for the first generation to pass over into the Wilderness (Joshua 3-4). The Ark went 2000 cubits ahead of the people. This again pointed to the Lord Jesus Christ who has gone 2000 years before the Church, conquering the waters of death, and leading His people into eternal rest. The Church will follow Him.

After the surrounding of Jericho for seven days, the seven priests blowing the seven trumpets leading the way, God caused the walls of Jericho to fall. The Ark of God lead the way in this victorious march of faith (Joshua 6-7). It is worthy to note in the Book of Revelation the seven Angels with the seven trumpets pertaining to the end of this age and the coming of Christ, when the kingdoms of this world become the kingdoms of our God and His Christ (Revelation 8:l-l4; ll:l5, l9).

When sin entered the camp. Joshua fell down before the Ark of the Lord and received instructions concerning the judgment of this sin of Aachan. There can be no victory in the camp while sin is undealt with (Joshua 7).

The Ark is positioned between Mt. Ebal, the Mt. of Cursing, and Mt. Gerizim, the Mt. of Blessing, in a great national convocation. The blessings and the cursings of the Law are uttered by the Levites as six tribes of Israel stand oneach mount (Joshua 8:30-35). All would be blessed or cursed according to their attitude towards the holy Ark of God and His commandments. This is also true when considered in the light of Christ's second coming. Blessing or cursing are measured out at the throne of His glory to all nations (Matthew 25:31-41).

The Ark seemed to be moving to different places in Canaan while the land was being allotted to the various tribes. It was possibly at Gilgal when the land was first entered (Joshua 9:6; 10:7-43). It was here the Lord gave the portions of the land to the tribes. Then the Ark was taken to Shiloh (Joshua 18:1-2). Here the rest of the land was divided according to the inheritance of the tribes. Then the Ark was possibly at Shechem for the great national convention (Joshua 24:1-28). And finally the Ark was taken back to Shiloh and it remained here for many years (Judges 20:18, 26, 27; 21:2, 12, 19; 1 Samuel 1:1-6; 3:3). It is at Shiloh we leave the Ark of the Covenant, set in the Tabernacle of Moses. Its history will be continued in the succeeding chapters.

One cannot read and meditate upon this brief outline of the construction, symbolism, and history of the Ark of the Lord without realizing the absolute importance of this article of furniture. Its construction and history symbolizes the person and ministry of the Lord Jesus Christ Himself in the midst of His redeemed people.

A proper understanding of this fact will help the student to appreciate more fully the subsequent transference of the Ark of God from the Tabernacle of Moses into the Tabernacle of David.

The Ark is symbolic of His Throne, His Presence, His Glory and His Fullness in the midst of His people.

(For a complete History of the Ark in outline form the reader is referred to the Appendix.)

THE ARK OF THE COVENANT

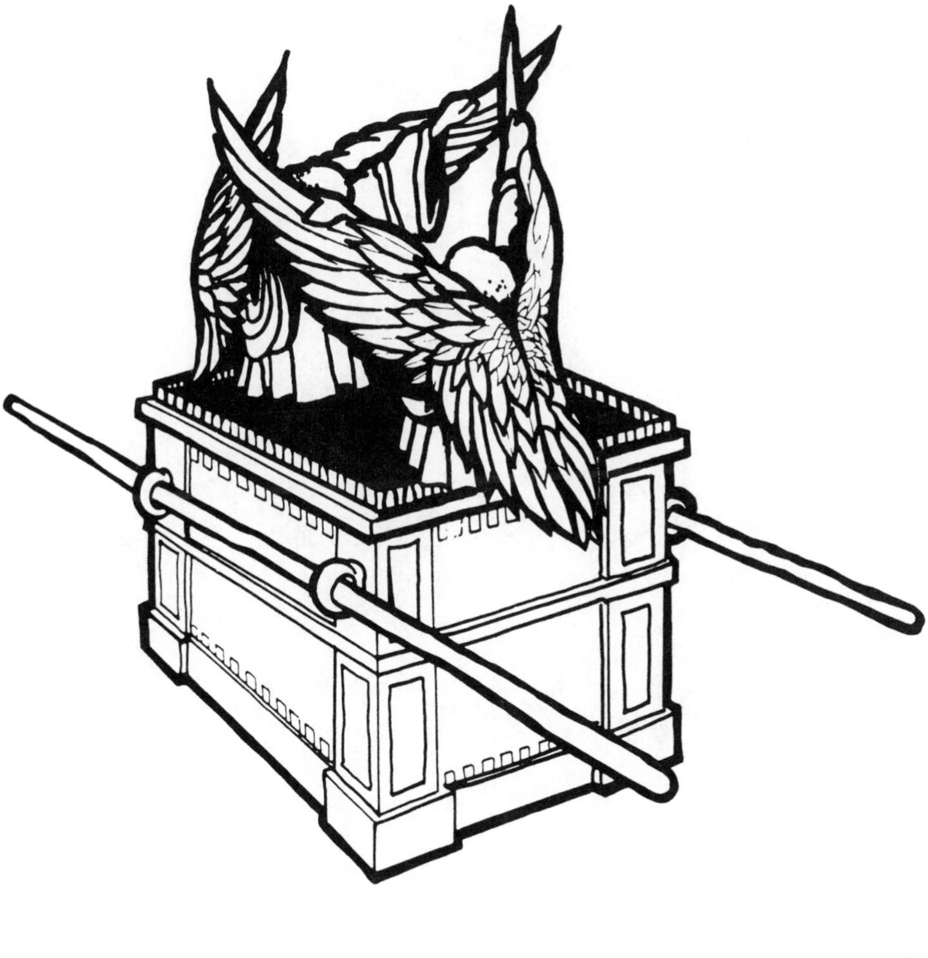

Chapter 14

GO BACK TO SHILOH

It is important to understand that which precipitated the need for and rise of the Tabernacle of David. If the student does not understand this then it can truly be questioned, Was David in the will of God setting up another Tabernacle when the Tabernacle of Moses was already in existence? If David did not have a revelation of the mind and will of God, it would have been absolute presumption on his part to place the Ark of the Covenant in another Tabernacle which he had set up in Mt. Zion.

Let us consider that which precipitated the rise of David's Tabernacle. In Jeremiah 7:1-16, the Word of the Lord came to Jeremiah the prophet. He was told to go and proclaim it in the Gate of the Lord's House, the Temple at Jerusalem. The burden of the prophetic word was a reproof to the people because they were boasting their trust in a material Temple. The House of Judah was in a state of apostasy and rebellion against the Lord and His Word through the prophet Jeremiah. As the worshippers came to the Temple through the Gate Jeremiah declared the Word of the Lord. He reproved them for their sins and their false sense of security, evidenced in their vain boastings in the Temple of God. They felt that God would never let the Temple be destroyed, as Jeremiah had prophesied. They felt that God would never let the Babylonians take them into captivity.

In the midst of these reproofs and denunciations, Jeremiah said to the people. "But go ye now unto my place which was in Shiloh, where I set my name at the first, and see what I did to it for the wickedness of my people Israel . . . Therefore will I do unto this house, which is called by my name, wherein ye trust, and unto the place which I gave to you and your fathers, as I have done to Shiloh" (Verses 12, 14).

The word is clear! "Go back to Shiloh and see what I did to it for the wickedness of My people Israel."

It will be remembered that Shiloh was the place where the Tabernacle of Moses was set up in the land of Canaan under Joshua. It seems as if it was there all through the period of the days of Joshua, the generation that outlived him and on through all the period of the Book of Judges; a period of several hundred years (Joshua 18:1; Judges 18:31).

It is worthy of note that the Ark is only mentioned once in the Book of Judges (Judges 20:27). Therefore, let us "go back to Shiloh" and see what did happen there. The details covered in this chapter are recorded for us in 1 Samuel 1-4. The student should familiarize himself with the historical account therein.

A. The Aaronic Priesthood - Eli and Sons.

At the time of the Divine judgments on Shiloh, the Aaronic Priesthood was represented in Eli and his two sons, Hophni and Phinehas. The spiritual condition of the nation is represented also in the spiritual condition of the Priesthood. It was in the last number of years closing off the period of anarchy. There was no king in Israel and everyone did that which was right in his own eyes. The Judge-Deliverers had come and gone. The nation had passed through periods of apostasy, servitudes, and deliverances.

At the time of Eli, things are again at a low ebb spiritually. It seemed that the corrupt condition of Eli and his sons precipitated the need and rise of the prophetic ministry of Samuel. Also, in time, the corrupt condition of Samuel's sons precipitated the rise of the Kings represented first in Saul. We glean the most prominent points which indicate the spiritual condition of the Priesthood at Shiloh.

1. Eli and his two sons, Hophni and Phinehas, are first mentioned as the Priests of the

Lord in Shiloh in 1 Samuel 1:3.

Eli's name means "The offering or the lifting up," or "Going up."
Hophni's name means "He that covers my fist," or "Fighter."
Phinehas' name means "A bold countenance," or "Brazen mouth."

The name in Scripture is usally significant of the nature and character of a person (Hebrews 7:2; 1 Samuel 25:25; Matthew 1:21).

2. Eli shows his lack of spiritual insight when, as he sat upon a seat by a post in the House of the Lord, he reproves Hannah in her intercessory prayer for a child. He does not discern between a woman in travail of soul and a woman in a state of drunkenness. He never realized that the son born of this woman would be called upon to confirm Divine judgments on his house (1 Samuel 1:9-28).

3. Eli's sons, though Priests at God's altar, were sons of Belial. They knew not the Lord (1 Samuel 2:12). Belial means "Lawless, Wrecklessness, Worthless." Thus Hophni and Phinehas were sons of Lawlessness, sons of wrecklessness. They were sons of the Devil, who is the Lawless and Wreckless one (cf., Deuteronomy 13:13). They were true to their interpreted names-- "Church saints and house devils."

4. Eli's sons were sacrilegious (1 Samuel 2:12-17). This passage shows that when the people did come to sacrifice to the Lord at Shiloh, Hophni and Phinehas would take much more than the Priest's portion of the sacrifice than the law of the offerings as given in Leviticus 1-7 allowed. The fat on the offerings was the Lord's portion, to be burned on the altar of God. When the people asked that the Lord receive His portion, these Priestly sons would take the offerings by force from the people. The result was that the people abhorred the offering of the Lord. They despised the atonement because of the way these sons behaved. Their sin was very great before the Lord. They were indeed sacrilegious.

5. Eli's sons were also immoral (1 Samuel 2:22). As the women who assembled at the Tabernacle came, these Priestly sons would become involved with some of them in acts of immorality. A corrupt and immoral Priesthood indeed. Though wearing the linen ephod and priestly robes, significant of righteousness, purity, and holiness, they were far removed from such.

6. Eli failed to properly discipline his sons (1 Samuel 2:23-25, 3:11-14). Although he heard of their immoral acts, he but mildly reproved them. They should have been out from the Priesthood. They failed in the qualifications. It is noteworthy that God would not touch these sons as long as they were under the covering of the father, Eli (1 Samuel 2:25). However, in time, because Eli would not discipline his sons, God would step in and judge the father and his two sons together. There would be Divine discipline if there was not human discipline! (1 Samuel 2:29).

These things reveal the spiritual state of the Priesthood in Shiloh where the Tabernacle of the Lord was. A Priesthood that was sacrilegious, lawless, wreckless, immoral, and undisciplined. Their sins were very great before the Lord and in great need of Divine discipline.

B. Declaration of Divine Judgment on Shiloh and Priesthood.

In 1 Samuel 2:27-36 the prophecy of Divine judgment on Eli and his sons is given.

There came a man of God to Eli to pronounce the mind of God. He reminded Eli of the Lord's choice of the Tribe of Levi to serve Him in the Priestly office, to offer sacrifice, burn incense, to partake of the offerings, and to wear the linen ephod before the Lord.

He reproved Eli for his lack of parental control and lack of discipline over his two sons in their Priestly ministrations. The man of God continued in the Word of the Lord by telling Eli of a threefold judgment that would come upon him and his house and Shiloh.

1. Judgment on Eli and his house.

The Priesthood would not continue in Eli's house forever. This was fulfilled in due time when the Priestly line was changed from Eli's line over to the Priesthood of Zadok. This will be taken up in the appropriate section (1 Samuel 2:30, 31, 33, 36).

2. Judgment on Eli's two sons, Hophni and Phinehas.

The sign to Eli of the judgment would be that his two sons would come under Divine discipline and would both die in the same day (1 Samuel 2:34).

3. Judgment on Shiloh and the Tabernacle.

Eli would see an enemy in God's habitation. The marginal reading says that Eli would see "the affliction of the Tabernacle." This statement actually involved the Ark of the Covenant being taken into captivity by enemy hands (1 Samuel 2:32; cf. Psalms 78:59-61). He forsook the Tabernacle of Shiloh.

The word of this man of God foretold the transference of the Priesthood of Eli over to another Priest also. God would raise up a faithful Priest, in contrast to the unfaithfulness of Eli in this office, and this Priest would perform the will and mind of God. God would build this Priest a sure house, and he would walk before the Lord's anointed forever.

As referred to in the judgment on Eli and his house, this prophecy was fulfilled in 1 Kings 2:26-27, 35, where Zadok was put into the Priestly office while Abiathar was thrust out. Abiathar was of Eli's line. The significance of this will be considered in that particular chapter on the Priesthood of Zadok.

C. Ministry of the Prophet Samuel.

During the period of time of the unfaithfulness of the Priesthood of Eli, God was preparing the prophet Samuel for ministry.

Samuel had been born in answer to Hannah's prayer, and given back to the Lord for His service (1 Samuel 1:19-24). It is beautiful to behold the growth and spiritual development of this child in spite of the corrupt conditions of Eli's household. The Lord preserved Samuel from the evil influence of Eli's sons. The particular verses are noted here.

1. Samuel ministered before the Lord and before Eli the Priest (1 Samuel 2:11). What a contrast to Eli's own sons. Samuel was a sensitive, submissive, and obedient child under Eli.

2. Samuel ministered before the Lord as a child being girded with a linen ephod (1 Samuel 2:18), clothed in Priestly garment.

3. Samuel grew spiritually before the Lord (1 Samuel 2:21).

4. Samuel grew on and was in favour with God and men; that is, he grew physically, mentally, and spiritually (1 Samuel 2:26).

D. The Word of the Lord confirmed to Samuel.

In 1 Samuel 3, the Lord confirmed to Eli through Samuel the word of judgment which He had spoken through the man of God previously. The Word of the Lord was precious (scarce) in those days, there was no open vision (vs 1). It attests to the lack of spiritual insight and Divine communications.

One evening, as Samuel was about to lay down to sleep, the Lord came and called to him. It is worthy to note that the Lord called "ere the lamp of God went out in the Temple of the Lord, where the Ark of God was . . . ." (vs 2). God never leaves Himself without a lamp of witness. God always calls before the lamp goes out.

The Lord called to Samuel four times before there came a recognition of the fact that it was the call of the Lord and not Eli. As soon as Samuel heard the voice he ran immediately to Eli. Eli told him to go back to sleep. Eli did not perceive as yet that the Lord was calling Samuel. Verse 7 says, "Now Samuel did not yet know the Lord, neither was the Word of the Lord yet revealed unto him."

After the third call, Eli perceived that the Lord was calling Samuel. He told him to respond to the voice by saying, "Speak Lord, for Thy servant heareth" (vs 9).

The Lord came and stood and called Samuel the fourth time. Samuel, as a sensitive, responsive, and obedient child responded, "Speak, for Thy servant heareth" (vs 10).

Note these four calls.

- The first call (vs 3-5).
- The second call (vs 6-7).
- The third call (vs 8-9).
- The fourth call (vs 10).

What must have passed through Eli's mind as he realized the Lord was calling and speaking to Samuel? Though under the same roof, the Lord was by-passing Eli and his house and the Word of the Lord was coming to a young man. Judgment was to begin at God's house (1 Peter 4:17).

As Samuel lay before the Lord, the Lord confirmed the word of judgment concerning the house of Eli. The declaration is solemn indeed (vs 11-14).

1. The judgment that God would bring on Eli and his house at Shiloh would make every one's ears tingle (vs 11).

2. Once God began the judgment, He would also finish it (vs 12).

3. God would judge Eli and his house forever because he knew of his sons' vileness and he restrained them not (vs 13).

4. The iniquity of Eli's house was unpardonable. No sacrifice or offering could cleanse it (I Samuel 3:14; cf., Hebrews 10:26-31).

In the morning, Eli asked Samuel what the Lord had spoken to him. Samuel fearfully told him all the words of the vision. Eli accepted the confirmation, for it was the same message as that spoken to him previously by the man of God. In the mouth of two or three witnesses will every Word of God be established.

The young prophet Samuel grew on before God and man. The Lord let none of his Words fall fruitless to the ground. God established his Word in the mouth of the prophet and all Israel recognized that Samuel was indeed a prophet of the Lord (I Samuel 3:19-20).

The chapter closes by saying, "And the Lord appeared again in Shiloh: for the Lord revealed Himself to Samuel in Shiloh by the Word of the Lord" (vs 21).

Before judgment fell upon Shiloh and the Priesthood of Eli and his sons, God called, prepared, and equipped the ministry that would arise to anoint David who would bring in the Tabernacle of David in Zion. God never closes off one act without preparing for the next.

E. <u>The Ark of God is Taken.</u>

The student should read carefully 1 Samuel 4. In this chapter we find the fulfillment of the prophetic word of judgment on Eli and his house as well as Shiloh. Here we see that which God did at Shiloh for the wickedness of His people Israel. One of the most momentous events in the history of the Nation takes place here.

A brief analysis of the chapter will be sufficient to bring these things into sharper focus.

1. <u>The Battle at Ebenezer</u> (I Samuel 4:1-2).

The Philistines came out in battle against Israel. Israel pitched over against Ebenezer, "The Stone of Help," or, "Hitherto hath the Lord helped us."

The Philistines were over against Aphek, "Strength," or "A Stream, Vigour."

In the course of the battle about 4000 Israelites were slain. God allowed the defeat to come, as in the days of the Judges, because of Israel's continued lapse into idolatry, wickedness, and immorality.

2. <u>The Ark of God brought into the Battle</u> (I Samuel 4:3-9).

The Israelites questioned why the Lord permitted them to be defeated in battle. In a spiritually decadent condition, they suggested that the Ark of the Covenant be fetched out of the Tabernacle of Shiloh and brought into the battle. Their faith in God had degenerated into superstitious belief in the material Ark of the Covenant, and not in the God who dwelt upon it.

The people in an act of presumption and superstition send to Shiloh to get the Ark. Eli's sons, Hophni and Phinehas, were at Shiloh where the Ark of God was. They also, as proper sons of Belial, presumed to bring the Ark of God out of the Tabernacle of Shiloh into the battle. Little did they realize that they were on the way to their own funeral. Little did they realize that the Ark once taken out of the Tabernacle at Shiloh would never ever return there again.

As they brought the Ark of God into the battle the people shouted with a great shout so that the earth rang with it. The people undoubtedly thought of the time when the Ark of God opened the way through the River Jordan. Undoubtedly they recalled the way the Ark of God had brought defeat to the Jericho city after the seven days march. The Ark of God had brought victory in various other battles. Surely it would do the same again here. The Ark was the most sacred of all the furnishings and it filled the Hebrew mind with the highest and noblest thoughts of God's mighty power in deliverance for His people.

Even the Philistines were fearful when they heard that the Ark of God was in the camp. They also associated the Ark with the power of God as in the plagues of Egypt, and the Divine judgment upon the Egyptians. They encouraged each other to be strong and fight like men so as not to become enslaved to the Israelites.

However, though the Israelites shouted with a great shout, it was but an empty hollow noise before God. It was an empty shout. God was not in it. There is a time to shout when God is in it. God told Israel to shout before the Ark on the day that Jericho collapsed (Joshua 5-6). There is a time to shout, but there is a time when a shout is nothing but a noise and farce. This certainly was the case here.

3. The Ark of God Taken by the Philistines (I Samuel 4:10-11a).

The battle continued. The Philistines fought. Israel was smitten and 30,000 footmen fell in the battle. Thus for several days battle 34,000 Israelites were slain. The worst was yet to come.

In the course of the battle the Philistines took the Ark of the Covenant captive. Such a thing had never happened before in the history of the Nation. Never had enemy hands touched the Ark of the Covenant. This was the fulfillment of God's word that the enemy would be in God's habitation (I Samuel 2:32 Amplified).

Psalm 78:60-61 describes this historical event.

> "So that He forsook the Tabernacle of Shiloh, the tent which He had placed among men; and delivered His strength into captivity, and His glory into the enemy's hand" (Judges 18:30-31 also).

The Ark was the Ark of His Strength, the Ark of His Glory.

The Amplified Old Testament reads this way. "So that He forsook the tabernacle at Shiloh, the tent in which He had dwelt among men (and never returned to it again), and delivered His strength and power (the Ark of the Covenant) into captivity, and His glory into the hand of (the Philistines) the foe."

4. The Death of Hophni and Phinehas (I Samuel 4:11b).

The judgment upon Eli's sons is fulfilled here. As the Philistines capture the Ark they slay the two Priestly sons of Eli. This was the sign of judgment on Eli's house.

These sons of Belial actually signed their "death-warrant" in their presumptuous acts concerning the Ark of the Covenant. It is worthy to note the commandments of the Lord they violated in this final act in the Tabernacle of Shiloh.

a. The Ark of the Covenant was placed in the Holiest of All in the Tabernacle of Moses. No one was to enter within the Veil except the High Priest alone, and this but once a year on the great Day of Atonement (Hebrews 9:1-12; Leviticus 16; Exodus 40).

b. On the Day of Atonement, even the High Priest could not enter without Blood Atonement, for his own sins as well as the sins of the people. He must also have the cloud of incense (Leviticus 16).

c. When the Ark was in transit, it had to be covered with the appointed cloths and with the covering Veil. No human eyes were to gaze upon it. It was to be always covered in transit (Numbers 4:5-6).

These were the most important commandments of the Lord through Moses concerning the Ark of the Covenant in His Tabernacle.

Did Hophni and Phinehas, these sons of Belial, worry about the commandments of the Lord? Did they care whether it was a Day of Atonement ceremony or not? Did they wait to bring the atoning blood and the cloud of incense within the Veil? Did they take time to fulfill the laws of approach to God as appointed for Priests? When they took the Ark out of the Holiest of All, did they take time to place the covering Veil over the Ark and the other cloths? Was God's order for transit followed by these sons? Undoubtedly not! There was a battle on. There was no time for religious formalities and obeying God's commandments!

Thus, these lawless Priests in great presumption rush the Ark off to the battle, never realizing that this would be the death of them both. They had filled their cup of iniquity to the full. Because they did not come under parental discipline they came under Divine discipline in due time.

5. The Death of Eli (I Samuel 4:12-18).

In the end of the battle, with the Ark of God in captivity to the Philistines, one of the army men of the Tribe of Benjamin ran back to Shiloh. His clothes were rent and earth was upon his head. Eli was sitting by a post at the House of God at Shiloh. His heart was trembling for the Ark of God. He knew the violations of God's commandments that his two wreckless sons were guilty of.

When the Benjaminite told the city of Shiloh that the Ark of God was taken by the Philistines they cried out in anguish. Eli heard the noise and asked what it was all about. As the Benjaminite told him of the battle, of the death of his two sons and of the Ark being taken, Eli took a stroke and died.

It is significant that it was not over the death of his two sons but at the mention of the Ark of God being taken that Eli died with shock. The physical condition of Eli in his death is also symbolic of the spiritual condition of Eli and the nation. Eli was old physically. His eyes were dim that he could not see. And when he died, he fell off the seat backward and broke his neck (vs 15, 18). Spiritually speaking, the nation's eyes were dim and unable to see. Spiritually, the nation had fallen backward into idolatry and apostasy and was stiffnecked towards the things of God.

What thoughts must have passed through the old man's mind over the Ark? The Ark had been with Israel all through the 40 years in the Wilderness from Mt. Sinai to the crossing of Jordan. The Ark of God's Presence had opened up the River Jordan for the nation to pass across into Canaan. The Ark had led the way to victory around Jericho. The land had been divided before the Lord at the Tabernacle in Shiloh.

Even through the hundreds of years in the period of the Judges, through the various servitudes and deliverances, God had never let enemy hands touch the Ark of the Lord. And now, here under his ministry, as Priest-Judge, God had permitted the Ark to fall into enemy hands.

Never in the history of the Nation had such a thing happened. It was Eli's own wayward sons that had precipitated it all. This was the worst tragedy so far in the history of Israel.

It is no wonder that when Eli heard that the Ark was taken that the shock of it all killed him. Here is fulfilled the judgment of God upon Eli who failed to discipline his sons. He honoured his sons above God's Word and did not restrain their vileness.

6. Ichabod - The Glory is Departed (I Samuel 4:19-22).

As if there had not been enough tragedy in Israel, further tragedy is seen in the passage here. Phinehas' wife is nearing the time of birth for her child. When she heard of the terrible news that the Ark of God was taken, that her father-in-law and her husband were dead, travail seized upon her. The end result was that a child was born, a baby boy, and she managed to name him just before she died in this travail.

The baby boy was named "Ichabod," which means, "Where is the Glory?"; "There is no Glory," or "The Glory is departed from Israel." This was because the Ark had been taken into captivity.

This child became a sign-child (cf. Isaiah 8:18) in Israel by the interpretation of his name. As long as that child was around it signified that the Glory had departed from Israel; there was no Glory. Without the Ark of God and the God of the Ark there could be no Glory. His Strength and His Glory was symbolized in the Ark. It was now in enemy hands. Tragic day for the nation indeed!

The tragedies of this chapter are summarized:

1. About 34,000 Israelites have been slain in battle by the Philistines.

2. The Ark of God has been taken in battle.

3. Hophni and Phinehas have been slain also.

4. Eli has died through shock.

5. Phinehas' wife also has died in travail.

6. A sign-child is born, named Ichabod, "The Glory is departed."

In the light of all these things and details given in 1 Samuel 1-4, we understand more fully and clearly the prophecy of Jeremiah to his wicked generation. Their boasting was vain in the Ark of the Lord and the Temple in the City of Jerusalem. Read Jeremiah 3:16 with 7:1-16; Psalms 78:54-62.

We repeat the particular references.

> "But go ye now unto My place which was in Shiloh, where I set My Name at the first, and see what I did to it for the wickedness of My people Israel ... Therefore will I do to this House ... as I have done to Shiloh" (Jeremiah 7:12, 14).
>
> "So that He forsook the Tabernacle of Shiloh, the tent which He placed among men; and delivered His strength into captivity, and His glory into the enemy's hands" (Psalms 78:60-61).

Chapter 15

CAPTIVITY & JOURNEYINGS OF THE ARK

(THE ARK IN CAPTIVITY)

The account of the captivity and journeyings of the Ark is given for us in 1 Samuel 5 and 6. The student should carefully read these Scriptures. The details therein are commented on in this section.

A. The Ark in Ashdod (1 Samuel 5:1-7).

With the capture of the Ark of the Covenant, the Philistines brought it from Ebenezer to Ashdod, or "Stronghold." This was a Philistine city between Gaza and Joppa, assigned to Judah (Joshua 15:47). The city was made famous by the Temple built to the god "Dagon." The Ark was placed in the House of Dagon, meaning "Fish." Dagon was the national idol of the Philistines. It was represented with human hands and face and a fish's body.

In the morning, when the Priests came to the Temple for their functions, they found that Dagon had fallen on his face before the Ark of the Lord. They promptly set him up in his place again.

The following morning they found Dagon fallen on his face again, but this time the head and hands had been cut off. All that was left of him was the stump or the "fishy" part of him! (King James Version, marginal reading).

Fear fell on the Priests and none dare tread on the threshold of that Temple again. They recognized that the Ark of the God of Israel was above all idol gods. All gods of the heathen must bow before the God of all the earth (Isaiah 42:8).

It is worthy to compare the event here with the captivity of the Lord Jesus Christ, "The Ark of God" in John's Gospel (John 18:1-6). When the Temple soldiers came to arrest Jesus in Gethsemane, He spoke the Name of God, "I AM"; that Name revealed to Moses at the burning bush and also later called upon the Ark of the Covenant, and these soldiers fell to the ground. It is significant of the fact that all will bow to Him. Idols and men are but vanity before the Ark of God personified in the Lord Jesus Christ.

Not only did Dagon and his temple fall into disuse, God smote the city of Ashdod with a plague of emerods (hemorrhoids or boils). The hand of God fell in judgment on Dagon and the Ashdodites who worshipped the fish-god. These plagues were part of the curses of the Law (Deuteronomy 28:27).

B. The Ark in Gath (1 Samuel 5:8, 9).

The Ashdodites sent and gathered the lords of the Philistines to discuss what to do with the Ark. The lords suggested that the Ark be sent to the city of Gath, meaning "Winepress." This was another of the five cities of the Philistines. That is, one of their five principal cities (Joshua 13:3; 1 Samuel 6:17).

This was later on, the home of Goliath the giant and defier of the God of Israel. (1 Samuel 17:4). It also became a refuge for David in the time of Saul's anger (1 Samuel 21:10).

Again, it is interesting to compare the questions which the Gathites asked concerning the Ark and those questions which were asked concerning the Lord Jesus in the New Testament.

"What shall we do with the Ark of the God of Israel?" (1 Samuel 5:8).

"What shall I do <u>with</u> Jesus which is called Christ?" (Matthew 27:22).

"What shall we do <u>to</u> the Ark of the Lord?" (1 Samuel 6:2).

"What will ye then that I shall do <u>unto</u> Him whom ye call the King of the Jews?" (Mark 15:12).

The Gathites carried the Ark about and so the Lord's hand fell on them and the city was smitten with a great destruction. They were also plagued with emerods as was Ashdod.

None dare touch the Ark of God. Otherwise it meant death, plagues and destruction.

C. <u>The Ark in Ekron</u> (1 Samuel 5:10-12).

The Philistines now send the Ark to the city of Ekron, which means, "Migration," or "Barrenness, Torn away."

The Ekronites had heard of the terrible plagues in the other cities and they cried out about the Ark being sent to their city. They called the lords of the cities and asked that the Ark be sent back to its own place. Deadly destruction was in their city, and men were smitten with emerods or struck dead. The cry of the Ekronites went up to heaven.

D. <u>The Ark sent to Bethshemesh</u> (1 Samuel 6:1-12, 13-20).

After 7 months of destruction in the land of the Philistines because of the presence of the Ark of God, the people called for the Priests and Diviners and asked them to find out what should be done.

The religious leaders said that the Ark should be returned to its own place in Judah. However, as all heathen religions had sacrificial rites of propitiation to the gods, they also realized they could not send back the Ark of the God of all the earth without some appeasement.

It seems evident that they had some measure of knowledge of the ways of the God of Israel, for they suggested that the Philistines send a Trespass Offering (cf. Leviticus 5) back with the Ark of God.

They reasoned that, if physical healing came to their people and land when the Ark was returned, then they would know it was the True God of Israel who had plagued and judged them. These priests actually exhorted the people and warned them not to harden their hearts as did the Egyptians when God had sent plagues on them because of their refusal to let Israel go.

The Philistines then made a new cart, placed the Ark on it, and a Trespass Offering beside it. The Trespass Offering consisted of 5 Golden emerods, and 5 Golden mice, according to the 5 lords of the 5 Philistine cities (1 Samuel 4:4, 5, 16, 17). These were the types of plagues they had been smitten with by the Lord. The number 5 is significant of the Atonement, symbolized in the nation of Israel in the 5 Levitical Offerings (Leviticus 1-7).

These two milch kine, upon which had come no yoke, were then tied to the new cart. Their calves were taken from them and left at home. The Philistines watched as the cows took the straight way to Bethshemesh, neither turning to the right hand or to the left. The lords of the Philistines followed them to the border of Bethshemesh.

How wonderful this thing was! The cows left their calves behind, lowing as they went. It was unnatural for them to do so. Also, not to turn aside to the right or to the left was contrary to the nature of the animals. It was supernatural. God overruled the animal nature, causing them to go the straight way to Bethshemesh , not stumbling as they went. Thus, the Ark left the land of the Philistines after 7 months captivity and returned to the land of Judah.

At Bethshemesh , it was wheat harvest time (Pentecost Harvest), and the reapers were reaping in the valley. As soon as they saw the Ark of God they rejoiced with real joy.

The Ark came to a stop in the field of Joshua ("Jehoshua is Salvation,") a Bethshemite , there, on the great Stone of Abel, they took the wood of the new cart that the Philistines had made and used it for fire as they offered the two kine as a burnt offering to the Lord.

The Levites handled the Ark and the Trespass Offerings the Philistines had sent with it. However, this blessed event was soon turned into great disaster. In vs 19,20, the men of Bethshemesh looked into the Ark of the Lord, and God smote 50,070 people with a great slaughter. Why? God did not permit the Philistines to handle the Ark. And even God's own people must learn respect for it and all that it represented. It was pride and presumption and vain curiosity which caused them to look into the Ark.

In order to do this, they had to remove the MERCY SEAT lid - that blood-stained Mercy Seat! And what would they behold? They would behold the 10 Commandments, the LAW, the ministration of death (2 Corinthians 3). The Law worketh wrath, destruction, and death. If mercy is put aside, man is then exposed to wrath (Romans 4:15).

Thus, God's people must respect the ways of a holy God.

E. <u>The Ark at Kirjath-jearim</u> (1 Samuel 6:21; 1 Samuel 7:1-2).

The men of Bethshemesh recognized that none could stand before such a holy God, and that He would only dwell in the midst of His people on His own terms.

Messengers were sent to Kirjath-jearim ("City of Woods"), a Gibeonite city which belonged to Judah (Joshua 9:17, Judges 18:12), asking them to come and get the Ark of God.

Possibly Psalm 132 is an historical reference to the Ark coming into the woods, or Kirjath-jearim, before it came into its new place of rest in the Tabernacle of David.

The men of Kirjath-jearim fetched the Ark and, after sanctifying Abinadab's son, Eleazar, charged him to keep the Ark in his father's house.

It seems that the Ark was here for about 100 years, and in the last 20 years the people of Israel lamented after the absence of the Glory of the Lord upon the Ark.

The Amplified Old Testament writes on 1 Samuel 7:2 as follows:

> "And the Ark remained in Kirjath-jearim a very long time (nearly 100 years, through Samuel's entire judgeship, Saul's reign, and well into David's, when it was brought to Jerusalem). For it was 20 years before all the house of Israel lamented after the Lord"

Hence, during this long period, Samuel, King Saul, and David are moving into their respective historical settings.

F. The Ark at Gibeah (1 Samuel 14:1-3; 15-19).

It seems from this Scripture that the Ark must have been at Gibeah ("Hill") for a time under King Saul.

King Saul is in a time of distress under the Philistines and asked that the Ark of God be brought to him. He had Ahiah, "Jehovah's Friend," son of Ahitub, Ichabod's brother, son of Phinehas, son of Eli of Shiloh, to be his priest.

Ahiah was a relative of Ichabod, "The Glory is departed." However, when Saul heard the noise of battle, he had no more time to wait for God to speak and thus asked the priest to withdraw his hand, as they stood before the Ark of God. Saul knew not at that time the God of the Ark, hence the Ark of God was superstitiously employed by him.

During the sad years that followed, Saul rose up against David, the freshly anointed of the Lord. On one occasion, in his chase after David, he discovered that Ahimelech, ("My Brother is King,"), a priest of the priestly city of Nob, had helped David. He had given David and his men some Shewbread and also Goliath's sword. Doeg, an Edomite overheard the conversation and told King Saul. The end result was that Saul caused Doeg, the Edomite, to kill 85 priests in that city because of helping David (1 Samuel 21:1-9, 22:9-23). Abiathar, one of Ahitub's sons, escaped and fled to David with an Ephod to enquire of God by.

It is no wonder that the Lord refused to answer King Saul by the Ark, the priest, Urim and Thummin, prophets or dreams, because of such actions against the Divine channels of communication (1 Samuel 28:6).

If Saul rejected these and silenced them, God certainly had nothing to say to him.

G. The Ark at the House of Obededom (2 Samuel 6:1-11; 1 Chronicles 13:11-14).

Possibly the Ark, after being at Gibeah for a short while, was then taken back and settled in Kirjath-jearim, or Baalah of Judah, in the house of Abinadab in the Gibeah area.

The time came when Saul and his son Jonathan were slain and David came to the throne of Israel. As noted previously, after David's third anointing as King over all Israel, David desired to see the Ark of God brought into its proper place in the nation.

David consulted with the captains and the leaders of the nation, expressing his desire for the Ark of God. He reminded them that they had not sought God at the Ark in the days of King Saul (1 Chronicles 13:3).

The people also were convinced that it was the right thing to do. David and the leaders with the people gathered together and went to Kirjath-jearim to bring up the Ark of God the Lord.

But what did David do? Lo and behold he followed in the footsteps of the Philistines and placed the Ark on A NEW CART, after taking it out of the house of Abinadab in Gibeah (cf. 1 Samuel 6:7; 1 Chronicles 13:7; 2 Samuel 6:3).

The Philistines' new cart had been burned in the fire. David had to make another new cart!

Uzza and Ahio, two priestly sons, began to drive the cart along. David and all Israel began to play before God with all their might. Harps, psalteries, timbrels, cymbals, trumpets, and singing resounded on the way (2 Samuel 6:5; 1 Chronicles 13:8).

But what happened? As they were rejoicing and shouting, the oxen came to the threshing floor of Nachon (or Chidon) and the oxen stumbled. Uzza put forth his hand to steady the Ark from falling off the new cart. God's anger is kindled against him and God struck him dead. He died before the Ark of God!

David the King was greatly displeased because of this. Fear gripped him. The happy occasion closed with death. David dared not proceed any further. He took the Ark aside and placed it in the house of Obededom, a Gittite. Here the Ark remained for 3 months and the blessing of God prevailed upon this house and all that was his (1 Chronicles 13:9-14; 2 Samuel 6:11). Thus, the Ark went from the house of Abinadab to the house of Obededom.

This step ended in tragedy. God must teach, even King David, that there is a Divine order which is to be followed. The Philistines may have their "new cart" and God will overrule the nature of the kine who bare the Ark. But when it comes to God's own people, God cannot permit any "new cart" nor can He have the hand of man steady the Ark.

God could have prevented the oxen from stumbling here, even as He supernaturally overruled the natures of the cows of the Philistines previously. But there is Divine order which His people must follow, even the pattern laid down in His Word.

God permitted the oxen to stumble. David was doing a right thing in a wrong way. The Philistines may have a new cart; the Israelites may not. "Others may; you may not" is an applicable statement here.

David and the Israelites knew that God had miraculously overruled in the case of the Philistines and that the new cart had been burnt and the oxen sacrificed to God. Therefore they should have known better than to make another cart for God.

There are tremendous spiritual lessons here for the people of God today.

It is possible for a spiritual leader and his congregation to recognize the need for the glory and presence and blessing of God. But all must learn that a right thing must not be done in a wrong way.

The Ark was only a piece of shittim wood, overlaid with gold - only a symbol. But it was what that symbol signified in the mind of God. To touch it with unsanctified hands meant plagues, destruction, and death.

The Lord says, "I will be sanctified in them that come nigh Me, and before all the people will I be glorified" (Leviticus 10:3). And again, "Be ye clean that bear the vessels of the Lord" (Isaiah 52:11).

Plagues and death had struck among the Philistines. Death had struck amongst the people of God at Bethshemesh. And now death strikes again upon Uzza as he tried to steady the shaking Ark on the new cart because of the stumbling oxen.

God permitted the oxen to stumble in order to drive David to seek His face and seek His order as laid down in the word given to Moses. David dare not presume any further.

Many organizations and groups of God's people today are resorting to "new carts" in order to get the presence and blessing of God back into their midst. What is a "new cart"? A "new cart" is significant of any man-made religious gimmick, contrary to the Word of God, which is used to get the Ark of God's presence back into a spiritually decadent congregation.

One must burn these "new carts" and seek God's face and study His Word for His order. The right thing must be done the right way. God's will done in God's way will never lack God's blessing!

The place where Uzza was struck dead was called "Perez-uzza," or "The Breach of Uzza," the breach caused by Uzza.

Thus, we have the record of the captivity and journeyings of the Ark from the Philistines on to the house of Obededom.

1. Ashdod
2. Gath
3. Ekron
4. Bethshemesh
5. Kirjath-jearim
6. Gibeah
7. The house of Obededom.

Its next step will be into the Tabernacle of David! The student is referred to the map of "The Journey of the Ark of the Covenant."

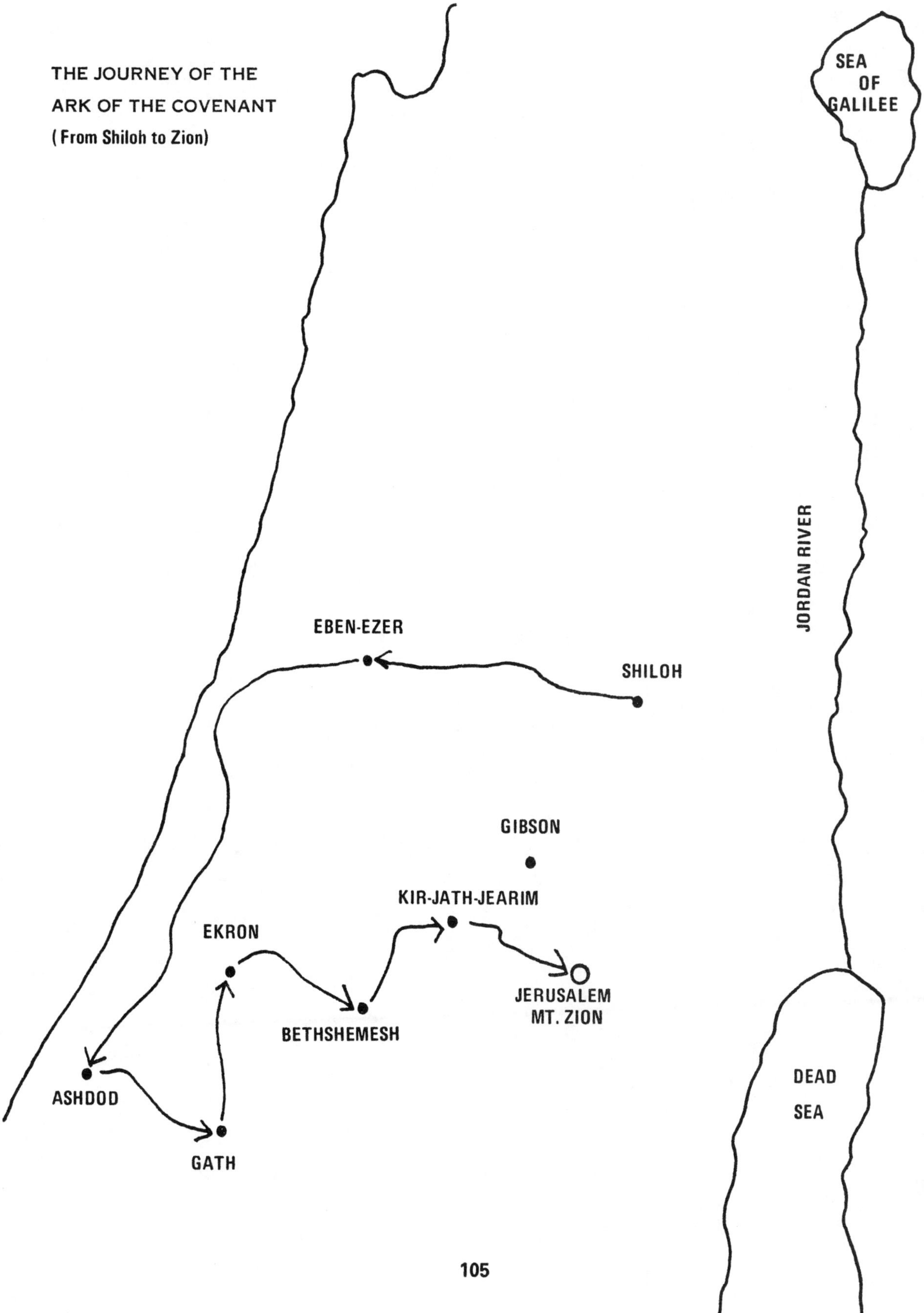

THE JOURNEY OF THE
ARK OF THE COVENANT
(From Shiloh to Zion)
SEA
OF
GALILEE
JORDAN RIVER
EBEN-EZER
SHILOH
GIBSON
KIR-JATH-JEARIM
EKRON
JERUSALEM
MT. ZION
BETHSHEMESH
ASHDOD
GATH
DEAD
SEA

Chapter 16

THE PREPARATION OF DAVID'S TABERNACLE

During the 3 months period in which the Ark of God was in the house of Obededom, David saw that the blessing of God came upon that household. He gave himself to seeking the Lord and searching His Word and it is certain that God gave to him understanding and insight into His will.

David now prepares a place for the Ark of the Lord. There is no doubt that David pitched the Tabernacle in the will of God. It may be questioned as to whether David was in the will of God setting up another Tabernacle when the Tabernacle of Moses was already in existence.

A brief review over the previous events concerning those who touched the Ark of God with unsanctified hands, be they Philistines or Israelites, reveals the fact that none dare to presume concerning the Ark of God.

If David dared to presume to set up another Tabernacle in opposition to or contradiction of the Tabernacle of Moses, he also would have been struck dead, even as death and plagues have judged so many so far. From the death of Hophni and Phinehas when the Ark was taken out of the Tabernacle at Shiloh through to the first bringing up of the Ark of God by David, death and judgment have prevailed. So if David was out of the will of God in establishing another Tabernacle, he certainly would have been judged by God. No! David was indeed in the will of God, as the following Scriptures show.

God testified of David the King, by saying, "I have found David the son of Jesse, a man after Mine own heart, which shall fulfill all My will" (Acts 13:22).

And again the Scripture states, "For David, after he had served his generation by the will of God fell on sleep ...." (Acts 13:36).

And yet again, "... the days of David, who found favour before God and desired to find a Tabernacle for the God of Jacob" (Acts 7:46).

There are several spiritual lessons which may be learned from the details given concerning the preparation of David for the bringing up of the Ark into this Tabernacle. The details are given for us especially in 1 Chronicles 15:1-24.

A. The Preparation of a Place.

Note the word "prepared" in 1 Chronicles 15:1, 3, 12. David prepared a place for the Ark of God. It was not a haphazard thing. There was a definite preparation of a place for the presence of God to dwell. Worthy of attention are the following Scriptures, for each of them show that God desired a place where he could dwell with His people and where His Name could be recorded.

> "... in all places where I record My Name I will come unto thee, and I will bless thee" (Exodus 20:24).
>
> "... I will prepare Him an Habitation" (Exodus 15:2).
>
> "But unto the place which the Lord your God shall choose out of all your tribes to put His Name there, even unto His Habitation shall ye seek, and thither thou shalt come" (Deuteronomy 12:5).
>
> "... a place which the Lord your God shall choose to cause His Name to dwell there; thither shall ye bring all that I command you; your burnt offerings, and your sacrifices, your tithes, and the heave offering of your hand, and all your choice vows..." (Deuteronomy 12:11).

Note also the use of the word "place" in these verses, Deuteronomy 12:2, 3, 13, 14, 18, 21; 16:2, 6, 7, 11, 15, 16.

The Tabernacle of Moses was a place of God at first. Now the Tabernacle of David becomes that place prepared for God here. God always desired a place to dwell with His people. Thus David prepared a place for the Ark of God.

The New Testament Local Church is that "place" now where the Lord gathers with His people gathered together in His Name (Matthew 18:20) "Where two or three are gathered together in My Name, there I AM in the midst of them."

B. David pitched a Tent or Tabernacle.

The Scriptures show that the place prepared by David for the Lord was a Tent or a Tabernacle in Zion, Jerusalem.

> "... for he had pitched a Tent for it at Jerusalem" (2 Chronicles 1:4).
>
> "... set the Ark in the midst of the Tent that David had pitched for it" (I Chronicles 16:I).
>
> "And they brought in the Ark of the Lord, and set it in his place, in the midst of the Tabernacle that David had pitched for it" (2 Samuel 6:17).

There are various words used in the Old Testament relative to the words "tent" or "tabernacle."

- The Tent (Hebrew "Ohel") of Moses (Exodus 18:7-12).
- The Tent (Hebrew "Ohel") of the Tabernacle of the Congregation (Exodus 33:7-11).
- The Tabernacle (Hebrew "Mishkan") of the Lord (Exodus 25:9, 26:1-35). Generally spoken of as the Tabernacle of Moses.
- The Tent or Tabernacle (Hebrew "Ohel") of David (1 Chronicles 16:1-3); 2 Samuel 6:17; Isaiah 16:5).

The Tabernacle was simply a Tent, pitched in Jerusalem, in Mt. Zion. It was there until the erection of the Temple of Solomon. It certainly could not be compared with the Tent or Tabernacle of Moses and its three places as far as structure was concerned. The very fact that David's Tabernacle was simply a Tent attested to the truth that its construction was temporary and transitional. It was not the ultimate as a structure. That which was established in it was incorporated in the Temple order. Both the revelation of the Tabernacle of David and the Temple of Solomon had been given to King David.

The Tent stages of God's movements in Israel are expressed clearly in 1 Chronicles 17:5, "For I have not dwelt in an house since the day that I brought up Israel unto this day; but have gone from tent to tent, and one tabernacle to another."

And again, "Whereas I have not dwelt in any house since the time that I brought up the children of Israel out of Egypt, even to this day, but have walked in a tent and in a tabernacle" (2 Samuel 7:6).

It is significant that God is always on the move, leading His people on in the unfolding and progressive revelation of Himself.

The Tent also speaks of the fact that we bear the character of pilgrims and strangers, and, like Abraham, Isaac and Jacob, we look for a City whose builder and maker is God. The Christian has no continuing City in this world, but has the pilgrim character symbolized in the Tents of the Patriarchal times, and David's Tabernacle as well as Moses' Tabernacle (1 Peter 2:11; Hebrews 11:8-16; 13:14; Revelation 21-22).

C. The Gathering Together of Israel.

The preparation for the upbringing of the Ark to David's Tabernacle also involved a great national gathering together of the people of God.

On the first occasion David gathered the leaders of the nation together, as well as the congregation of Israel (1 Chronicles 13:1-4). Then 3 months later there is another great assembling together. This time to do the thing in God's way (1 Chronicles 15:25).

This gathering of the people was for one purpose. The unifying factor was the bringing up of the Ark of the Lord and a restoration of true worship in Israel after the sad years of decline from Samuel's time and through the reign of King Saul.

The spiritual lessons are evident for the Church today. If the Church desires to see the restoration of the Presence of the Lord - our Ark - then there must be unity of purpose and a true gathering together unto Him.

> "Unto HIM shall the gathering of the people be" (Genesis 49:10).
>
> "Gather My saints together unto ME, those that have made a covenant with Me by sacrifice" (Psalms 50:5).
>
> "Where two or three are gathered together in My Name, there I AM in the midst" (Matthew 18:20).

It is where the brethren dwell together in unity that the Lord commands His blessing -- one accord, one purpose, one people (Psalm 133; Acts 2:1-4).

The leaders must come together (cf. Exodus 4:29). The people must gather together (cf. Acts 14:27).

God generally comes to the leaders first, and then to the congregations. How the nation of Israel would have been robbed of the truth of the Tabernacle of David if the leaders had fought and opposed the revelation that God had given King David!

The same is applicable to today. Congregations of God's people are robbed of the revelation of David's Tabernacle because their leaders resist it. How blessed and glorious that David had the captains and the leaders one with him in this event, as well as the congregation of Israel.

D. The Due Order (1 Chronicles 15:13).

As David was preparing the Levites and the people for the upbringing of the Ark of God, he exhorted them to follow God's order. He said to them, "For because ye did it not at the first, the Lord our God made a breach upon us, for that we sought Him not after the due order."

What was this "due order"? It was important that David learn that God had a particular order to follow, even though God was revealing progressive truth to David.

God is a God of order. Creation reveals order. Redemption reveals order. There is order in the Eternal Godhead. And so when it comes to the House of the Lord, there must be Divine order in the service. Of course, much that is man's order is not necessarily God's order, and perhaps to man, God's order may seem disorder! But God has laid down in His Word the order of worship that His people are to follow.

The word "order" has the thought of "Divine decree, Law, sentence, style" (S.C. 4941).

It is worthy to note the order that God commanded in things pertaining to Himself and the approach of His people to Him in worship.

1. The sacrifices on the Brazen Altar have order. The wood, the inward parts of the animals were laid upon the altar in "order"; God's order (Leviticus 1:7, 8, 12, 6:12). The word "order" here is "to set in a row, arrange, put in order" (S.C. 6186).

2. The Golden Candlestick and its 7 lighted lamps had to be "ordered" evening and morning (S.C. "arranged" Exodus 27:21, 39:37, S.C. 6186 and 4634).

3. The Table of Shewbread had the bread set "in order" (S.C. 6186 and 6187, "arrangement") upon it (Exodus 40:4, 23). Note also 2 Chronicles 13:11 (S.C. 494, "Bread of Order," or "Bread of Arrangement").

4. The Priests waited in their courses according to Divine order. The word "order" here means "Verdict, sentence, formal decree." (S.C. 4941). Note also, Luke 1:8, (S.C. 5010), "Regular arrangement." Zacharias waited before God in order after his course as Priest.

5. The revelation of Christ's Priesthood is "after the order of Melchisedek" (Hebrews 5:6, 10; 7:11, 17, 21). (S.C. 5010, "Regular arrangement in time, fixed succession of rank or character, official dignity".)

6. There is order even in the resurrection of the saints. Every man will be resurrected in his own order. S.C. 5001, "Something orderly in arrangement."

Thus all that pertains to God and His service is according to God's "due order."

The same truth is brought over to New Testament for the Local Churches to follow. Paul, the Apostle, established Churches according to Divine order which was given to him. He exhorts them to follow this order. He rejoices when the believers do, and warns them that he will have to adjust things if they do not follow God's due order.

7. To the Corinthian Church he writes, "Let all things be done decently and in order" (1 Corinthians 14:40). (S.C. 5010, "Regular arrangement... etc.) There must be order in the operation of spiritual gifts in the Church.

1 Corinthians 16:1, "As I have given order (S.C. 1299, "To arrange thoroughly") to the Churches." There was order relative to the offerings of the believers in the Churches.

"The rest will I set in order when I come" (1 Corinthians 11:34; S.C. 1299). There must be order at the Lord's Table.

Luke 1:1, 3, Luke wrote his gospel "to set forth in order (S.C. 1299) a declaration of those things which are most surely believed among us."

Paul writes to the Colossian believers telling them that he was with them in spirit "joying and beholding your order" (S.C. 5010; Colossians 2:5).

Thus the Scriptures, Old and New Testaments, clearly reveal that God demands order in all that which pertains to worship and Divine service. Order in the sacrifices, order at the altar, order at the lampstand, order in the priesthood.

The New Testament continues the same truth. The Apostle Paul established an order in the Church. He systematically arranged things according to the pattern and revelation that was given to him.

Order in the gifts of the Spirit, order at the Lord's Table, order in the worship and gathering of the believers. Even the resurrection of the saints will follow Divine order, Divine arrangement into the various glories.

Hence, the lesson that David learned in the setting up of this Tabernacle was that there is "due order" to be followed. The same lesson of "due order" in the New Testament Church must be recognized and followed in order to have God's blessing and presence. Without Divine order in the service, all will be anarchy, lawlessness, and chaos." God is not the author of confusion, but of peace, as in all the Churches" (1 Corinthians 14:33). People will "do their own thing" like the Corinthian Church without having Divine order in the Church. But there is real joy in beholding the order of the saints of God (Colossians 2:5). The saints need to know how to behave themselves in the House of God, which is the Church of the Living God, the pillar and ground (stay, support) of the truth (1 Timothy 3:15).

E. The Ark on the Shoulders of the Levites (1 Chronicles 15:2, 12, 14, 15).

The "due order" expressly referred to in David's time was that which pertained to the bearing of the Ark of God. The Lord had commanded through the mouth of Moses that the Ark was to be borne by the Levites on their shoulders. It was to have the staves of shittim wood overlaid with gold always in them, whether stationary or in transit (Exodus 25:10-15). In vs 15, the Lord says, "The staves shall be in the rings of the Ark; they shall not be taken from it." The staves were always to be in the Ark while in its pilgrimage character. When at last the Ark was taken from the Tabernacle of David into the Temple of Solomon, then the staves were removed (2 Chronicles 5:9; 1 Kings 8:8). Here the journey was over and rest and permanency typified in the Temple, was to be revealed. Until that time, the staves remained in the Ark of the Lord. Not only was this to be so, the Ark in transit had to be borne upon the shoulders of the Priests - not a new cart! (Numbers 4:4-6, 15; 7:9 with Joshua 6:6, 7). Various parts of the Tabernacle of Moses were carried on wagons with the oxen drawing the same, but not the Ark of God (Numbers 3:36, 37; 7:7-9).

The "shoulder" in Scripture is symbolic of government, support, and strength in responsibility.

1. The shoulder and the breast were given to the Priest out of certain of the sacrifices offered to the Lord (Leviticus 7:32-34; 8:25, 26; Numbers 18:18).

2. The shoulder was waved for a wave offering before the Lord and brought for certain of the offerings (Leviticus 9:21; 10:14, 15).

3. The shoulder was a special portion to be given to the Priests (Deuteronomy 18:3).

4. The prophet Samuel gave the special portion of the shoulder to the anointed King Saul (1 Samuel 9:24). Significant of the government and responsibility that was to fall upon his shoulders in the matter of the Kingdom in Israel as a nation.

5. The 12 names of the Children of Israel were engraven on two onyx stones as pertaining to the garments of the High Priest. These were placed upon the shoulders (Exodus 28:12, 39:7).

6. The government of God is placed upon the shoulder of Jesus Christ, the King-Priest after the order of Melchisedek (Isaiah 9:6). He also is the one who has the key of David laid upon His shoulder (Isaiah 22:22).

All of this is symbolic of the fact that proper government, support, and strength of responsibility is of the Lord. He designates such to whom He wills and whom He chooses.

The New Testament Church has in it the ministry of governments. The government of God, through Christ, by the Spirit is laid upon the shoulders of qualified and ordained Eldership (1 Corinthians 12:28; Hebrews 13:7, 17). Believers are not to despise government that God sets in the Church (2 Peter 2:10).

God did not permit any Israelite to run around with the Ark on their shoulders, but only those who were ordained to that responsibility. So God has placed the government of His Church on the shoulders of those whom He has called, equipped, qualified, and ordained to that responsibility under Christ (1 Chronicles 15:2).

The Glory of the Lord will settle where His order is followed in the life of the Spirit, not merely the letter of the Law.

F. <u>The Time of Sanctification</u> (1 Chronicles 15:12, 14).

The preparation of David's Tabernacle also involved a great process of sanctification among the Levites in their office. David called the Priests and Levites to sanctify themselves to bring up the Ark of God. He reminded them that judgment fell on them in their first attempt because they failed to do so.

The word "sanctify" means "to separate oneself, to set apart as holy to the Lord, or for holy use." The laws of sanctification and consecration for the Priesthood are to be found in Exodus 29 and Leviticus 8.

Their sanctification involved:

1. Cleansing by <u>blood</u> sprinkled on the right ear, thumb, and toe.

2. Bathing in <u>water</u>.

3. Anointing with holy <u>oil,</u> on the blood which had been sprinkled on the right ear, the right thumb and the right toe.

Blood, water, and oil were used in the sanctifying of the Priests unto the service of the Lord. They also had to be clothed in the clean and white fine linen robes (Exodus 28). Then their hands were filled with certain parts of the offerings which were then offered to the Lord in their consecration to Priesthood ministry. Only after this could they minister unto the Lord. Thus in David's time, a great process and work of sanctification of the priests took place before the Tabernacle of David was established in its order in Zion.

All of this symbolic truth points to that which is confirmed in the New Testament concerning God's people. Believers are called to be Kings and Priests unto God after the order of Melchisedek

(Revelation 1:6; 5:9-10; 1 Peter 2:5-9). The believer must be cleansed by the blood of Jesus, baptized in water and then anointed with the Holy Spirit. He must be clothed with the fine linen which is the righteousness of Christ in His saints in order to move in Priestly ministration in the New Testament Tabernacle, which is the Church (Revelation 19:8).

The believer must experience the "three witnesses" in his life; the:

Witness of the Blood,

Witness of the Water of the Word,

Witness of the Holy Spirit (1 John 5:8-10).

This threefold work of God brings about the sanctification and consecration of the believer to Priestly duties.

We are sanctified by:

1. The Blood (Hebrews 13:12).

2. The Word (John 17:17).

3. The Spirit (1 Peter 1:2).

Separated from all evil, consecrated unto the Lord for Priestly service in God's Tabernacle, we can stand in His Presence to worship in the beauty of holiness (Psalms 29:1-2).

The preparation of David's Tabernacle was no mean thing. The preparation of a place, the gathering together of the people, following Divine order and the great time of sanctification -- all were involved. Each of these teach spiritual and practical lessons for any Local Church that desires to have the Presence of the Lord in their midst.

Chapter 17

THE ARK TAKEN INTO THE TABERNACLE OF DAVID (THE DAY OF DEDICATION)

In the bringing up of the Ark into David's Tabernacle, we see a distinct order in the Priests and Levites and in the chosen singers and musicians.

- The Order of the Priests and Levites (1 Chronicles 15:4-11).

- The Order of the singers and musicians (1 Chronicles 15:16-24).

The significance is seen in the truth of the numbers as used in Scripture. Each had their particular function in the dedicatory service of the Tabernacle of David. It must have been a solemn yet glorious procession. The details of this order are given in 1 Chronicles 16:4-29.

A. The Procession of the Ark.

For a clearer focus of the service of dedication, the assembly of the Priests and Levites is set out according to what the numerical arrangement possibly might have been.

David the King
Leader and Commander
(Isaiah 55:4; I Chronicles I5:25)

The Elders of Israel
(I Chronicles I5:25)

The Captains of Israel
(I Chronicles I5:25)

The High Priests
Zadok and Abiathar
(I Chronicles I5:4-II)

The Chiefs and Levites (I Chronicles I5:5-I0)

1.	Uriel and I20 Kohathites	vs 5	)	
2.	Asaiah and 220 Meraites	vs 6	)	Of Levi
3.	Joel and I30 Gershomites	vs 7	)	
4.	Shemaiah and 200 Sons of Elizaphan	vs 8		
5.	Eliel and 80 Sons of Hebron	vs 9		
6.	Amminadab and II2 Sons of Uzziel	vs I0		

Numerically, the Priests and Levites here numbered 870 persons. That is, two High Priests plus 6 Chiefs and then 862 Levites.

The 7 Trumpeters
(1 Chronicles 15:24)

Two Doorkeepers
(1 Chronicles 15:23)

THE ARK OF THE LORD
(1 Chronicles 15:12-15)

Two Porters
(1 Chronicles 15:18)

The Singers and Musicians
(1 Chronicles 15:16-24)

1. Chenaniah - Chief Singer
(1 Chronicles 15:22)

2. Heman, Asaph, Ethan
3 Chief Singers - Musicians
1st Degree
(1 Chronicles 15:17, 19)

3. Twelve Singers
2nd Degree
(I Chronicles 15:18-21)

Singers and Musicians

The CONGREGATION OF ISRAEL FOLLOWING

Thus we have another 28 persons listed here. The total persons distinctly listed equaled 898 persons. Then the congregation of Israel following.

By reading Psalm 87:7 and Psalm 68:25, we gain a little glimpse of what the possible order of bringing up the Ark of God was. The singers went first, then the players on instruments and weaving in and out and amongst them were the damsels playing their timbrels. Then the congregation followed in the glorious procession. It certainly was no mean service of dedication.

King David led the way. The Elders and Captains of Israel were with him, then the High Priests, the Chiefs and the Levites. The trumpeters sounded before the Ark. Following them there were the doorkeepers of the Ark, then the Ark of God "in the midst", then doorkeepers, and after this the singers, the musicians and the damsels playing their timbrels. Then following the procession would be the tribes of Israel who gathered for the occasion.

It is interesting to remember the journeys of the Ark of the Lord in the light of its present journey to David's Tabernacle.

- The Ark's first journey had been 3 days journey, as it went to seek out a place of rest for the people of the Lord (Numbers 10:33-36).

- The order of Israel's march in the wilderness always showed that the Ark of the Lord was wrapped in the veil, badger's skins, and then covered with a cloth of blue (Numbers 4:4-6). There was the proper marching order for the 12 tribes in relation to the Ark of God and the rest of the Tabernacle furniture carried by the Priestly tribe of Levi.

- The crossing of the River Jordan also had Divine order relative to the Ark of the Lord. The Priests held the Ark of the Lord in the midst of Jordan while the whole nation passed over into Canaan from the wilderness (Joshua 3-4).

- The compassing of the city of Jericho revealed that the Priests bearing the Ark of the Lord were preceded by 7 Priests with the 7 trumpets (ram's horns) as the congregation of the Lord followed them (Joshua 6).

- So here under David, with the great procession of the Ark of God into the Tabernacle of David, there is wonderful order given.

It must have been a grand and glorious procession, of triumph and rejoicing at the new thing God was doing in the nation.

B. The Ark Taken out of the House of Obededom (1 Chronicles 15:25; 2 Samuel 6:12).

As seen earlier, the Ark of God had been taken aside and placed in the house of Obededom This certainly was an act of faith on his part. To accept the Ark of God into his house, when destruction had followed upon any who dare touch it, was trust in the Lord. The Lord blessed the house of Obededom during the 3 months it was there. Here the blessing of the Lord was in a house meeting. However, the house meeting of Obededom was only temporary. It was transitional.

The time came when the Ark of God was taken out of the house of Obededom into the Tabernacle of David. What was his reaction? It seems evident that his response was good to this next step in the plan of God. There was no argument with the elders of Israel. He was willing to move from the "house stage" to the Tabernacle of David stage and the order of God established there. He was willing to move with what God was doing.

The Holy Spirit has given us in the several Scriptures concerning Obededom a typical picture and foreshadowing of the coming in of the Gentiles into priestly ministry.

The following outline sets this forth.

1. The name "Obededom" means "Servant of the Red, or Servant of Edom" (2 Samuel 6:12). Edom is the name of Esau, the flesh seed of Isaac, and twin brother of Jacob. The name is significant of the nature or character of the person. It seems to shadow forth that which speaks of the "remnant of Edom, and the heathen upon whom the name of the Lord would be called" as foretold in Amos 9:11, 12 (Acts 15:16-18).

2. Obededom was a Levite of the family of the Korhites (1 Chronicles 15:18, 24; 1 Chronicles 16:38). He is called a Gittite, or Gathite, from his birthplace in the Priestly or Levitical city of Gath-rimmon in the Tribe of Dan (Joshua 21:24, 25).

3. Obededom was willing to take the Ark into his house. When others rejected it because of the plagues, he was willing as a faithful priest to accept it. This was true faith in God (1 Chronicles 13:13-14; 2 Samuel 6:10).

4. Obededom and his household must have lived a sanctified life unto the Lord because of the fact that the blessing of the Lord was upon his household during the 3 months the Ark was there (1 Chronicles 13:14).

5. Obededom was willing to move with God on into David's Tabernacle. He accepted the fact that the "house stage" was but transitional. It was not intended to be the ultimate. Once David found God's due order (1 Chronicles 15:13), the Ark was taken out of the house into the Tabernacle of David (1 Chronicles 15:25; 2 Samuel 6:12).

6. Obededom was appointed to be amongst the musicians in the order of worship in David's Tabernacle in Zion (1 Chronicles 15:21; 16:5, 38). He came into the ministry of music here.

7. Obededom was blessed with 8 sons from whom came mighty men of valour, strong for the service of the Lord. These were in the divisions of the porters (1 Chronicles 26:4-8).

These Scriptures concerning Obededom set forth a character study of those who are willing to receive the Ark of God's presence into their home and yet continue to move on with God in His time into proper order.

Only those who have the servant spirit and attitude are best fitted for priestly ministry in the Tabernacle of Jesus Christ, the Son of David. These find themselves amongst the worshippers there.

Another Obededom, the son of Jeduthan, was a doorkeeper in the house of God (1 Chronicles 16:38). Perhaps David was referring to this when he said, "I had rather be a doorkeeper in the house of my God, than to dwell in the tents of wickedness" (Psalms 84:10).

The cameo picture that God has given here certainly finds its fulfillment in the New Testament revelation. Many of the Local Churches in Apostolic times began or met in the home setting. The Gospel of Christ came to the house of Cornelius by Peter and here a whole household received a sovereign outpouring of the Spirit. Here we see the Gentiles coming into the Tabernacle of David order, into New Testament priesthood ministrations (Acts 10-11 with 15:15-18). These house settings were certainly a great contrast to the old Mosaic economy and ritualism of the Tabernacle of Moses and the Temple times of Messiah.

C. The Dedicatory Sacrifices (1 Chronicles 15:26, 16:1-2; 2 Samuel 6:13, 17-18).

With the removal of the Ark from Obededom's house into the Tabernacle of David, certain dedicatory animal sacrifices were offered to the Lord. The first group of sacrifices consisted of 7 bullocks and 7 rams. The significance is seen here.

- Number seven speaks of perfection, completeness, fullness. It is symbolic of and points to Christ's perfect, sinless, and once-for-all sacrifice at Calvary (Hebrews 10:1-14).
- The bullock is symbolic of service, strength for service. The ox was used to tread out the corn and to serve man. It was also used in the consecration of the Priests as a sin offering (Exodus 29:1, 12-14).
- The ram is symbolic of substitution and consecration. It is seen in this connection in these Scriptures: Genesis 22:13, 14; Exodus 29:1-3, 15-28. It was also used in the consecration of the Priests.

The student should familiarize himself with the spiritual significance of the Levitical offerings in Leviticus 1-7.

The account in Samuel (2 Samuel 6:13) says, "And it was so, that when they that bare the Ark of the Lord had gone six paces, he (David) sacrificed oxen and fatlings."

Possibly the 6 paces pointed back to the 6 places that the Ark had been in its journeyings from Ashdod, to Gath, to Ekron, to Bethshemesh, to Kirjath-jearim, to Gibeah, before it came into the house of Obededom.

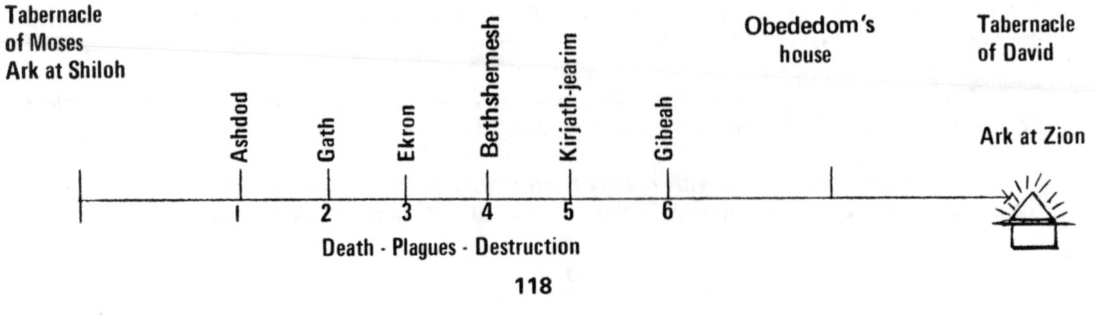

There were further animal sacrifices when the Ark was brought into David's Tabernacle (I Chronicles 16:1-2; 2 Samuel 6:17-18). David offered before God:

- Burnt offerings -- refer to Leviticus 1.
- Peace offerings -- refer to Leviticus 3.

Both of these were voluntary offerings, offered as a freewill offering to the Lord. They are indicative of Christ's voluntary offering at Calvary. He came to do the Father's will and was offered as a freewill sacrifice on the Cross (Hebrews 10:5-7; Psalms 40:7-8; John 10:17, 18).

Thus sacrifices were offered when the Ark was taken from Obededom's house and then into the Tabernacle of David. God never takes His people from something He has blessed unless He takes them into the next step in His plan. Many times the Lord's people hesitate to come from something God is blessing into the fresh visitation of the Spirit through fear of the unknown. But God always desires to lead His people into a fuller revelation of Himself in each step.

The major point here is that there were sacrifices offered at the dedication of the Tabernacle of David.

1. There were animal sacrifices offered at the dedication of the Tabernacle of Moses and the dedication of the altar (Numbers 7, Exodus 29; Leviticus 8; Leviticus 9; Leviticus 10).

2. There were animal sacrifices offered at the dedication of Solomon's Temple also (2 Chronicles 6-7; 1 Kings 8) in the Feast of Tabernacles.

3. There were animal sacrifices offered at the dedication of the Tabernacle of David (1 Chronicles 15:26, 16:1-2; 2 Samuel 6:13, 17-18).

The writer to the Hebrews tells us that everything involved in the making of a Covenant or Testament had to be dedicated with BLOOD, sacrificial blood (Hebrews 9:11-22).

Each of these dedicatory sacrifices pointed to Calvary. Here the greatest dedicatory sacrifice took place. The cross was the altar to which all other altars pointed. It fulfilled and abolished all such. Here Jesus Christ, the greater Son of David, offered His own body and blood as the perfect, sinless, once-for-all dedicatory sacrifice to God. His blood was shed for the dedication of His Tabernacle -- the Church! It was the blood of the NEW Testament, the NEW Covenant (Matthew 26:26-28).

It is noteworthy that there is no account of animal sacrifices ever being offered again in the Tabernacle of David. After the initial dedicatory sacrifices, the only sacrifices were "sacrifices of praise and joy." These were offered by the Priests and Levites in David's Tabernacle.

The New Testament fulfillment should be evident. When Jesus Christ was offered on Calvary, His perfect once-for-all sacrifice fulfilled and abolished animal sacrifices. No animal sacrifices since Calvary are acceptable to God. All such are an abomination to Him (Isaiah 66:1-4; Hebrews 9-10; John 1:29, 36). God will never again accept animal sacrifices, now that He has the body and blood of His only begotten Son. To do so would be the greatest insult to Calvary and would be a reversal of the New Covenant to reestablish the Old and Mosaic Covenant.

The only sacrifices God accepts since the Cross are "spiritual sacrifices" in His Tabernacle, the Church (1 Peter 2:5-9; Romans 12:1-2). This will be taken up in the appropriate chapter.

The Church, the Tabernacle of Jesus Christ, had its dedicatory service founded in sacrificial blood at Calvary. Animal sacrifices are required no longer. David is doing typically what Jesus Christ would fulfill actually and spiritually. David and his Tabernacle pointed to Christ and the Church.

D. The Ark Enters the City of David (1 Chronicles 15:26-29; 2 Samuel 6:14-16).

These Scriptures record for us the glorious entrance the Ark had coming into the City of David, which is Zion. The important place Zion held in the Hebrew mind will be considered in another section.

God helped the Levites which bare the Ark. He strengthened them that there was no stumbling. It was several miles from the house of Obededom to Zion. The great procession could truly have sung the famous hymn of the church:

> "We're marching to Zion, beautiful, beautiful Zion,
> "We're marching upward to Zion, that beautiful City of God."

The processional march was accompanied by singing, shouting, sound of the cornets, trumpets, cymbals, psalteries, and harps. The women of Israel danced in and out and between those in the great procession. It was certainly not a quiet service, but one of great joy, gladness, excitement, and enthusiasm. David played and danced with all his might before the Lord. The singers and musicians sang and played with all their might. The Ark was the center of attraction. Read again Psalms 87:7 and Psalms 68:25.

How would many of God's people today have reacted to such a meeting, such a Divine service? Such a service and procession would be charged as not being "decent and in order." But this was God's order - not man's!

All over the world, there are those who see the Ark of God's presence coming into the Church in a greater way and are rejoicing in like manner before the Lord.

E. Michal - The Wrong Side of the Window! (1 Chronicles 15:29; 2 Samuel 6:16, 20-23).

In the midst of all this joy and gladness and this hilarious service, the Holy Spirit has caused to be recorded another side of the picture. Here in the given references we have a person whose character represents the very opposite to all the joy that is going on over the return of the Ark of the Lord.

This concerns Michal, the daughter of Saul. Instead of being down with the multitude, she looks out of her window and despises all that is going on. A few salient points are noted here.

1. "Michal" means "Who is like God?" or "Who is perfect?"

2. She was the daughter of a King, of the line of royalty, a princess, the daughter of King Saul, of the Tribe of Benjamin (1 Samuel 25:44).

3. She was bought by David with the blood of circumcision to be his wife, his bride (I Samuel I8:I7-28).

4. She saved David, her husband, from death by the hand of her father, Saul (1 Samuel 19:11-17).

5. She was taken from David and given to another man to be his wife (1 Samuel 25:44).

6. She was restored to David in due time (2 Samuel 3:13-15). He loved her.

7. She despised her husband in her heart, and then reproved her husband and king for his joy and dancing over the Ark coming to Zion.

What a tragedy! Here Michal could have lived up in measure to her name, as she was partaker of the Name of God. She was a king's daughter, bought with the price of blood, and she became the bride of a King of the Tribe of Judah. After a time of separation from him, her bridegroom king, she is restored to him. But what happens? As her bridegroom king is shouting and rejoicing before the Ark of God, as leader and commander in Israel, Michal looks out of the window and despises him in her heart.

What was she doing at home? Looking out of the wrong side of the window? She could have been down in the procession, rejoicing and praising the Lord along with the women in Israel.

What does she see? All she sees is "flesh." She does not see the ARK of God. She despises David. What was in the heart now comes out, for "out of the abundance of the heart the mouth speaketh" (Matthew 12:34). She sarcastically reproves her husband's behavior, charging him with indecency in his hilarious and vigorous playing and dancing before the Lord.

She did not see the Ark of God and the return of the Lord's presence. She missed the whole significance of what God was doing. Her attitudes were totally wrong.

The end of this story is that Michal had no child until the day of her death. Barrenness became her portion from this time on (2 Samuel 6:23).

The character study that the Holy Spirit has given us certainly contains exhortation and warning. How many "Michal's" are among God's people today? Bought with blood, children of royalty, to be joined to the King of Kings; yet because of despising expressions of worship, manifestations of the Spirit, they are smitten with spiritual barrenness until the day of their death!

Such a thing may happen individually as well as corporately!

F. <u>David - The King-Priest</u> (1 Chronicles 16:1-3; 2 Samuel 6:17-19).

The Lord set forth David to be a witness, leader, and commander of His people (Isaiah 55:4). The role that David takes here in the inauguration of the Tabernacle called by his name shows that David actually touched something in God after the Order of the Melchisedek Priesthood.

Melchisedek was King Priest of the Most High God. He ministered bread and wine to Abraham and blessed him in the Name of God, possessor of heaven and earth (Genesis 14:18-20; Hebrews 7:1-3; Psalm 110).

The student is reminded of the points already covered in an earlier section.

1. David was a King of the Tribe of Judah.

2. David wore a linen ephod, a Priestly garment. Symbolic of righteousness (2 Samuel 6:14; 1 Chronicles 15:27).

3. David acted as a King and Priest when he offered burnt and peace offerings before the Lord (2 Samuel 6:17).

4. David set up a Tabernacle and placed the Ark of the Covenant therein, even as Moses had set up his Tabernacle and placed the Ark therein centuries before (1 Chronicles 16:1).

5. David officiated in the Aaronic Priesthood blessing in the Name of the Lord (1 Chronicles 16:1-2; Numbers 6:24-27).

6. David ministered bread and wine and flesh to the people (1 Chronicles 16:3). A great time of communion.

Thus, David foreshadowed in these things the ministry of his greater Son, Jesus Christ, ministering after the Order of Melchisedek.

The Lord Jesus is our King Priest, "King of Righteousness and King of Peace." He offered Himself as the sacrifice for sin before He established His Tabernacle, the New Testament Church. It is He who ministers the bread and wine (His flesh and blood) in communion and blesses His people in the Name of the Lord. He is our Melchisedek, our King Priest forever, living in the power of an endless life, and unchangeable Priesthood.

G. The Ark Set in the Tabernacle of David (1 Chronicles 16:1-3; 2 Samuel 6:17-19).

With the great festivities of the day of dedication, the Ark is finally placed in the Tabernacle of David.

> "So they brought the Ark of God and set it in the midst of the tent that David had pitched for it ..." (1 Chronicles 16:1).
>
> "And they brought in the Ark of the Lord and set it in His place, in the midst of the Tabernacle that David had pitched for it ..." (II Samuel 6:17).

The implications in these references are rich in thought. The Ark had been taken out of the Tabernacle of Moses at Shiloh under the corrupt Priesthood of Eli and his sons. It had been through the great ordeal in the land of the Philistines, bringing death, plagues, and destruction in its journeyings. Even when it was returned to the land of Judah, death followed in its train. None dare to touch it or to presume upon God's order. And now after all this period of time, David had received revelation from God and has set up another Tabernacle, called by his name, for the Ark of God. This would have been great presumption indeed if David was not in the will of God.

Here David brings the Ark on this dedication day, amidst the thousands of Israel, placing it - not in the Tabernacle of Moses - but in the Tabernacle of David. It is called "His place." Moses' Tabernacle, used to be "His place" but no longer is this to be. There is to be a transference of the Ark from the Tabernacle of Moses to the Tabernacle of David.

Thus the Lord went from tent to tent and from one tabernacle to another (1 Chronicles 17:5; 2 Samuel 7:7). The Ark finds its place in a new setting, a new Tabernacle, a new order! No longer in the Holiest of All in Moses' Tabernacle, but set in the Tabernacle of David.

The significant fact drawn to our attention here is that once the Ark of the Covenant was taken out of the Tabernacle of Moses, it never ever returned to it again!

The Glory had departed from that Tabernacle never to return to it again. God had moved on. The final step would be that it would be taken from the Tabernacle of David into the Temple of Solomon.

The truths foreshadowed by implication here will be considered in a subsequent section. Sufficient for the present is to recognize that this act of David foreshadowed the transference of the Glory, symbolized in the Ark, from the Old Covenant Tabernacle (Temple) to the New Covenant Tabernacle (Temple) -- the New Testament Church.

The Scripture is silent as to whether the Ark was covered in this journey to David's Tabernacle. It was possibly left hanging upon its four pillars at the Tabernacle of Moses in Gibeon, as God was indeed doing a "new thing" here, foreshadowing the rending of the veil of the Mosaic economy which was to take place under New Covenant times.

Chapter 18

TWO TABERNACLES -- MOSES' AND DAVID'S

It is to be noted that from now on until the building of the Temple of Solomon, there are two Tabernacles in existence at the same time. Each had its particular function. Each had its own company of priests. Each was in a particular mountain. The approximate period of time would be about 35 to 40 years from the establishment of David's Tabernacle to the building of the Temple (B.C. 1042-1004).

The two Tabernacles with their attendant Priests were the Tabernacle of Moses and the Tabernacle of David. The two special mountains (or hills) in which these Tabernacles were functioning were Mt. Gibeon and Mt. Zion.

Let us consider the spiritual significances of both Tabernacles being in existence and functioning at the same time. What Divine lessons was the Lord setting forth to the Church of New Testament times? The Scripture tells us "All these things happened unto them for ensamples (types), and they are written for our admonition, upon whom the ends of the world (age) are come" (1 Corinthians 10:11).

The Old Testament sets out the type and shadow; the New Testament sets out the antitype and substance.

THE TABERNACLE OF MOSES AT MT. GIBEON.

Study these Scriptures: 1 Chronicles 16:37-43; 21:28-30; 2 Chronicles 1:1-6. These Scriptures show that David set Zadok the Priest and his brethren the priests to minister before the Tabernacle of Moses that was in the high place at Gibeon. Their ministry was to offer the morning and evening sacrifices on the Brazen Altar, according to the Law of Moses. (Compare 1 Chronicles 16:39-40 with Exodus 29:38, and Numbers 28:3, 6).

Jamieson, Fausset & Brown Commentary comments on 1 Chronicles 16:40-43, saying that Heman and Jeduthan presided over the sacred music; the sons of Jeduthan were door-keepers, and Zadok, with his suite of attendant priests, offered the sacrifices. Thus, at the Tabernacle of Moses certain of the Priests ministered with musical instruments, cymbals and trumpets.

When David presumed to number the people without the required Atonement money, he built an altar to the Lord and sacrificed in the threshing floor of Ornan. The reason is stated that he was afraid to go to Mt. Gibeon where the Tabernacle of Moses was because of the terrible plague that the Lord had sent among the people (1 Chronicles 21:28-30; 2 Samuel 24).

Later on when Solomon came to the Throne of David, he went with the congregation of Israel to the Tabernacle of the Lord which was in Gibeon, and there offered 1000 burnt offerings on the Brazen Altar (2 Chronicles 1:1-6; 1 Kings 3:3-4). It was at Mt. Gibeon that the Lord appeared to Solomon and there he was granted Divine wisdom, knowledge, and understanding (2 Chronicles 1:7-13; 1 Kings 3:5-15). Gibeon means "Lofty Hill." This mount stands out as one of the important mountains or high places in Israel's history because of the period in which the Tabernacle of Moses was there.

Thus, at Mt. Gibeon we have a company of Priests, maintaining the legal order of Moses, functioning in the Tabernacle there with its Outer Court, and Holy Place and Most Holy Place.

However, the significant thing about this company of Priests is that they have in this Tabernacle an empty Most Holy Place. There is no Ark of the Covenant there! They minister before an empty Holiest of All!

What spiritual truth was the Lord demonstrating here? After all, what valid functioning of ministering Priests counted if the Ark of God's Presence was not in its proper place?

The fact must not be ignored that God did bless that which attended the Tabernacle of Moses. But God did have something else in mind in that which functioned in the Tabernacle of David.

THE TABERNACLE OF DAVID IN MT. ZION.

The student should read these Scriptures: 2 Samuel 6:15-19; 1 Chronicles 15:29; 16:1-3; 1 Kings 8:1; 2 Chronicles 5:2; 1 Chronicles 16:37-43. A careful consideration of these Scriptures shows that the Tabernacle of David was pitched in Mt. Zion, and Zion was called the City of David. Here David placed a company of Priests and Levites who had been taken from the "old order" that they had known for years as in Moses' Tabernacle. In David's Tabernacle, these Priests came into a "new order" as pertaining to worship.

In contrast to the Tabernacle of Moses and the Priests at Mt. Gibeon, these Priests in the Tabernacle at Zion did not offer animal sacrifices. They offered sacrifices of praise and joy and thanksgiving. Here the ministry of the singers and musicians was in full operation. They were to offer up "spiritual sacrifices" in Mt. Zion in the Tabernacle of David.

Again, the Tabernacle of David had no Outer Court with its attendant furniture, no Holy Place with its attendant furniture, in contrast to the Tabernacle of Moses at Gibeon.

These Priest and Levites simply had the Holiest of All, or the Most Holy Place and in it the Ark of the Covenant. One wonders what transpired in the minds of these two companies of Priests, at two different Tabernacles in two different places.

The questions that the student needs to ask himself are, "Why did God allow this to be? What did God have in mind? What was being foreshadowed here?"

In Old Testament actuality, David had transferred the Ark of the Covenant from the Tabernacle of Moses to the Tabernacle of David. There was simply a transference of the Holiest of All. The Priests in David's Tabernacle could simply and boldly enter into the Most Holy Place. They had access before the Ark of the Lord. There was no standing veil between them and the Ark, as there had been for centuries in the Tabernacle of Moses. They had boldness (typically) to enter in "within the veil" because that veil belonged to the Tabernacle of Moses, NOT to the Tabernacle of David.

Once the dedicatory sacrifices had been offered, no more animal sacrifices were offered in David's Tabernacle, only spiritual sacrifices. What joy and praise must have been in the hearts and on the lips of those Priests and Levites who had been transferred from the form of Moses' Tabernacle to the glory of David's Tabernacle.

Jamieson, Fausset & Brown Commentary on 1 Chronicles 16:39-43, says, "Thus, in the time of David, the worship was performed at two places, where the sacred things that had been transmitted from the age of Moses were preserved. Before the Ark at Jerusalem, Asaph and his brethren officiated as singers -- Obededom and Hosah served as door-keepers - Benaiah and Jehaziel blew the trumpets - while at the Tabernacle and burnt offering in Gibeon, Heman and Jeduthan presided over the sacred music; the sons of Jeduthan were door-keepers, and Zadok, with his suite of attendant priests, offered the sacrifices." (Matthew Henry's Commentary and The Preacher's Homiletical Commentary also state that David set musical instruments in both places at this time. Up to this time no such ministry had been in Moses' Tabernacle.)

There has always been music by singing and instruments in Israel, but it seems that there was something seeded in the days of the prophet Samuel with music and prophecy in the "school of the prophets". Then it developed into a fulness in the time of David, especially after Samuel's anointing David to be king over Israel in God's appointed time. David himself was very musical and called the sweet psalmist and singer in Israel (1 Samuel 10:5-7; 16:12-13; 2 Samuel 23:1-2).

A.Z. Idelsohn in "Jewish Liturgy and its Development" (p. 37) on quoting 1 Chronicles 16:37-42 writes, "Thus we see long before David there were professional singers at the Sanctuary in Gibeon, some of whom he removed to the new Sanctuary in Jerusalem." He quotes R. Kittel to support his view; "The singing of Psalms and chanting of prayer during the service dates back to the very beginnings of Israel."

The following diagram and summarized comparison brings the truth into sharper focus.

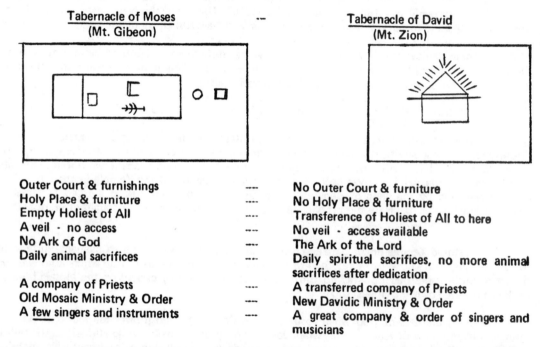

Tabernacle of Moses (Mt. Gibeon)	--	Tabernacle of David (Mt. Zion)
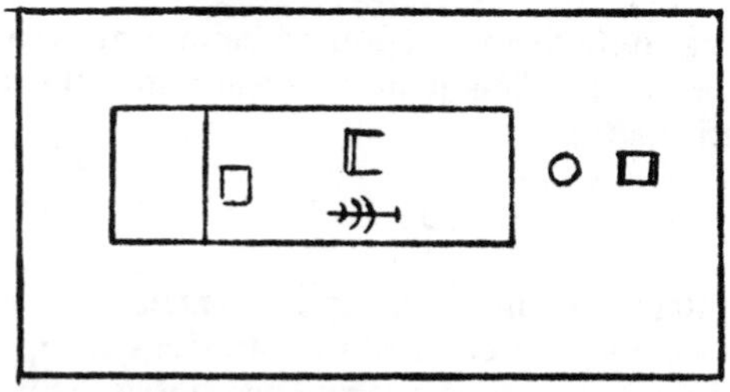		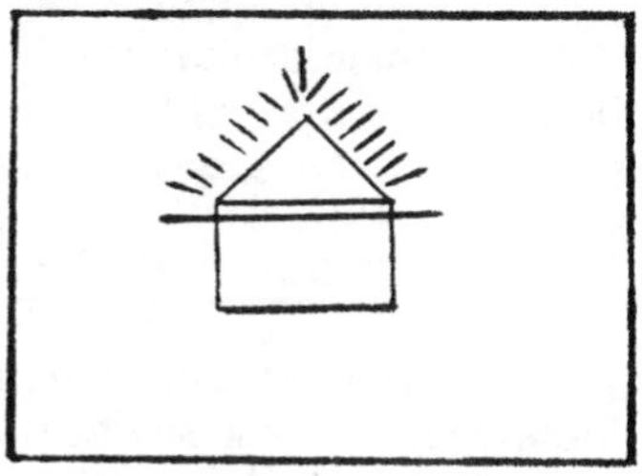
Outer Court & furnishings	---	No Outer Court & furniture
Holy Place & furniture	---	No Holy Place & furniture
Empty Holiest of All	---	Transference of Holiest of All to here
A veil - no access	---	No veil - access available
No Ark of God	---	The Ark of the Lord
Daily animal sacrifices	---	Daily spiritual sacrifices, no more animal sacrifices after dedication
A company of Priests	---	A transferred company of Priests
Old Mosaic Ministry & Order	---	New Davidic Ministry & Order
A few singers and instruments	---	A great company & order of singers and musicians

The contrast and comparisons of these two Tabernacles surely portray that which would find its fulfillment in the New Testament. However, before seeing the antitypical fulfillment there, the experience of King Solomon should be considered.

Solomon experienced a progressive relationship with God in three typical structures. The Tabernacle of Moses, the Tabernacle of David, and then the Temple. Consider his experience with God in relation to these two Tabernacles.

SOLOMON AT THE TABERNACLE OF MOSES - THE BRAZEN ALTAR.

God visited Solomon in Mt. Gibeon in relation to the order of the Tabernacle of Moses. Here God gave him wisdom, knowledge, and understanding. Here Solomon's first approach to God was by way of animal sacrifice and the Brazen Altar (2 Chronicles 1:1-13; 1 Kings 3:3-15).

SOLOMON AT THE TABERNACLE OF DAVID - THE ARK OF THE COVENANT.

After Solomon had been met by the Lord in the Tabernacle of Moses, and after he had experienced the Brazen Altar, he came to Jerusalem. Here he also, as David his father, offered up burnt offerings and peace offerings in dedicatory sacrifice at the Tabernacle of David. After this Solomon stood before the Ark of the Lord (1 Kings 3:4-5, 15).

Thus Solomon began with the Brazen Altar in the Tabernacle of Moses in Mt. Gibeon, and then came unto the Ark of God in the Tabernacle of David in Zion. First the Altar, and finally the Ark; this is God's order!

In due time he would bring the Ark of God from David's Tabernacle to the Temple in Mt. Moriah, place it within the veil, and draw out the staves from it. The pilgrimage would be over.

The setting of these two Tabernacles, on two different mountains with their different companies of Priests certainly was a foreshadowing of Messianic Times and the New Testament era. It foreshadows the Old and the New Covenants, the Covenants of Law and Grace (John 1:17).

We consider now the New Testament antitypical fulfillment. It should be remembered that the substance is always more glorious than the shadow, the fulfillment always greater than the promise, spiritual realities greater than the natural and material outline.

THE TABERNACLE OF MOSES - THE LAW COVENANT - THE GOSPELS.

The Gospels reveal the closing years of the Law Covenant and the Mosaic order and the Aaronic Priesthood. Animal sacrifices and Temple ritualism were still in operation in Messiah's times. The Outer Court, the Holy Place functions continued. But the Ark of the Covenant was not in the Holiest of All. In fact, the Ark has never been seen since the destruction of the Temple in the days of the Prophet Jeremiah by the King of Babylon. The final mention of the Ark in the Old Testament is found in Jeremiah 3:16. Here the prophet says it will not be remembered or sought after, nor visited any more.

The restored Temple under Ezra and Nehemiah never had the Ark of the Covenant, and for this reason the Shekinah Glory never returned to this restored material Temple. And when Jesus was here on earth, the Temple had no Ark, no Glory, and even though they carried on the Mosaic laws, no Shekinah hovered over the Holiest of All.

However, the acts of God when Jesus died on Calvary settled forever the fact that God had finished with the Law Covenant. For, when Jesus died on the Cross, offering Himself as the sinless, perfect, once-for-all sacrifice, He fulfilled and abolished forever all animal sacrifices. He abolished forever the Mosaic economy. It will never ever be reinstituted by God. If the Jew reinstitutes it again, it will be the greatest insult to Calvary ever offered (Isaiah 66:1-4, John 1:29, 36, Hebrews 10:1-10).

The seal of God to His Son's sacrifice was the rending of the veil of the Temple (Matthew 27:51). Probably about the time of the evening sacrifice, during the Feast of Passover, the Aaronic Priesthood stood before the veil and God rent it from top to bottom. In effect, God was saying to them that He had finished with the Mosaic economy, the Law Covenant, the Aaronic Priesthood and all that pertained to the Tabernacle of Moses order as carried out in the Temple of Herod. Once God rent that veil in two, He would never have it sewed up again. The way of access was opened into the Holiest of All.

The great tragedy in Jewish history is that they continued to offer up animal sacrifices, maintaining the Mosaic order and Aaronic Priesthood until A.D. 70 (about 40 years after Calvary) when God allowed Prince Titus to smash the whole abominable set-up. Truly, the Glory had departed, no Ark, no Glory, a rent veil, a corrupt Priesthood, and an abolished Mosaic order.

THE TABERNACLE OF DAVID - THE NEW COVENANT - ACTS & EPISTLE.

That which David did typically and prophetically was fulfilled historically and actually by Jesus Christ. When Jesus died on the Cross, and God rent the veil of the Temple in twain, the Holiest of All was opened. Access was made available for all who would enter in through Christ Jesus. There was a transference of the Holiest of All, or Most Holy Place, from the Old Law Covenant Church - Israel after the flesh - to the New Covenant Church in grace - Israel after the Spirit.

The Epistle to the Hebrews clearly confirms that which took place in the Gospels. It gives us the true spiritual significance of the rent veil. The Gospels record the historical account of the rent veil, but the Epistle to the Hebrews interprets that account for us.

The Epistle to the Hebrews clearly shows us that we have access into the Holiest of All, "within the veil." No longer does the veil (Literally, "That which divides") stand between us and God. No longer do we need a material earthly Tabernacle, with its Outer Court and Holy Place. The Most Holy Place, the Holiest of All in a greater and more perfect Tabernacle, is now open to us. It is this that is typified and prophetically set forth in the Tabernacle of David.

THE GOSPEL HISTORICAL ACCOUNT

"And, behold the veil of the Temple was rent in twain from the top to the bottom..." (Matthew 27:51).

"And the veil of the Temple was rent in twain from the top to the bottom" (Mark 15:38).

"... the veil of the Temple was rent in the midst" (Luke 23:45).

"Jesus said ... 'It is finished ...' " (John 19:30).

THE EPISTLE'S INTERPRETATION

"... The Holy Ghost this signifying, that the way into the Holiest of All was not yet made manifest, while as the first Tabernacle was yet standing: which was a figure for the time then present ... imposed on them until the time of reformation" (Hebrews 9:8-10).

"... which hope we have as an anchor of the soul, both sure and steadfast, and which enters into that within the veil; whither the forerunner is for us entered, even Jesus..." (Hebrews 6:19-20).

"Having therefore, brethren, boldness, to enter into the Holiest by the blood of Jesus, by a new and living way which He hath consecrated for us, through the veil, that is to say, His flesh ... let us draw near ..." (Hebrews 10:19-22).

Jews and Gentiles now have access to God in Christ (Ephesians 2:18). Access, entrance within the veil and boldness to do so is made possible by the blood of Jesus. The Priests and Levites in David's Tabernacle had this typically.

No wonder the Book of Acts says, "And a great company of Priests were obedient to the faith" (Acts 6:7). As the Gospel news spread, these Priests must have realized the futility of carrying on animal sacrifices, the Aaronic Priesthood, and the Mosaic economy in a material Temple that God had finished with. Once the veil was rent in two, it was useless to carry on the form. The Lord Jesus Christ was the sacrifice. He was the True Temple. He was the Priest after the Order of Melchisedek. It is through His sacrifice, His body and blood, that all may have access to God. Why then need the Priests carry on that which God Himself had finished with in connection with His Only Begotten Son?

The diagram illustrates the position of the Cross in relation to the Temple or Mosaic economy.

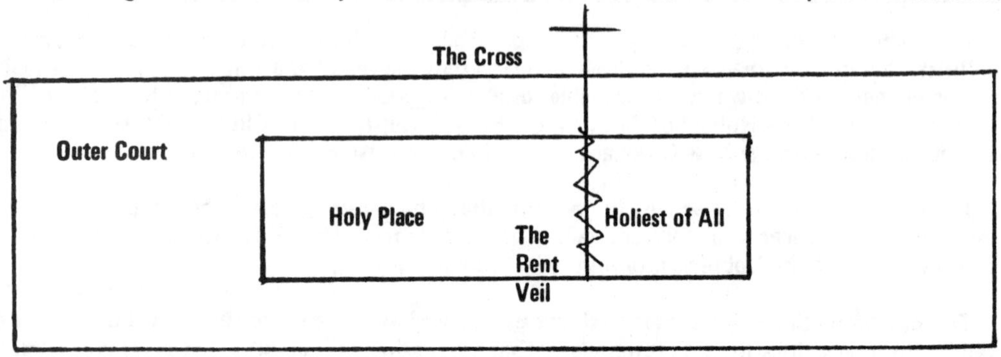

Under the Old Covenant the Priests entered the Outer Court and the Holy Place, accomplishing the daily ministrations. Only the High Priest, however, could enter the Holiest of All, and that once a year on the great Day of Atonement (Hebrews 9:1-10; Leviticus 16).

The rending of the veil in connection with the Cross of Jesus shows vividly that the Holiest of All was opened then and there for all who believe, be they Jew or Gentile. Jesus Christ is the Great High Priest, and the Cross was the whole of the sacrificial system compounded into one perfect sacrifice. All the sacrifices offered on the various Feast Days were compounded in that one sacrifice of Jesus. Passover and Day of Atonement were united in the Cross, as far as the body and blood sacrifice of Jesus was concerned. This is why He could enter "within the veil" and why we also have boldness to enter in after our forerunner. He was both Priest and sacrifice because of the union in His person of the Divine and human natures.

CONCLUSION AND SUMMARY

In concluding this chapter, we again focus on the antitypical fulfillment of the two Tabernacles in existence at the same time.

As there were two Tabernacles, two companies of Priests functioning on two different mountains in David's time for approximately 40 years, so there is that which answers to this in the New Testament times.

Many in Judaism carried on the Old Mosaic Covenant for about 40 years after the death, burial, resurrection, and ascension of Jesus Christ. They continued to offer up animal sacrifices. They must have sewed up the rent veil to continue the Aaronic Priesthood until in A.D. 70 God allowed the material Temple to be destroyed (Hebrews 10:1-4; Matthew 24:1-2).

However, a remnant according to the election of grace (Romans 11:5) believed on the Lord Jesus Christ, accepted His once-for-all offering and oblation and came in under the Melchisedek Priesthood, thus finding access "within the veil." This was in a greater and more perfect Tabernacle under the New Covenant order. Read Hebrews 7-8-9-10.

The diagram illustrates the truth and the contrasting summary confirms it.

The Old Tabernacle — The New Tabernacle

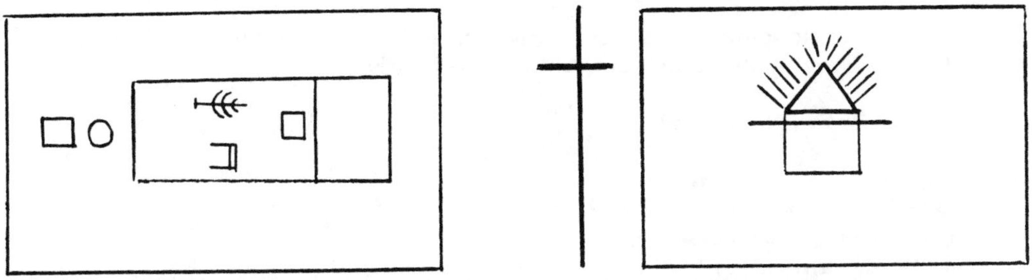

The Old Mosaic Covenant	---	The Messianic New Covenant
Many sacrifices	---	One perfect sinless sacrifice
Animal sacrifices and oblations	---	Divine-Human sacrifice of Jesus
The Aaronic Priesthood	---	The Melchisedek Priesthood
No access to Holiest of All	---	Access to Holiest of All
The rent veil	---	Entrance within the veil
Work never finished	---	A finished work
Priests carry on old order	---	Great company of Priests come to the faith
For Jewish nation and Gentile proselytes	---	For all nations, Jew and Gentile
The Glory departed	---	The Glory of the Lord (Colossians l:27; Ephesians 3:21).
House left desolate Matthew 23:38; 24:1-2).	---	His Church is His House (Hebrews 3:1-6; 1 Timothy 3:15).
The Cross rejected	---	The Cross accepted
Typically - Mt. Sinai	---	Spiritually - Mt. Zion (Isaiah 28:16; Hebrews 12:22-24; 1 Peter 2:6-9).

The Tabernacle of Moses was like a guardian to bring the Priests to the Tabernacle of David, even as "the law was a schoolmaster to bring us to Christ" (Galatians 3:24).

Solomon's experience shadows forth the experience of those Jews who believed in Christ. First they experienced the Tabernacle of Moses; the Old Covenant, Aaronic Priesthood, Brazen Altar, animal sacrifices, or that set out in Mt. Gibeon. Then they experience the Tabernacle of David; the Ark as personified in Christ, the New Covenant, Melchisedek Priesthood, and spiritual sacrifices in Mt. Zion.

Philip Mauro (p. 224-225) in commenting on George Smith's "Harmony of the Divine Dispensations" says,

> "Thus, the Tabernacle of David is evidently replete with typical meaning, concerning which it will suffice for our present purpose to remark, that, to David, the man after God's own heart, who was himself a conspicuous type of Christ, and who is more closely associated with the Gospel than any other of the patriarchs (Matthew 1:1; Acts 13:22, 34; Romans 1:3; 2 Timothy 2:8; Revelation 22:16) it was given to know the mind of God concerning real spiritual worship; and that he," being a prophet, and knowing that God had sworn with an oath to him, that

of the fruit of his loins according to the flesh, He would raise up Christ to sit on His throne" (Acts 2:30) was permitted to give in the tabernacle pitched by him on Mt. Zion, a wonderful foreshadowing of the worship, by prayer, preaching and song, which characterizes the gatherings of God's people in this Gospel dispensation." (Emphasis his)

Thus, the two Tabernacles in existence at the same time in David's time surely typify that which took place in Messiah's times, in the Gospels, the Acts and the Epistles.

No wonder the Song writer exclaims:

"O Behold the Man of Sorrows,
O behold Him in plain view,
Lo! He is the mighty conqueror
Since He rent the veil in two."

N. B. Herrell

(Note: – Without wanting to confuse the issue here, the following diagram sets out in sharper focus the "Tabernacles" in the time of David with their distinctives. It shows that there were actually three "Tabernacles" in this period of time with their respective truths. However, it is the two Tabernacles relative to redemption and worship that are under consideration in this section).

"TABERNACLES" IN THE TIME OF KING DAVID

The Psalms speak of "Tabernacles" in a number of places in the plural.
Psalm 43:3. Let them bring me to Thy holy hill and to Thy Tabernacles.
Psalm 46:4. The holy places of the Tabernacles of the Most High.
Psalm 84:1. O Lord, how amiable are Thy Tabernacles.
Psalm 118:15. The voice of rejoicing and salvation in the Tabernacles of the righteous.
Psalm 132:7. We will go into His Tabernacles.

There were three special Tabernacles in David's time with their distinctives as set out in brief here.

(1) THE TABERNACLE OF THE LORD	(2) THE TABERNACLE OF DAVID	(3) THE TABERNACLE OF DAVID
Built by Moses	Pitched by David	Built by the Lord
Mosaic Covenant	Covenant of the Lord	Davidic Covenant
In Mt. Gibeon	In Mt. Zion	In Mt. Zion
2 Chronicles 1:3	2 Samuel 6:17	Isaiah 16:5
Holy Places & Furniture	Ark of the Covenant	Throne of David
Outer Court & Furniture	"Holiest of All"	
No Ark of God	2 Chronicles 1:4	Amos 9:11, 12
	1 Chronicles 15:1; 16:1	Psalm 132:3
	Psalm 27:2; 76:2; 132:5	
	Acts 7:45-47	
	Acts 15:16, 17	Acts 15:16, 17
	Amos 9:11, 12	

Chapter 19

WALK ABOUT ZION

The Psalmist exhorts his people to "walk about Zion ..." (Psalms 48:12). With the establishing of the Tabernacle in Mt. Zion, Zion from this period on takes on special significance in the Old Testament Psalms and Prophets. This significance is taken up by the New Testament writers also.

Mt. Zion was the city of David the king, and it was also the place of the Tabernacle of David. Many of the hymn writers over the years have seen that Zion had spiritual significance for the Church of New Testament times. For many years the author sang hymns about Zion and never ever understood what was being sung. What was Zion? Why is Zion so important? What has the Church got to do with Zion? Truly, many believers today do not realize the significance of the following hymns.

"Come ye that love the Lord,
And let your joys be known,
Join in a sing with sweet accord,
And thus surround the throne.

Chorus:

We're marching to Zion,
Beautiful, beautiful Zion,
We're marching upward to Zion,
The beautiful city of God.

The hill of Zion yields
A thousand sacred sweets,
Before we reach the heavenly fields
Or walk the golden streets."

The song writer certainly caught a glimpse of the truth of the City of Zion.

Another great hymn writer sings:

"Glorious things of thee are spoken,
Zion, city of our God;
He, whose word cannot be broken
Formed thee for His own abode,
On the Rock of Ages founded,
What can shake thy sure repose?
With salvation's walls surrounded,
Thou mayest smile at all thy foes.

Many other hymns could be quoted. The Spirit of God today is quickening in our generation many of the Scriptures concerning Zion, and these are being sung around the world by the people of the Lord.

In the light of these comments, we turn to the Scriptures and consider what they have to tell us about Zion.

Historical Background.

Zion, or Sion, as it is sometimes translated, in its literal and restricted sense was the celebrated mount in Jerusalem, the highest and southernmost or southwesternmost of the city. It was the original hill of the Jebusites. The Jebusites settled in Jebus, the name of the city of Jerusalem when the Canaanites held it (Joshua 15:63; Judges 19:10, 11; Judges 1:8; Bible Dictionary, by James P. Boyd). The territory was given to the Tribe of Benjamin as part of their inheritance (Joshua 18:28). However, the Jebusites never lost the citadel for they held it or part of it until the time of David.

Zion was captured during the time of King David. After he captured it, the stronghold of Zion became known as the city of David. He greatly enlarged and strengthened its fortifications (2 Samuel 5:6-9; 1 Chronicles 11:5-8; 1 Kings 8:1; 2 Chronicles 5:2).

"Zion" is suggested by various authors of Bible Dictionaries to mean "Mount, Sunny, Fortress, Elevated, Highest." Some also suggest it means, "Lofty, A Monument, Sepulchre, Turret." It was the ancient name of Mt. Hermon. Zion is mentioned approximately 153 times in the Bible, or more especially in the Old Testament. Twice it is translated "Sion" in the Old Testament, and in the same way in the New Testament seven times.

Significance of Zion City.

From David's time on, the city of Zion takes on much meaning. The Old Testament poets and prophets exalted the word "Zion" by frequent use and gave it a sacred meaning, so that in time it became typical of a sacred capital. It is used of a place, and also becomes a name for God's chosen people in both Old and New Testaments.

There are two dominant themes associated with Zion in both Testaments -- that which is political and that which is religious.

Zion -- The city of King David, the capital city, the governing city of the nation, sets forth the governmental or political aspect of Zion.

Zion -- The city of the Tabernacle of David, the sacred city, the religious capital of the nation, sets forth the spiritual or ecclesiastical aspect of Zion.

In bringing these thoughts together, Zion is seen as the political and the ecclesiastical city of the nation of Israel. Here King David ruled and reigned over the people of the Lord. Here the government of God was revealed in the Kingdom of David and the Kingdom of God is the chosen nation.

It was here also that David led the nation in the order of worship, as established in his Tabernacle. Here the worship of God was seen and heard, as the musicians and singers functioned in their proper courses.

Thus, Zion combines in itself the political and religious unity of the nation and King David exemplifies the ministry of a KING (Political or Governmental), and PRIEST (Religious or Ecclesiastical) unto God.

The typical truth becomes evident in the light of the New Testament revelation. Jesus Christ, the greater Son of David, is King in Zion, the city of God. He rules and reigns. His government is revealed. He is King of Kings and Lord of Lords (Isaiah 9:6-9; Revelation 19:16; 1 Timothy 6:15).

He is also Priest. He leads the host of the redeemed, the true Israel of God, in worship to the Father (Hebrews 2:12; Psalms 22:22). He is King-Priest after the Order of Melchisedek, combining in Himself the governmental and spiritual administrations over the people of God.

Let us consider two groupings of Scriptures which set forth Zion in its political and ecclesiastical function. This combination in King David and in Zion shadows forth the same in Christ and His Church.

A. Zion - The Governmental City of God.

1. Zion - The City Where the King Dwells.

"Yet have I set (margin, Anointed) my King upon my holy hill of Zion. I will declare the decree: The Lord hath said unto me, Thou art my Son; this day have I begotten thee" (Psalms 2:6-7). Read also, Psalms 48:l-2.

This Psalm is classified as being one of the great Messianic Psalms. King David was the anointed king in Zion in the Old Testament, but the New Testament writers apply this Psalm specifically to Christ Jesus. He is the King in Zion. Read Acts 4:23-26 with Acts 13:33, and Hebrews 1:5.

2. Zion - The City of the King-Priest.

"The Lord shall send the rod of Thy strength out of Zion: rule Thou in the midst of Thine enemies" (Psalms 110:2).

This whole Psalm deals with the Priesthood of Christ after the order of Melchisedek. Read Psalms 110:1-7. It is taken up in detail in the Epistle to the Hebrews. The Lord Jesus Christ is the King-Priest, after the Order of Melchisedek. He is King-Priest in Zion, in His Church. Read Hebrews, Chapter 7.

3. Zion - The City Where the Lord Reigns.

"The Lord shall reign for ever, even Thy God, O Zion, unto all generations" (Psalms 146:10). Read also Isaiah 60:14.

These several Scriptures clearly show forth the governmental aspect of the city of Zion. It is the city where the King rules and reigns over the people of God. David the anointed King in Zion shadowed forth the Lord Jesus Christ, the anointed King over the Church. The Divine government is placed upon His shoulders. He is the Head over all things, and His rule and reign - His Kingdom - is to be manifested in the Church.

B. Zion - The Spiritual City of God.

In this grouping of Scriptures, we consider the things that are to be done in Zion in its spiritual function.

1. Zion is the Place Where the Lord Dwells.

"Sing praises unto the Lord which dwelleth in Zion . . ."(Psalms 9:ll). Read also Psalms 74:2, 76:1-2; Joel 3:16, 21; Isaiah 8:18.

2. Zion is the Place of the Salvation of Israel.

"Oh that the salvation of Israel were come out of Zion . . ."(Psalms l4:7). Read also Psalms 53:6, 69:35.

"And the Redeemer shall come to Zion ..." (Isaiah 59:20). Read also Zechariah 9:9; Isaiah 46:13, 62:11.

3. Zion is the Place of Strength for God's people.

"Send thee help from the Sanctuary, and strengthen thee out of Zion. . ." (Psalms 20:2,3 along with Psalms 84:4-7).

4. Zion is the Place of Joy for the Whole Earth.

"Beautiful for situation, the joy of the whole earth, is Mount Zion, on the sides of the north, the city of the great King. . . " (Psalms 48:2, II). Read also Psalms 97:8, 149:2, Isaiah 61:3.

5. Zion is the Place Where God's Beauty Shines Forth.

"Out of Zion, the perfection of beauty, God hath shined" (Psalms 50:2). Read also Lamentations 2:15.

6. Zion is the Place Where the Lord is Praised.

"Praise waiteth for Thee, O God, in Sion: unto Thee shall the vow be performed" (Psalms 65:1). Read also Psalms 147:12.

7. Zion is the Place Chosen by God.

"But chose the tribe of Judah, the Mount Zion which He loved" (Psalms 78:68). Read also Isaiah 14:32.

8. Zion is the Place that God Loves More Than any Other.

"His foundation is in the holy mountains. The Lord loveth the gates of Zion more than all the dwellings of Jacob. . . " (Psalms 87:1-3).

9. Zion is the Place Where People are Born and Established.

"And of Zion it shall be said, this and that man was born in her: and the highest Himself shall establish her. . . " (Psalms 87:5, 6).

"As soon as Zion travailed, she brought forth her children" (Isaiah 66:8).

10. Zion is the Place Where the Lord Reigns.

"The Lord reigneth; let the people tremble: He sitteth between the Cherubims, let the earth be moved. The Lord is great in Zion; and He is high above all the people" (Psalms 99:1-2).

Here is a reference to the Lord sitting upon the Ark of the Covenant between the Cherubims in the Tabernacle of David in Zion. Read also Isaiah 24:23, 52:7.

11. Zion is the Place Where the Lord Appears in Glory.

"Thou shalt arise, and have mercy upon Zion; for the time to favour her, yea, the set time is come ... When the Lord shall build up Zion, He shall appear in His Glory" (Psalms 102:13, 16). Read and connect this with Colossians 3:4.

12. Zion is the Place Where the Lord's Name is Declared and Praised.

"To declare the Name of the Lord in Zion, and His praise in Jerusalem" (Psalms 102:21).

13. <u>Zion is a Place of Blessing.</u>

"The Lord shall bless thee out of Zion ..." Psalms 128:5.

a. God's people bless Him in Zion (Psalms 135:21).

b. The Lord blesses His people in Zion (Psalms 134:3).

14. <u>Zion is God's Rest and Habitation For Ever.</u>

"For the Lord hath chosen Zion; He hath desired it for His habitation. This is My rest forever, here will I dwell; for I have desired it" (Psalms 132:13, 14). The whole Psalm has to do with the Ark of God coming into rest in Zion, in the Tabernacle of David. Note especially verses 5-9, 13-17.

15. <u>Zion is to Have Her Captivity Turned to Laughter.</u>

Note the brief references in these Scriptures. One cannot "sing the songs of Zion" in a strange land, or in Babylonian captivity (Psalms 137:1-4).

"When the Lord turned again the captivity of Zion. . . " then there is laughter and joy and singing (Psalms 126:1-4).

16. <u>Zion is the Place Where the Word of the Lord is Taught.</u>

". . . for out of Zion shall go forth the Law, and the Word of the Lord from Jerusalem . . ." (Read Isaiah 2:1-5 with Micah 4:1-2).

17. <u>Zion is a Place of Shouting, Singing and Comfort.</u>

"Cry out and shout, thou inhabitant of Zion; for great is the Holy One of Israel in the midst of thee" (Isaiah 12:6).

"Therefore the redeemed of the Lord shall return, and come with singing unto Zion; and everlasting joy shall be upon their heads; they shall obtain gladness and joy; and sorrow and mourning shall flee away" (Isaiah 51:11 [3], 35:10; Zechariah 2:10; Joel 2:1, 15, 23; Zephaniah 3:14-16).

". . . And the Lord shall yet comfort Zion, and shall yet choose Jerusalem" (Zechariah 1:17 [14].

18. <u>Zion is a Name for the People of God.</u>

" ... and say unto Zion, thou art My people" (Isaiah 51:16).

19. <u>Zion is a Place that Publishes Good Tidings.</u>

"O Zion, that bringest good tidings ... " (Isaiah 40:9). Read also Isaiah 52:1, 2, 7, 8, 41:27; Micah 4:13.

Christ is the One who brought good tidings to Jerusalem, and it is the Church who now publishes those good tidings.

20. Zion is a Place Where Sinners and Hypocrites are Dealt With.

"The sinners in Zion are afraid; fearfulness hath surprised the hypocrites. . ." (Isaiah 33:14 [15] with Isaiah 33:5, 31:9, 1:27; and Amos 6:1).

"When the Lord shall have washed away the filth of the daughters of Zion ..." (Isaiah 4:3-4).

21. Zion is a City of Solemnities.

"Look upon Zion, the city of our solemnities; thine eyes shall see Jerusalem a quiet habitation, a tabernacle that shall not be taken down ..." (Isaiah 33:20 [21-24]).

Here we have another reference to the Tabernacle of David.

22. Zion is Where the Foundation Stone is Laid.

"Behold, I lay in Zion for a foundation, a stone, a tried stone, a precious cornerstone, a sure foundation; he that believeth shall not make haste" (Isaiah 28:16).

There is no mistaking the interpretation of this Scripture, for the New Testament writers take it and apply it to Jesus Christ. He is "the foundation stone in Zion." Christ is the foundation of His Church (1 Peter 2:6-8; Matthew 21:42; Acts 4:11).

23. Zion is the place where God has a Faithful Remnant.

"For out of Jerusalem shall go forth a remnant, and they that escape out of Mount Zion; the zeal of the Lord of Hosts shall do this" (Isaiah 37: [31] 32; Jeremiah 3:14; Micah 4:7; 2 Kings 19:31).

24. Zion has the Glory Cloud Upon Her Assemblies.

"And the Lord will create upon every dwelling place of Mount Zion, and upon her assemblies, a cloud and smoke by day, and the shining of a flaming fire by night; for upon all the glory shall be for a defence (a covering). And there shall be a Tabernacle for a shadow in the daytime from the heat, and for a place of refuge, and for a covert from storm and from rain" (Isaiah 4:5-6).

The Tabernacle of David is referred to again here.

25. Zion is a Place Where Saviours Minister.

"And Saviours shall come up on Mount Zion to judge the mount of Esau; and the Kingdom shall be the Lord's" (Obadiah 21 with Nehemiah 9:27; Judges 2:14).

The Lord Jesus Christ is THE Saviour. "And it shall come to pass that whosoever shall call on the Name of the Lord shall be delivered; for in Mount Zion and in Jerusalem shall be deliverance ..." (Joel 2:32 with Acts 2:21).

The other "saviours" mentioned here speak of the judge-deliverers who delivered Israel out of their bondages and servitudes. This ministry pointed to the ministry in the New Testament Church era; to that deliverance from the bondage and servitude of sin.

Thus Zion is taken up by the poets and the prophets and used to express the Kingly and

Priestly functions and the relationship of the people of the Lord to the same.

It should be evident to the thoughtful reader that the fulness of truth cannot possibly apply just to the small geographical hill of Mount Zion. The writer stood on the Mt. of Olives at one time and gazed over toward Mount Zion, the hill of David. These Scriptures flooded his mind. He thought, surely the Lord had something higher and greater in mind than merely the geographical location in Palestine. Indeed, that was simply the earthly, the geographical, the natural place but it pointed to the heavenly, the spiritual, and that place which is eternal.

And this is so. The earthly Zion with its Kingly and Priestly functions, its sorrows and joys, its defeats and triumphs, its worship, its people -- all shadowed forth the heavenly and spiritual Zion.

This is seen by what the New Testament writers do with that which pertains to Old Testament Zion. The several Scriptures referred to are example Scriptures of interpretation and application of the theme of "Zion."

Let us consider the New Testament truths concerning Zion. Here we have Apostolic interpretation and application of some of these verses from the Old Testament.

New Testament References to "Zion."

- "Tell ye the daughter of Sion, Behold, thy King cometh unto thee, meek, and sitting upon an ass, and a colt of the foal of an ass" (Matthew 21:4, 5; John 12:15, 16). This is the fulfillment of Zechariah 9:9. The great tragedy was seen in the fact that Jesus Christ came to earthly Zion, and His ministry there fulfilled actually many of the Old Testament prophecies concerning earthly Zion, but earthly Zion rejected Him. They crucified their King of Zion.

- "Behold, I lay in Sion a stumbling stone and rock of offence; and whosoever believeth on him shall not be ashamed" (Romans 9:33).

Here the Apostle Paul tells how the Jewish nation, as a whole, stumbled over Christ Jesus, the foundation stone in Zion. He is the stumbling stone and rock of offence to Jewry. This is quoted as being the fulfillment of Isaiah 8:14 with Psalms 118:22. Refer also to Isaiah 28:16 and Matthew 21:42.

- "And so all Israel shall be saved; as it is written, there shall come out of Sion the Deliverer, and shall turn away ungodliness from Jacob" (Romans 11:26).

This is quoted from Isaiah 59:20. It confirms once again the fact that Jesus Christ is the Deliverer out of Sion. He is the only One through whom Israel can be saved.

- "But ye are come unto Mount Sion, and unto the city of the living God, the heavenly Jerusalem. . . " (Hebrews 12:22).

The writer to the Hebrews here encourages the believers concerning the true and heavenly Jerusalem and Zion. Leaving the earthly Temple, the animal sacrifices, the Aaronic Priesthood, earthly Zion, and Jerusalem, they come to a spiritual Temple, to spiritual sacrifices, to the Priesthood of Melchisedek and to heavenly Zion and Jerusalem.

The whole Epistle of Hebrews sets forth the contrast between that which is natural and spiritual, that which is earthly and heavenly, that which is temporal and eternal. Hence, Zion and Jerusalem are certainly greater than the earthly Zion and Jerusalem, for, the latter was only the shadow of the former.

● "Wherefore also it is contained in the scripture, Behold, I lay in Sion a chief corner stone, elect, precious, and he that believeth on him shall not be confounded" (1 Peter 2:6). The verses in the surrounding context should be read also (1 Peter 2:4-9). This verse is quoted from Isaiah 28:16 and finds its fulfillment in the Lord Jesus Christ as being the foundation stone in His Church.

● "And I looked, and lo, a Lamb stood on the mount Sion, and with him an hundred and forty four thousand, having his Father's name written in their foreheads" (Revelation 14:1).

This is the final distinct reference to Sion in the New Testament. A consideration of the verse certainly shows that the Lamb of God does not stand on literal or earthly Mt. Zion in Palestine. That was where the Lamb was slain. The Mount Zion He stands in is the spiritual and heavenly Sion.

In concluding our "walk about Zion" we note the connotations in the Word of God concerning Zion. We find that there are three aspects to Zion. The diagram and the following comments will clarify this for us.

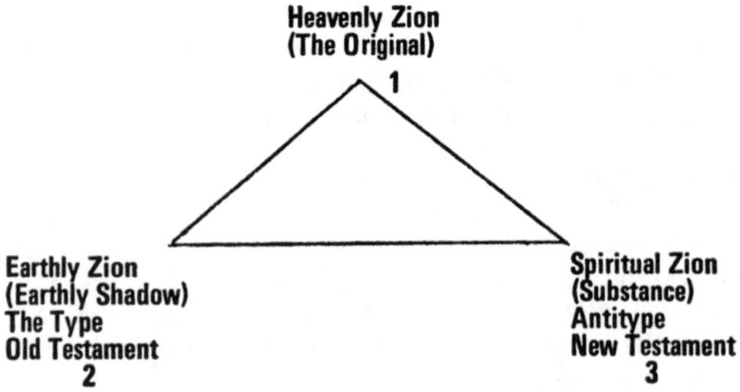

THERE WAS THE HEAVENLY ZION. The original of all things shadowed on earth. This is unseen, and eternal. Earthly Zion was meant to be the shadow of the heavenly Zion, the heavenly Jerusalem. The things that are not seen are eternal (2 Corinthians 4:18; Hebrews 12:22; Revelation 14:1).

THERE WAS THE NATURAL OR EARTHLY ZION, WHICH WAS TEMPORAL. It was but the shadow of a greater Zion. This is the type as seen in the Old Testament in Israel and in the geographical situation in Palestine. The things that are seen are temporal (2 Corinthians 4:18).

THERE IS THE SPIRITUAL ASPECT OF ZION IN THE CHURCH, THE PEOPLE OF GOD. The believers are born again and become children of Zion. The Church worships the Lamb in Zion. Christ is the foundation stone in Zion. Zion is the place of joy, singing, shouting and praise.

Thus we have the three aspects of the significance of Zion in the Scriptures. The original in heaven, the type in the Old Testament, and the antitype in the Church.

The student would do well to refresh himself on all the things that Zion signified to the Israel of God in the Old Testament. There it will be seen that God indeed had the true, the heavenly, and the spiritual Zion in mind. Many of the Scriptures become meaningless if applied to the geographical location in Palestine. The eternal Zion is the New Testament reality of the Old Testament shadow. It finds its glorious fulfillment in Christ and His Church. The New Testament writers are the infallible interpreters of the Old Testament prophets. They give us the "key" to the significance of Zion. It is impossible to disassociate the Tabernacle of David from the significance of Zion.

It may well be said that He who came from heavenly Zion to earthly Zion was crucified and now He takes His place as the risen Lord in the spiritual Zion - the Church - as the foundation stone upon which His Church is built.

The Hymn writer was quickened by the Spirit when he wrote this verse concerning Zion.

> "Savior, if of Zions's City,
> I, through grace, a member am,
> Let the world deride or pity,
> I will glory in Thy Name.
> Fading is the worlding's pleasure,
> All his boasted pomp and show,
> Solid joys and lasting treasure
> None but Zions's children know."

Chapter 20

ACCORDING TO THE COMMANDMENT OF DAVID

With the setting up of the Tabernacle of David in Zion we see David establishing a complete new order of worship for the priests and Levites there.

It is evident by a consideration of a number of Scriptures that David must have received revelation from the Lord and then given commandments concerning this order. These commandments particularly involved the ministry of music, both of the singers and the musicians. It will be seen that the godly Kings of Israel who brought Israel back to the Lord always restored the order of worship that was established by David the King in the Tabernacle of David.

Let us consider what the Scriptures have to say concerning the commandments of David which were also the commandments of the Lord.

A. Interpretation of Israel's History.

1. The Tabernacle of David, B.C. 1048 (1 Chronicles 15-16).

Here we have the origin of the order of David. David appointed and ordained singers and musicians to sing and play before the Lord in His Tabernacle (1 Chronicles 15:14-29, 16:4-6, 37-43). It will be seen that at this time even the Tabernacle of Moses had some singers and musicians set there, even though such had not been in Moses' Tabernacle ever before. However, the great courses of singers and musicians were at the Tabernacle of David in Mt. Zion (1 Chronicles 25). Thus David appointed certain of the Levites to be singers with instruments of music, psalteries and harps and cymbals, sounding, by lifting up the voice with joy. These were to minister before the Ark of the Lord continually, as every day's work required.

2. The Temple of Solomon, B.C. 1012 (2 Chronicles 3-5).

King Solomon built the Temple according to the pattern that was given to King David, his father. We find by a study of the Scriptures that the very order of worship which was established in the 24 courses in the Tabernacle of David was later on incorporated into that order of worship in Solomon's Temple.

For approximately 30 years or more the Tabernacle of David had been functioning before the Temple of Solomon was built. When the day of dedication came, the singers and the musicians played a tremendous part. The Ark was taken out of the Tabernacle of David at Zion and placed in the Holy Oracle - the Holiest of All - in the Temple. The staves were taken out. As soon as the priests came out of the Holy Place, the singers and the musicians began to minister before the Lord as they stood at the east end of the brazen altar.

The Scripture tells us, "It came to pass, as the trumpeters and singers were as one, to make one sound to be heard in praising and thanking the Lord; and when they lifted up their voice with the trumpets and cymbals and instruments of music, and praised the Lord, saying, "For He is good; for His mercy endureth forever; that then the house was filled with a cloud, even the house of the Lord; so that the priests could not stand to minister by reason of the cloud; for the glory of the Lord had filled the house of God" (2 Chronicles 5:11-14).

The Tabernacle of David was preparatory to this day of dedication. And as the ministry of the singers and instruments blended into one accord and one sound, the Shekinah Glory Cloud filled the Temple and no flesh could minister in the presence of the Lord. All of this was according to the revelation given to David and according to that which he ordained.

3. The Godly King Jehoshaphat, B.C. 896 (2 Chronicles 20).

In this Scripture we see how the Moabites and the Ammonites came to battle against King Jehoshaphat. Jehoshaphat set himself to seek the Lord by prayer and fasting and all Judah with him. The king went to the house of the Lord and there in the new court made intercession before God. As he stood in prayer and the congregation with him, the Spirit of the Lord came upon Jahaziel and the prophetic word of encouragement came forth. The Lord said He would fight the battle for them. King Jehoshaphat and the congregation with him fell before the Lord in worship. The Levites stood and began to praise the Lord with a loud voice on high as they were in the Temple court.

Early in the morning, Jehoshaphat, after consulting with the people, appointed singers unto the Lord who were to praise the beauty of holiness and the mercy of the Lord. As the singers began to praise the Lord, He set ambushments amongst the enemy and they began to destroy one another. Judah was three days in gathering the spoils from such a victory. Thus, God used the ministry of the singers, that which was ordained by David, to bring victory out of apparent defeat.

4. The Godly King Hezekiah, B.C. 726 (2 Chronicles 29-30).

In these two chapters we are given the account of the cleansing of the Temple under the rule and reign of godly King Hezekiah. The preceding king, wicked Ahaz, had allowed the Temple of the Lord to become polluted and eventually closed down. When Hezekiah came to the throne, he set his heart to seek the Lord. He repaired the house of the Lord and re-established the order of the Lord's house and its daily ministrations. He encouraged the priestly tribe to sanctify themselves in order that they could fulfil their ministry unto God. After a number of days, all the filthiness was cleansed out of the Temple. Once again the atoning sacrifices were offered on the altar and the Temple was dedicated afresh to the Lord in the Feast of Passover.

Not only did Hezekiah do this, but he also revived the ministry of the singers and musicians as ordained by David many years before. 2 Chronicles 29:25-28 tells us, "And he set the Levites in the house of the Lord with cymbals, with psalteries, and with harps according to the commandment of David, and of Gad the king's seer, and Nathan the prophet; for so was the commandment of the Lord by His prophets. And the Levites stood with the instruments of David, and the priests with the trumpets... And when the burnt offering began, the song of the Lord began also with the trumpets, and with the instruments ordained by David king of Israel. And all the congregation worshipped, and the singers sang, and the trumpets sounded; and all this continued until the burnt offering was finished."

What a wonderful service this must have been! It was a restoration of that order of worship established by the commandment of David.

5. The Godly King Josiah, B.C. 623 (2 Chronicles 35:1-19).

Once more we see a godly King, Josiah by name, raised to the throne of Judah. The previous King, Ammon, had been a wicked king, following the sins of wicked Manasseh. Josiah had the Temple of the Lord cleansed again under the Feast of Passover, even as Hezekiah had years previous. He charged the priests and the Levites to prepare themselves after their courses "according to the writing of David king of Israel, and according to the writing of his son Solomon" (2 Chronicles 35:4).

The service was prepared, and the priests stood in their places and the Levites in their respective courses (2 Chronicles 35:10). Then we are told, "And the singers the sons of Asaph were in their place, according to the commandment of David, and Heman, and Jeduthan the King's seer . . ." (2 Chronicles 35:15).

Here there was a restoration of that order of worship as established by David in his Tabernacle. All was according to the writing and commandment of David and of Solomon.

6. The Restoration of Judah from Babylon, B.C. 536 (Ezra 2:65; 3:1-13; Nehemiah 12:27-47).

A study of the books of Ezra and Nehemiah show the number of the house of Judah who responded to the call to come out of Babylon at the close of the 70 years captivity.

The dominant godly leaders of these returns were Ezra the scribe-priest and Nehemiah the governor. The first thing involved in the restoration of the people to the land was the rebuilding of the Temple. The altar was set up and blood sacrifices once again offered to the Lord. The Temple foundation was laid in the Feast of Trumpets, the very Feast in which the Temple of Solomon had been dedicated many years before (I Kings 8:1-2).

As one reads the Scriptures given above we discover once more the restoration also of the order of David in the singers and musicians. Two hundred "singing men and singing women" returned to Judah from Babylon (Ezra 2:65).

When the foundation of the Temple was laid "they set the priests in their apparel with trumpets, and the Levites the sons of Asaph with cymbals, to praise the Lord, after the ordinance of David king of Israel. And they sang together by course in praising the giving thanks unto the Lord. . ." (Ezra 3:10, 11).

A number of years later, another company of people came up out of Babylon to Judah and we are told the Levites who were "with their brethren over against them, to praise and to give thanks, according to the commandment of David the man of God . . . "(Nehemiah 12:24).

Then when the walls of the city were dedicated, the Levites were sought out of all the places to come to Jerusalem and to keep the dedication with gladness. They had thanksgivings, singing and praise with cymbals, psalteries and harps. They were in companies "with the musical instruments of David the man of God, and Ezra the scribe before them" (Nehemiah 12: 27, 36).

The Levites were appointed once again to their ministry, "And both the singers and the porters kept the ward of their God, and the ward of purification, according to the commandment of David, and of Solomon his son. For in the days of David and Asaph of old there were chief of the singers, and songs of praise and thanksgiving unto God. And all Israel in the days of Zerubbabel, and in the days of Nehemiah, gave the portions of the singers and the porters, every day his portion . . ." (Nehemiah 12:44-47).

7. The Prophecy of Amos, B.C. 787 (Amos 9:11-13).

Surely the prophecy of Amos given about 60 years before Hezekiah's time, during a period of national apostacy and spiritual decline takes on more significance in the light of the various awakenings in Israel and Judah under the reign of the above mentioned godly kings.

To build again the Tabernacle of David which is fallen down; to close up the breaches thereon; to raise up its ruins and to build it as in the days of old (Amos 9:11; Acts 15:16), certainly signified a restoration of the order of worship established in that Tabernacle, not a restoration of the material tent.

Each of the above awakenings in the nation's history followed a period of spiritual lapse and each constituted a restoration of the order of worship according to the commandment of David, which was also the commandment of the Lord through His prophets.

Each period of time in spiritual decline represented "a breach," a rent, a leak, a cleft or a gap in the nation's favour with God. These "breaches" could only be closed up by their return to the Lord who is "the repairer of the breach, and the restorer of the paths to dwell in" (Isaiah 58:12). Read also, Nehemiah 4:7, 6:1 and Psalms 106:23.

Every visitation in Judah was accompanied by a return to a renewal of the order of worship. Wicked and ungodly kings brought about these breaches, and godly kings sought to mend these breaches.

The following diagram illustrates the fact of these "breaches of time" in which there was decline and apostacy, and then shows those godly leaders who sought to repair the breach by restoring the Temple - the House of the Lord - and the order of worship according to the commandment of David in his Tabernacle.

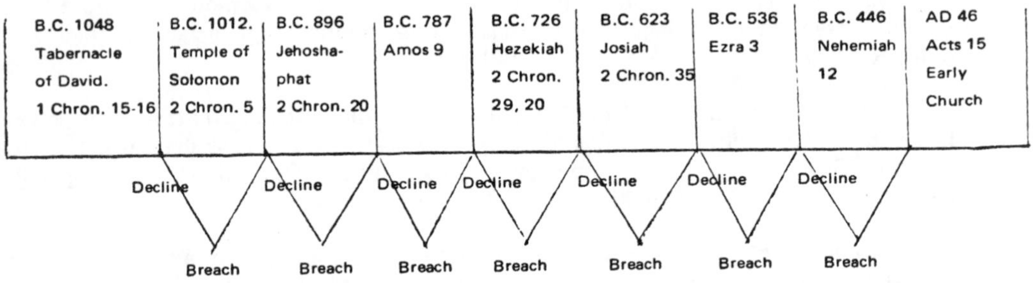

B. Application to Church History.

Who can fail to see the application to Church history? Under the outpouring of the Holy Spirit in the Book of Acts we see Jew and Gentile coming into the spiritual order of the Tabernacle of David (Acts 15:13-18).

The ministry of true worship (John 4:24), the ministry of Psalms, hymns, and spiritual songs (Ephesians 5:18-19; Colossians 3:16; James 5:13) was confirmed in the Early Church. Song, praise and joy abounded even as it had in the days of old under David's Tabernacle.

However, over the years of Church history, decline and apostacy set in even as in Israel's history. The Church departed from the faith once delivered to the saints (Jude 3). The ministry of true worship, of music and the song of the Lord departed. Spiritual death settled on the people of God.

But, even as in Israel's history, so in Church history, God had a faithful remnant who sought the Lord to recover the days of old. God began to visit His people, to restore that which was lost over the years, to repair the breaches of the Dark Ages (Joel 2:23-26).

Reformation and restoration began to move the Church of God. Music and song started to be heard in the congregation of God. God began to raise up godly reformers, godly leaders, and gave to them the songs of the Lord. The breaches began to be stopped. Thus, every awakening, every movement of the Spirit of God has had some particular "new song" associated with it.

As the Lord began to recover the lost truths to the Church, these truths were taught and practiced. These truths were clothed in song and God's people began to sing, teaching and admonishing one another in Psalms, hymns and spiritual songs, singing and making melody in their hearts to the Lord (Ephesians 5:18-19; Colossians 3:16).

A cursory glance over Church history and over the various awakenings or revivals show that each carried "a song of the Lord" peculiar to that awakening, and the things which the Spirit of God was quickening. A brief history concerning the development of music will be taken up in a subsequent chapter. Sufficient for the present is to mention the fact that the Lutheran, Presbyterian, Methodist, Baptist, Anglican, Plymouth Brethren, Salvation Army, Pentecostal, as well as many others have each been characterized by their own particular "new song" emphasizing the fact of truth or experience God gave to them (Revelation 5:9; 14:3). Also in this present time there is a new emphasis on music and the song of the Lord in the Church.

One thing should be clear and this is the fact that God is seeking to restore worship according to the commandment of David, the anointed sweet singer and Psalmist of Israel (2 Samuel 23:1-2).

As there were various awakenings under Israel's history and a measure of recovery of the song of the Lord, so Church history has been a repetition of the same.

The following diagram illustrates this in relation to Church history.

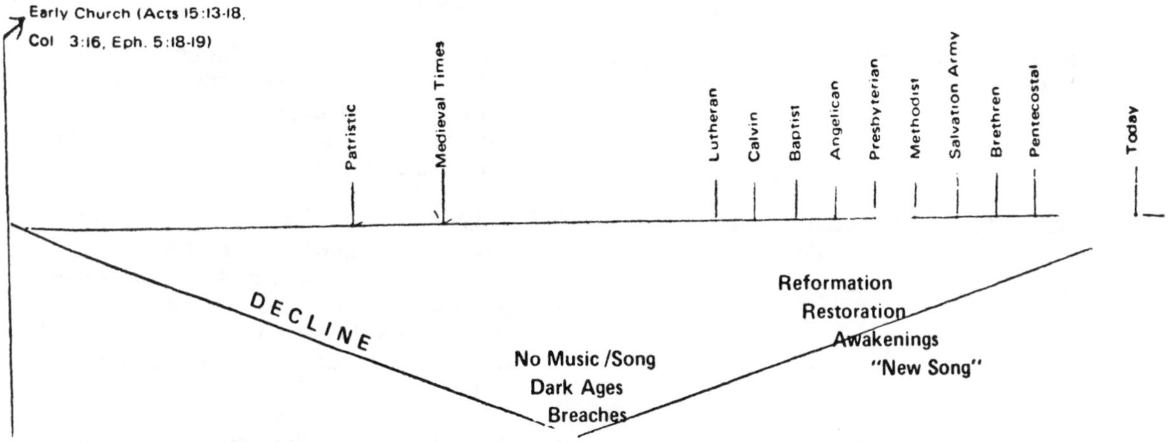

The words of the Psalmist are being fulfilled. God is turning again the captivity of Zion. Mouths are being filled with laughter and song (Psalms 126:1-4). While the Church was in spiritual Babylon, the harps were hung on the willow tree, the weeping trees. There could be no singing of the Lord's song in a strange land. But now the Church is coming out of Babylon, "religious confusion," and her captivity is being turned. Once again the songs of Zion are being heard in the earth. Harps and other musical instruments are being taken off the willow tree and the singers and musicians are rising to minister in worship according to the commandment of David.

It is important to note that each of the visitations in Israel's history was in connection with the Temple of the Lord. All pointed to the true Temple, the Church, God's spiritual house and the music and songs in His house (Ephesians 2:20-22; I Corinthians 3:16; I Peter 2:3-9).

In bringing our chapter to its conclusion, the following summary needs to be considered. Godly kings of the dynasty of king David always sought to bring about a restoration of the Tabernacle of David order or worship. Ungodly kings ignored or neglected this Davidic worship as they sought to maintain their Davidic throne. The Davidic throne (Kingship) and the Davidic worship (Priesthood) were not meant to be separated in their distinctives. Both tabernacles pointed to the Lord Jesus Christ, the greater Son of David who would unite both in Himself and the Church, the New Covenant order of King-Priests after the order of Melchisedek. The two columns emphasize and show the relationship of the house and throne of David (the Davidic-Kingdom Tabernacle), and the Davidic order of worship (the Davidic-Worship Tabernacle).

TABERNACLE OF DAVID-KINGSHIP	TABERNACLE OF DAVID – WORSHIP-PRIESTHOOD
1. Davidic throne, kingdom, house, government, Davidic covenant. 1 Chronicles 17; 2 Samuel 7	1. Tabernacle of David, singers, musicians, praise, worship. Foundation laid in Zion. 1 Chronicles 15-16; 2 Samuel 16; Isaiah 28:16
2. Solomon, the King. 1 Kings 1-2	2. Temple of Lord dedicated with singers and trumpeters in one accord. 1 Chronicles 5:11-14
3. Jehoshaphat the King. 2 Chronicles 17-18-19	3. Jehoshaphat set singers of the Levites to praise the Lord and win the battle. 2 Chronicles 20
4. Hezekiah, the King. 2 Chronicles 29-30-31-31	4. Hezekiah restored the order of the temple of the Lord according to the commandment of David, Gad and Nathan, with the singers and instruments of David. 2 Chronicles 29; 31:2
5. Josiah, the King. 2 Chronicles 34	5. Josiah restored the Ark of the Lord to the temple of the Lord according to the writing of David, king of Israel and according to the writing of Solomon his son. The singers were in their place according to the commandment of David. 2 Chronicles 35:1-18
6. Nehemiah, the Governor of the tribe of Judah. Nehemiah 12	6. Nehemiah's book lists the names of the Levites who were to praise and give thanks according to the commandment of David, the man of God, with singing and instruments, at the dedication of the rebuilt and restored walls of Jerusalem. Nehemiah 12:24-47. In the days of David and Asaph of old they sang and praised the Lord.

The Davidic-Kingdom Tabernacle and the Davidic-Worship Tabernacle are thus seen to be distinguishable but inseparable as both were in Mt. Zion, one the governmental pertaining to the Kingdom, the other ecclesiastical, pertaining to the worship.

Chapter 21

DIVINE ORDER OF WORSHIP

Having considered the Scriptures which clearly show that worship was according to the commandment of David and the commandment of the Lord, we here consider a variety of expressions pertaining to this ministry.

The word "worship" means "to honour, revere, adore, pay homage, render devotion and respect" to someone, especially to God. It is used here in this chapter in its broadest sense to encompass all ministry unto the Lord. All our service should sprina from a true spirit of worship and praise.

The Lord Jesus said that the Father was seeking those who would worship Him "in spirit and in truth" (John 4:24). Man was created to be a worshipper of God. Of himself, man does not know how to worship God, yet he longs to worship. It is for this reason that man designs forms of worship or some sort of program for religious services and then asks God to bless his program. Also, because man does not know how God desires to be worshipped, he develops a variety of forms. People generally congregate to the particular form that suits their tastes, their spiritual disposition and which does not offend their mentality.

It is worthy to ask ourselves what Jesus meant when He said that the Father desired us to worship in spirit and in truth. How can we worship in spirit? How can we worship in truth?

To worship "in spirit" is to allow the Holy Spirit to move upon the believer's redeemed spirit, causing love, adoration, devotion, honour and respect to ascend to God. The believer is born again in his spirit by the Holy Spirit (John 3:l-5). His spirit is to be in union with the Spirit of God (Romans 8:l6; I Corinthians 6:l7). And as the Holy Spirit moves upon the redeemed spirit, then worship "in spirit" ascends to God who is Spirit (John 4:20-24).

To worship "in truth" is to worship according to the Word of God. Jesus said, "Sanctify them through Thy truth: Thy Word is truth" (John l7:l7). The Word of God is the Scripture of truth. God has laid down in His Word how we are to worship Him. He has shown His acceptance of a variety of expressions of praise and of worship from those who truly love Him. To worship "in truth" is to worship according to the Word of God.

Thus "worship in spirit and in truth" involves the believer honouring and adoring God by the quickening of the Holy Spirit and according to the Word of the Lord. The Spirit and the Word are both needed in proper worship. Both must be there. If the Spirit is not there, then worship is dead, lifeless. It is according to the letter which killeth. All becomes empty form. If the Word is not there, then the worship can become mere sentimentalism, emotionalism and can lead to fanaticism. There is need of the Spirit and the Word in true Biblical worship. There is nothing wrong with form or order.

In Genesis l:2 we find the earth in a state of being without form and void and darkness on the face of the deep. The Spirit of God moved on the face of the deep and then God spoke.

By the ministry of the Spirit and the Word order was brought out of chaos, light out of darkness, form out of disorder (Genesis l:l-5). Thus, Divine worship is dependent upon the Spirit and the Word operating in the midst of the worshipping congregation.

Expressions of Worship.

Following are a number of expressions of worship associated with the order of the Tabernacle of David, as well as in the history of Israel over the years. It should be recognized that each of these can become mechanical, lifeless forms unless the life of the Spirit is maintained by the congregation.

Also, it is not to say that each or all of these have to be in every service. Those responsible in leading worship will be sensitive to the Spirit of God and dependent upon the mind of the Lord for any particular service. They will follow the flow of the river of the Spirit of God for that service.

The variety of ways of ministry before the Lord listed below are briefly commented on because several of them will be taken up in further detail in the succeeding chapters. The contrast between that order of the Tabernacle of Moses and the Tabernacle of David will be noted also.

1. <u>Ministry of the Singers and Singing</u> (I Chronicles 15:16-27; 25:1-7).

David appointed certain Levites to be singers in the Tabernacle of David. The ministry of the singers in the song of the Lord was very prominent here. No singers ever sang in the Tabernacle of Moses.

2. <u>Ministry of the Musicians with Instruments</u> (I Chronicles 23:5; 25:1-7).

King David also ordained musicians with a variety of instruments to play and sing before the Lord in His Tabernacle. No musical instruments were ever played in the Tabernacle of Moses.

3. <u>Ministry of the Levites before the Ark</u> (I Chronicles 16:4,6,37).

The Levites were appointed to minister before the Ark of the Covenant continually, day by day as every man's work required. This was indeed in great contrast to the order of the Tabernacle of Moses. Only the High Priest on the great Day of Atonement ever dared to enter into the Holiest of All and stand before the Ark of God. Then it was in great silence and solemnity. If any other had dared to presume into the Most Holy Place judgment would have fallen on them. But here in David's Tabernacle stood a group of Levites of the priestly tribe. They stood in their courses day by day to minister before the Ark of God. It will be remembered that the Tabernacle of David signified the transference of the Holiest of All from the Tabernacle of Moses to Mt. Zion. Thus these Levites had access "within the veil", so to speak (Hebrews 6:19-20; 9:7-9; 10:20-21).

4. <u>Ministry of Recording</u> (I Chronicles 16:4; 28:12,19).

King David set Levites in his Tabernacle to "record." The word "record" means to "Set it down so that it can be remembered." It involved the ministry of the scribe. Many of the Psalms, especially those which concern Zion, must have been given by the inspiration of the Holy Spirit in connection with the Tabernacle of David. The title of Psalm 80 as well as the whole Psalm is an example of this. Asaph prayed a prophetic prayer as he stood before the Ark of the Covenant and the Shepherd of Israel who dwelt between the Cherubims (Psalm 80:1). The Psalms would be recorded by the Levitical scribes and thus set down so that they could be remembered. What a vast treasure would have been lost if the Psalms had not been recorded. Moses was the only one who wrote inspired Scripture in relation to the Tabernacle called by his name. Psalms 90-91 have been attributed to Moses. In the Tabernacle of David many Levites wrote the Psalms, as well as King David.

5. <u>Ministry of Thanking the Lord</u> (I Chronicles 16:4,8,41).

David appointed the Levites to thank the Lord also. Many of the Psalms exhort God's people to thank the Lord for His mercy. Giving thanks is an expression of gratefulness and appreciation to the giver of all things. Unthankfulness is a sign of the Last Days. Those who were set in the Tabernacle of David were to give thanks continually for all things (Psalms 116:17; 2 Chronicles 29:30-31; I Thessalonians 5:18). Under the Tabernacle of Moses, Israel could render a voluntary "thank offering" to the Lord (Leviticus 7:12,13).

6. Ministry of Praise (I Chronicles 16:4,36).

Part of the order in David's Tabernacle was to praise the Lord for His goodness and mercy. There were always Levites in their respective courses praising the Lord. One just needs to check the concordance and count the numerous references to "praise" to realize the importance of this unto the Lord.

It is Scriptural to "say" praise (Isaiah 12:1,4; Jeremiah 33:10-12). It is Scriptural to "sing" praise also (Psalms 47:6-7; 98:1-6; 100:2). The Psalms especially exhort the people of the Lord to "sing praise." There are over 70 references in the 150 Psalms to "sing praise." There was no singing of praise in the Tabernacle of Moses. All was silent order. But in the Tabernacle of David there was a continual sound of praise.

7. Ministry of Psalms (I Chronicles 16:9; Psalms 98:6).

On the day of the dedication, David delivered a Psalm to the singers and musicians. The Tabernacle of David was characterized by the writing and singing of Psalms. The greater majority of the Psalms are linked with David's Tabernacle. This is seen by the many references to Zion. This is in contrast with the Tabernacle of Moses where only one or possibly two Psalms were written, these being Psalms attributed to Moses (Psalms 90-91, Title). The New Testament exhorts us to sing the Psalms (Colossians 3:16; Ephesians 5:18,19; James 5:13; I Corinthians 14:26), thus continuing the ordinance of David. The Church in general recognizes that the Psalms are an integral part of worship, either chanting or singing them in Divine service. Many centuries of history show that often the Psalms only were chanted or sung.

8. Ministry of Rejoicing and Joy (I Chronicles 16:10,16,25-31).

Joy and rejoicing characterized the order of Tabernacle of David also. The Canaanite religions, as well as most religions outside of Christianity had no real joy. Even the Tabernacle of Moses was characterized by great solemnity; not the joy of David's Tabernacle. Numerous Scriptures exhort the believer to rejoice in the Lord (Philippians 3:3; 4:4).

9. Ministry of Clapping of Hands (Psalms 47:1; 98:8; Isaiah 55:12).

One of the Psalms for the sons of Korah exhorts the people to clap hands. One of the most natural of all human responses to joy and appreciation is the clapping of the hands. From the baby in the cradle, to the youth, to the adult, clapping of hands is an expression of happiness, thanks, appreciation, and joy. How much more shall God's people clap unto the Lord as they did in Bible times? There was no such expression of joy in the Tabernacle of Moses.

10. Ministry of Shouting (I Chronicles 15:28; Psalms 47:1,5; Isaiah 12:6).

When the Ark of God was taken into David's Tabernacle, there was much shouting unto the Lord. A number of Scriptures speak of shouting in Israel's history. When Israel shouted on the 7th day on the march around Jericho, God caused the walls to fall down flat (Joshua 6:5). There are times when a shout is just an empty noise (I Samuel 4:5-9), but when God is in it and it is an act of worship unto the Lord, then God works with the shout of His people. The Lord Jesus will return for His people at the second coming with a shout (I Thessalonians 4:16).

11. Ministry of Dancing (I Chronicles 15:29; 2 Samuel 6:14; Psalms 149:3; 150:4).

There was the expression of dancing before the Lord at the dedication day of the Tabernacle of David. Michal despised David dancing before the Ark of the Lord. There is a time to dance (Ecclesiastes 3:4). Most of the Canaanite dancing was sensuous, lustful, and done amidst the orgies of idolatrous festivals. The dancing of Israel was to be in joy, praise, and as a part of worship unto the Lord. It was particularly associated with festival occasions. Miriam and the women with her danced at the deliverance from Egypt after the crossing of the Red Sea (Exodus 15:20).

12. Ministry of Lifting up of Hands (Psalms 134; 141:2).

The Levites in their courses in Zion also lifted up their hands as an act of worship to the Lord in David's Tabernacle. Lifting hands in Scripture has several suggested meanings. It is an act of surrender, of a person taking a vow before the Lord, of prayer and worship. It is part of Old and New Testament worship (Genesis 14:22; Leviticus 9:22; Luke 24:50; I Timothy 2:8). The Psalmist says, "Let my prayer be set forth before Thee as incense; and the lifting up of my hands as the evening sacrifice" (Psalms 141:2). Only Aaron would lift up hands in blessing in the Tabernacle of Moses. In the Tabernacle of David all could lift their hands to the Lord. So it is today. All believers as ministering priests may lift their hands in worship. We are to lift up our heart with our hands (Lamentations 3:41).

13. Ministry of Worship (I Chronicles 16:29; Psalms 29:1-2; 95:6).

Although the word "worship" is being used in this chapter in its broadest sense, in its strictest sense the word means "to bow down, to stoop very low, to prostrate oneself."

The Levites in David's Tabernacle were not only to sing, praise, play instruments, clap hands, lift hands to the Lord, they were to worship. There was a bowing before the Lord, a prostration of themselves in deep adoration and devotion. This aspect of worship is the highest expression before God of all expressions of worship in spirit and in truth (John 4:20-24; Revelation 5). All believers should experience times of deep prostration of the spirit before God in the Holiest of All in this aspect of worship (Revelation 11:1-2; Matthew 28:9,17). At Mt. Sinai the people worshipped afar off (Exodus 24:1-2). In the Tabernacle of David worship was near to God. Much nearer is it in New Testament times through the blood of Jesus.

14. Ministry of Seeking the Lord (I Chronicles 16:10-11; 2 Chronicles 7:14).

David exhorted the Levites to seek the face of the Lord in His Tabernacle. This is also part of worship; seeking God's face with our whole heart. Only those who seek Him with their whole being will find Him. We are to rejoice as we seek Him (Psalms 27:8; 63:1-2; 70:4). The Tabernacle of David was a place where priests and Levites sought the Lord.

15. Ministry of Spiritual Sacrifices (Psalms 27:6; I Peter 2:3-5; Hebrews 13:15,16).

David's Tabernacle was a place where spiritual sacrifices were offered to the Lord by priests and Levites. As already noted, animal sacrifices were offered at the dedicatory service but only spiritual sacrifices were offered after that day in the Tabernacle of David. This was in great contrast to the continual animal sacrifices in the Tabernacle of Moses. We list several of these spiritual sacrifices as mentioned in Scripture.

The sacrifices of joy (Psalms 27:6).
The sacrifices of thanksgiving (Psalms 116:17; Leviticus 7:12; Jonah 2:9).
The sacrifices of praise (Jeremiah 17:26; 33:11, with Hebrews 13:15).

These are "spiritual sacrifices" offered up by the royal priesthood in the spiritual house, the Church. No more animal sacrifices are needed since the once-for-all sacrifice of the body and blood of Jesus. The New Testament believer, as a ministering priest unto the Lord, offers his body (Romans 12:1-2), his praise (Hebrews 13:15) and his substance (Hebrews 13:16) as spiritual sacrifices to God through Christ.

16. Ministry of Saying "Amen" (I Chronicles 16:36).

In Hebrew the word "Amen" means "Sure." It is translated "Amen, so be it, truth." It involves faithfulness and truth. In Greek the same word means "Firm, trustworthy" (so be it) and is translated "Amen, verily." The saying of "Amen" from the heart is an expression of support, approval of faith, of certainty that the thing spoken is true, and it shall come to pass.

It is worthy to note that Israel only responded with "Amen" to the curses of the Lord in Deuteronomy 27:15-26 and Numbers 5:22. In the Tabernacle of David it was the "Amen" of blessing. This is an Old Testament and New Testament expression of worship also (Nehemiah 5:13; 8:6; Psalms 89:52; 106:48; I Corinthians 14:16; Ephesians 3:21; Revelation 7:12).

The various expressions of worship related to, or in, David's Tabernacle have been briefly considered. Any or all of these may be in a given service. They are all Scriptural, they are all a part of God's Word. Both Old Testament and New Testament believers may enter into these expressions of worship and praise. It is vain to say that these things are only for Old Testament Israel and not for the New Testament Church because some of these things are not expressly mentioned in the New Testament. The New Testament Church arose out of the Old Testament Church. The early believers continually appealed to the Psalms as well as the rest of the Old Testament, in their teaching, preaching and worshipping. The New Testament does not write off the Old Testament. The New interprets the Old. The New Testament does show that animal sacrifices and the Mosaic economy were fulfilled and abolished at the Cross. But nowhere does it say that worship was abolished, nor these expressions of worship. It is inconsistent to accept some of these expressions and reject others, for all are Scriptural expressions unto the Lord. Worship is lifted into a greater and higher realm in the New Testament because of the cross of Jesus and the power of the Holy Spirit, and because all New Testament believers are to be kings and priests unto God through Christ, after the order of Melchisedek.

The New Testament Church worshipped the Lord as set out in the Psalms. If these things be not so, then the Church today should not accept anything of the Psalms as being applicable to our times. However, the Psalms generally are a revelation of Christ in the midst of a worshipping Church. "In the midst of the Church will I (Christ) sing praise to Thee (God)" (Psalms 22:22-31). "Is any merry, let him sing Psalms" (James 5:13). "Singing to yourselves in Psalms, hymns and spiritual ..." (Ephesians 5:18,19; Colossians 3:16).

The following diagram and its respective columns bring into sharper focus the contrast between the Tabernacle of Moses and the Tabernacle of David and the expressions of worship briefly considered in this chapter. The distinction in worship between the two Tabernacles is clear. The student should read the Scriptures in the right hand column and notice how the New Testament confirms the Old Testament order of worship as in David's Tabernacle.

ORDER OF WORSHIP ESTABLISHED

	Tabernacle of David (New Testament Church) (Mt. Zion Order)		Tabernacle of Moses (Old Testament Church) (Mt. Sinai Order)
			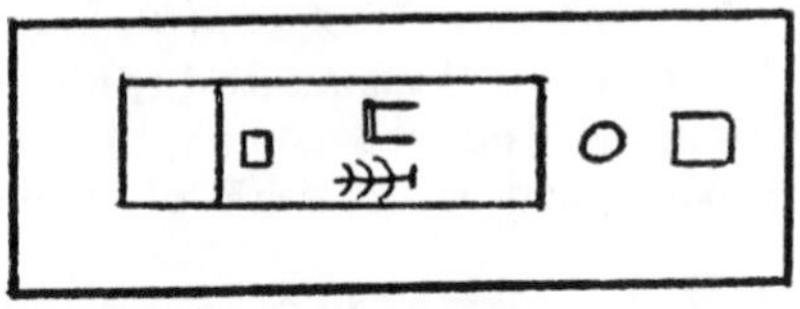
1.	Singers & Singing (I Chronicles 15:16-2 7; Colossians 3:16).	1.	None (Mt. Gibeon - a few. I Chronicles 16:37-43).
2.	Instruments of Music (I Chronicles 23:5; 25:1-7; Ephesians 5:18-19).	2.	None
3.	Levites minister before Ark (I Chronicles 16:37; Hebrews 6:19-20;10:19-21).	3.	High Priest only
4.	Recording (I Chronicles 16:4; Psalms 80:1; Revelation 1:10-11).	4.	None
5.	Thanking (I Chronicles 16:4,8,41; I Thessalonians 5:18).	5.	None
6.	Praise (I Chronicles 16:4, 36; Hebrews 13:15).	6.	None
7.	Psalm Singing (I Chronicles 16:7; Ephesians 5:18-19; I Corinthians 14:26; James 5:13).	7.	None (Psalm 90 only)
8.	Rejoicing and Joy (I Chronicles 16:10,27,31; Acts 13:52).	8.	Commanded
9.	Clapping (Psalms 47:1).	9.	None
10.	Shouting (I Chronicles 15:28; I Thessalonians 4:16).	10.	None (Except Jericho, Joshua 6)
11.	Dancing (I Chronicles 15:29; Psalms 149:3; Luke 15:25).	11.	None (Except Exodus 15)
12.	Lifting up hands (Psalms 134; I Timothy 2:8).	12.	None
13.	Worship - Access - Bowing (I Chronicles 16:29; John 4:20-24).	13.	Worship - Afar off
14.	Seeking the Lord (I Chronicles 16:10-11; Acts 15:17).	14.	Sought the Tabernacle
15.	Spiritual Sacrifices (Psalms 27:6; 116:17; I Peter 2:3-5; Hebrews 13:15,16).	15.	Animal Sacrifices
16.	Amen (In Blessing) (I Chronicles 16:36; I Corinthians 14:16).	16.	Amen (To Curses) (Deuteronomy 27:15-26).

Jamieson, Fausett and Brown, in "Commentary on the Whole Bible" (p. 679) comment on Amos 9:11-12, saying:

> "In that day - quoted by St. James (Acts 15:16,17), 'After this.' i.e., in the dispensation of Messiah (Genesis 49:10; Hosea 3:4,5; Joel 2:28; 3:1). Tabernacle of David - not "the house of David" ' which is used of his affairs when prospering (2 Samuel 3:1), but the tent or booth, expressing the low condition to which his kingdom and family had fallen in Amos' time, and subsequently at the Babylonian captivity before the restoration; and secondarily, in the last days preceding Israel's restoration under Messiah, the antitype to David (Psalm 102: 13,14; Isaiah 12:1; Jeremiah 30:9; Ezekiel 23:24; 37:24)...
>
> 'Tabernacle' is appropriate to Him, as His human nature is the tabernacle which He assumed in becoming Immanuel, 'God with us' (John 1:14). 'Dwelt,' lit., tabernacled 'among us' (cf., Revelation 21:3). Some understand 'the tabernacle of David' as that which David pitched for the ark in Zion, after bringing it from Obededom's house. It remained there all his reign for thirty years, till the temple of Solomon was built; whereas the 'tabernacle of the congregation' remained at Gibeon (2 Chronicles 1:3), where the priests ministered in sacrifices (1 Chronicles 16:39).
>
> Song and praise was the service of David's attendants before the ark (Asaph, etc.); a type of the Gospel separation between the sacrificial service (Messiah's priesthood now in heaven) and the access of believers on earth to the presence of God, apart from the former (cf., 2 Samuel 6:12-17; 1 Chronicles 16:37-39; 2 Chronicles 1:3)."

It is no wonder that the writer to the Hebrews tells the believers that we are not come to Mt. Sinai but to Mt. Zion; not to the Tabernacle of Moses with its silent order of worship, with its form and solemnity, after the letter of the Law that kills, but we are come to the Tabernacle of David, to the ministration of the Spirit which gives life.

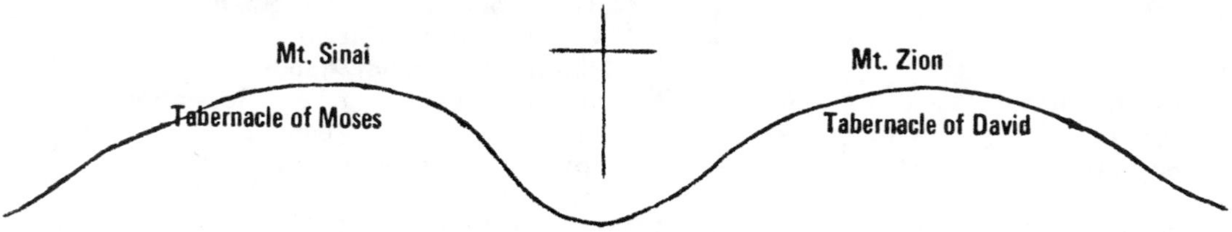

For those who have responsibility in leadership it is a good thing to remember the principle set out in Ecclesiastes 3:1-8 which says "To everything there is a time . . ." (vs 1). There is a time to sing, a time to clap, a time to lift up the hands, a time to rejoice and dance before the Lord, a time to praise, and a time to worship. There is a time for everything. Sensitivity to the Holy Spirit will be the guideline in all expressions of worship.

As has been seen in previous chapters, a principle of Biblical interpretation is to bring all things in the Old Testament to the cross. The cross becomes what may be called, "the hermeneutical filter" through which everything must pass. Some things from the Old Testament pass to the cross and are abolished there. Some things pass to the cross and through the cross and are validated and elevated there.

Worship in its purest sense, and expressions of worship, pass to and through the cross. Worship was not abolished at the cross. Worship will never be abolished. Worship is for time and eternity, that worship which must be in spirit and in truth (John 4:20-24).

We columnize the various expressions of praise and worship as seen in the Old Testament and are validated in the New Testament as a whole. Such show that these expressions should not be relegated or limited to Old Testament Israel, but are valid expressions in the New Testament church, which is the continuation of the people of God.

1. OLD TESTAMENT ORDER (Kingdom Tabernacle)		NEW TESTAMENT ORDER
Davidic Covenant	—	New Covenant
Mt. Zion	—	Heavenly Mt. Zion
Tabernacle of David	—	The Church, N.T. Dwelling place of God
Kingdom, Kingship	—	Messiah's Kingdom, Kingship
Seed of David	—	Messiah, David's Son
House of David	—	Messiah's House
Throne of David	—	Messiah sits on David's throne
Subdue enemies	—	Subdues His enemies under feet
Conquers Gentile nations	—	Gentiles come into His Kingdom
King David	—	King-Priest Jesus, Son of David

2. OLD TESTAMENT WORSHIP EXPRESSIONS (Worship Tabernacle)		NEW TESTAMENT WORSHIP EXPRESSIONS
Order of Praise and Worship	—	Praise and Worship. Revelation 4-5
The Ark of God	—	The Throne of God and the Lamb
David, sweet Singer and Psalmist	—	Jesus-Worship Leaders; Hebrews 2:12
Singing	—	Hebrews 2:12; Colossians 3:16
Clapping	—	Not mentioned in New Testament
Praising	—	Hebrews 13:15. Sacrifice of praise
Uplifting of hands	—	1 Timothy 2:8. Lift holy hands
Bowing down	—	Falling down before the Lord. Revelation 4
Rejoicing	—	Luke 1:47; Acts 13:51. Leaping
Worshipping	—	In spirit and truth. John 4:20-24
Kneeling	—	Kneeling. Luke 22:41
Standing	—	Standing. Revelation 20:12
Psalms singing	—	Psalms, Hymns, Spiritual Songs. Ephesians 5:18, 19
Shouting	—	The great shout. 1 Thessalonians 4:16
Dancing	—	Dancing. Luke 15:25
Musical Instruments	—	Harps of God. Revelation 5:8

The ultimate of all expressions of praise and worship is edification! Does it edify the saint? Does it glorify the Lord? Does it draw the unregenerate to Christ or drive them away? Let all things be done unto edifying (1 Corinthians 14:3, 4, 5, 12, 26).

Chapter 22

A BRIEF HISTORY OF MUSIC

Because the ministry of music plays such an important part in the order of David, a few selective sketches from the development of the history of music become necessary. This is particularly so in the light of the fact that Church history reveals the varying degrees of conflict and controversy over the place of music in the Church.

The place of vocal and instrumental music as part of the Church order of worship has been much contended over the centuries. Most present-day denominations accept at least vocal singing of the congregation as well as some instrument to accompany the same, either the piano or the organ. The struggle, however, has been long and hard, even to come thus far. There are denominations who deny the right of the Church to use musical instruments in Christian worship but will allow a limited amount of vocal singing.

The winds of change are blowing across the Church in our day. This brief history of music should be helpful to see the Biblical importance of this ministry before the Lord. More competent authors have dealt exhaustively with the history of music, hence this present chapter will only touch briefly on the main points as they relate to this present text.

A. The Heavenly Origin of Music

1. The Harmony of the Universe.

There should be no doubt as to the origin of music. Music either originated with God or the Devil or man. Scripture revelation of music suggests that music originated in the very heart of God. Before mankind was created, and even before the angelic hosts were created, music was in the very being of God.

Webster's Dictionary defines music as being "the art and science of combining vocal or instrumental sounds or tones in varying melody, harmony, rhythm, and timbre, especially so as to form structurally complete and emotionally expressive compositions."

Creation itself is really God's "Musicale." The universe of galaxies of worlds presents a melody and a harmony that reveals the musical heart of God. When God created the worlds, He set them all in their orbits, moving in one grand and glorious harmonious musicale. There was no discordant sound to be heard. All creation moved in triumphant major mode of music. The universe was God's orchestral arrangement!

2. The Angelic Choir.

The Scriptures teach that God created the angelic hosts and they also imply that the angelic hosts were the "heavenly choir" at the dawn of creation. This heavenly choir was led by Lucifer, the Day-Star, the Son of the Morning.

Most Bible expositors believe that Lucifer (Ezekiel 28:11-19; Isaiah 14:12-17) was Satan before his fall. Assuming this to be so, the description of Lucifer suggests that he was heaven's Song-leader, Heaven's choir-director. Note the major points as set forth in the verses here.

a. His name was Lucifer, which means "Day-Star," Son of the Morning.

b. He was an Anointed Cherub, given a distinctive anointing for ministry.

c. He was the "covering Cherub," covering the Throne of God in the Mountain of God.

d. He was created perfect in beauty, full of wisdom.

e. He was the heavenly Archangel, in the Eden (Paradise) of God.

f. He was clothed as a priest with precious stones in his garments.

g. He had the workmanship of tabrets and pipes in him in the day that he was created.

Thus, it is implied that Lucifer had the ministry of music in him and that he was anointed to this ministry before God, to lead the angelic hosts - the heavenly choir - as the celestial choir leader. What heavenly music, what celestial symphonies must have been heard in that original creation throughout the universe. The angels were created to worship God as well as to be ministering spirits (Hebrews 1:13,14; 12:22; Daniel 7:10; Luke 2:13; Revelation 5:1,11).

The Book of Job tells us that "the Morning Stars SANG together, and all the Sons of God SHOUTED for joy" at creation (Job 38:4-7). Again, most expositors accept the Morning Stars or the Sons of God here as being the angelic hosts. The angels sing the "Song of creation" but not the "Song of redemption" (I Peter 1:12; Revelation 5:1-12).

Singing and shouting took place at the time of creation, for all creation and creatures were in perfect harmony with Divinity. There were no minors or discords known then!

3. The Discord of Sin.

Only eternity will reveal clearly the full details of the entrance of sin into the universe. Suddenly, in the midst of the Divine music and harmony of creation and creatures, Lucifer, the Anointed Cherub, rises to assert his will against the Divine will. Heaven's music and song director beholds his own beauty, wisdom, anointing, and ministry and thus becomes lifted up in pride, arrogancy, and self-will. Rebellion manifests itself. Discord, which is simply the lack of harmony, a conflict of musical notes, is heard in the universe. Self-will is manifested against God's will.

The angelic hosts are put to the test in their will. Some choose to follow Lucifer and are cast out of the Paradise of God. Sin breaks the harmony of God's universe. Sin brings in discord. The majestic music major is now turned to depressing music minor. Another note is heard in the universe. The Divine harmony has been broken.

God casts Satan out of the third heaven, but now in the universe the sound of music is heard in two conflicting keys; the minor and the major; discordant and harmonious. It is worthy to note that God did not strip Lucifer (Satan) of his wisdom nor his ministry of music. He still has it and all through the history of mankind Satanically inspired music has had the power to debase, degrade, and eventually destroy mankind.

Music in itself is neither moral nor immoral. It is amoral! It is the use of music which makes it evil or good, destroying or edifying.

Hence, Lucifer did not forfeit his ministry of music; he corrupted it. Today it is one of the master-weapons which he is using to draw people away from God and the Lord Jesus Christ. He knows the power of it.

B. The Music of the Gentile Nations

It seems that nearly all primitive peoples of the earth believe that music was of divine origin. Every civilization has some kind of legend concerning the origin and creation of music. In practically every case a god discovers it and passes it on to mankind.

History reveals that, from earliest times, music was used exclusively for worship. Whether men worshipped the true God, or idols, or demon spirits, music was used originally in worship. All tribes, no matter how primitive, had musical instruments of some kind or another. God planted in the heart of man a desire to worship. God gave man the ability to express this urge for worship and man does this by music, vocal or instrumental. We note briefly some of the nations and references to music.

1. The first specific mention of musical instruments in the Bible is in the ungodly line of Cain. There were those who handled the harp and the organ. Jubal was the father (first teacher) of all these musicians (Genesis 4:21).

2. Genesis 31:27, Laban, the Syrian, rebuked Jacob for fleeing with his wife and possessions before the whole family could have a musical farewell of festivity "with mirth, and with songs, with tabret and with harp."

3. Job 21:12, Job, possibly the oldest Book of the Bible, refers to the wicked dancing with timbrel (tambourine) and harp (pipe) and rejoicing at the sound of the organ. Vocal and instrumental music were generally linked together.

4. The Egyptians were especially fond of stringed instruments. They gave percussion instruments a minor place. Archeologists inform us of a great variety of harps, guitars, lyres and flutes which were used for temple worship, and at times for leading people to battle, being found in Egypt.

5. It seems that the worship of the Canaanites was of the grossest kind. Festivity, idolatry, and immorality were carried on amidst the most debasing kind of music. Israel was totally forbidden to have anything to do with the Canaanite religions and sensuous worship.

Exodus 32:17-18 is an example showing how Israel acted in the worship of the golden calf. The people were singing, dancing and fell into sensuous acts. It reveals the influence of Egypt as well as other corrupt religions that Israel needed cleansing from.

6. The Assyrian, Babylonian, and Persian empires had musical instruments, predominately harp-like instruments. One of the harps was of triangular shape. The dulcimer was composed of a square wooden box, with metal strings intended to be struck by a hammer. Actually this was the great-great-great grandfather of the modern piano. Daniel 3 is an example of music associated with the worship of the Babylonian king in the role of divinity. Cornet, flute, harp, sackbut, psaltery, dulcimer are mentioned as instruments used in the festival of worship of King Nebuchadnezzar in vs. 5, and 15. The power of music was used to cause all to surrender to the influence of worshipping this earthly king.

7. The Greeks, as a nation, were fond of pipe organs particularly. The "pipes of Pan" are spoken of in Greek history.

8. The Chinese, especially, were fond of percussion instruments, such as drums, bells, stones beaten with wooden mallets, cymbals, and wooden tubs beaten on the inside and outside. They also had instruments of bamboo tubes. Stringed instruments were rare. Musical instru-

ments in Chinese history date as far back as B.C. 3000. A Chinese legend states that the Emperor sent his Master of Music to the Promised Land. In this land he saw bamboo trees from which he fashioned twelve tubes, each one to match the twelve notes sung by the Phoenix bird.

9. The Japanese had instruments very similar to the Chinese; drums, bell rattles, wooden clappers, and sometimes flutes. One instrument was made of a certain sea-shell with a tube inserted into it and it was used like a trumpet.

10. India and Africa, as well as other nations, developed various primitive types of instruments.

11. The Sumerians said that the goddess Nina was the creator and originator of the art of music.

12. The Greek god, Hermes, was the god of eloquence, interpretation and the arts. He is said to have tripped over a tortoise shell and made the first lyre. He gave it to Apollo whose beautiful playing gave him the title of "The god of music."

These things show that many of the legends of civilization accredit the origin of music to the gods, which they passed on to mankind. It does indeed help to confirm the thought that music did originate with the true God.

All music is a combination of sound, rhythm, and pitch, whether primitive or modern. No doubt many instruments arose out of incidental tappings or sounds on sticks and stones, metals, etc., which were pleasing to the ear of man. Thus from the most primitive tribe to the most advanced nation mankind has sought to express his emotions in vocal or instrumental music, especially as part of worship. From the worship of idols, demon spirits, to hero-worship of kings or warriors, music has played an integral part of devotion.

C. The Music of the Hebrew Nation

The great majority of references to music in the Old Testament have to do with the chosen nation, Israel. These references are generally in relation to their worship of Jehovah, the true God. It will be seen that God commanded music, whether vocal or instrumental, to be used in worship.

If the Lord God was against music, or if music originated with Satan or the godless nations, then the Lord would certainly have forbidden and warned Israel against such. However, the very opposite is true. The Lord commanded Israel to worship Him with singing, praising, shouting, and all kinds of musical instruments. The Hebrew nation, in its highest spiritual moments, was a singing nation, a musical people. Songs of worship were born in this nation concerning the true God that were and still are incomparable with the corrupt and sensuous songs of the heathen. The worship of the gods of the Canaanites was vile, lustful and sensuous. The music which accompanied these filthy orgies was certainly Satanically inspired and totally unfit for the redeemed people of God.

Israel's music, on the other hand, was of the highest, richest, purest, and noblest type and it pleased God, the originator of holy music.

We consider a number of references to music, vocally and instrumentally, in the Hebrew nation.

1. <u>Music - Vocally.</u>

There are numerous references to vocal music -- singing to God with the voice.

a. Exodus 15:1-19, the song of Moses and the children of Israel is recorded here after the great deliverance from the bondage of Egypt. Note also the "Song of Moses and the Lamb" in Revelation 15:3,4.

b. The song of Moses in Exodus is the first recorded song from the time of Adam.

c. Exodus 15:20-21, Miriam the prophetess took a timbrel in her hand and all the women went after her, singing and praising the Lord in the dance for the victory at the Red Sea.

d. Numbers 21:16-18, Israel sang a song to the well in the desert. As the princes and nobles dug the well with their staves, the people sang to the well and the Lord caused the waters to flow.

e. Joshua 6, at the collapse of the walls of Jericho, the priests blew the ram's horn trumpets and the people shouted to God. God worked with this vocal expression of faith and obedience to His Word.

f. Judges 5, the song of Deborah and Barak is recorded for us in this chapter. It was a song of praise to the God of Israel. Read especially vs. 1-3.

g. 1 Chronicles 15-16, David especially established the ministry of the singers in his Tabernacle. There were twenty-four courses of singers in David's Tabernacle and then later on in the Temple of Solomon (1 Chronicles 23:1-7; 1 Chronicles 25).

h. 2 Chronicles 5:11-14, at the dedication of the Temple of Solomon the singers played an integral part.

i. 2 Chronicles 20, godly King Jehoshaphat used the ministry of the singers to lead the battle against the Moabites and Ammonites. God worked with the singers, and brought a great victory over the enemy.

j. 2 Chronicles 29:25-28, godly King Hezekiah knew what the song of the Lord was in the great awakening that he led in the nation of Israel.

k. 2 Chronicles 35:1-19, King Josiah, another godly king, also revived the ministry of the singers in his reign.

l. Ezra 3:1-13, the priestly scribe, Ezra, had the singers minister at the laying again of the foundation of the Temple after the remnant had come out of Babylon. The Levites wore their robes, and sang and played with instruments. The singing men and the singing women were there (Ezra 2:65).

m. Nehemiah 12:27-47, Nehemiah also, the governor of Judah, used the ministry of the singers in the day of dedication of the rebuilt walls of Jerusalem.

n. 1 Kings 4:29-32, Solomon, the son of David the sweet Psalmist and singer in Israel, was also musically talented. He wrote 1005 songs. The "Song of Songs" is recorded for us (Song of Songs 1:1).

o. 2 Samuel 19:35; Eccles 2:8, there were "singing men and singing women" in the courts of King David and King Solomon. The age of Samuel, David, and Solomon was Israel's golden age of poetry and music (Also read Ezra 2:65; 1 Chronicles 13:8; 25:5, 6).

p. Isaiah 16:10, in harvest time, Israel would sing as they trod out the grapes, producing the "new wine."

q. Psalms 136; Psalms 24, much of the singing of the Hebrew nation was antiphonal (i.e., one group responding to another group), and these Psalms illustrate the responsive chorus or parts that would be sung. However, most of the singing was in unison.

2. Music - Instrumentally.

Although there are many references to vocal music, there are many more which include both vocal and instrumental. Both were generally combined and they played an important part in divine worship. God's blessing and approval was on it. There is not one commandment of God either in Old or New Testament against the use of music in divine worship. For those believers today who would deny the right of the Church to use musical instruments in Christian worship and only allow singing, it would be profitable to consider the Scriptures listed below.

a. Exodus 15:20-21, percussion instruments (tambourines) were used, along with responsive singing under Moses, Miriam, and the children of Israel at the Red Sea.

b. Joshua 6, wind instruments (trumpets made of ram's horns) were used as well as shouting at the fall of Jericho.

c. 1 Chronicles 15-16, David particularly set the order of twenty-four courses of singers and priestly musicians in the Tabernacle of David. Of the 4800 in the tribe of Levi, 4000 praised the Lord with the instruments David had made. Of these were 288 skilled musicians divided into twenty-four courses, twelve in each, headed by the twenty-four sons of Heman, Asaph and Jeduthan. The rest of the 4000 were "scholars" (1 Chronicles 23-25). This was the Temple orechestra.

d. 2 Chronicles 5:11-14, singers and instrumentalists were combined in the dedication of Solomon's Temple, when the glory of God filled the place.

e. 2 Chronicles 29:25-29; 30:21, vocal and instrumental music were combined at the cleansing of the Temple under the reign of godly King Hezekiah.

f. 2 Chronicles 35:1-19, both vocal and instrumental music were heard again under godly King Josiah.

g. Ezra 3:1-13, in the restoration of Judah from Babylon under Ezra, singers and musicians combined to worship the Lord.

h. Nehemiah 12:27-47, under the return from Babylon with governor Nehemiah, singers and musicians were used in the dedication of the walls.

i. 1 Samuel 10:5-6, the prophet Samuel had schools of the prophets in different places. Music played a great part in the spiritual influences upon those coming into the prophetic office. Undoubtedly David came under this influence also (1 Samuel 19:19, 20; 2 Kings 2:5-7).

j. 2 Samuel 6:5, 12-16, David and all Israel played much music at the bringing up of the Ark into his Tabernacle.

k. 2 Kings 3:15, 16, Elisha had the ministry of a minstrel release the prophetic word to the kings of Israel and Judah here.

l. 1 Samuel 16:16-23, David played before Saul when the evil spirit was troubling him. The evil spirit would depart for a season. It showed the power of anointed music over the troubling power of an evil spirit.

m. Numbers 10:1-10 (2 Chronicles 13:12), the two silver trumpets were used in Israel for a number of occasions, especially festival times, as well as for battle and the journeyings of the camps.

n. Isaiah 5:12 , instruments were used much in banquets in Israel.

o. Psalms 87:7; 68:25, the order generally recognized is set out in these verses. The singers first, then the players on instruments following, with the damsels playing timbrels.

p. 1 Kings 10:12, Solomon also made harps and psalteries for the singers in his time.

It should be noted clearly that these instruments were used by the commandment of God, as well as the commandment of David and Solomon (2 Chronicles 29:25-28). They were expressly called "the instruments of God."

> " ... and with the musical instruments of God" (1 Chronicles 16:4, 5, [42]).
>
> " ... and 4000 praised the Lord with the instruments which I made, said David, to praise therewith" (1 Chronicles 23:5).
>
> " ... who prophesied with a harp, to give thanks and to praise the Lord" (1 Chronicles 25:3).
>
> "And the priests waited on their offices: the Levites also with instruments of music of the Lord, which David the king had made to praise the Lord, because His mercy endureth for ever, when David praised by their ministry; and the priests sounded trumpets before them, and all Israel stood" (2 Chronicles 7:6).

The most information given to us in the Bible concerning music, vocal and/or instrumental, is that of the Hebrew nation, the people of God. Never ever did God condemn singing or instrumental music, unless it was done in hypocritical worship. In Amos 8:3 He threatened to turn "the songs of the temple" into howlings because of Israel's sins.

References to songs in Biblical Hebrew history are plentiful. We list a number of these.

1. The Song of Moses, Exodus 15, is the first recorded song.
2. The Song of Miriam, the prophetess (Exodus 15:20).
3. The second Song of Moses (Deuteronomy 31:19-20; Deuteronomy 32).
4. The Song of Israel at the well (Numbers 21:16-18).
5. The Song of Deborah and Barak (Judges 5).
6. The Songs of David (2 Samuel 23:1-2; 1 Chronicles 16:7).
7. The 1005 and Songs of Solomon (1 Kings 4:29-34).
8. The Song of Solomon (1:1)

9. The Song of the Morning Stars (Job 38:4-7).
10. The Songs of Isaiah. The prophet mentions songs and singing quite a number of times.

    Isaiah 5:1, The Song of the Beloved and His Vineyard.
    Isaiah 12, The Song of Praise.
    Isaiah 26:1-4, The Song of the Strong City.
    Isaiah 35, The Songs of the Redeemed.
    Isaiah 42:10, The New Song.
    Isaiah 44:23, The Song of Creation.
    Isaiah 54:1, The Song of the Barren Woman.

11. The Songs of King Hezekiah (Isaiah 38:20; Songs of Degrees, Psalms 120-134).
12. The Songs of Jeremiah (Jeremiah 31:12, 13).
13. The rejected Song of Ezekiel (Ezekiel 33:32).
14. The Song (Psalm) of Jonah (Jonah 2:9).
15. The Song of the Lord in Zephaniah (Zephaniah 3:14-17).
16. The Song of Messiah in the Church (Psalms 22:22, 25; Hebrews 2:12).
17. The Songs of Moses and the Lamb (Revelation 15:3, 4).
18. The Songs of the Redeemed (Revelation 5:8, 9; 14:2, 3).
19. The Singing Men and Singing Women (Exodus 15:20; 1 Chronicles 25:5, 6; Eccles 2:8; Ezra 2:65; Nehemiah 7:67; 2 Samuel 19:35; 2 Chronicles 35:25).

Women in Israel were involved in leading the dances with timbrels, singing antiphonally, playing instruments and prophecying, singing with men in the Temple choir as well as the women's choirs.

No music in Israel was actually a sign of judgment and the curse in the land (Isaiah 24:8, 9; Jeremiah 7:34; Ezekiel 26:13).

Phil Kerr, in Music in Evangelism (P. 34), comments on the close of the Old Testament period of Jewish history by saying that it was a time of idolatry, apostacy, and unbelief. The Jews had allowed the worship of Jehovah to degenerate into great formalism. The Synagogues were bound by the letter of the law. This apostacy was reflected in their singing. The joyful songs of the nation's earlier history had gone. The songs of Moses, Miriam, David, Cheneniah, Asaph and Solomon were no longer heard. Musical instruments were used with less frequency in Synagogue worship. The religious music of the nation became more formal and mournful. Musical singing was abandoned by the laity, and Synagogue singing was confined to the ritualistic chanting of the priests.

The Pharisees especially held the strictest views concerning music in Temple and Synagogue worship. After the destruction of the Temple in A.D. 70, the Pharisees forbad the use of instruments, their reason being that the clarinet, cymbal, gongs, and drums were used by the pagan mystery cults of Asia Minor in demon worship. Hence Paul's probable allusion to such when he mentions trumpets giving an uncertain sound, "sounding brass and tinkling cymbals" in 1 Corinthians 13 as an expression of lovelessness. However, Paul never condemned music; he encouraged Psalms (Greek Psalmos, "song with instrumental accompaniment"), hymns and spiritual songs (Ephesians 5:18, 19 and Colossians 3:16). The spirituality of the Hebrew nation can be ascertained by the rise and/or decline of the ministry to the Lord in music and song.

In closing this section concerning music in the Hebrew nation, it is worthy to note the attitude of the modern day Jew concerning music and singing. The Central Conference of American Rabbis compiled and published in A.D. 1897, A.D. 1914, and A.D. 1932 editions of the Jewish "Union Hymnal," the one most used in the Synagogues. It was compiled under the direct authority of the spiritual governing body of Reform Judaism.

The three main branches in American Judaism, Reform, Conservative and Orthodox criticized the effort. The Orthodox will not use a hymnal. A male singer sings in Hebrew, he sings unaccompanied, as organs are not permitted in Orthodox Synagogues. The Reform will allow a hymnal and organ, yet they are unfriendly towards the "Union Hymnal" because of its lack of Jewishness in music as well as text.

Stevenson (p. 178) quotes Rabbi Isaac Moses, a hymnbook editor of the Central New York Synagogue, as saying,

> "It is eminently proper that hymnbooks intended for Jewish worship should be Jewish in character, and that the hymns of prayer should be the products of Jewish authors ... A collection of fine poems and melodies culled from the hymnals of the different (Christian) Churches has no place in the Synagogue. Has the Jewish genius produced nothing of value that we must needs go begging at the doors of every denomination?"

The "Union Hymnal" was a collection of fine poems and melodies taken from hymnals of different Christian Churches. Each edition has shown an endeavour to have more Jewish features rather than Christian sources. The national style of music, as well as the Jewish Faith, is being asked for. Jews express themselves by saying that the reign of Gentile organists and singers in the choir will come to an end, as Jewish organists and singers replace them. The Jew no longer desires to depend on Gentile talent.

Stevenson (P. 183) quotes Leonid Sabaneev in The Jewish National School of Music (July, 1929), as saying,

> "On the average the Jewish race is by nature more musical than any other and the number of Jewish musicians is considerably greater than that of other nationalities ... The Jews have always been a nation of singers, have always found in song an outlet for their agitating griefs, their temptations, their wrath. And now when that nation has singled out from itself an intellectual class, it not only can but must speak to the world in a musical language of its own."

It is a tragic comment on the history of a nation chosen by God to declare His glory in vocal and instrumental music. After rejecting their long-promised Messiah, they continue to worship God whom they know not. It is ironical that the hymns they selected from the Christian Churches deal only with God the Father, but show manifestly a rejection of the Son of God, Messiah and Saviour of the world, both Jew and Gentile. Only those who come to know Christ as their Saviour will really be able to sing the songs of redemption as heard in the Christian Church around the world.

D. The Music in the New Testament (Apostolic Period A.D. 26-95).

Music, both vocally and instrumentally, is carried over into the New Testament period also. Church history records the conflict over whether there should be singing in the Church worship, whether there should be instruments used or not. It has been a centuries-long struggle for various denominations to allow singing and instruments to be used in Christian worship.

One of the prominent arguments put forth was that musical instruments were for Old Testament worship in Israel only. Because they lived under the Law, the age of the ceremonial, then all of this was fulfilled and abolished by Jesus at the cross. They contended that the only "instrument" that the New Testament allowed in worship was the heart in tune with God. There are still those in Christianity today who hold forth the same argument.

It is true that God wants the heart in tune with Himself; otherwise all is hypocrisy and unacceptable to Him. But, we will find, that the New Testament interprets the Old Testament. Though ceremonialism was abolished at the cross, WORSHIP and all its related expressions was never abolished. It never will be. Worship began in eternity; it was continued in the history of the redeemed and it will continue into the eternities. Worship cannot be confined to periods or dispensations! It is for all times!

Jesus condemned the formalism and the hypocrisy of His times. Jesus abolished animal sacrifices and all other forms of ceremonialism of the Law, but He never repudiated Old Testament vocal or instrument music. Let us consider the New Testament references to music ministry.

1. Luke 15:25, Jesus spoke of "musick and dancing" at the return of the prodigal son to the Father's house. He spoke of the attitude of the elder brother also. Most Christians admit that the story is a picture of the heart of the Father God over a returning child. One cannot accept the rest of the parable and discount the "musick and dancing" which was part of the joyous occasion.

2. Matthew 26:30; Mark 14:26, Jesus sung a hymn (Greek "Humneo", i.e., "To hymn, sing a religious ode; by implication, to celebrate (God) in song; one of the Psalms), at the establishing of the Lord's Table.

It is generally accepted that it was the Great Hallel or Paschal Hymn which was usually sung after Passover by the Jews (Psalms 113-118).

3. 1 Corinthians 14:26, the Apostle Paul, in writing to the Gentile Corinthian believers concerning Church order encouraged them to have a psalm, as well as other functions of edification. The Greek word for psalm is "Psalmos," and means "a set piece of music, i.e., a sacred ode (accompanied with the voice, harp or other instrument)."

4. Ephesians 5:18, 19, Paul exhorts the Ephesian believers to sing psalms, hymns, and spiritual songs and make melody in their heart unto the Lord. It is part of the Spirit-filled life to do so. That is, to sing a set piece of music, a sacred ode, accompanied by the voice, harp or other instrument (Greek "Psalmos"). "Making melody" is the Greek word "Psallo" as used also in James 5:13.

5. Colossians 3:16, the same exhortation to sing psalms, hymns, and spiritual songs with grace in the heart to the Lord is given by Paul to the Colossian believers. It is the same Greek word as mentioned in Ephesians 5:19.

6. James 5:13, James also exhorts the believer, "... Is any merry? Let him sing Psalms." The Greek word is "Psallo"' and means "to rub or touch the surface; to twitch or twang, i.e., to play on a stringed instrument (celebrate the divine worship with music and accompanying odes)."

7. Acts 16:25, Paul and Silas sang praise (Greek "Humneo," or Hymn) to God at the midnight hour and God worked with their praise. The jailor and his household were saved that night.

8. Hebrews 2:12, this verse is a prophecy of Christ quoted from Psalms 22:22. It states "In the midst of the Church (the worshipping congregation) will I sing praise (Greek "Humneo," or Hymn) to Thee." Thus Christ sings praise to the Father in the midst of His worshipping people.

9. Romans 15:9 with Psalms 18:49, the Lord Jesus said, "For this cause I will confess to Thee among the Gentiles, and sing [(Greek "Psallo," to rub or touch the surface; to twitch or twang), i.e., to play on an stringed instrument (celebrate the divine worship with music and accompanying odes, as James 5:13)] unto Thy Name."

10. 1 Corinthians 14:5, Paul said that he would sing (Greek "Psallo," as in James 5:13) with the spirit and he would also sing with the understanding.

11. Revelation 5:8-10, the four living creatures and the twenty-four elders "sung a new song" before the Lord God and the Lamb on the throne. They also had harps, musical instruments to accompany them. Thus music, vocal and instrumental is seen before the very throne of God. Who can fail to see here an allusion to the twenty-four courses of singers and musicians in the Tabernacle of David? The Greek word for song is "Odee," the same as in Ephesians 5:19, and Colossians 3:16.

12. Revelation 14:1-5, the 144,000 sung "a new song" (Greek "Odee" or Ode) before God and the Lamb, and accompanied themselves with harps, stringed instruments.

Vocal and instrumental music are blended together in worship here. Once again we have an allusion to the twenty-four courses of the singers and musicians in the Tabernacle of David.

13. Revelation 15:2-3, those who overcome the mark of the beast take their positions on the Sea of Glass before the throne. They have musical instruments of God, harps, and they sing the song of Moses and of the Lamb. This reminds us of Israel gaining the victory over Pharoah (The Beast) at the Red Sea and the Song of Moses and Miriam and the power of the deliverance of the Passover Lamb (Exodus 12, 13, 14, 15).

In the light of these Scriptures from the New Testament, it is impossible to discount the ministry of music unto the Lord, both vocally and instrumentally.

Neither the Lord Jesus, nor the Apostles ever condemned the use of music in Church worship. They endorsed it and encouraged it. The eternal order of worship in the Book of Revelation confirms it. The New Testament believers continually appealed to the Psalms in preaching and teaching as well as things pertaining to worship.

The singing of Psalms in Christian worship was undoubtedly carried over from the Synagogue worship, from the Jewish tradition into the Church. There is not a word against the use of music in Christian service in the New Testament. The heart, the hand, and the mouth should be used in worship to God and the Lamb. Praying, singing, praising, worshipping are all expressions of worship; so also is the playing of musical instruments.

The use of music in worship never seemed to be a serious problem before the 4th Century. David Appleby in History of Church Music (P. 31), states that Psalms singing in the early Christian Churches was of three types.

a. Direct psalmody, the singing of a complete Psalm, or a number of verses, without textual addition or modification.

b. Responsorial psalmody, taken directly from the Jewish Synagogue, in which the entire Psalm was sung by a soloist, while a choir or congregation responded with a short affirmative exclamation such as "Amen" or "Alleluia."

c. Antiphonal psalmody, thought to have been introduced by Ambrose, who used two alternating half-choruses, according to the practice in Syria.

Thus we have the ministry of music as mentioned by the New Testament writers through to the close of the Apostolic era under the Apostle John, A.D. 26-95.

E. Music in Church History.

The history of music with regard to Church history can only receive the briefest attention. The student is encouraged to refer to those works which deal exclusively with this subject. Church music will be considered under five periods: the Patristic Period; the Medieval Period; the Reformation Period; the Post-Reformation Period; and the Modern Period.

1. The Patristic Period (A.D. 95-600).

The earliest Christian hymns are the Songs of Elizabeth (Luke 1:42-45) and Mary (Luke 1:46-55). The Psalms also were sung by believers. In time, Christians began to write their own spiritual songs along the lines of Apostolic teaching and thousands have been found to be in existence. Ancient manuscripts show many poems of praise to Christ in the Greek language; these being called "Christian Odes."

Some of the Church fathers indicate the attitude to music during the Patristic Period.

a. Ignatius (A.D. 30-107) wrote a hymn just before he was martyred.

b. The Roman Emperor appointed Pliny (Born A.D. 79) to investigate the customs, methods, and beliefs of the Christians. In his report, Pliny stated that "They have a custom of meeting before dawn on an appointed day, and singing by turn hymns to Christ."

c. Josephus, a noted Jewish historian, accounts how often the Christians in the Coliseum arena, as they waited the coming of the lions to destroy them, would sing so loud and triumphantly that their singing could be heard above the roars of the lions and the shouting of the blood-thirsty Roman spectators.

d. Clement of Alexandria (A.D. 150-220) was one of the earliest hymn writers. He composed many hymns. Clement, however, condemned the use of instruments in public worship because of their use in Pagan rituals and superstitious rites. Questions were raised in the Post-Apostolic era as to whether music should be instrumental or only vocal; whether the Psalms and sacred poems should be sung to new tunes or Jewish and heathen melodies.

Clement seems to "allegorize" the musical instruments of Psalm 150 to be significant of the believer worshipping God with his whole being (Anti-Nicene Fathers, Vol. II, P. 248-249). All of this was a reaction against the worldy and ungodly use of musical instruments. He once wrote a letter to a friend saying, "We cultivate our fields praising; we sail the seas, hymning; our lives are filled with prayers and praises and Scripture readings, before meals and before bed, and even during the night. By this means we unite ourselves to the heavenly choir."

e. Athenagoras (A.D. 177) also left a hymn behind him before he was martyred. This was used by Christians for several centuries afterwards.

f. Tertullian (A.D. 150-225) in Apology 39 records that at the Love-Feasts (Agapae), after the water was furnished for the hands, and the lights lit, according as any remembered Scripture or could compose (cf., 1 Corinthians 14:26, improvised Psalms) he was invited to sing praises to God for the general good. He left many accounts of the habits of the early Christians of the First Century. He mentions that their meetings had plenty of songs, verses, sentences, and proverbs.

It was interesting also to note that false teachers (such as Arius) made use of music to instill their particular doctines into the minds and hearts of people in this period.

g. Eusebius Pamphilius of Caesarea (A.D. 260-340) records in his History of the Church:

> "When someone had started to sing a psalm to a soft melody, the congregation, at first, would listen in silence, and only sing in chorus the last verses of the hymn."

h. The 3rd Century tells of great controversy which arose over the use of the Psalms of David and the use of humanly-composed hymns. Some contended that only that which was inspired by the Spirit of God, as the Psalms, should be sung. They contended that other songs were sacrilegious. Others felt that God could inspire hymns of praise and worship for New Testament saints as much as He did the Old Testament saints. These contended that the Psalms of David pointed prophetically to Christ, while Christian songs testified of their fulfillment. This controversy was to last until A.D. 1600 and even beyond that time.

i. John Chrysostom (A.D. 354-407) warned his people against the licentious character of various chants. He taught that there was no need of instruments, or trained voices, but the true song that came from the heart of the worshipper. This was the New Testament "instrument."

j. Jerome (A.D. 340-420) confirmed that music was an aid to worship by exhorting believers to sing psalms, hymns, and spiritual songs from the heart. He warned against the turning of the house of God into a theatre.

k. The Synod of Laodocia (A.D. 343-381) passed a regulation that "psalms composed by private men must not be used in the Church." This Council of Laodocia also ruled that none should sing in the Church except those regularly appointed singers. Women were later excluded from choirs in A.D. 578, except in convents. This is interesting in the light of Christ's letter to the Church at Laodocia in Revelation 3:14-22.

l. Basil the Great (A.D. 330-378) preferred the use of the psaltery over all other instruments in accompanying the singing of the Psalms.

m. Ambrose (A.D. 337-397) encouraged congregational singing, wrote many hymns, and also strongly favoured humanly-composed hymns.

n. Augustine (A.D. 350-430), though having mixed emotions about music, does write an exposition on Psalm 146 in which he seems to favour Psalm singing accompanied by the musical instrument, the psaltery according to Appleby (P. 25).

o. Bishop Gregory (A.D. 540-604), one of the greatest Popes of the Catholic Church had a great influence on Christian singing. He rejected congregational singing, believing that the laity should not participate. He said that singing was a clerical function. He reformed much of the current religious music and originated the "Gregorian Chants" as being more stately and solemn monotone for the Church music. He founded a school for religious music in Rome, and sent out its graduates throughout Europe to teach his theories and principles.

p. The Council of Braga (A.D. 563) forbad all singing except the Psalms of David.

In our brief sketch of the Patristic period we note the decline of worship in contrast to that joyful, spontaneous and full-hearted singing of the Apostolic era. The use of musical instruments in Christian worship seemed to be frowned upon as the decline set in. As the Church became more official, the people became less spiritual, so worship became more formal and liturgical. Congregational singing was discarded, humanly-composed hymns were suppressed, and what singing there was passed into the hands of the clergy. Instead of joyful and melodious hymns and spiritual songs, solemn and mournful chanting of the Psalms was brought in. Creativity in music almost perished. Church trials, divisions, wranglings, charges of heresy and excommunications characterized this period in the long battle over the place of music in Christian worship.

2. The Medieval Period (A.D. 600-1517).

The period of the Middle Ages has been called "The Dark Ages" or "The Church's Babylonian Captivity." The song of the heart almost died during this one thousand year period. Congregational singing became almost extinct, singing being confined to the clergy. A few voices endeavoured to revive the lost art of Christian song.

a. Bernard of Clairvaux wrote many beautiful songs and urged Christians to sing.

b. St. Francis of Assissi (A.D. 1182-1225) also emphasized the importance of Christian singing. Many joyful songs were composed by him.

c. Musical instruments were ruled out in the Church. The Catholic Church frowned upon the development of music. Outside the Church, the 14th Century revealed an important development of musical instruments. The period abounded with all types of instruments coming into their own -- string, woodwind, and percussion instruments of various types. Viols, harps, psalteries, lutes, trumpets, drums, chimes, cymbals, bagpipes, reeds, horns, and flutes are mentioned. The organ was called "king of all instruments."

Secular music as an art developed, but music in the Church remained stagnant, owing to the Papal denunciations of secular music. This stifled creative effort in the Church. Musicians were forced to flee to the secular world to find freedom of expressions and recognition. The organ was generally accepted in the Church.

d. Songs to the Virgin Mary, as well as to other saints, dominated the scene of the Middle Ages, in the 11th and 12 centuries. Very few songs were composed to God or Christ. Mary and the saints seemed to be more sympathetic to the needs of the people, while God the Father and Christ were presented in anger and sternness. The sad depressive spiritual state of the previous centuries deepened in this era.

Perhaps this period could be summed up in the stand of the Catholic Church concerning Church music as Stevenson in Patterns of Protestant Church Music (p. 147) states it: The teaching of Pope Pius X (1903) on Church music is "that the Gregorian Chant has always been regarded as the peculiar heritage of the Catholic Church, and therefore a type of music that is her very own - regarded as the supreme model for sacred music." He also says that the congregation as well as the choir should learn how to sing chant, as long as Gregorian music or other music following the musical ideals embodied in the Gregorian Chant are used. This has been the stand of the Catholic Church for centuries, especially since the time of Gregory the Great, and the introduction of the "Gregorian Chants."

In summarizing this period, Psalms 137 may well be applied here. As in Israel's Babylonian Captivity, so in the Church's spiritual captivity. How could any sing the Lord's song in a strange land?

How could any take their musical instruments off the willow tree when the Church was in bondage? No music or song in the Church was evidence of the lack of divine blessing on His people. It was evidence of judgment.

3. The Reformation Period (A.D. 1517-1600).

With the Renaissance and the spread of Protestant Reformation in the 15th and 16th Centuries, religious music, amongst other arts, began to come into its own again. With the revival of true religious experience came a revival of Christian music. The Lord began to "turn again the captivity of Zion." Mouths were filled with laughter, tongues with singing. Music and singing began to be heard in the earth once again, an evident sign of the blessing of the Lord beginning to flow again "as the streams in the south" (Psalms 126).

Again, we note only several of the most important vessels that the Lord used in the Reformation period in the restoration of song and music in the Church.

a. Martin Luther (A.D. 1483-1546), the father of the Reformation period, played one of the greatest parts in the restoration of music to the Chruch. Others before him had prepared the way, but Luther gave Christian music the forward thrust that was needed.

John Huss (Martyred A.D. 1415), leader of the Bohemian Brethren, and his followers sang. He circulated the first congregational song book in 1504.

Luther not only gave the German people the Bible in their own language, he gave them Christian songs in their own language. The Roman Catholic Church had confined singing to the clergy in the Latin tongue, a tongue that the people understood not (cf. 1 Corinthians 14:13-17). Luther composed new hymns and encouraged others to do so. With the printing press having been recently invented, this aided the wide distribution of Bibles and hymnbooks. Hymns to the Virgin Mary and to the saints became obsolete. Some people who were in possession of Luther's hymnbooks were imprisoned, tortured or put to death.

Music was a vital part of Luther's fame. Thousands would sing the song of the Reformation, singing the truth into their own hearts as also the hearts of others. Luther recognized that Catholic music was too solemn. He contended for beauty and melody, cheerfulness and joy in Christian song. He ranked music second only to theology. Though condemning much of Roman practice, he never condemned music itself.

Luther was well acquainted with the Gregorian Chants. Luther held out for polyphonic (use of other parts) music, which has been resisted for centuries. He felt that the whole domain of music was a vast storehouse, from which the Church should take and use the best to praise God. Some conscientous people believed that elaborate music was sensuous, as was ungodly music. They failed to distinguish between good and evil use of music, not that music was evil in itself. Luther used German folk tunes, popular songs and set them with suitable words to glorify God.

Robert M. Stevenson, in Patterns of Protestant Church Music (P. 4), after documentation and examination lists eight specific reasons which made Luther's principles of Church music attractive, both then and today. These are as follows:

1. He showed admirable discrimination in his own evaluation of contemporary composers and this set a standard of correct musical judgment;

2. He defined music as an art which to be appreciated properly must be studied rather than listened to;

3. He made music study a mandatory part of the curriculum in all schools organized under his auspices;

4. He required the ministers who followed his lead to study singing and made an understanding of music a prerequisite to ordination;

5. He overrode the scruples of those who, following St. Augustine's example, feared elaborate Church music on moral grounds;

6. He spoke often and ardently in behalf of excellence in Church music;

7. While exalting the role of the congregation he never minimized the role of the organist or of the choir in Church music;

8. He upheld the right of musicians to an adequate and assured income from Church sources.

These were Luther's ideals in music. They are still in good standing. The spiritual battle song of the Reformation was Luther's own Hymn, "A Mighty Fortress is our God." Though not majoring on musical instruments in the Church, Luther did allow the organ along with congregational and choir singing. He allowed human-composed hymns as well as Psalm singing. He never allowed instruments to be destroyed, as did Calvin's followers.

Thus, even as Luther was used to plant properly the seed-truth of "justification by faith," so he was used to restore the seed-music of singing of hymns and songs unto the Lord. This "seed" would be watered by the Spirit in due time, and bring forth the harmony of God, in the Church.

b. <u>John Calvin (A.D. 1509-1564).</u>

About the same period of time that Luther was shaking Germany, John Calvin (Presbyterians hold to him) was doing the same thing in France and Switzerland. Though differing doctrinally from Luther in some areas, he did preach personal salvation with God through Christ. Multitudes experienced salvation under his ministry.

Calvin, as Luther, realized his people needed vocal expression for Christian experiences. He encouraged congregational singing. However, in contrast to Luther, he strongly disapproved of humanly-composed hymns. He insisted that only the inspired Psalms of David could be sung in Christian worship. The Psalms, in time, were arranged metrically and many of them sung to commonly known ballad tunes. When eventually the 150 Psalms were arranged metrically, they were known as "The Genevan Psalter," all Psalms having tunes for them, some tunes being used for several psalms. Most of the Psalters used in England and Scotland trace their parentage to that original Genevan Psalter. Congregational singing was revived in France and Switzerland; most believers brought their own Psalter to the services.

Again, Calvin allowed no instrumental (organ) music in the Churches of Geneva. He also opposed the introduction of any part-singing into congregational singing. Stevenson (P. 14, 15) states that Calvin taught that instrumental music was only tolerated in Israel under the Law because the people were then in infancy. Calvin, in commenting on Psalms 92:4 concerning musical instruments speaks of these things as being shadows of a departed dispensation. He comments on Psalms 149 that "musical instruments .... were peculiar to this infancy of the Church, nor should we foolishly imitate a practice which was intended only for God's ancient people!" On 1 Corinthians 14:13, as an argument against musical instruments, Calvin makes Paul say that we must pray and praise God only in a known tongue.

Under Calvin, in Europe, England, and Scotland, organs in Churches were destroyed or melted down in order to retain the tin from the pipes. Calvinists taught that "singing with instruments was typical, and so a ceremonial worship and therefore is ceased."

Because Calvin knew the emotional power of music, and feared it, he had a distaste for organs, a distaste for hymns, and a distaste for part-singing in Church music. He denied the power of the Holy Spirit to inspire men to praise God in fresh ways, therefore limited the Church music to the inspired Psalms of David only.

It was upon the foundation Calvin laid in Psalm singing that the English and Scottish singing was built. The Church of England and the Church of Scotland favoured only singing from the Psalter.

There was a period of time in England, under Charles the First and Queen Mary ("Bloody Mary") when Psalm singing and hymn singing were totally banned in Church services. However, nothing could suppress the song in the heart. Accounts tell how often thousands of people would gather together after the services and sing and praise God. In time the ban was lifted and singing began to take its place more in Christian services.

It was not until over three hundred years later, or about A.D. 1866-1883 that some of the branches of the Presbyterian Church allowed organs within their buildings, along with hymns of human composure, and the singing of parts in congregational singing. However, some branches still reject such today. Very few Presbyterians today hold with Calvin's music philosophy regarding hymns and organs.

Adam Clarke in, A Commentary and Critical Notes of the Old Testament (P. 610), expresses clearly the view of those who rejected musical instruments in Christian services. In commenting on 1 Chronicles 16:42 concerning the musicians which David placed at Gibeon in Moses' Tabernacle, he writes;

> "Query, Did God ever ordain instruments of music to be used in his worship? Can they be used in Christian assemblies according to the spirit of Christianity? Has Jesus Christ, or his apostles, ever commanded or sanctioned the use of them? Were they ever used any where in the apostolic Church? Does the use of them at present, in Christian congregations, ever increase the spirit of devotion? Does it ever appear that bands of musicians, either in their collective or individual capacity, are more spiritual, or as spiritual, as the other parts of the Church of Christ? Is there less pride, self-will, stubbornness, insubordination, lightness, and frivolity, among such persons, than among the other professors of Christianity found in the same religious society? Is it ever remarked or known that musicians in the house of God have attained to any depth of piety, or superior soundness of understanding, in the things of God? Is it ever found that those Churches and Christian societies which have and use instruments of music in Divine worship are more holy, or as holy, as those societies which do not use them? And is it always found that the ministers which affect and recommend them to be used in the worship of Almighty God, are the most spiritual men, and the most spiritual and useful preachers? Can mere sounds, no matter how melodious, where no word nor sentiment is or can be uttered, be considered as giving praise to God? Is it possible that pipes or strings of any kind can give God praise? Can God be pleased with

sounds which are emitted by no sentient being, and have in themselves no meaning? If these questions cannot be answered in the affirmative; then, query, Is not the introduction of such instruments into the worship of God antichristian, and calculated to debase and ultimately ruin the spirit and influence of the Gospel of Jesus Christ? And should not all who wish well to the spread and establishment of pure and undefiled religion, lift up their hand, their influence, and their voice against them? The argument from their use in the Jewish service is futile in the extreme when applied to Christianity.

The great lesson one can learn from this is that resistance to change can become a source of strength and/or weakness when it comes to progress in the Church. Especially has this been so in the realm of Church music.

4. The Post-Reformation Period (A.D. 1600-1800).

The Reformation period was certainly a revival of singing (if not of musical instruments) in the Church, with particular emphasis on Psalm singing. The battle was long and hard even to restore this to the Church in her worship to God.

The Post-Reformation was a period in which the great struggle concerning music in the Church continued. The point of contention in this time centered around the recovery and use of HYMN singing! That is, humanly-composed hymns. Luther had contended for both Psalm and hymn singing, as well as limited use of instruments, and congregation and choir part singing. Calvin had contended for congregational Psalm singing only; no organs, no instruments, no choirs, no part singing. The Psalter, generally speaking, won the battle for centuries in most Churches.

In A.D. 1623, King James in England sanctioned a book of "Hymns and Songs of the Church," along with the Metrical Psalms. He was forced to withdraw it because of the greatest of opposition in the Church.

The musical giants of this period (1700-1750) were Bach and Handel, as far as Church music and opera music were concerned. Both had their battles for expression and recognition of the talents given to them.

The Puritans were very antagonistic to choirs and musical instruments. Humanly composed hymns were counted sacrilegious. The Puritans looked upon with disfavour any joyful or pleasant hymns. Their preaching centered around holiness, death, and hell. In A.D. 1640, the "Bay Psalm Book" was printed and all singing was confined to the Psalter. Psalm singing became a lifeless expression for multitudes. But, music and song within the hearts of God's people was bursting for expression, some other form than the lifeless singing of Psalms. We mention only several persons who stand out preeminently because of their contribution to Christian music in the area of hymn singing.

a. Isaac Watts (A.D. 1707), gave new impetus to humanly-composed hymns, as well as Metric Psalm singing. He maintained that the Psalms was primarily a Hebrew book and that many of the Psalms were not written in the spirit of a New Testament worshipper.

Because the Church would not listen to anything unless it was Davidic he used "Psalm Imitations" (paraphrase of the Psalms) as a point of departure from the customary singing and thus opened the way for hymns of human composure. He wrote many hymns, as well as compiled others. Hymn singing as part of the congregational life was strenuously opposed by the established and dissenting Churches of England and Scotland. Watts, though holding heretical views of Christ's person (Arianism tendency) wrote many hymns which are noble as pertaining to Christ's humanity. Also there was a note of joy in many of these hymns. The 20th Century owes this much to Watts, that he pioneered strongly the use of hymns in congregational singing amidst great opposition.

b. The Moravians were the first Christians in America to freely allow the use of musical instruments in their services. Disciples of John Huss (A.D. 1722), and also known as United Brethren, early references speak of violins,clarinets, trumpets, trombones, harps, and organs being used in their services.

c. John & Charles Wesley (A.D. 1737-1784).

The Wesley brothers gave great impetus to singing, especially hymn singing. Wesley was greatly influenced by Watt's psalms and hymns as well as the joyful and triumphant singing of the Moravian believers.

After John's conversion, the Wesleys became convinced that congregational singing was important in the place of worship. It is interesting to note that in A.D. 1737, while Wesley was in the Anglican Communion he was called before a Grand Jury to answer charges of changing the order of the Liturgy, singing versions of the Psalms which were changed, and then singing hymns which had not been inspected by the proper authorities.

In A.D. 1737-1784 several issues of "Collection of Psalms and Hymns" had been published. In fact, the first Anglican hymnal later became the first Methodist hymnal.

The Wesley brothers wrote over six thousand hymns, dealing with theological and experiential topics. Thousands were attracted by these hymns and enjoyed singing them. There is more sound theology in the hymns of Wesley than others. The Wesleys would take any secular or popular tunes which came out and convert them to the use of the Church, as well as compose their own tunes.

The American colonies were swept by the influence of the Wesleyan awakening. People began to break with the lifeless Psalm singing to enjoy hymn singing. The revivals under Charles Finney, Jonathan Edwards, and Whitefield (during the 1700's) gave great thrust to the singing of Isaac Watt's hymns.

With the coming of American independence, hymn authors and composers began to come into their own place of expression. As in previous generations, so at this time, hymn singing met with fierce opposition. The Congregational, Baptist and Presbyterian Church, which came to favour humanly composed hymns, became satisfied with Watt's Hymnals. The Methodists were satisfied with Wesley's Hymns.

The question of musical instruments continued to be controversial for many generations. The organ had been rejected by the early Baptists and Presbyterians. The early Methodists also were slow to accept the use of instruments in Church worship, following the example of the Wesleys of the Anglican Church.

5. The Modern Period (A.D. 1800-1976).

a. The Salvation Army (A.D. 1879 --).

William Booth, founder of the Salvation Army, had been baptized into the Anglican communion, but his religious life had been nurtured in Methodism. When the time came that he separated himself from the Methodist Church, he and his wife betook themselves to their life passion, the saving of souls. His motto was "Go for souls and go for the worst." This they did.

The Salvation Army, in due time, developed their own hymn book, compiling hymns from various others, especially the Methodist hymn book, as well as composing many of their own based on the experiences of the early converts.

As to the origin of Salvation Army Bands, the record provides interesting reading. Booth and some of his officers saw a Presbyterian group using brass instruments in street meetings. From this he gained the idea of forming a band. Thus when the Salvation Army was born, band music became a vital part of Army worship. Booth, like Luther, Wesley, and others, also took well-known tunes and melodies from the secular world and converted them to praise and testimony of the Lord.

For people who have been accustomed to Church organ music and a more solemn approach in congregational singing, the Salvation Army services, with clapping of hands, beating of tambourines, shouts of "Hallelujah," along with brass band instruments and drums, are quite a shock! However, all of these things are indeed Scriptural expressions of worship unto the Lord. What opposition and resistance the early Salvationists experienced is now a matter of history.

b. The Gospel Song.

As the previous centuries had witnessed the struggle in the Church to accept singing of the Psalms, and later periods to accept the singing of hymns, the modern period saw the difficult rise of the gospel song.

By the early 19th Century, hymns of German, English, and American composers were more accepted and new hymnals were published. By the middle of the century many hymnals appeared on the scene. Many names could be mentioned. Originally many of the hymnals had only the words printed, then later on some had a few select tunes in a section. In due time many had the words and tunes published. The hymn book had won the battle for its right to exist and had found its place in the Church. Musical instruments also gradually appeared in many Churches after the long hard struggle. It was during the 19th Century that the gospel song came into its own. Phil Kerr (P. 56) stated it well when he wrote, "Just as, a century earlier, Psalm-singers had objected to the use of hymns, now hymn-singers opposed the use of gospel songs."

The gospel song came to meet a specific need; the need of a popular song in which people could express the experience of the heart born as a result of evangelistic emphasis. The gospel song was born in an emotionally charged atmosphere of the camp meeting, prayer meeting, and evangelistic preaching.

Of the many that could be mentioned by name, Ira D. Sankey stands out as the most prominent channel that the Lord used in this area. He was D.L. Moody's campaign singer and under his ministry of song and music he stirred untold thousands into the kingdom of God. He overcame opposition to the gospel song even as previous men of God had overcome opposition to the use of hymns and Psalms.

Kerr (P. 57) makes his distinction between Psalms, hymns, and gospel songs in the following manner:

1. A psalm is a praise song, and may be set to music. Especially seen in the use of the Psalter.

2. A hymn is a prayer song and may also be set to music. Generally hymns are addressed to Father, Son and Holy Spirit.

3. A gospel song is a testimony song set to music. It is addressed to people, generally in the way of testimony or exhortation.

It is to be recognized that some Christian songs cannot be strictly categorized in the above as some may be a combination of praise, prayer, or testimony. Only the language of the verses will show this.

The gospel song has been America's most typical contribution to Christian music, as the hymn has been England's and the psalms have been Europe's contribution.

Church history certainly reveals that human nature fears and resists change. This has been so in the history of the place of music in the Christian Church and her worship.

c. The Pentecostals (A.D. 1900 - 1950).

In the 1900's God poured out His Spirit upon hungry believers waiting upon Him to receive the Baptism of the Holy Spirit, according to Acts 2:4. The "Pentecostal revival" spread around the world in a short number of years. Again there was a distinctive type of song which characterized the Pentecostals. Their singing was alive, spontaneous, and whole-hearted. They used hymns and gospel songs, and also numerous choruses to express their faith. Some of these hymns were born out of the distinctive truth entrusted to them. With all the variety of Churches in the Pentecostal framework, most of them accept the use of musical instruments of all kinds in their services. Some of the larger Pentecostal denominations have large orchestras and music plays a large part in their services.

d. The Charismatic Renewal (A.D. 1950 ---).

In the last twenty to thirty years there has been a definite outpouring of the Holy Spirit upon the Church. It has been identified by various names, by reason of various truths that were recovered to the Church in these years. For the sake of simplicity the word "charismatic" is used in a very broad sense to embrace the truths which God has been emphasizing in the Church during these years. It is beyond the purpose of this text to deal with these truths. (For the student interested in these things, "Present Day Truths" by Reverend K.R. (Dick) Iverson may be purchased at the publishers.)

In the years of 1948-1950 God poured out His Spirit upon some people who were praying and fasting and seeking the Lord for a renewal of the ministries and gifts of the Spirit which belonged to the Church. God visited this company of people and gave specific revelation of things which He desired to restore to the Church in these Last Days.

In those days of waiting upon God, people gathered together under this visitation of the Spirit and sought the face of God. The Spirit of the Lord moved upon the congregation in holy worship. Many heard the "Heavenly Choir." Others heard heavenly music. The congregation was swept upon by the Spirit of God and praise and song of the Lord came forth as the "sound of rushing waters." Spiritual songs were born in the midst of the times of waiting upon God.

Since that time, that "seed" that was sown in that outpouring of the Spirit has brought forth fruit, and now across the world, there is heard praise among the people of God. Spiritual songs are coming forth, congregational praises are being sung, vocal and instrumental music is being heard in many Churches. God's people are seeing that there is a new level of worship in music and song that the Lord is wanting to bring His people into.

The winds of change are blowing across the Church. Many Churches are being challenged with what the Lord is doing today. As usual, resistance to change is being evidenced. But many hungry hearts, tired of death and formalism, are responding to a fresh expression of the life of Christ.

One of the things which distinctly characterize the ministry of music in those believers who are responding to God is the singing of the Scriptures. Perhaps as never before in Church history, the Scriptures are being sung -- Scriptures from Old and New Testament. Songs, melodies, and tunes are being used to sing the Scriptures into the hearts and minds of Christians. Not melancholy or mournful tunes, but melodies of joy, praise, triumph, and rejoicing.

e. Psalms, Hymns and Spiritual Songs.

The author believes that God is desirous of having a balanced Church, a Church that can sing and make melody in her heart unto the Lord in "... psalms and hymns and spiritual songs..." (Colossians 3:16; Ephesians 5:18, [19]).

God has given to the Church a threefold expression of music and song. There is no need for reaction of one against the other. Church history has revealed the resistance to music in the Christian worship; the reaction to Psalms, then to hymns and then to gospel songs, and in our day to spiritual songs.

In a subsequent chapter, guidelines for the choice of proper music, music that is suitable to the house of the Lord, will be dealt with. For the present it is helpful to recognize the need of the three areas of music listed in Colossians and Ephesians.

1. Psalms (Greek "Psalmos")

A Psalm is a song accompanied by a musical instrument, especially the harp. No one knows the exact style or tunes of the Hebrews when they sang the Psalms. However, God is a God of infinite variety. He can give suitable tunes to the Psalms. There is no need of the mournful dirgy chanting of the Psalms. The Psalms are Psalms of praise and worship, generally speaking. God is inspiring good tunes to many verses of the Psalms today that are suitable for congregational singing and which minister life.

2. Hymns (Greek "Humneo")

There are many, many wonderful hymns of the Church. One cannot take his theology from the hymn book, but many of the great hymns have sound theology in them. One of the dangers today is the cry that hymns are dead. It should be remembered than many of the hymns were born out of a genuine experience with God and that life was originally ministered when first sung. The problem was that suceeding generations lacked the experience and spirit of the hymn and had not been quickened by the Spirit themselves. How then could people "dead in sins" sing a hymn that had been "quickened by the Spirit"? The problem was not with the hymn but with those who sang the hymn. It was this that made many of the hymns appear dead and lifeless to those who centuries later sang them. Some of these same hymns, made alive by the Spirit of God to a congregation alive by that same Spirit minister life to those that sing. There is a place for hymns which have good sound theology as well as experiential truth in them.

3. Spiritual Songs (Greek "Odes")

A spiritual song is a song that is quickened by the Holy Spirit. It may be spontaneous in a given service. It may be a song quickened to a believer that all may learn and be edified. It is not to be mistaken for the "Negro spiritual" which was the particular expression of the Negro people in their worship to God. It is not to be mistaken for the "gospel song" as dealt with under Ira D. Sankey's era. Both of these have their place. The "spiritual song" is more of a spontaneous expression of the heart as believers gather together for worship, or as an individual worships God in his own devotions.

> "O sing unto the Lord a new song ..." (Psalms 96:1; 98:1).
> "I call to remembrance my song ..." (Psalms 77:6).
> "He hath put a new song in my mouth..." (Psalms (40:3).
> "...his song shall be with me ..." (Psalms 42:8).
> "... and with my song will I praise Him ..." (Psalms 28:7).

In concluding our sketch of music in Church history with the above, it is the WORD OF GOD which becomes the final test for all music in the Church.

> "Let the WORD OF CHRIST (The Anointed) dwell in you richly in all wisdom; teaching and admonishing one another in psalms and hymns and spiritual songs, singing with grace in your hearts to the Lord" (Colossians 3:16).

All music and song must be tested by the Word of the Lord. If it is contrary to the Word, if it does not teach or edify, then it does not qualify for music in the house of the Lord.

The Church has only just begun to enter into the realms of the music of heaven. Surely Church history reveals the many attempts to return to that order of worship which was established in the Tabernacle of David.

Evangeline Booth of the Salvation Army truly said, "Music is the gift of God to man! The only art of heaven given to earth and the only art of earth we take back to heaven. But music like every gift is only given to us in the seed. It is for us to unfold, and cultivate, that its wondrous blossoms may bless our own path and bless all those who meet us upon it. Sing these songs in your heart or do not sing them at all."

The author believes that a proper understanding of the relationship of the Tabernacle of David to the Church order of ministry and worship would have helped solve many of the obstacles and much of the opposition which came in Church history over the place of music in Christianity.

MINISTRY OF MUSIC IN SCRIPTURE
(CHRIST'S MINISTRY)

Col 1:10-19. Rev 22:16.
Prov 8:23-31. Heb 2:12.

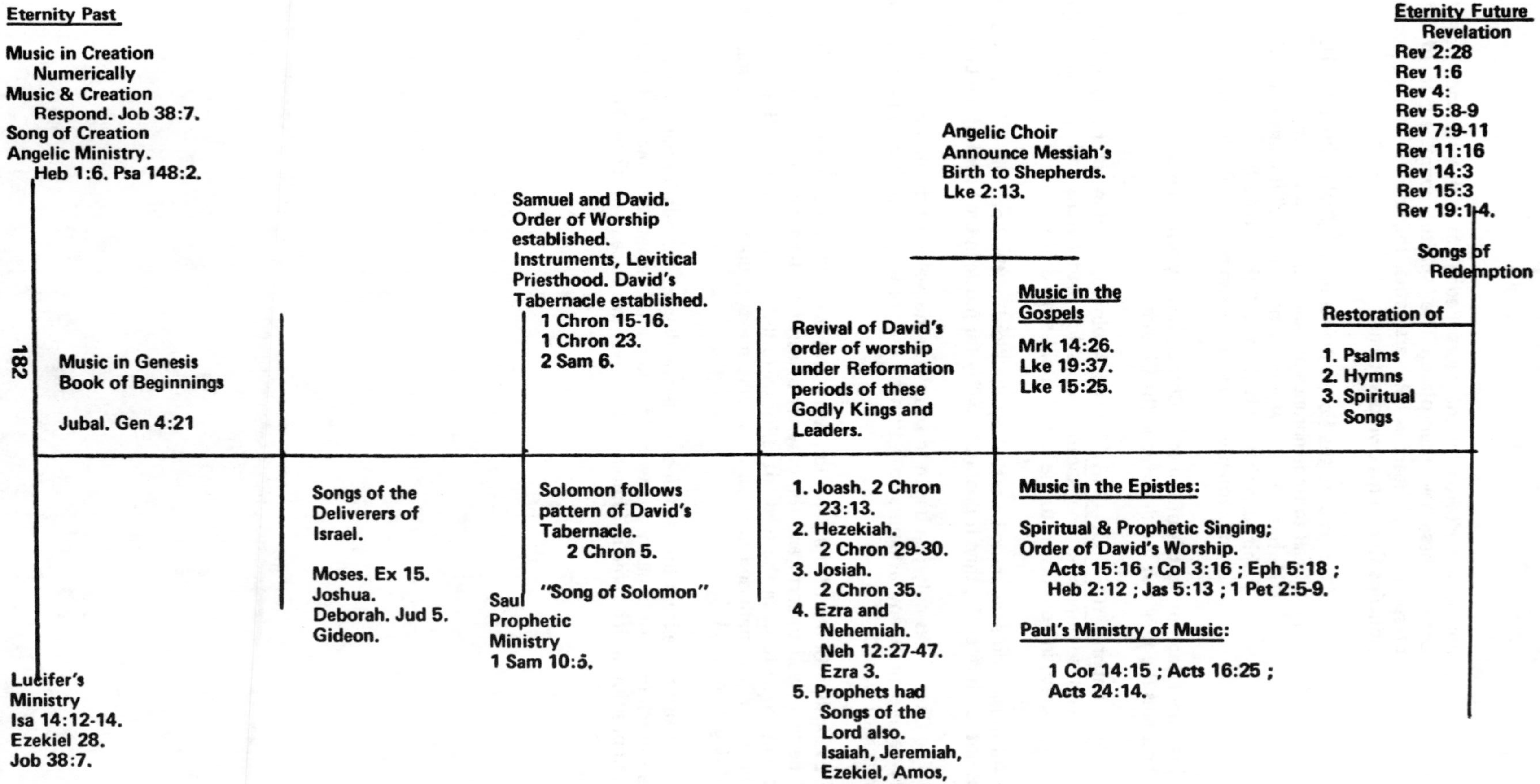
Eternity Past
Music in Creation Numerically
Music & Creation Respond. Job 38:7.
Song of Creation
Angelic Ministry. Heb 1:6. Psa 148:2.
Music in Genesis Book of Beginnings
Jubal. Gen 4:21
Lucifer's Ministry
Isa 14:12-14.
Ezekiel 28.
Job 38:7.
Songs of the Deliverers of Israel.
Moses. Ex 15.
Joshua.
Deborah. Jud 5.
Gideon.
Samuel and David. Order of Worship established. Instruments, Levitical Priesthood. David's Tabernacle established.
1 Chron 15-16.
1 Chron 23.
2 Sam 6.
Saul Prophetic Ministry 1 Sam 10:5.
Solomon follows pattern of David's Tabernacle.
2 Chron 5.
"Song of Solomon"
Revival of David's order of worship under Reformation periods of these Godly Kings and Leaders.
1. Joash. 2 Chron 23:13.
2. Hezekiah. 2 Chron 29-30.
3. Josiah. 2 Chron 35.
4. Ezra and Nehemiah. Neh 12:27-47. Ezra 3.
5. Prophets had Songs of the Lord also. Isaiah, Jeremiah, Ezekiel, Amos, Habukkuk, Zephaniah.
Angelic Choir Announce Messiah's Birth to Shepherds. Lke 2:13.
Music in the Gospels
Mrk 14:26.
Lke 19:37.
Lke 15:25.
Music in the Epistles:
Spiritual & Prophetic Singing; Order of David's Worship.
Acts 15:16 ; Col 3:16 ; Eph 5:18 ; Heb 2:12 ; Jas 5:13 ; 1 Pet 2:5-9.
Paul's Ministry of Music:
1 Cor 14:15 ; Acts 16:25 ; Acts 24:14.
Restoration of
1. Psalms
2. Hymns
3. Spiritual Songs
Songs of Redemption
Eternity Future
Revelation
Rev 2:28
Rev 1:6
Rev 4:
Rev 5:8-9
Rev 7:9-11
Rev 11:16
Rev 14:3
Rev 15:3
Rev 19:1-4.

Diagram Arranged by
Mike Herron.

Chapter 23

THE ORDER OF SINGERS AND MUSICIANS

The ministry of the singers and musicians was given prominence in David's time. It was u doubtedly the peak of Israel's national history in many ways, especially in the area of worship.

In outline form we will consider the order of David and the privilege, ministry, and respons bility of the singers and musicans in the Tabernacle of David, and later on, in Solomon's Templ

1. The Singers and Musicians were appointed (1 Chronicles 16:9, 23; 15: 16-28).

   2 Chronicles 20:21, the word "appointed" means "to cause to stand." They were assign ed an office, ordained, equipped for this function. It was not merely the use of a talent but was a ministry to the Lord in Israel.

2. The Singers and Musicians were separated (1 Chronicles 25:1).

   The word "separated" means that they were selected and set apart to this function Separated to the ministry of song.

3. The Singers and Musicians were instructed (1 Chronicles 25:1-7; 2 Chronicles 23:13)

   The singers and musicians were instructed in the songs of the Lord. There were thos who taught them to sing praise to God. The 288 singers needed instruction in order to releas that which God had placed in their hearts.

4. The Singers and Musicians had a Director (1 Chronicles 15:22, 27).

   Chenaniah, which interpreted means "preparation, made by God, favour of God" was chosen to be the Master of the Song. He was actually the choir leader and director. The singers and musicians were taught under his hands.

5. The Singers and Musicians were in various ranks (1 Chronicles 15:16-18).

   There were three chief singers and musicians. Then there were others of the "second degree," that is, the second order and rank. So there are those in the house of the Lord who have their various skills in the ministry of music.

6. The Singers and Musicians were chosen by name (1 Chronicles 16:37-41).

   David chose these Levites and they were expressed by name. Those who had a ministry in song were recognized. Their gift made room for them.

7. The Singers and Musicians were skillful (1 Chronicles 15:22; 2 Chronicles 34:12; Psalms 33:3).

   The word skillful speaks of those who were practiced, those who were expert and had the ability to understand, perceive and perform in the service of the Lord. Ignorance and lack of skill find no virtue in the things of God. David could play well, and skillfully when he ministered before King Saul (1 Samuel 16:16, 17, 23). So those who have this ministry should seek to be skillful before the Lord.

8. The Singers and Musicians were employed in that work (1 Chronicles 9:22, 26-33: Ezekiel 40:44).

Various priests had their particular services in the Temple. Some of these were employed in the service of praise in the temple day and night. Many nations in Bible times had the highest talented musicians to minister in their palaces, and employed them to do so.

9. The Singers and Musicians had charge of the service of song (1 Chronicles 6:31-32).

The service of song (or song service) was the distinct charge given to the Levites in the Tabernacle of David, then later on incorporated in the Temple of Solomon. There are those whom the Lord gives a distinct ministry for leading the song service in His house.

10. The Singers and Musicians waited on their office (1 Chronicles 6:31-32; 2 Chronicles 7:6; 35:15).

Those who had this ministry had to wait on their office according to their order. It was not a haphazard thing but a sense of responsibility before the Lord. As others in the Body of Christ today have to wait on their ministry, attending to it as a priest, so does the singer and musician need to wait on their ministry (Romans 12:7).

11. The Singers and Musicians received their portions (Nehemiah 7:1, 44, 73; 10:28, 39; 11:22-23; 12:28-47; 13:5, 10).

In the restoration from Babylon, the singers and musicians were to be given their portion out of the Lord's house. Nehemiah lamented the fact that they had not been given their portion so that they could function in the ministry of song. So in the Church today. Those who minister in song and music should receive their portion from the Lord's storehouse. Without this spiritual portion, their function will cease.

12. The Singers and Musicians functioned in their courses (1 Chronicles 25:1-31).

The singers were numbered by David into twenty-four courses. There was someone on duty in their course throughout the twenty-four hours of the day and night praising the Lord (Psalms 134). There was a continual service of praise ascending to the Lord as the Levites waited in their particular course. What a glorious atmosphere to live in. God inhabits the praises of His people (Psalms 22:3).

Thus in the Church today, God has talented those who are singers and musicians. It is their ministry to the Lord and to the people of God. It is not just to display talent or skill but it is a service for which God had anointed and ordained them. Those who have this ministry have a responsibility to seek the Lord and wait on their office, so that in the service of song they will be able to lead God's people into the realms of worship which God desires.

The Church is the New Testament fulfillment of this order in David's Tabernacle. The ultimate vision of this order is found in the Book of Revelation. There we see the order of David represented in the twenty-four Elders who have harps and vials of incense which are the praises and prayers of the saints. These twenty-four Elders lead the hosts of the redeemed in the "new song" of worship and redemption to God and the Lamb, even as the twenty-four courses were the representative leaders of worship in Old Testament Israel (Revelation 4:4; 5:1-14). An understanding of the twenty-four courses of priests and its multiples of 144,000 in David's Tabernacle, which was incorporated into the Temple order, helps the believer to understand the order of worship in Revelation. There we see the twenty-four Elders with instruments of worship, singing a new song, as well as the 144,000 sealed ones out of the true Israel of God (Revelation 5:9-10; 14:1-3).

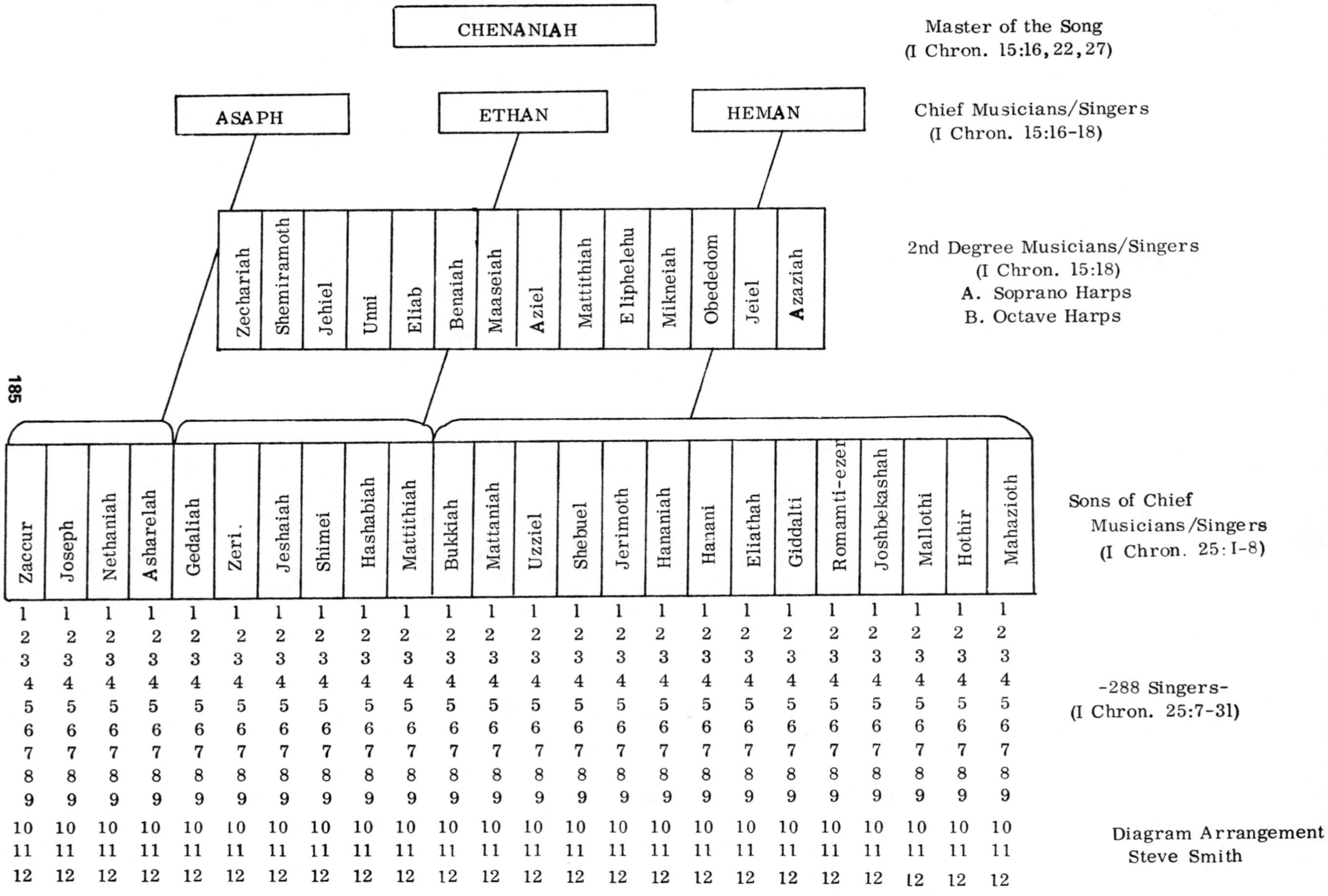
CHENANIAH
Master of the Song
(I Chron. 15:16, 22, 27)
ASAPH
ETHAN
HEMAN
Chief Musicians/Singers
(I Chron. 15:16-18)
Zechariah
Shemiramoth
Jehiel
Unni
Eliab
Benaiah
Maaseiah
Aziel
Mattithiah
E liphelehu
Mikneiah
Obededom
Jeiel
Azaziah
2nd Degree Musicians/Singers
(I Chron. 15:18)
A. Soprano Harps
B. Octave Harps
Zaccur
Joseph
Nethaniah
Asharelah
Gedaliah
Zeri.
Jeshaiah
Shimei
Hashabiah
Mattithiah
Bukkiah
Mattaniah
Uzziel
Shebuel
Jerimoth
Hananiah
Hanani
Eliathah
Giddalti
Romamti-ezer
Joshbekashah
Mallothi
Hothir
Mahazioth
Sons of Chief
Musicians/Singers
(I Chron. 25: I-8)
1 2 3 4 5 6 7 8 9 10 11 12
-288 Singers-
(I Chron. 25:7-31)
Diagram Arrangement
Steve Smith

Chapter 24

PSALM TITLES AND INSCRIPTIONS

The Book of Psalms was Israel's national hymnal or praise book. It was a book of sacred songs, songs of praise, prayer, worship, confidence, trust, thanksgiving, joy, history, prophecy, and theology. Almost every other theme that could be named is to be found in the Book of Psalms.

A. The Definition of the word.

1. The Hebrew title of the Book is "Sepher Tihillim," which means "praise" or "hymns," or "The Book of Praises."

Another Hebrew title calls it "Tephilloth," meaning "prayers." By bringing these two thoughts together the Book of Psalms becomes "The Book of Praise and Prayer."

2. The Greek title, from the Septuagint, "Psalmoi" means "songs," or "songs accompanied by a musical instrument." The Early Christian Fathers called it "The Psalter," from "Psalterion," meaning "a harp or other stringed instrument."

3. The English title is "The Psalms" (Luke 20:42; 24:44; Acts 1:20; Acts 13:33; 1 Corinthians 14:26).

4. A Psalm is a pruned song, an ode, or song intended to be sung, accompanied by a musical instrument, especially the harp. Many psalms are lyrical songs adpated to musical instruments for sanctuary worship (1 Chronicles 16:4-8; 2 Chronicles 5:12-13).

B. The Use of Psalms in the Early Church.

A study of the New Testatment shows clearly how the Early Church made good use of the Psalms.

1. The Psalms were used in worship in the assembly life (1 Corinthians 14:26).
2. The Psalms were used for joy and praise (James 5:13).
3. The Psalms were used for teaching, admonition and instruction in the Word of the Lord (Colossians 3:16).
4. The Psalms were sung along with hymns and spiritual songs (Ephesians 5:19).
5. The Lord Jesus and His disciples sang Psalms or hymns at the Last Supper (Mark 14:26; Luke 24:44-45).
6. The Lord exhorts His people to make a joyful noise to Him with Psalms (Psalms 81:2; 95:2; 98:5; 105:2; 1 Chronicles 16:9).

Saints of Old Testament and New Testament times used the Psalms in worship.

C. Psalm-Titles and Inscriptions.

Over approximately one hundred Psalms there are prefixed inscriptions (Authorized Version). These titles and inscriptions have been a matter of mystery over the centuries and difficult of explanation. The early Scriptures had no spaces between the Psalms, just the various numbers, making it difficult to see whether these inscriptions belonged to the end of one Psalm and/or the beginning of another. The solution to this puzzle has possibly been discovered in more recent times.

The Companion Bible, and J. Sidlow Baxter in Explore the Book (pp 91-97) supply some interesting information on these titles. According to these writers the super-inscription of these Psalm titles should be the sub-scription of the previous Psalm.

For a fuller treatment of these Psalm inscriptions, the reader should refer to the particular authors mentioned. Sufficient for the purpose of this text is to note five areas which these Psalm titles suggest to us. It should be remembered that some Psalms have none of these directions; others have one or more. However, when all viewed or brought together they provide interesting material and light on Israel's worship and use of the Psalms. All together they give instructions and directions for their proper and best use.

We consider these five areas which are suggested to us in the various Psalm titles and inscriptions, treating them as they are generally found in the Authorized Version.

1. <u>The Instructions to the Chief Musician.</u>

There are about fifty-five Psalms which have the inscription "To the Chief Musician" upon them. Psalms 4, 5, 6, 44, 45, 46, 60, 61, 64, 109, 139, 140 are some examples of this.

In David's Tabernacle, Chenaniah was the Chief Musician (1 Chronicles 15:1 6, 22, 27). He was the overseer, the music conductor, the Master of the song, the choir leader. As such, the Psalms were directed to him. His responsibility was to determine the direction of the music and the song. Hence, the inscription "To the Chief Musician."

2. <u>The Name of the Author of the Psalm.</u>

Not all of the Psalms have authorship ascribed to them, but many of them do. There are about 73 Psalms attributed to King David, 12 Psalms attributed to Asaph, about 10 or 12 to (or for) the sons of Korah; then there are Psalms attributed to Heman, Ethan, Moses, and Solomon.

It will be seen that these authors were godly men when they wrote the Psalms. No Psalm found its way into Israel's Hymn Book that did not have the divine seal upon it. Refer to these Psalms as examples of some of these authors: Psalms 6, 23, 24, 25, 27, 44, 46, 47, 49, 88, 90, 127.

It shows that the compilers checked out the language of the Psalm first. The lesson we may learn from this today is that those who are responsible for hymns and songs that are to be sung in the congregation of the Lord should see that all conform to the Word of God. The Word of God should be the standard and test for all singing and poetry in the Church (Colossians 3:16).

3. <u>The Historical Setting of the Psalm.</u>

A number of these Psalms also have the subject or historical occasion of the writing in their title. Psalms 3, 7, 18, 24, 51, 52, are some examples of this. An understanding of the Psalm becomes richer when considered in the light of its historical backdrop. Many hymns and songs of the Church are also much more appreciated when the spiritual occasion of the writing is known.

4. <u>The Style of the Music and Poetry.</u>

Some of the Psalms intimate in their titles the style of the music which is to be played. Several examples in Scripture are Psalms 7, 8, 92, 102 and Habakkuk 3:19. Sometimes the poetry lends itself to music that is joyful and victorious. Other times it may have music that is minor, descriptive of the trials, distresses, and conflicts of the author. At other times the language may call for music of deepest devotion and worship. The style of the poetry will determine the style of the music. Hence, it would be the responsibility of the Chief Musician to censor the style of both poetry and music before it was rendered to the Lord by the singers and musicians.

5. <u>The Instrument to accompany the Psalm.</u>

Under this sub-heading we will note a number of special musical expressions in particular Psalm titles. This will include those which have their own special significance as well as those which suggest the kind of instrument to accompany the singing of the Psalm. Certain Psalms lend themselves to certain kinds of instruments.

NOTE: Various authors differ at times in their definitions of these inscriptions under consideration. The writer of this textbook in researching this area simply puts under this sub-heading what seems to be the most significant explanation of these inscriptions. The dominant thing that should be seen is in the fact that the Psalms with their titles and/or inscriptions did intend to convey some measure of instruction to the singers and musicians.

a. <u>Aijeleth-Shahar.</u>

This appears in the title of Psalm 22. Amplified Old Testament says, "To the Chief Musician; set to [the tune of] Aijeleth Hashshahar [the hind of the morning dawn]." Other writers suggest the Psalm title to mean "Hind of the Morning," or "The Day Dawn," or "Morning Twilight."

b. <u>Alamoth</u> (1 Chronicles 15:19-21; Psalms 46 title).

The Amplified Old Testament states, "To the Chief Musician; a Psalm of the Sons of Korah, set to treble voices. A Song."

Alamoth (S.C. 5961. Hebrew) is the plural of Almah, "a lass, damsel, veiled or private, a virgin." It is suggested to be a choir of singing maidens, or song of the virgins; treble or soprano. Psalms 68:25 speaks of the damsels ("<u>almah</u>") playing their timbrels along with the singers and players on instruments.

In Revelation 14:1-4 we see 144,000 virgins singing a new song upon their harps according to the order established by David the king.

Concerning 1 Chronicles 15:20, other writers suggest that Alamoth could simply mean "treble voices" whether young men or girls because of eight men who played psalteries ("<u>Nebel</u>") upon Alamoth.

c. <u>Al-Tashchith.</u>

The titles of Psalms 57, 58, 59 and 75 carry this inscription. Amplified Old Testament has "To the Chief Musician; set to the tune, Do not Destroy." Strong's Concordance (S.C. 516) suggests meaning, "thou must not destroy; probably the opening words of a popular song."

d. <u>Gittith.</u>

The word "Gittith" comes from "Gath," meaning "winepress." Psalms 8, 81 and 84 bear this inscription. Amplified Old Testament, "To the Chief Musician; set to a Philistine lute or (possible) a particular Hittite tune."

Strong (S.C. 1665) suggests this to be a Gittite harp; the musical instrument to accompany the Psalm. The word is derived from the Hebrew root meaning "wine press." The fruit which came in the Feast of Tabernacles was the time for the treading out of the wine. The ones treading out the wine would dance, and march and sing for joy and call to each other of the goodness of the Lord. Jesus went to Gethsemane," Winepress," for us that we might receive the wine of the Spirit and be able to sing and rejoice before the Lord in our worship.

e. Jeduthan.

Concerning Jeduthan the Amplified Old Testament writes, "To the Chief Musician; for Jeduthan (founder of an official musical family)." Jeduthan was one of the 3 Chief singers in the temple worship (1 Chronicles 16:41, 42; 25:1-6; 2 Chronicles 5:12). Psalms 39, 62, and 77 have his name in their titles. His name interpreted means "praise-giver," or "let them give praise." His name suited his ministry. All believers are called to give praise to the Lord. There are those, however, who have a distinct ministry in praise and music.

f. Jonath-elem-rechokim.

This is only to be found in the title of Psalm 56. "To the Chief Musician; to the tune, Silent Dove Among Those Far Away." (Amplified Old Testament). Strong (S.C. 3128) suggests the title to be a melody entitled "The Dove of the Distant Woods." The Song of Solomon likens Christ and His Church to be like two doves responding in love to each other (Song 2:14).

g. Mahaleth.

Psalms 53 and 88 bear this inscription. Amplified Old Testament states, "To the Chief Musician; in a mournful strain. A skillful song or didactic or reflective poem of David." Strong (S.C. 4257) suggests that the word means "sickness" and that the title was the initial word of a popular song. Others suggest that means "Melodious Song," "The Great Dancing," or that it was a lute, accompanied by stringed instruments.

Whatever may have been the case, it does show that the Psalm was a song and involved certain instruments to express its message.

h. Maschil.

Amplified Old Testament, "A skillful song, or a didactic or reflective poem." Maschil is used on about eighteen Psalms; Psalms 32, 42, 44, 45, 52, 53, 54, 55, 74, 78, 88, 142. Strong (S.C. 4905) says that Maschil means "didactic" or "melody." It was a Psalm of instruction, understanding, or an instructive song. The Psalms are indeed full of instruction for the Church today.

i. Michtam.

Psalms 16, 56, 57, 58, 59, 60 bear this title and musical term on them. Amplified Old Testament states this to be "A Poem of David (probably) intended to record memorable thoughts." Strong (S.C. 4387) says, "engraving, a poem," indicating emphasis and permanence by reason of being engraven. The spiritual lesson we may derive from Michtam is that by prayer and meditation the Word of God may be engraven and engrafted into the believer's heart (James 1:21).

j. Muth-Laben.

This inscription is only found in the title of Psalm 9. The Amplified Old Testament says "To the Chief Musician; set for [possibly] soprano voices."

Strong (S.C. 4192) says that it means "to die for the son," and that it was probably the title of a popular tune. [The writers who follow the thought that these inscriptions belong to the previous Psalms suggest that "The Death of the Son" refers to the death of the champion, the giant Goliath (1 Samuel 17:4, 23)]. Whatever may be the true meaning of this title, we know that through the death of the Son of God, He conquered all the giants of Satan's domain.

k. Neginoth.

Psalms bearing this title are Psalms 4, 54, 55, 61, 67, and 76. Also Isaiah 38:20 uses this thought. Amplified Old Testament states, "To the Chief Musician; on stringed instruments." Strong (S.C. 5058, from S.C. 5059) says that it is "instrumental music; by implication a stringed instrument; a poem set to music." The word is translated "stringed instruments, music, Neginoth, song" in Isaiah 38:20 and Habukkuk 3:19.

Neginoth is the plural of Neginah. The Hebrew word means "to strike a chord," to beat a tune with the fingers. It speaks of stringed musical instruments. In 1 Samuel 16:16, 18, we see David who could "play well, thrum, beat a tune with the fingers, play on a stringed instrument, make music" (S.C. 5058. "Nagan") being brought before King Saul to calm his troubled spirit and mind. This word Neginoth is one of the clearer inscriptions, and confirms the fact that songs with musical instruments may be used before the Lord in worship and praise.

l. Nehiloth, or Nahaloth.

Psalm 5 only has this title. Amplified Old Testament writes, "To the Chief Musician; on wind instruments." Strong (S.C. 5155) says it means "a flute." Thus Nehiloth means "perforated," or means "the flute and similar wind instruments."

m. Sheminith.

This inscription is found on Psalms 6, 12 along with 1 Chronicles 15:21. Amplified Old Testament has this inscription, "To the Chief Musician; on stringed instruments, set [possibly] an octave below." Strong (S.C. 8067, from 8066, meaning eight) says, probably an eight stringed instrument, as a lyre.

Some suggest that it refers to the eighth group or division in the procession of bringing back the Ark (1 Chronicles 24:1, 5; 26:1, 12). Others state that it simply means an octave, either voices (or instruments), in the bass cleft range, for men singers, being eight notes lower than the Alamoth in the treble or soprano range for women singers.

n. Shiggaion, or Shigionoth.

Psalms 7 title has this, along with Habakkuk 3:1. The Amplified Old Testament says, "An ode of David (probably) in a wild, irregular, enthusiastic strain." On Habakkuk 3:1, 19 the Amplified says that it was "Set to wild, enthusiastic, triumphant music." Strong (S.C. 7692) interprets it to be "a rambling poem, or a mournful poem, or dirge, a plaintive song, a crying aloud (either of joy or grief)."

Shiggaion is interpreted variously to mean "mournful erratic, a song of trouble." Shigionoth is interpreted to mean "wanderings; according to variable tunes." For the Church triumphant there will be times when music is exciting, enthusiastic and triumphant because of the work of the Lord in behalf of His people. The Church has had plenty of plaintive and mournful dirgy songs in her history. But victory is God's ultimate for the Church.

o. Shoshannim.

Psalms 45, 69, titles carry this inscription. "To the Chief Musician; set to Lilies [probably a popular air. A Psalm] of the Sons of Korah. A skillful song, or a didactic or reflective poem. A Song of Loves" (Amplified Old Testament).

Strong's Concordance (S.C. 7799) interprets it to mean "a lily, from its whiteness, as a flower or ornament; also a straight trumpet from the tubular shape." Shoshannim is variously construed to be "a melody, bridal-song, and a musical instrument."

p. Shoshannim-Eduth, or Shushan-Eduth.

Psalm 60 title, and Psalm 80 title. This is very much related to the previous title. Amplified Old Testament introduces it as "To the Chief Musician; set to the tune of The Lily of Testimony." Strong (S.C. 7802, from S.C. 7799 and 5715) interprets it as "Lily or trumpet of assemblage; the title of a popular song." It's generally accepted meaning is "Lilies of Testimony." It possibly suggests the assembling of the congregation of the Lord to the Testimony of the Law (Deuteronomy 31:10-13). Jesus Himself is the Lily of the Valley (Song 5:13; 6:2-4; Luke 12:27). The Spirit of Prophecy is the Testimony of Jesus (Revelation 19:10).

q. Higgaion.

Psalms 9:16, Strong (S.C. 1902) interprets Higgaion to be, "A murmuring sound, i.e., a musical notation." It is translated in the Authorized Version by the words "higgaion," (Psalms 9:16), "meditation" (Psalms 19:14), and "solemn sound" (Psalms 92:3). Amplified Old Testament translated it as to be "meditation." It means to speak to one's self, to meditate, thought, reflection. It is also suggested to be a harp murmuring a musical interlude in the Psalm. Thus Higgaion would be a musical pause for meditation. Meditation is part of the worship of the Church also.

r. Selah.

The word Selah is used about seventy-one times in the Psalms, and three times in the Prophet Habakkuk. Habakkuk seemed to be a priest-prophet associated with the Temple singers (Habakkuk 3:1, 3, 9, 13, 19). Strong (S.C. 5542) interprets it to mean "suspension of Music, i.e., pause." Examples of the use of this word in the Psalms are Psalms 3:2, 4, 8; 39:5, 11; 46:3, 7, 11; 89:4, 37, 45, 48; 140:3, 5, 8. The Amplified Old Testament on Psalms 9:16 says "Selah," [pause, calmly think of that!].

Its derivation has uncertainty about it. It is variously interpreted to be "to pause, to lift up," a thought link, and a connecting of two passages; a music rest, think it over, Amen, repeat, pause, either over a note, or rest, or end of a piece or refrain, and make prominent."

John Stainer (pp 82-83) writes on the word Selah, saying, "The term Selah which occurs three times in the Book of Habakkuk, and no less than seventy-one times in Psalms, has been variously interpreted as indicating (1) a pause; (2) repetition (like Da Capo); (3) the end of a strophe, (a stanza); (4) a playing with full power (fortissimo), (5) a bending of the body and obeisance; (6) a short recurring symphony ('Ritornelli'). In a lecture on the subject, given by Sir F. Ouseley, a Psalm was sung into which such 'ritornelli' on stringed instruments and trumpets were introduced at every occurrence of the word 'Selah'. The effect was considered imposing and devotional. The fact that 28 of the 39 Psalms in which this word occurs have musical superscriptions seems to compel belief that it was a direction to musical performers." Stainer comments that Selah would attempt to paint a picture in sound, as a musical interlude.

It seems then that Selah is a musical interlude. It is meant to be descriptive, according to the language of the poem being sung or played. Stainer suggests that these Selahs were sound-pictures and the particular instrumental music was meant to be descriptive of that poetic picture. He describes several kinds of Selahs considered categorically here.

1. <u>The Flight or Storm Selah</u> (Psalms 55:1-7; 61:4).

The Psalm references here describe the fury of the storm as the frightened dove beats its way to a peaceful wilderness. Clapping hands,beating feet, and clash of cymbals would be descriptive of the storm and lightning. These would supply the sound effects. Thus this Selah - musical interlude - would then be the "Flight and Storm" Selah.

The Prophet Habakkuk presents a most vivid picture of a tropical storm, with thunder and lightning and God coming into action for the salvation of His people (Habakkuk 3:3, 9, 13). Each of the Selahs here would have their own distinctive message.

2. <u>The Death Nell Selah</u> (Psalms 52:5; 55:19; 57:3; 59:5, 13).

Judgment, affliction, and death are noted in these references. In this particular kind of a Selah - musical interlude - the reed pipes would wail a funeral dirge, sounding the death notes, descriptive of the final judgments of God on the wicked. This Selah would certainly cause the listeners and players to "pause and meditate" on the Word of God.

3. <u>The Sacrificial Selah.</u>

Stainer (p. 92) comments on this Selah also saying "It is known that the sound of trumpets accompanied the ritual of the altar, a blare of silver trumpets blowing, as it were, the sacrificial smoke heavenward. Once the victim was consumed, the offertory music was silent. Here is an explanation of the difficult words, "God is gone up with a shout, the Lord with the sound of a trumpet" (Psalms 47:5). The Selah preceding this verse was the sacrificial interlude of trumpets augmented with loud Hallelujahs, which die away as the smoke grows thinner until, over the dying embers of the sacrifice, the Levites come in again to say that the LORD, who had seemed to them to stoop from highest heaven to receive the gift, had returned once more to His lofty throne."

4. <u>The War Selah</u> (Psalms 60:4; 76:1-3).

The War Selah is to be found in these references. There God brakes the weapons of war, and the Lord of Hosts comes into battle. The Lord is revealed as a "Man of War." The trumpets, probably the "Shophar," the curved ram's horn, would be used here. This trumpet was especially used for war, the sounding of the alarm, and when the leaders in Israel blew this trumpet, God would come into action in the behalf of His people. Note these references: Joshua 6:5, 20; Judges 3:27; 6:34; 7:16, 18; 1 Samuel 13:3; Nehemiah 4:18, 20; Jeremiah 4:19, 21; 42:14.

This War Selah - this musical interlude - would certainly be descriptive of the rage and fury of the battle.

5. The Triumphal Selah (Psalms 49:15).

Here the Psalmist declares "But God will redeem my soul from the power of the grave; for He shall receive me. Selah."

In vs. 13, 14 the Death Selah is noted, as the pipes or flutes would play a mournful funeral dirge over the wicked. But the musical interlude (Selah) of vs. 15 would be the blast of the trumpet that would sound - picture the triumph and resurrection of the dead.

Perhaps this points to the triumphant resurrection of the righteous dead at the second coming of Christ at the sounding of the Last Trump. (1 Corinthians 15:51-57; 1 Thessalonians 4:13-18). That will be the "Triumphal Selah" indeed. "Thanks be unto God who giveth us the victory through our Lord Jesus Christ."

The Selahs, in this interpretation of the term, surely help to teach truth. Sometimes the verses are understood only by their Selahs. The Selah is not just "a stop, pause, or think about that;" it is also a descriptive musical interlude that illustrates and interprets that which comes before and after it. It gives it a sound-colour and staging for the stirring of the imagination of the listeners. The Temple orchestra and musicians thus helped the singers by these descriptive Selahs, Selahs of melody symphony, sacrifice, war, flight and storm, peace and triumph. The particular type of instrument, whether stringed, wind or percussion would be used for that particular type of Selah. This would indeed make vivid to the minds of the singers and worshippers that which God was saying through the words of the Psalms.

In concluding our remarks on the Psalm Titles and inscriptions, we find that the Psalms become much more meaningful to the Church, even though some uncertainty surrounds the exact interpretation of these inscriptions. They do, at least, show that various Psalms lend themselves to certain types of instruments and melodies and that singing and instruments did play an important part in the worship of the Old Testament Church, Israel. Therefore the New Testament Church should be able to use the Psalms in a richer and fuller light because of the revelation of the Lord Jesus Christ and the finished work of the cross.

Chapter 25

MUSICAL INSTRUMENTS IN BIBLE TIMES

Musical instruments used in Bible times, as today, fall into three main categories: stringed, wind, and percussion instruments. Instruments of themselves have no ability to convey life-giving sound, but in the hands of a musician can convey a distinct message to the hearer (1 Corinthians 14:7).

It seems that there were about four thousand instruments of music used in the Temple Orchestra (1 Chronicles 23:5). These were called the instruments of David, the instruments of the Lord. Although a full and exact description of instruments of Bible times is not possible, archeologists have provided some very interesting information on these three categories. Psalm 150 calls upon the redeemed to praise God with everything we have. This Psalm includes a list of stringed, wind, and percussion instruments. We consider briefly some of the instruments mentioned in Scripture.

A. Stringed Instruments.

1. Kin-nohr (S.C. 3658, Hebrew, The Harp).

The first stringed instrument mentioned in Scripture is the "kin-nohr" which is always translated harp. John Stainer in The Music of the Bible suggests that this was probably a "portable lyre." The Hebrew comes from an unused root "to twang" and is translated harp. It is the only stringed instrument mentioned in the Pentateuch (Genesis 4:21). Stainer suggests it was probably of Syrian origin.

This instrument is referred to in many Scriptures of which the following are a few: 1 Samuel 10:5; 16:16, 23; Job 21:12; 30:31; Psalms 33:2; 43:4; 49:4; 108:2; 147:7; 149:3; 150:3; Isaiah 5:12; 16:11; 23:16; 1 Chronicles 15:16, 21, 28; 16:5; 25:1; 2 Chronicles 5:12.

The Greek word "kitharizo" (S.C. 2789) means "to play on a lyre." Scripture references from the New Testament are 1 Corinthians 14:7; Revelation 5:8; 14:2; 15:2; 18:22.

The redeemed are called upon to worship and praise the Lord with the harp. There were those in David's Tabernacle who prophesied with the harp. Music and worship release the Spirit of prophecy in the midst of God's people.

The following diagrams suggest what the earliest forms of harps could have been like.

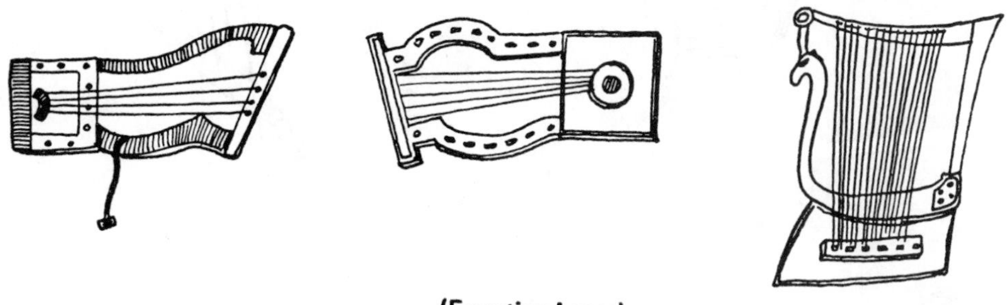

(Egyptian Lyres)

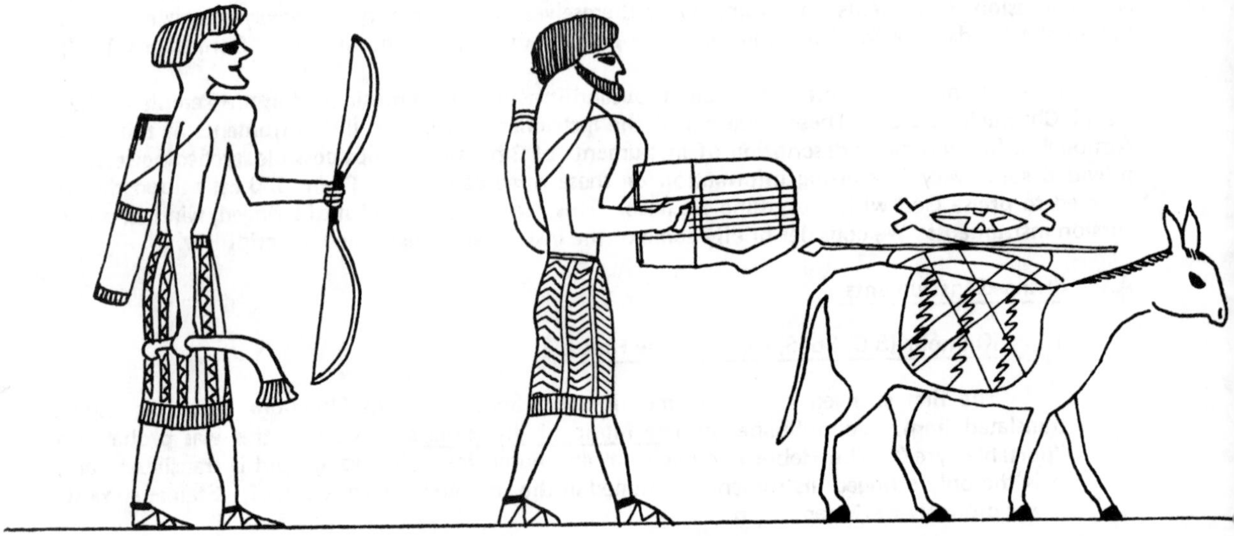

(A company of strangers in Egypt, believed to be Joseph's brethren)

(The earliest form of harps - atone time believed to be the Kinnor)

2. Neh-vel (S.C. 5035, Hebrew, The Psaltery).

The Hebrew word for psaltery is "neh-vel" and is used of a skin-bag for liquids, also a lyre. It is translated by the words, bottle, pitcher, psaltery, vessel and viol. Unger's Bible Dictionary states that Rabbinic tradition asserts the harp was called "nebel" because it was shaped like a skin bottle. The word is used twenty-seven times concerning a musical instrument.

The first appearance of the word is in 1 Samuel 10:5. Other Scripture references which speak of the psaltery are as follows: 2 Samuel 6:5; 1 Kings 10:12; 1 Chronicles 13:8; 15:16, 20, 28; 16:5; 25:1, 6; 2 Chronicles 5:12; 9:11; 20:28; 29:25; Nehemiah 12:27; Psalms 33:2; 57:8; 71:22; 81:2; 92:3; 108:2; 144:9; 150:3; Daniel 3:5, 7, 10, 15. It is translated by the word viol in Isaiah 5:12; Amos 5:23.

Following are some suggested shapes of the psalteries of different nations. John Stainer suggests it was probably of Phoenecian origin.

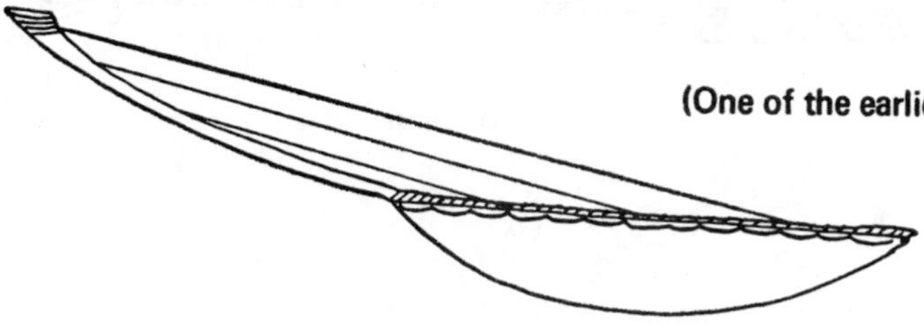

(One of the earliest forms of Neh-vel)

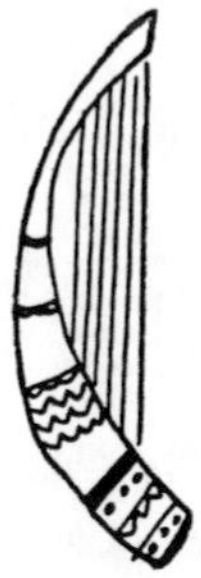

(Egyptian)

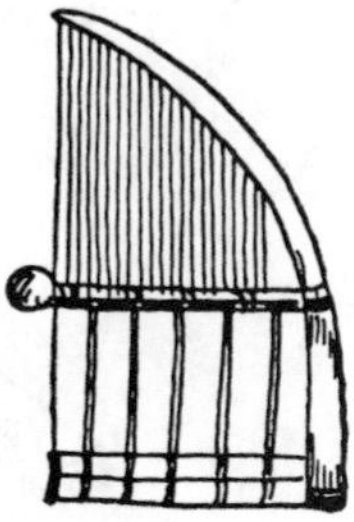

(Assyrian)

(Burmese)

3. P'san-teh-reen (S.C. 6460, The Psaltery).

The Chaldean word "p'san-teh-reen" is a transliteration of the Greek word "psalterion", which means, a lyre. It is translated by the word "psaltery" in Daniel 3:5, 7, 10, 15.

(Italian)

(Chinese)

4. Sab-b'chah (S.C. 5443, Chaldee, The Sackbut).

The Hebrew "sah-vach" (S.C. 5440) is from a primitive root meaning "to entwine." Strong's Concordance refers to it as a lyre. According to the Bible Study Source Book (Donald Demaray, p. 256) the sackbut is also translated "trigon." This was, in its earliest form, a harp-like instrument which was tied to the players wrist and held upright as he walked and played.

The sackbut was one of the instruments used in the worship of the image of Nebuchadnezzar (Daniel 3:5, 7, 10, 15).

The diagrams illustrate what the "trigon" possibly looked like, along with Egyptian forms of this large, powerful harp.

(Other writers suggest that in later times the sackbut was a wind instrument.)

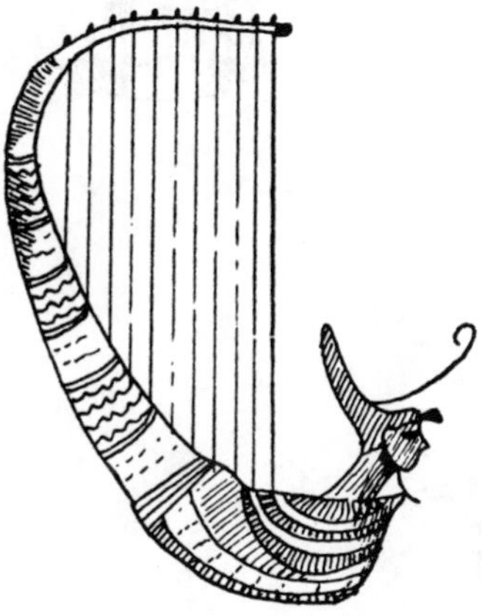

(Egyptian Forms)

(Trigon)

5. **Kee-thah-rohs (S.C. 7030, Chaldee, The Harp).**

The Chaldee word "kee-thah-rohs" is a transliteration of the Greek word "kithros," which means a lyre. It is translated as "harp" in Daniel 3:5, 7, 10, 15. The diagrams show that this was a more fully developed lyre.

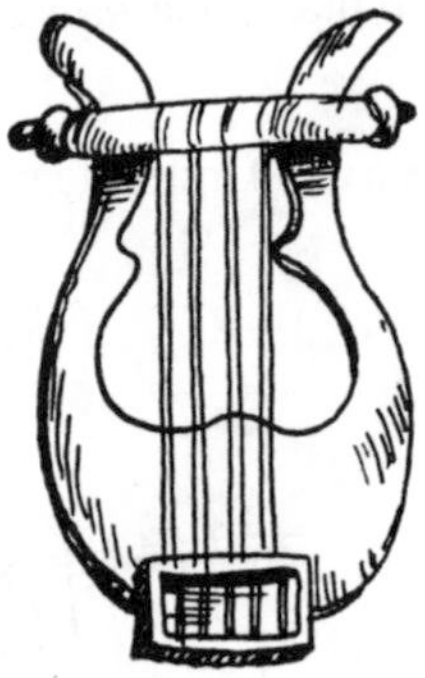

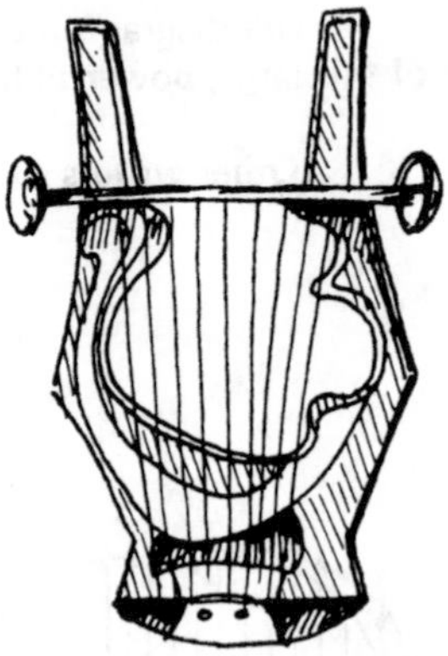

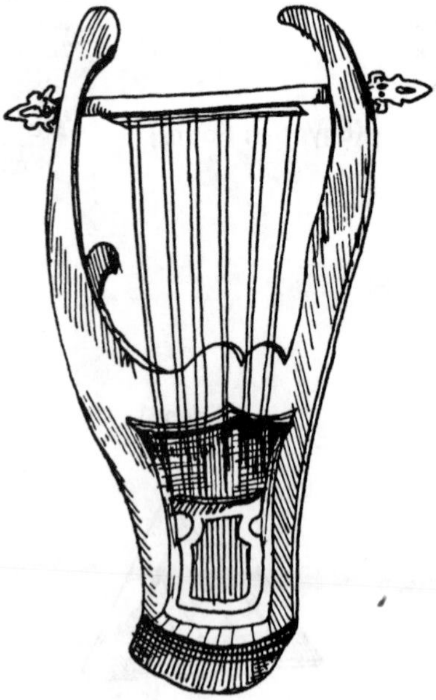

6. <u>Gah-sohr (S.C. 6218, Hebrew, The Instrument of Ten Strings, Zither).</u>

"Gah-sohr" means ten, and by abbreviation "ten strings," and so a deca-chord. It is translated as being an instrument of ten strings in Psalms 33:2; 92:3; 144:9. Some consider this to be the <u>zither</u> of ten strings, but mostly it seems to be considered as a ten-stringed lyre.

Psalm 150:4 exhorts the people of the Lord to play upon "stringed instruments." It refers to a family of stringed instruments and not to any particular one.

Whatever may have been the exact shape or style of the stringed instruments it is evident that this type of musical instrument was used much in Bible times, both in the nation of Israel and other nations.

John Stainer summarizes his conclusions by suggesting that these instruments were the major stringed instruments in Bible times. (Hebrew spelling as per Stainer.)

1. Kinnor - A portable lyre.
2. Nebel - A harp of moderate size, but portable.
3. Psanteriyn - A psaltery or dulcimer.
4. Sabbekaw - A triangular harp.
5. Qiytharoc or Kithros - A more fully developed harp.
6. Nebel-asor - A ten-stringed harp.

B. **Wind Instruments.**

1. **Ghah-leel (S.C. 2485, from S.C. 2490, The Pipes).**

The "ghah-leel" means "a flute (as perforated)" and is translated by the word pipe in these Scriptures: 1 Samuel 10:5; Isaiah 5:12; 30:29; 1 Kings 1:40; Jeremiah 48:36. It was a wind instrument, spoken of also as the flute or oboe.

2. **Mash-roh-kee-thah (S.C. 4953, Chaldee, The Flute).**

This Chaldee word is translated as flute in Daniel 3:5, 7, 10, 15. It was a musical pipe, from its whistling sound and part of the Chaldean symphony orchestra in the worship of Nebuchadnezzar's image.

These diagrams suggest some of the various types of flutes or pipes.

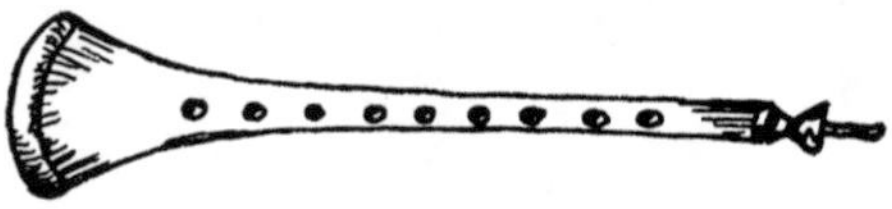

(Arab Zamr)

(Egyptian Reed Flute)

3. Goo-Gahv [(or Goog-gahv) S.C. 5748, comes from S.C. 5689, The Organ].

This Hebrew word "goo-gahv" S.C. 5748 comes from S.C. 5689 in the original sense of breathing; a reed instrument of music; translated organ (Genesis 4:21; Psalms 150:4; Job 21:12; 30:31).

This particular wind instrument is only mentioned four times in the King James Authorized Version of the Scriptures. It is the first instrument mentioned in the Bible, perhaps only being a series of pipes bound together from the shortest to the tallest, as the following diagram suggests.

4. Soom-poh-n'yah (S.C. 5481, Chaldee, translated The Dulcimer).

This Chaldee word is of Greek origin ("sumphonia"); meaning a bagpipe (with a double pipe) and translated by the word dulcimer (Daniel 3:5, 10, 15).

The diagram suggests what these may have been like.

(Arabian)

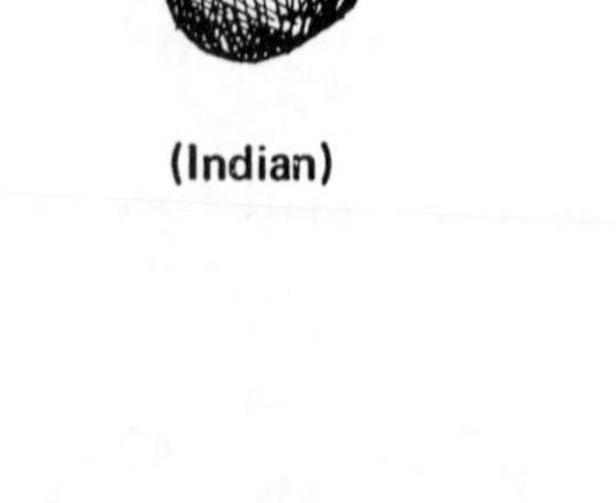

(Indian)

5. The Trumpet.

There are three particular words used to speak of the trumpets in Israel's history. These are the "keh'-ren," "shoh-phahr" and "ghatzoh-tzrah."

a. Keh'-ren (S.C. 7161, Hebrew, The Cornet or Horn).

The Chaldee word "keh'-ren", S.C. 7162 comes from S.C. 7161, meaning "a horn," literally, or for sound. It is translated horn or cornet. It is spoken of as cornet in Daniel 3:5, 7, 10, 15. It is called the horn in Joshua 6:5; 1 Samuel 2:1; 1 Chronicles 25:5. In David's Tabernacle there were those appointed to prophesy in song lifting up the horn. This was used as a musical instrument.

The horn probably came from some sacrifice, from the bullock or the ram. In Joshua 6, the trumpets were made of the ram's horns and were used to blast out the note of shouting at the collapse of the walls of Jericho. It seems that the "keh'-ren" was used synonymously with the "shophar," or ram's horn.

Suggested shapes of the horns are seen in the following diagrams.

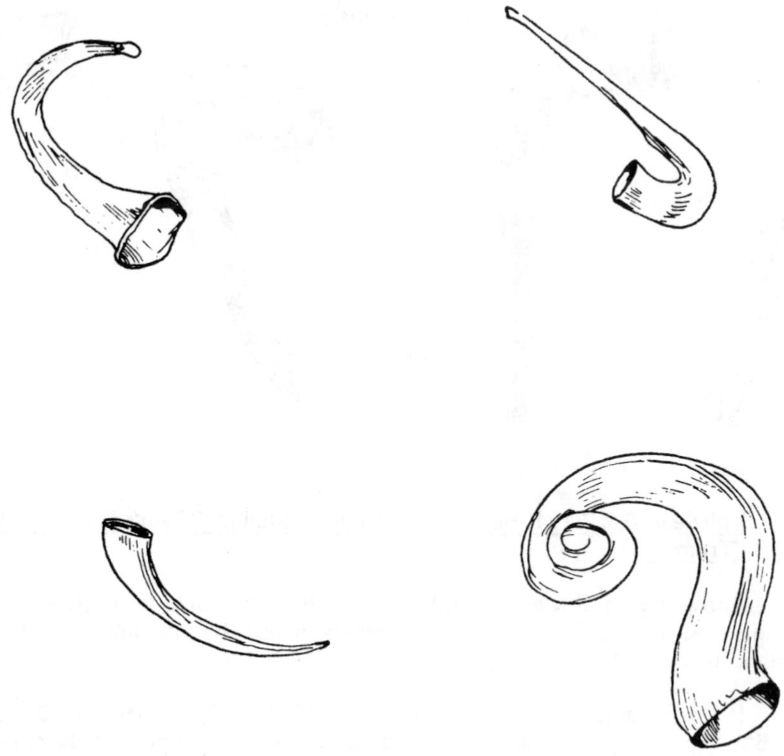

b. Shoh-phahr (S.C. 7782, Hebrew, The Cornet, or Trumpet).

The Hebrew word "shoh-phahr" (or, "shofar") is from S.C. 8231 in the original sense of incising; a cornet, as giving a clear sound, or curved horn. It is translated as cornet or trumpet.

This trumpet is most significant in Israel. It is mentioned about seventy times in Scripture.

The trumpet (shoh-phahr) sounded at Mt. Sinai (Exodus 19:16, 19; 20:18). The trumpet sounded in the Jubilee year (Leviticus 25:9). The trumpet of Jubilee, made of ram's horn, sounded around the walls of Jericho (Joshua 6:5, 20).

Read also these Scriptures: 1 Samuel 13:3; Judges 3:27, 28; Judges 6:34; Isaiah 18:3; 27:13; Joel 2:1, 15; Zechariah 9:14; Ezekiel 33:3-6; 2 Samuel 6:15; Psalms 47:5; 81:3; 150:3.

It was used extensively in troubled times but not necessarily as a musical instrument. Also used for Jubilee years, and New Moons.

(The Shoh-phar)

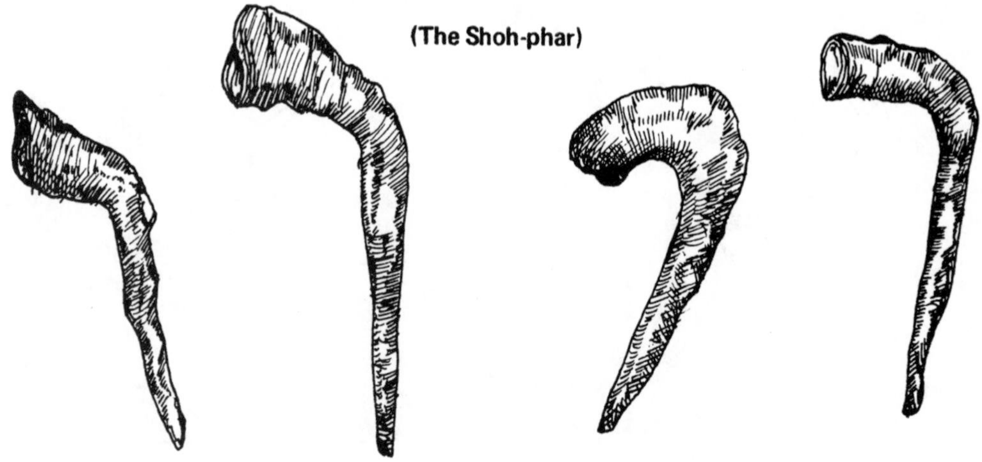

c. Yoh-vehl (S.C. 3104, Hebrew, Translated "Jubile," "Ram's Horn," and "Trumpet").

According to Strong, "yoh-vehl" was the blast of a horn (from its continuous sound); spec. the signal of the silver trumpets; hence the instrument itself and the festival thus introduced.

It is translated "jubile" in Leviticus 25:10, 11, 12, 13, 15, 28, 30, 31, 33, 40, 50, 52, 54; "ram's horn," in Joshua 6:4, 6, 8, 13, and "trumpet," only once, in Exodus 19:13.

d. Ghatzoh-rehr (S.C. 2689. The [Silver] Trumpets)

The trumpet here seems to speak more particularly of the silver trumpets which God commanded Moses to make in Numbers 10:2. The word "ghatzoh-rehr" (by reduplication from S.C. 2690) means a trumpet, from its sundered or quavering note and is translated trumpet. Some suggest that it was a straight trumpet with a bell. The Arch of Titus (Rome) shows straight trumpets like in the accompanying diagram (80 A.D.). Numbers 10: 2,8,9,10; 29:1, Silver trumpets were used for a number of purposes, especially in the Feast of Trumpets. Trumpets were used at the dedication of Solomon's Temple (2 Chronicles 5:12-13).

Read also: 2 Chronicles 7:6; 15:14; 1 Chronicles 13:8; 15:24,28; 16:6, 42; Ezra 3:10; Nehemiah 12:35, 41; Hosea 5:8; 2 Kings 11:14; Psalms 98:6.

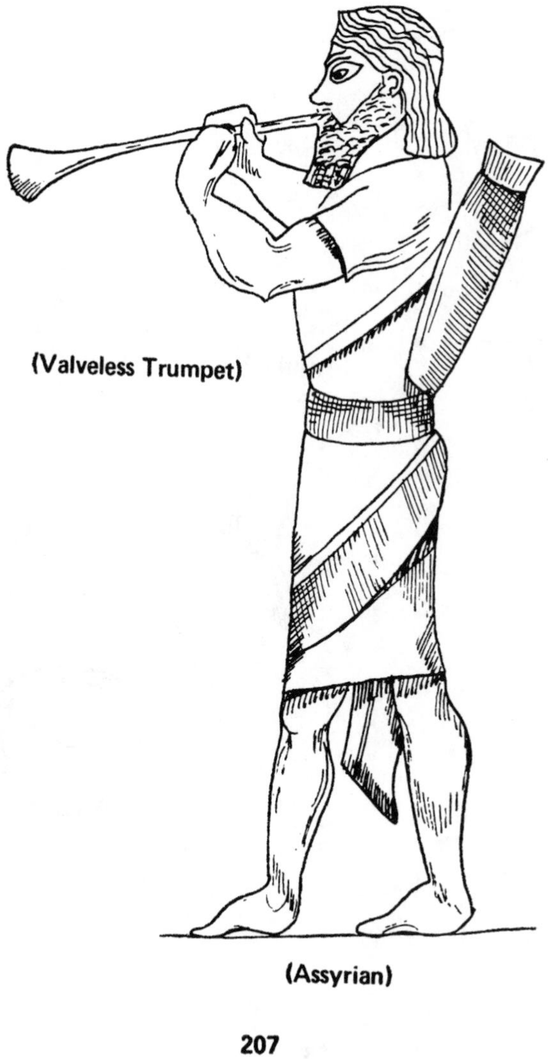

(Assyrian)

C. Percussion Instruments.

1. Tz'lah-Tzahl, Hebrew (S.C. 6767., from S.C. 7850. The Cymbals, which is with 6749 through the idea of vibration; to tinkle, i.e., rattle together). The cymbal means "to clatter"; a cymbal as clanging together. This word is used in 2 Samuel 6:5, Psalms 150:5.

2. M'tzil-Tah-Yim, Hebrew (S.C. 4700., from S.C. 6750, only dual, The Cymbals, double tinklers; i.e., cymbals). This word is used in these scriptures: I Chronicles 13:8; 15:16, 19, 28; 16: 5, 42; 25:1, 6; 2 Chronicles 5:12, 13; 29:25; Ezra 3:10; Nehemiah 12:27. It is translated "bells" in Zechariah 14:20.

3. Kumbalon (S.C. 2950, Greek, The Cymbal). The cymbal spoken of here is a hollow cymbal (I Corinthians 13:1). It seems that there were two main types of cymbals used. The loud cymbals and the high-sounding cymbals (Psalms 150:5).

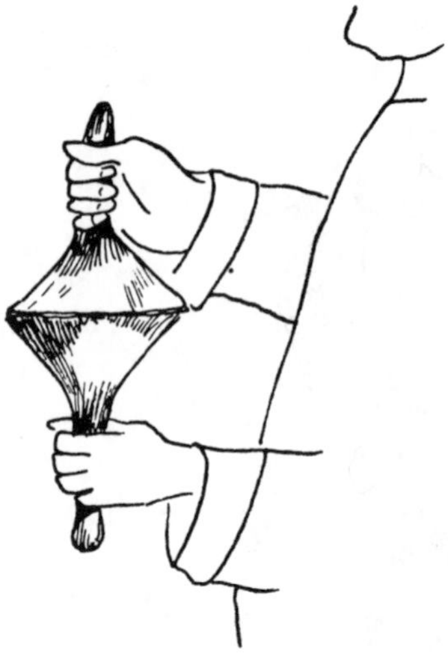

(Assyrian)

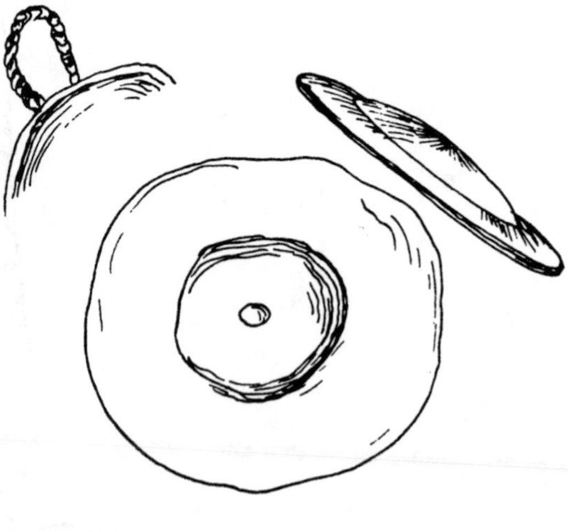

4. Pah-Gamohn, Hebrew (S.C. 6472, The Bells).

The word simply means "as struck." It is translated bell just twice in Exodus 28:33, 34; 39:25, 26. The bells were not used as musical instruments but were heard upon the garments of the High Priest in sanctuary ministry. The bells were percussion sounding.

5. M'nah-Gan-Geem, Hebrew (S.C. 4517, The Sistrum).

M'nah-Gan-Geem is wrongly translated "cornets" in 2 Samuel 6:5. The word means "a sistrum," so called from its rattling sound. It means " to waver, to shake to and fro." The sistrum was an instrument made of metal, with metal rods on which metal rings moved up and down or to and fro. Perhaps "the sounding brass" spoken of in I Corinthians 13:1 is an allusion to this instrument.

6. The Shah-Leesh, Hebrew (S.C. 7991, from 7969, Chaldee).

A triple, i.e., as a musical instrument, a triangle, perhaps rather a three stringed lute. The word is only used once and this is in I Samuel 18:6, when David came from the slaughter of the Philistines, the women of Israel met him with singing and dancing and three-stringed instruments of music (Marginal reference, Hebrew). Probably something very simple for the women to play and sing and dance with, keeping a rhythmic beat for their style of dancing.

The diagrams suggest possible shapes of these percussion instruments.

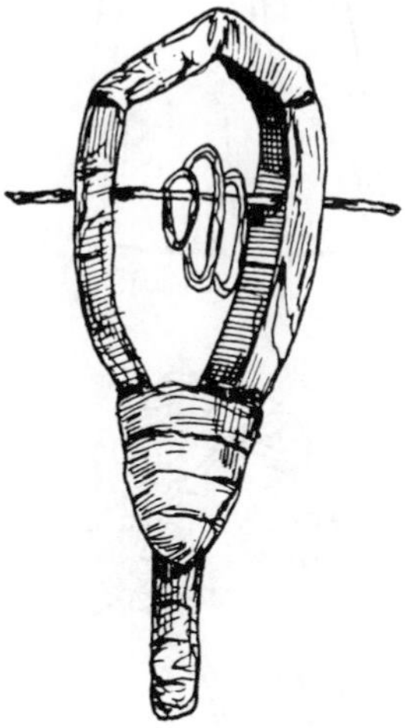

(Egyptian)

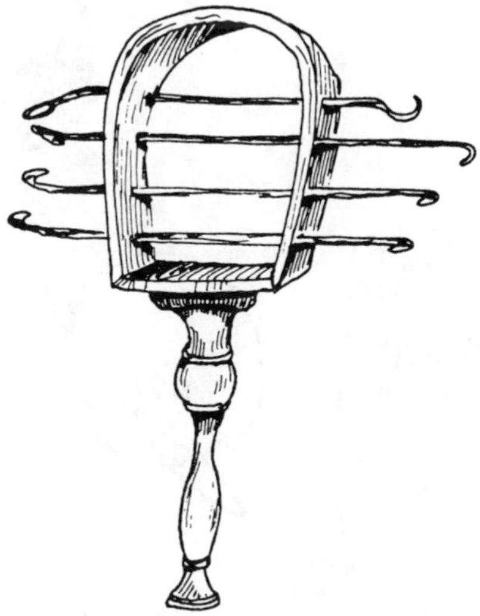

7. Tohph, Hebrew (S.C. 8596, from 8608 (to drum), play as on a tambourine. It is translated tabret, timbrel).

The word "Tohph" is used about eighteen times in the Bible. The word "timbrel" is used in a number of scriptures, Exodus 15:20; Job 21:12; Psalms 81:2; 149:3; 150:4; Judges 11:34; 2 Samuel 6:5; I Chronicles 13:8; Psalms 68:25. The same Hebrew word is translated "tabret" in the following references: Genesis 31:27; I Samuel 10:5; Job 17:6; Isaiah 5:12; I Samuel 18:6; Isaiah 24:8; 30:32; Jeremiah 31:4; Ezekiel 28:13.

The references in Genesis show how ancient the timbrel or tambourine is as a percussion instrument.

The diagram shows some of the variety of tambourine or hand-drums of several nations.

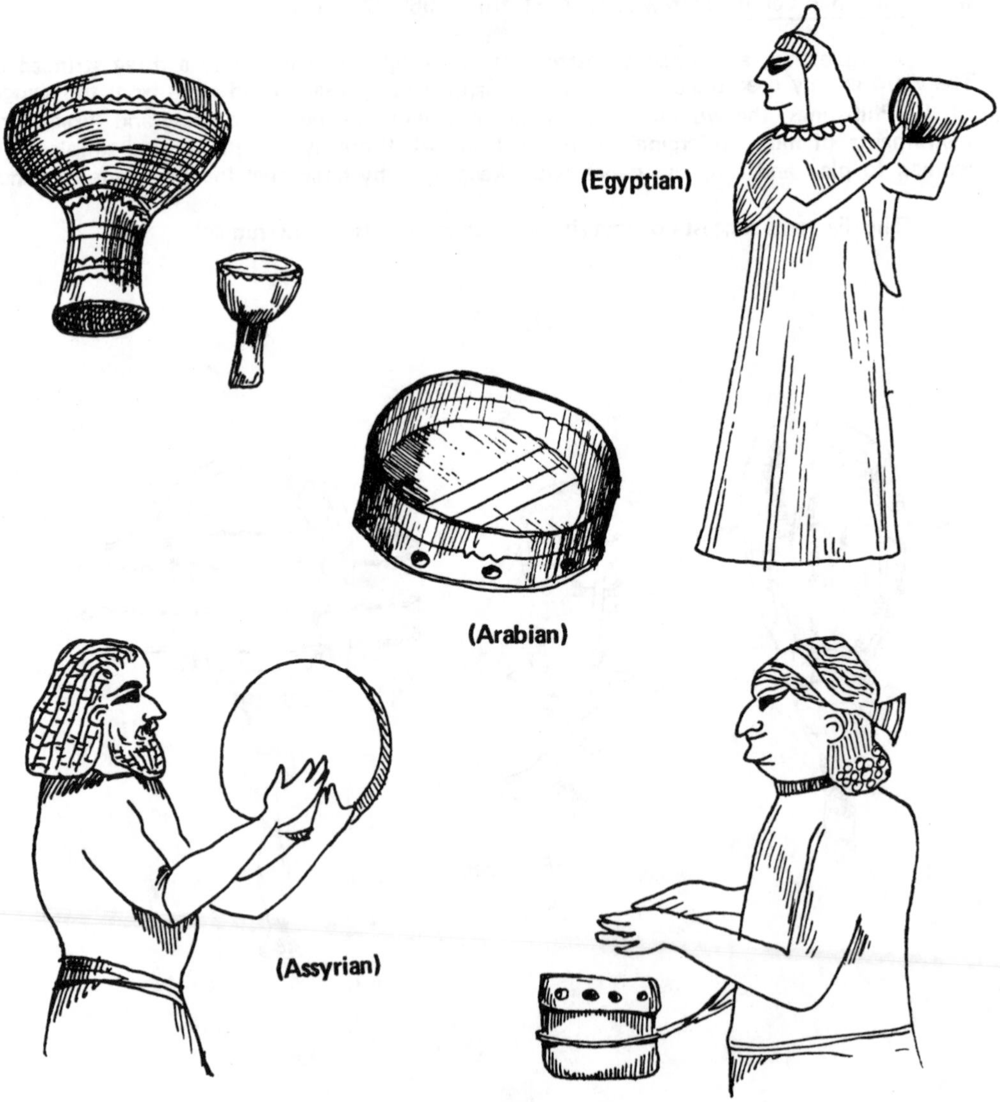

8. The Tympana, or Drums.

The Book of the Maccabees 9:39 is the first specific mention of a drum in Hebrew. "And the bridegroom came forth and his friends and brethren to meet them with drums ("tympana") and instruments of musick and many weapons."

Pictured as an illustrated hand-drum.

Although there is very little to be found in archeological findings in Hebrew history concerning musical instruments, other surrounding nations supply a reasonable measure of information. The Hebrew nation, following the strict letter of the law which forbad the making of any form of images or sculpture strictly refrained from such in contrast to other nations. Whatever may have been the exact description of the instruments of Bible times, enough information shows that they fell into the same basic categories as mentioned in Psalm 150. That is, stringed, wind, and percussion instruments. The making of instruments in today's world certainly excels that of previous history. These musical instruments can be used in praise to the Lord. Psalms 150 is a fitting conclusion to this chapter.

Praise ye the Lord.
Praise God in His sanctuary:
Praise Him in the firmament of His power.
Praise Him for His mighty acts:
Praise Him according to His excellent greatness.
Praise Him with the sound of the trumpet:
Praise Him with the psaltery and harp.
Praise Him with the timbrel and dance:
Praise Him with stringed instruments and organs.
Praise Him upon the loud cymbals:
Praise Him upon the high sounding cymbals.
Let everything that hath breath praise the Lord.
Praise ye the Lord.

Thus: Stringed instruments: psalteries, harps.
Wind instruments: trumpet, and organs.
Percussion instruments: loud cymbals, high sounding cymbals.

Chapter 26

SATAN'S COUNTERFEIT "MUSICALE"

Having seen that music originated with God and that music of itself is neither moral nor immoral, we consider how Satan is using the power of music to draw people to himself. With a revival of music and worship in the Church, Satan is counterfeiting this revival by bringing in a corrupt kind of music. He does this with everything that God seeks to restore to the Church.

A. Lucifer - Heaven's Music Director.

As noted in the history of music, Lucifer was originally heaven's music director, heaven's choir leader. He was the anointed Cherub and given the ministry of music as the guardian Cherub of the throne of God. When he fell, God did not divest him of his wisdom or his musical ability and ministry. It is a solemn thought to reflect upon the fact that sin and discord entered the universe through a rebellious archangel, a song-leader and musician.

Since his fall, Satan has used the power of music to divert worship from the true God to himself. Satan desires to be worshipped. One of the most powerful expressions of worship is through music. Thus, music may be corrupted by the evil use of it.

B. The Evil Use of Music.

Music, as already mentioned, is neither moral nor immoral. It is amoral. Music in itself is not evil. Only the perverted use of a thing makes it evil. We note some of the wrong uses of music mentioned in Scripture.

1. Genesis 4:21 is the first specific mention of musical instruments in the Bible. They were used in the ungodly line of Cain. This line consisted of murderers and polygamists. Undoubtedly the use of music would not be of a godly character.

2. Exodus 32:17-19, Israel, after their deliverance from Egypt, soon lapsed back into idolatry. Aaron set up a golden calf, made out of the earrings of the people. The people gathered together for great festivity. The festivities caused the people to sing, shout, and dance themselves naked. The Satanic use of music is evident here. The music must have been lewd and boisterous to make the people strip themselves naked, throwing off all proper restraint.

   There was a great difference in the holy dancing of Miriam and the women in Exodus 15:20 and this sensuous dancing before the golden calf.

3. Job 21:7-12, Job lamented over the way the wicked danced, using the timbrel, harp, and organ in their musical activities. The era of modern dancing has been associated with much wickedness also.

4. Psalm 69:12, David was mocked in the song of the drunkards. The singing that generally comes from drinking bouts is coarse and vile, certainly not glorifying to God.

5. Isaiah 23:15, 16, in Bible times, harlots would play harps (guitars) to attract men to themselves. One can imagine the sensuous type of song and music that would be played to seduce men to evil.

6. Amos 6:5 with 5:21-23, there were those in Israel who invented for themselves instruments of music, like David. God declared how He despised the Temple music and song because of their hypocrisy. Such music is not pleasing to God when the heart is far from him. He will judge such (Amos 8:10).

7. Daniel 3, music was used to influence all in Babylon to fall down and worship King Nebuchadnezzar's image. Here we see a Satanic use of music in worship to make man worship men as god. Music and worship cannot be separated, whether directed to the true God or false gods or men.

8. Leviticus 18:21; 2 Kings 23:10; Jeremiah 32:35, history records that the worship of Molech by the Canaanites was of the vilest and basest sort. In the sacrificing of their children, the priests would beat the drums to drown out the cries of the children being offered in the fire to Molech. In their idolatrous festivities, music played an important part. As the priest would ascend the steps of the altar, he would gradually divest himself of his clothing. At the given signal, the people would join in all kinds of vile orgies. The music was Satanically inspired to produce these results. It was for this reason that God did not allow steps to His altar in Israel, so that no nakedness would be seen (Exodus 20:25, 26; Acts 7:43).

9. Mark 6:22; Matthew 14:6, Herod had the head of John the Baptist taken off because of the sensuous dancing of his daughter.

10. Revelation 18:22, 23, Babylon is characterized by musicians in the Last Days. God will cause Babylon's music to cease. Babylon is significant of "religious confusion." Babylon certainly will not be characterized by godly music.

Thus, through these Scriptures we can plainly see that music is an instrument that can be used for evil as well as good. Just as a hammer, though neither good or evil of itself, may be used to build or destroy, so the laws of music, which were created by God for good, may be corrupted to produce ungodly music that will destroy those who listen to it. Though originally an instrument of God, music has become one of Satan's most powerful tools. He has used many different styles and forms to lead generations, cultures, and nations astray. Whether they be savage or sophisticated Satan has used the many styles of music to motivate mankind to evil and to tie the heart's affections to all that is not of God. He has used primitive "jungle" music to keep men bound by sensuality and demonic superstition. He has used military "march" music to inspire men to slay each other en masse on the battlefields. He has even used the sophisticated "classical" music to get men to worship music as an end in itself. In modern Western civilization Satan has implemented various styles of music in affecting the hearts and minds of men. The contemporary music scene is highly complex and constantly changing. To thoroughly evaluate it would be a gigantic task. Therefore, one modern form, "Rock Music," has been chosen out of them all to demonstrate Satan's powerful use of music.

C. <u>Rock Music.</u>

Undoubtedly one of the greatest challenges to the believer and the Church today is the so-called "Rock Music." Church history has shown that there have been various crises over music in the Church and "Rock Music" is just another one of these crises.

"Rock Music," both secular and religious, actually took its place in the world about the years 1960-65. It has been on the increase since. (The student is referred to the Bibliography for books dealing with information about, and analysis of, this kind of music).

A careful and prayerful consideration of "Rock Music" should be done by any believer who personally desires a high standard of music. In the Church, "Rock" is one of Satan's master-weapons to corrupt the gospel of the Lord Jesus Christ. The Devil's motto has always been "If you cannot beat them, join them; if you cannot destroy them, corrupt them." Music is just one of the avenues through which Satan can do this to the Church.

"Rock Music" seems to fall into two basic categories: Secular Rock, which is entirely the product of the godless, anti-Christal world, and, Christian Rock, a mixture of the music of the Rock world and Christian or ethical lyrics. Secular Rock has a wide variety and range; the heaviest kind belonging to the world of drugs. The various designations, such as "Acid Rock," "Hard Rock," "Satan Rock," "Love Rock," come and go in the changing world of "Rock Music." "Psychedelic" is a word generally applied to "Acid Rock" with its mixture of sounds. It is to be recognized that this scene of music changes over the years in its presentation but the same basic root problems and principles remain the same. "Rock Music" is associated with the world of drugs, sensuality and the occult.

"Christian Rock" also varies in its range, and is known under such titles as "Gospel Rock," "Jesus Rock," or "Christian Rock." Because of the vastness of such an area of music, we will content ourselves with some of the most important facts associated with "Rock Music," be it secular or so-called "Christian."

The Scriptures clearly teach that a tree is known by its fruit. A corrupt tree can only bring forth corrupt fruit; a good tree can only bring forth good fruit. If the fruit is evil, then the root is evil (Matthew 7:16-20). Many times the fruit on a tree looks good, and even has a sweet taste to it, but its poison is soon made evident in the being of man. The root is the problem.

Another illustration of the same thing is the Parable of the wheat and the tares. The Devil sowed tares amongst the wheat, thus producing a mixture of seed (Matthew 13:24-30, 36-43). "Rock Music" is the tares among the wheat of holy music. Tares and wheat look alike at the beginning, to the undiscerning. Tares are really an imitation wheat, but, when matured, a poisonous seed causing diziness if eaten with bread, is seen. "Rock Music" looks and sounds like "music." It is just another style of music to many evangelicals, who, desperate to relate to the world on its level, use it as an outreach to the "now" generation.

Only the harvest time will really expose it for what it is. This music, like the tare, has a deadly poison in it. It causes spiritual dizziness to those who are fed this mixture in the "bread of life." Nothing can change the tare because the root is wrong.

Let us outline some facts concerning "Rock Music" and its evil associations:

1. <u>Rock Music Is Associated With Evil Descriptions.</u>

It is generally difficult to give an exact description of "Rock Music." LOOK MAGAZINE (August 22nd, 1967) gives a good description of this type of music.

> "Referred to as 'love-rock' or 'acid-rock,' rock music is a vital ingredient in their whole way of life. In its ideal form - Rock Music,-fast and almost too loud for the normal ear to withstand, it blanks the mind, stuns the senses and forcibly reaches out and commands all the nerve fibres and viscera of the body to the extent that you find yourself leaping and twitching to the contagious drum rhythm with unconscious abandon."

The essentials of "Rock" are drums, lead, rhythm, and bass guitars (sometimes a brass section) and jarring beats. The very essence of "Rock" is its beat, rhythmic pounding beat. When a person can differentiate between (1) melody, (2) harmony, and (3) rhythm (the three basic ingredients of music), then "Rock Music" can be more easily defined. It is because of the many varied types of "Rock Music" that it is difficult to give a precise definition.

However, "Rock Music" is identified by its overriding beat and fast rhythm. The emphasis of the music is more on the beat than the melody. Proper music reveals the melody. "Rock Music" subordinates the melody. The music is pulsating and syncopated, having the accent on the off-beat, appealing to the rhythm of the human body.

2. Rock Music Is Associated With Heathen Origin.

Heathen Africa has for centuries been noted for its witch-doctor activities, along with the tribal dances amidst jungle music beat. The wild incessant beat of drums, the gyrations and sensuous twisting of the body and the climactic sexual atrocities were only the forerunner of the modern "Rock Festivals" of the Western world.

Bob Larson in "The Day Music Died" (pp 109, 179) tells of a Missionary who tested "Rock" type of music out in an uncivilized region of Africa. Good classical types of music produced pleasureable attitudes; "Rock" type of music stirred up cannibalistic tendencies. Much of the Negro soul music has its influence from African tribal dances.

3. Rock Music Is Associated With Rebel Cultures.

Rebel cultures seek to make Jesus Christ the founder of their movement. "Rock Music" had its birth in rebellion and it has reproduced rebellion in society. It expressed the sound of overthrowing the establishment. Its sound is the sound of rebellion, the sound of iniquity and discord. It calls you to "do your own thing" - an expression of self-will. The hair-styles, dress styles, and music styles are generally the symbols associated with rebellion - the Spirit of Antichrist.

4. Rock Music Is Associated With Drugs.

Drugs and "Rock Music" have a direct relationship. Drugs, meditation, and immorality are all interrelated. Some believe that drugs open the doorway to a God-consciousness. "Rock" extols the virtues of drugs. It is worthy to note that the word used in the New Testament for "sorcery" comes from the Greek word "Pharmakia," which is "a maker, enchanter and user of drugs."

Note these Scriptures where it is so used: Galatians 5:20; Revelation 9:21; 18:23; 21:8. A sign of the Last Days is drug users and makers. Evil spirits are sometimes associated with the use of drugs.

5. Rock Music Is Associated With Immorality.

Rock type of music has an appeal to the body, to its carnal appetites. It is often effeminate and lascivious in character. It is identified with sensual arousal. Drugs and sex seem to be siamese twins. Under the cloak of "love," lust and physical gratification are exploited. The "Rock Festivals" in America, with their music, rock bands, nudity, and shameless sensuous hip movements and sexual orgies are nothing less than a repetition of the Canaanite religious orgies. Israel had a lapse into this in Exodus 32:17-25 in the worship of the golden calf.

These type of "Rock Festivals" are a replica of African heathen dances, contortions, and immorality. It is the music of the white man's "witch doctors." Most "Rock" heroes are worshipped as gods and their personal lives are corrupted by sin.

6. Rock Music Is Associated With Evil Spirits.

Spirits work with music. The Holy Spirit works with wholesome music; evil spirits work with corrupt music. From Hinduism in India to the African witch-doctor, spirits work with tribal music and dances. The whole purpose of the music and dance, the beat of drums, the body rhythm, the chanting tone, is to call the evil spirits to take possession of one's faculties. Unnatural torture of the human body can be taken under the power of "Rock," because of the supernatural power given by demon spirits. This is evidenced in heathen countries. Satan worship and occult practices are often accompanied by liturgical music of the "Rock" type.

Demon spirits are very definitely involved with certain types of music. Many times those who become believers in Christ Jesus find the power of these spirits broken only as they destroy "Rock" records.

7. Rock Music Is Associated With Hinduistic Meditation.

"Rock Music" helps to tune the Western mind to the Eastern mind. Especially is this so in the realm of Hinduism, the religion of millions of people in the East. Mysticism or transcendental meditation can be practiced without any repentance or turning from sin. Hinduism believes in sun-worship, reincarnation and the development of the god within. "Rock Music" helps one in this kind of meditation which opens the mind for the influence of evil spirits. This is Satan's counterfeit of true meditation in the Word of God (Psalms 1:2; 19:14).

8. Rock Music Is Associated With Lyrics Exalting Sin.

In Galatians 5:19-21 there are seventeen works of the flesh listed. Adultery, fornication, uncleanness, lasciviousness, have to do with the works of the flesh, sins of the body.

Idolatry, witchcraft, have to do with demon worship. Hatred, variance, emulations, wrath, strife, seditions, heresies, envyings, murders, drunkenness, and revellings are sins of soul, mind, and body. "Rock Music" glorifies these sins, stirring sensual desires and unbridled lusts.

Many of the lyrics are nothing less than a perverted use of words, having double meanings. A hidden meaning known to those who are involved in that world of evil. The words are suggestive, and heavy with implications of the works of the flesh. Music of discord, clashings, frenzied beat, sounds of confusion and conflict characterize such music. The musicale "Hair" is but one example of obsenity.

All of this is totally opposite to the nine fruits of the Spirit. Love, joy, peace, longsuffering, gentleness, goodness, faith, meekness and temperance are the fruit of the Holy Spirit in the believer.

In today's changing world of "Rock Music," certain types of classical music are highly revered and the style is used to reproduce a kind of peace and create a sort of melancholy mood. This is just the human counterfeit of the fruit of the Spirit of God. However, the end result reveals the true fruit or the counterfeit. Anything that glorifies and produces the works of the flesh is not of God.

9. Rock Music Corrupts The Gospel of Christ.

It is about this final area that evangelicals are confused. Most of the so-called "Christian Rock," "Jesus Rock," or "Gospel Rock" groups use religious lyrics. However, many of these are anti-Scriptural and untheological indeed. Many times the words are a corruption and distortion of the Gospel of Christ. Some of the good gospel songs have been distorted by a "Rock" musical presentation. The motivation has been to reach the sinner where he is, but the "end does not justify the means."

The use of religious themes in "Rock Music" does not make it right. It is possible to do a right thing in a wrong way. Such groups who use these style of music hope that the Holy Spirit will move with it, not realizing that evil spirits generally move with this style.

Satan does not mind a religious garb, and will even use the name of Jesus Christ as it suits his ends. "Jesus Christ Superstar" is just one of many examples of the corruption of Gospel and music. Changing the label on the bottle does not alter its poisonous contents.

"Rock Music" is simply using the "new cart of the Philistines" (I Chronicles 13:1-14) to try and communicate with the sinner and it ends up in death. The Gospel of Christ is compromised to a subjective sentimentality, or a low ethical approach to get them to accept Christ. Rock fans themselves recognize this deceitful approach.

The fundamental doctrines of the cross, the blood of Jesus, repentance, and salvation through faith in Christ are neglected. In the desire to become "all things to all men to save some" (I Corinthians 9:22) Rock groups have discarded the language of the Bible as obsolete and resorted to "sub-culture" language, psychodelic colored texts, and "Rock Music."

It should be remembered that one does not become a drunkard to win the drunkard; one does not become a harlot to win the harlots. Jesus Christ did come down to our level to win us to Himself, but He never became a sinner to win the sinner. Neither should Christians become loose in styles of appearance or music to win them. The Church does not have to be like the world to win the world. God was very particular about the clothes, hair or beard styles, and the worship of Israel in the Old Testament. Anything that flavoured of the Canaanitish religion and worship was an abomination and forbidden by the Lord.

This is not a plea for music of the "Dark Ages," nor a plea for dirges, but for wholesome, healthy music that causes the believer to worship God, and the sinner to be convicted. Most adults, and even many of the unregenerate reject "Rock Music." Not merely for spiritual reasons, but because of its cultural shock and its immoral implications. Yet some Christians resort to its use, "aping" the world. The Church should not be governed by world styles, as it generally seems to be. Many sinners, becoming disgusted with the "Rock" world are more disgusted to find this type of music in the Church under the guise of religion. They generally recognize that "Rock Music" is just another "golden calf" made out of the "earrings" of the "Rock" sounds and religious words, around which some Christians like to dance.

Generally speaking a thing that is doubtful is dirty! The very fact that "Rock Music" glorifies drugs, sex, homosexuality, rebellion, and sedition shows its evil nature. It belongs to the unfruitful works of darkness (Ephesians 5:11; 2 Corinthians 6:14; Romans 13:12).

The progress of "Satan's Musicale" seems to have followed in the "musical score" of jazz, "Rock and Roll," rebel culture and drugs, "Rock," transcendental meditation, culminating in the occult and Satan worship. This seems to have been the trend of the last number of years, from A.D. 1930-70's.

In concluding our chapter, the believer should check the words and melodies of all music in the Church. One can have the right words and the wrong style of music, or one can have the right music and the wrong words. Or, one can have words and music that are wrong or a mixture.

Those men that God used in Church history contended for melodies and lyrics that would be true to Scripture and glorify God and edify the believer. "Rock Music" does not qualify to be in the house of the Lord.

It is not just a matter of a listener's appreciation for different music styles. It is not enough to justify "Rock" by saying that each generation has its own rhythm and beat and must be accommodated to in order to reach them. Each generation does have its heart beat and must be reached, but it will be by music and lyrics which glorify God, appealing to the spirit of man, not to his carnal appetites! Music, to enter the house of the Lord, must be purified by the fire of God (cf. I Corinthians 3:9-15 with Numbers 31:21-24).

The early Church had no orchestras, musicals, choirs, festivals of music to win a pagan world. They preached the Word in season and out of season (2 Timothy 4:2). The Word took first place; music second. Therefore the ministry of music should never take the place of the ministry of the Word. When music relegates the Word of God to second place, then God's order is violated (Psalms 138:2).

There will certainly be no "Rock Music" in heaven when we stand before the throne of God and the Lamb. No jarring discordant note will be heard; only the harmony of heaven and the redeemed of earth worshipping God and the Lamb. Therefore no music that would not stand in the light of the throne of God in heaven should ever find its place in the Church, the house of the Lord on earth.

(NOTE: Obviously over the last decade there have been many changes in the area of "Rock Music". As this textbook is not intended to cover this subject comprehensively, the author recommends the following excellent resource materials by other more qualified writers.

- ROCK, by Bob Larson
- WHY KNOCK ROCK? by Dan and Steve Peters
- SATAN'S MUSIC EXPOSED by Lowell Hart
- ROCK REVISED, by Steve Lawhead

Refer to Bibliography for further information on these books. The student is encouraged to prayerfully read these books and make his own personal evaluation before the Lord).

Chapter 27

THE POWER AND EVALUATION OF MUSIC

There should be no doubt about the fact that music is a power and can be a ministry either for good or evil over mankind. Music may have beneficial or harmful results. Under the influence of wholesome music a person can be lifted to lofty heights and energized to spiritual activities. Under the influence of corrupt music a person can be brought down to Satanically inspired, vicious, and demoralizing activities. Both of these influences can be seen in the history of Israel as well as the history of mankind in general. It also is evident in today's world of music. The power, evaluation, and ministry of music will therefore be considered here.

A. The Power of Music.

1. The Positive Effect of Music.

a. Doctors find that good music in hospitals has a positive effect. Nervous tensions are eased. Phil Kerr in, Music in Evangelism (p. 18), says that music has been known to soothe violently insane persons and even some cases of epilepsy have been prevented by good music. Both doctors and dentists use music to enable patients to withstand pain. King Saul was eased of the trouble of an evil spirit by the good music that David played (I Samuel 16:15-17, 23).

b. Industrialists have found that music in factories or large stores helps business, both to relax nerves and speed up production.

c. Scientists also have discovered that music helps cows to give more milk and hens to lay more eggs. Even plant life growth and development is affected by good or bad music.

d. Music is used constantly to stir patriotism in every nation on earth. National anthems are used to stir the emotions and the will to sacrifice and loyalty.

2. The Negative Effect of Music.

a. Repetitive hypnotic music was a Tribal inducement to stir the mind, emotions, and body to war, lust or engage in cannibalistic orgies. Abnormal reactions and unnatural behaviour are the result of evil music.

b. Certain types of jazz and more especially "Rock Music" have brought about demoralizing results in recent generations of Western culture. The suggestive and sensuous movements enflamed by this kind of music have brought about a moral breakdown in society.

Thus music carries its own power. It can be soothing or reviling, invigorating or demoralizing. It can be used for evil or good purposes.

3. Music and Emotion.

Music is vitally connected in its power to the emotions. According to Phil Kerr (pp. 18-23) in speaking of the power of music he says that music is an expression of human emotions. The basic law of human nature is that emotions seek expression. God has provided two normal channels for this, rhythmic physical movement, and vocal sound.

a. All emotions include either pleasure or pain. The infant expresses joy by clapping or beating hands. Most people express impatience by tapping the foot. Sorrow may be expressed by people bending over in pain, or groaning. Anger or temper often expresses itself in shouting wildly at someone or something. Joy and pleasure find expression in laughter, or sometimes in tears.

b. All human emotions seek a vocal or physical expression. Kerr (p. 24) says that physical expression of emotion is the foundation of rhythm. Dancing is such an expression. Also he says that vocal expression of emotion is the foundation for music. Therefore, these two, rhythm and music are vitally related, each of them being channels for the expression of emotion.

Kerr (p. 8) suggests that a person's individual capacity for emotion often determines their ability to produce music. The great composers and musicians have been, practically without exception, highly temperamental and intensely emotional. There is nothing wrong with having emotion: it is when emotions control us instead of being controlled by us that problems arise. Emotions directed into proper channels and under proper control are part of the human makeup that God intended for man in the beginning.

c. Music and emotional responses are vitally connected. All music whether vocal or instrumental can be classified into three groups.

1) Music which expresses emotion.

Any emotion can be expressed or incited by music. Emotions of love or hate, anger, fear or courage, faith or despair, laughter or tears, shouting and every other emotion in the depths of the human heart can be expressed through the power of music.

2) Music which incites emotion.

People react to music through their emotions, either in a good way or bad way. Music affects and incites people emotionally, phychologically, and physically for good or evil.

3) Music which is descriptive.

Any picture may be painted by the sound of music. Pictures of storm, war and danger, turmoil, or trust and peace. Music may be used to describe beauty and harmony, or used to debase. Thus one of the things by which to judge music is the fruit that it produces in the realm of the emotions. Is it the fruit of the Spirit of God, expressing and inciting holy emotion, or is it the works of the flesh, expressing and inciting sensuality and all manner of works of the flesh which pertain to the kingdom of darkness.

B. The Evaluation of Music.

In attempting to evaluate music it will be profitable to ask some specific questions regarding it. Just what is music? What kind of music does God enjoy? What kind of music should believers enjoy? Are there any definite guidelines by which music may be evaluated?

These questions may be answered if there is a general understanding of what music really is and what its components are. There are certain integral parts to music which can determine whether music is good or bad. These parts play an important role in evaluating music as to whether it should be in the house of the Lord or in a believer's life. There are three basic parts to music which we will consider here, these being, melody, harmony and rhythm.

1. Melody.

The fundamental part of music is its melody. This is the most creative part of music, therefore it should be the strongest. Melody appeals to the spiritual or to the spirit of man. Good and proper melody should be able to be sung by itself and not necessarily have to have an instrument to accompany it.

The first basic test and primary evaluation of music is whether it has good melody or not. The Scripture speaks of melody in these references.

Isaiah 23:16. "Take an harp . . . make sweet melody, sing many songs. . . "

Isaiah 51:3. ". . . joy and gladness shall be found therein, thanksgiving, and the voice of melody" (i.e., a musical piece or song to be accompanied by an instrument, S.C. 2172).

Amos 5:23. " . . . I will not hear the melody of thy viols . . . "

Ephesians 5:18. "Speaking to yourselves in psalms, hymns and spiritual songs, singing and making melody in your heart to the Lord."

All melody should be balanced in tension and relaxation, or rise and fall. Rise in music is its tension (melody up), and fall in music is its relaxation (melody down). If the melody does not have proper rise and fall then the effects of imbalance are seen. Too much tension brings the effect of frustration, lack of fulfillment, or creates passion. Too much fall creates depression and despair. Rise and fall in melodious music is significant of the various experiences of mankind in his earthly pilgrimage.

Rise and fall in music may be likened to mountains and hills, valleys and plains. All are necessary to give good melody. If all were on one repetitious note, then all would become dull and monotonous as a plain or lowland. If all were on the rise or tension then all would be mountainous. If all were on the fall, then there would be valley experience. But melody, good melody, will include in itself rise and fall, or mountains and valleys, hills and plains which give variety and actually constitute melody.

2. Harmony.

The next important part of music is its harmony. What is harmony? Harmony is simply the arrangement of chords which are meant to support the melody. Webster's Dictionary defines harmony in relation to music to be "agreeable sounds; the pleasing combination of tones in a chord, structure in terms of the arrangement, progression of chords." To harmonize is "to add chords to a melody so as to form a harmony."

A Scripture which illustrates the "chord principle" is found in Matthew 18:19-20,

> "Again I tell you, if two of you on earth agree (harmonize together, together make a symphony) about - anything and everything - whatever they shall ask, it will come to pass and be done for them by My Father in heaven. For wherever two or three are gathered (drawn together as My followers) in (into) My name, there I AM in the midst of them" (Amplified New Testament).

Harmony appeals to the psychological or to the mind and soul of man even as melody appeals to the spirit of man. Harmony should follow the melody. It should never dominate or subordinate the melodic line. Often times musicians have so great a mass of harmonic sound that no one can hear or recognize the melody. The melody should dominate the harmony and not the reverse. One should not get lost in the arrangements and miss the message of the melody.

No harmony of earth is perfect; hence in adding chords to a melody there is both consonance and dissonance in music. Webster's Dictionary defines consonance in music to mean accord or agreement of sounds; a pleasing combination of sounds simultaneously produced. Agreement, congruity, harmony are synonyms of the same word.

Webster's Dictionary defines dissonance in music to mean disagreeable in sound; a chord which sounds harsh and incomplete until resolved to a harmonious chord. Discordant or inharmonious sound or combination of sounds describes dissonance.

Again, there must be that delicate balance in harmony. Too much consonance tends to showmanship or sentimentalism. Too much dissonance creates confusion and rebellion in the emotions. In harmony one should be careful to avoid prolonged minors (dissonance) with no major (consonance) variations. Excessive use of altered chords should also be avoided.

Harmony will carry its minors and majors. The minor chord is generally significant of sadness, loneliness, melancholy, and tragedy. It is used to express the depths of the human spirit. War, solemnity, sorrow, plague, famine, tears, despondency, and death are the characteristics of the minor key.

Funeral music is often in the minor key. Heathen music and wailing is often in the minor. It was sin that introduced into creation the minor note. One note can transform a major chord into a minor (e.g., C, E and G equal a major chord. By changing one note, E to Eb the result is a minor key). When sin entered the glorious harmonious universe, the major symphonies of God felt the shock of discord. The minor key was also introduced. All nature was thrown off key when Adam sinned. Birds, animals, creation, and man himself heard and experienced the minor note.

The major chord generally is used to express joy and gladness, praise, exaltation and victory. It is the mode of the triumphant march. Christianity generally majors in the music that is major. It is significant of the resurrection.

This is not to say however, that music in its present state will not have touches of the minor key. The trials, sufferings, tribulations, pressure and sorrows of the saints are expressed in the minor. The sorrows of Calvary and the events surrounding the death of Christ were significant of the minor. But it was the resurrection that transformed the minor into the major. That which began in minor ended in the major. Therefore the victorious believer majors in the major, even though at times the minor is experienced. Minor becomes victorious when merged into the major.

There are twenty four keys - - twelve major, twelve minor. All music is conveyed to us through twenty four keys. When an end is made of sin all shall return to full harmony. Discords will disappear because God's kingdom will be filled with melody, harmony, and rhythm after God's eternal order.

3. Rhythm.

The third part of music is rhythm. It appeals to the physical, the body. Again, this part should be dominated by the melody. Melody naturally produces rhythm but rhythm should always be subservient to both melody and harmony.

In music, rhythm is the regular (or, occasionally somewhat irregular) recurrence of grouped strong and weak beats, or heavily and lightly accented tones, in alternation. It is the particular beat of music. There must also be that balance as in melody and harmony.

If there is no beat or rhythm, then the music is lifeless and dead. It is like having no pulse. If the beat is throbbing or pulsating then the music is sick. If the beat is concealed in the harmony with the melody dominating then the music is healthy. The so-called "Rock Music" majors on the beat, tension and repetition, or dissonance and totally distorts the melody. It actually reverses the proper order of music because of that which it is appealing to, the physical passions and appetites of the fallen nature.

With rhythm there will be repetition and variation. However, if there is too much repetitious beat it tends to sensuality; if too much variation there is too much distraction. Again there must be proper balance.

Music evaluation can be guided by these basic principles of melody, harmony and rhythm. Pulsating beat, clashing discords, psychodelic sounds which produce physical and sensuous responses are certainly not the style of music to be found amongst God's people. To reverse melody (spirit), harmony (soul), and rhythm (body) is to reverse God's intended order for man's being and music as a proper healthy expression of the emotions (I Thessalonians 5:23).

Bill Gothard, in Basic Youth Conflict seminars (1974-75) uses the following diagram in his lectures when dealing with music evaluation. It summarizes the content of this section on evaluation of music.

BASIC PRINCIPLES OF MUSIC EVALUATION

I Thess. 5:23	Basic Parts of Music	Basic Drives in Music	Tension/Relaxation	Basic Effects of Imbalance
SPIRIT	MELODY To dominate	Spiritual Drive	Rise / Fall	Tension, Unfulfillment, Frustration, Passion, Depression, Despair
SOUL	HARMONY To support the melody	Psychological Drive	Dissonance / Consonance	Confusion, Rebellion, Pride, Sentimentalism
BODY	RHYTHM To be concealed in the harmony and subordinate to the melody	Physical Drive	Repetition / Variation	Sensuality, Distraction

C. Other Guidelines For Evaluation.

Several other guidelines for evaluating music should be helpful here. These have to do with origination, identification, and communication. This will conclude with a brief consideration of the positive ministration of music.

1. Origination.

It is helpful to ask "Where did the music originate; who wrote it?" "Did it originate in the heart of a genuine believer out of Christian principles or out of the principles of the flesh?"

The Scripture in John 3:6 is applicable for "that which is born of the flesh is flesh." All that the flesh can produce is flesh. All that the world can produce is that which belongs to the spirit of the world, and the world systems. Music which has its origin in the flesh will have the characteristics of the flesh. It will appeal to the fallen nature of the unregenerate man. It will appeal to the unfruitful works of darkness (Ephesians 5:II). If one sows to the flesh, then of the flesh one can only reap corruption. One can only reap what is sown. Music which finds its origination in the flesh will produce responses in the flesh (Romans 8:5-8). The believer should keep himself unspotted from the spirit of the world (James I:27; 4:4; Ephesians 2:2; Galatians 6:7-9).

On the positive side we find that God is the great originator of all things. He can inspire in the heart of the saints the music of heaven. Surely in God there is a realm of divine music that man has never dreamed or heard of but is available to the Church in these last days as well as in the eternities to come. Thus, music should be checked as to its origination.

2. Identification.

Not only should music be checked as to its origin but also its identification should be discerned. With what will the listener identify the particular style of music that is being played?

Music is generally identified with something or someone; either God, the world, the flesh, or the Devil. Certain styles of music are identified with sensuality and other works of darkness.

Therefore another guideline is to endeavour to have music that identifies with the things of God.

3. Communication.

Finally, music is primarily a means to an end. All music is meant to convey a message and bring a response to the same. One should ask, "What does this music communicate? What response does it bring? What is the fruit of it?" Music should convey a message that is founded in the Word of God. Music is a blessed means to an end, and that end is to glorify God.

The test of all hymns, gospel songs, and lyrics is the "Word content" (Colossians 3:I6). Is it Scriptural? Is it theological? Does it teach, admonish and edify according to the standards of the Word of God? If not, then it should be rejected as being unworthy of God and His people. If music fails to communicate a message then it has missed the very purpose of its existence as an instrument of communication. Therefore, what message is being communicated becomes a definite guideline in evaluating music.

D. Ministration.

In concluding our remarks concerning guidelines for the evaluation of music, looking at such from negative and positive aspects, we consider music as a positive ministration.

Music which originates with God, with which the believer can identify, and which communicates a message, is a definite ministry. As such it falls into three areas or levels: ministry to the Lord, ministry to the saints, ministry to the sinner.

1. Ministry to the Lord.

The highest ministry in music is to the Lord in worship, prayer, and praise. This sets the believer as a ministering priest unto God in the Church (I Peter 2:5, 9; Matthew 18:20; Hebrews 13:15; Ephesians 5:19-20; Acts 2:46-47; 2 Chronicles 29:11; I Samuel 3:1; Acts 13:1-3). There are psalms, hymns, and spiritual songs which are wholly given over to ministry to the Lord.

2. Ministry to the Saints.

Saints should also minister to one another, teaching, admonishing, and edifying one another in psalms, hymns, and spiritual songs. This also is part of priestly ministry in the Sanctuary, the Church (Acts 2:42-46; John 13:34, 35; Galatians 6:2; Ephesians 5:19). Songs of joy, victory, trust, assurance, and encouragement are all part of this ministry to the believers (Isaiah 51:11). How much spiritual ministry the saints have received from one another in the realm of music will only be revealed in eternity.

3. Ministry to the Sinner.

God also uses the ministry of music to reach the sinner. Untold numbers of sinners have been converted to Christ through the Gospel in song. Sometimes when a sermon would never reach them, a sermon in song has brought them to the Lord. This also is a ministry and a way of communicating the good news to the unsaved (Matthew 5:14-16; Mark 16:16-20; Luke 10:17-20; Acts 2:43, 47; Matthew 24:14). This is a part of priestly ministry for the Lord has given to the believer the Word of reconciliation.

It is good to test all music as to its ministry. Will it minister to the Lord? Does it minister to the saints or the sinner? What does it minister? Therefore music can, as a whole, be evaluated with these guidelines. Music is a glorious ministry. It carries its own power and when quickened by the power of the Holy Spirit it becomes a source of great blessing. A proper understanding of these things will help us to sing praise with understanding (Psalm 47:7).

Chapter 28

THE TABERNACLE IN THE BOOK OF HEBREWS

The theological implications in the Tabernacle of David are greatly enhanced by the truths set forth in the Epistle to the Hebrews. The Book of Hebrews sets forth the great doctrine of Christ's priesthood after the order of Melchisedek. It is a book of comparison and contrast. The glory of the person of the Lord Jesus Christ is vividly seen in these comparisons and contrasts of that which was under the Old Covenant and that which is under the New Covenant.

An outline of the chapters by topic will show these main contrasts.

1.	The Son and the Prophets. (Hebrews 1:1-3)	The Two Spokesmen.
2.	The Son and Angelic messengers. (Hebrews 1:4-14)	The Two Messengers.
3.	The Son and the First Man. (Hebrews 2)	The Two Adams.
4.	The Son and the Servant Moses. (Hebrews 3)	The Two Mediators.
5.	The Son and Joshua's Canaan Rest. (Hebrews 4)	The Two Rests.
6.	The Son and Melchisedek. (Hebrews 5)	The Two Priests.
7.	The Son and Abraham. (Hebrews 6)	The Two Covenant Men.
8.	The Son and the Aaronic Priesthood. (Hebrews 7)	The Two Priesthoods.
9.	The Son and the Old Covenant. (Hebrews 8)	The Two Covenants.
10.	The Son and the Sanctuary Ministry. (Hebrews 9)	The Two Sanctuaries.
11.	The Son and Animal Sacrifices. (Hebrews 10)	The Two Sacrifices.
12.	The Son and the Heroes of Faith. (Hebrews 11)	The Two Faiths.
13.	The Son and Earthly Jerusalem. (Hebrews 12)	The Two Jerusalems.
14.	The Son and the Law. (Hebrews 13)	The Two Laws.

Just a cursory glance over this outline shows that the Epistle is a Book of contrasts and comparisons. However, the main burden of the Epistle is the contrast and comparison between the Old Covenant with its Aaronic priesthood, animal sacrifices, Sanctuary service and the New Covenant with its Melchisedek priesthood, spiritual sacrifices and heavenly Sanctuary services.

The book was written more particularly to the Hebrew believers to warn them against lapsing into apostacy and returning to Judaism. It was written to wean them from Moses wholly over to Christ. The writer desired to wean them from:

the natural to the spiritual,
the earthly to the heavenly, exchanging
the human for the Divine,
the temporal for the eternal,
the visible for the invisible,
the old for the new,
the good for the better,
the shadow for the substance,
the promise for the answer,
the prophecy for the fulfillment,
the type for the reality.

The modern believer cannot fully understand or appreciate the inner and outer conflict that the Hebrew believers experienced. In accepting Christ, they apparently had no temple, no visible priesthood, no animal sacrifices, no Jewish rites or ceremonies. They had to come into the realm of the eternal, to the spiritual temple, to spiritual sacrifices, to the royal priesthood in Christ and His Church (1 Peter 2:5-9; 2 Corinthians 4:18).

It was the contrastive - and comparative - mention principle of interpretation which made the strongest appeal to the Hebrew believer that showed him that all he had "in Christ" was "better" (one of the key words in this Epistle, used about 13 times) than all he ever had under the Old Covenant.

Hence, as the writer contrasted and compared the Aaronic priesthood with Christ's priesthood, animal sacrifices with Christ's perfect once-for-all sacrifice, the Old Covenant with the New Covenant, the climax of his argument is reached in Hebrews 12 where he contrasts Moses in Mt. Sinai with his Tabernacle and Jesus in Mt. Zion with the true Tabernacle.

A consideration of the Epistle in the light of these comments clearly shows that the Epistle may be summarized as being a contrast and comparison of the two Tabernacles, the Tabernacle of Moses and the Tabernacle of David. This becomes increasingly clearer as one meditates upon these things.

Philip Mauro (p. 223), says that as Mr. George Smith "points out, the most remarkable and significant feature of this great historical event is that it constituted a decided break with the Levitical ordinances given through Moses, in that the ark of God's presence was no longer in the holy of holies at the Tabernacle of the Wilderness (which was then at Gibeon), but in the midst of the Tabernacle of David on Mount Zion; and further that there were no animal sacrifices there only sacrifices of praise and thanksgiving; and no priests, but only Levites, whom David appointed "to minister before the ark of the Lord, and to record, "that is literally to make mention of, or bring to remembrance, or in other words to proclaim or preach the mercies and the marvellous acts of God," and to thank and praise the Lord God of Israel (1 Chronicles 16:4). This was a very remarkable suspension of the system of the Law, and an equally remarkable foreshadowing of that of the Gospel."

Following are a number of these contrasts and/or comparisons as related to these two Tabernacles.

1. The Tabernacle of Moses spoke of the Old Covenant, a Covenant of Law and works (Romans 9:32; 3:27).

The Tabernacle of David spoke of the New Covenant, a Covenant of grace and faith (Romans 4:16; 3:27; Matthew 26:26-28; Hebrews 8).

2. The Tabernacle of Moses spoke of the Aaronic Priesthood, and the Levitical order, only one tribe being priests (Hebrews 7).

The Tabernacle of David spoke of the Melchisedek priesthood, the Church order where all believers are called to be kings and priests (Hebrews 7; 1 Peter 2:5-9; Revelation 1:6; Revelation 5:9-10).

3. The Tabernacle of Moses was concerned with those who were only priests.

The Tabernacle of David involved David who acted as a "king-priest" after the order of Melchisedek (Revelation 1:6; Exodus 19:3-6; Revelation 5:9-10; 1 Peter 2:5-9).

4. The Tabernacle of Moses had dedicatory and continual animal sacrifices offered (Exodus 29; Numbers 28-29; Leviticus 1-7).

The Tabernacle of David only had dedicatory animal sacrifices and after that only ever spiritual sacrifices of joy, thanksgiving and praise. (Psalms 27:1-6; 1 Peter 2:5-9; Hebrews 13:15, 16).

5. The Tabernacle of Moses had an Outer Court, Holy Place, and a Most Holy Place with a dividing veil (Exodus 26:31-35; Hebrews 9:1-10).

The Tabernacle of David had no veil, just the Most Holiest Place, which signified a transference of the Holiest of All (Hebrews 6:19-20; 9:8-9; 10:19-20).

6. The Tabernacle of Moses lost the Ark of Glory after having had it for years (1 Samuel 1-2-3-4). The Ark never returned there after this.

The Tabernacle of David had the Ark of God's presence. It became the habitation for the Ark until the building of the Temple of Solomon. (2 Chronicles 1:4; 1 Kings 8:1-3).

7. The Tabernacle of Moses had a Brazen Altar but no Ark of the Covenant.

The Tabernacle of David had the Ark of the Covenant, but no Altar. This signified a finished work for the priests ministering therein.

8. The Tabernacle of Moses had no seat except the Mercyseat upon the Ark which used to be there. However, none could sit upon it.

The Tabernacle of David had the Ark and the prophet Isaiah foretells of someone who would sit in the throne in the Tabernacle of David (Isaiah 16:5; cf. Hebrews 1:3; 10:11-14; 12:2).

9. The Tabernacle of Moses had only one High Priest and many other priests, but only the High Priest had access within the veil once a year on the Day of Atonement (Leviticus 16; Hebrews 9:1-10).

The Tabernacle of David had High Priests and many priests and Levites but all had access as there was no veil (Hebrews 10:19-20; 6:19-20).

10. The Tabernacle of Moses still carried on its sacrificial system even though the Tabernacle of David was pitched and functioning in Zion. (2 Chronicles 1:1-3).

The Tabernacle of David had only spiritual sacrifices of praise, joy and thanksgiving in Zion (Psalms 27:1-6; 1 Chronicles 16; 2 Chronicles 1:4; I Peter 2:5-9).

11. The Tabernacle of Moses pointed to Mt. Sinai, in Arabia, and it typifies earthly Jerusalem which is in bondage with her children (Galatians 4:22-31; Hebrews 12:18-29).

The Tabernacle of David pointed to Mt. Zion, that is that which is in the heavenly Jerusalem, which is free and the mother of all believers (Galatians 4:22-31; Hebrews 12:18-29; 11:10-16; 13:12-14).

12. The Tabernacle of Moses ministry was after the Law and order of Moses, the Old Covenant Mediator (Hebrews 3:1-5).

The Tabernacle of David ministry was after the Law and order of David, who was a type of the New Covenant Mediator, the greater Son of David, Jesus Christ (Hebrews 12:22-24; Hebrews 8).

13. The Tabernacle of Moses had Moses as prophet, priest and king as its builder and founder (Hebrews 3:1-5).

The Tabernacle of David had David as prophet, priest and king as its builder and founder (I Chronicles 15-16; 2 Samuel 6:12-19).

14. The Tabernacle of Moses had no ministry of singers, musical instruments, Psalms, or songs of praise within its walls. All was a silent order and old form of worship.

The Tabernacle of David had the ministry of singers, musical instruments, Psalms, hymns and spiritual songs in its tent. There was a new order and a continual sound of worship (Psalms 134; I Chronicles 16; Colossians 3:16).

15. The Tabernacle of Moses was especially for the one chosen nation, Israel.

The Tabernacle of David is opened for the coming in of all nations, both Jew and Gentile, circumcision or uncircumcision (Ephesians 2:11-22; Acts 15:15-18).

16. The Tabernacle of Moses was a typical representation and prophetic symbol of the Law Age or arrangement before the cross.

The Tabernacle of David was a typical representation and prophetic symbol of the Church Age or that arrangement which would be after the cross.

Philip Mauro (pp. 227-228), quotes George Smith as saying:

> "Circumcision fell and perished from the Christian Church before the Divinely inspired quotation of the prophecy of Amos by the Apostle James. Sacrifice was abolished with circumcision. For that institution formed no part of the worship offered to God on Mount Zion.
>
> 'With circumcision and sacrifices the priesthood was also abolished. Indeed an unsacrificial priesthood is a contradiction of terms; for every priest is 'ordained to offer gifts and sacrifices' (Hebrews 8:3). But there was nothing of that kind in the tabernacle of David, whose sacred services therefore vividly represented the worship proper to that Church which is redeemed by the blood of the Lamb, Whose 'one sacrifice for sins' is universally and everlastingly efficacious - 'once for all' (Hebrews 10:10). Nor must it be forgotten that, with those elements of the Mosaic economy, every existing typical and symbolical thing was swept away" (That is to say all the "shadows" of the law were abolished and replaced by the corresponding spiritual realities). (Emphasis his.)

Meditation on these things will show that these are the great theological truths typified in these two Tabernacles, these two tents, these two mountains. Even as God used persons, places and things to shadow forth the Gospel of Jesus Christ, so He used these two structures to shadow forth the Old and New Covenant eras.

Although the present writer does not follow fully the analogy of Horger in Fundamental Revelation in Dramatic Symbol, he does note these two Tabernacles as being significant of the two Covenants and that David's Tabernacle typified the Church of New Testament times.

> Horger (pp. 204-207) says, "However, another most significant constitutional trait that characterizes this typical city is the fact that it was built upon two small elevations, called Mt Zion and Mt Moriah. To the mind of the writer, this is suggestive of the two covenants on which the plan of salvation is built, and, therefore, indicative of the two works of grace; namely, the new birth and the baptism of the Spirit. . . As already stated, the heart, life, and glory of the Tabernacle was the Ark of the Covenant in the Holy of Holies; and when the Ark was captured by the Philistines, as recorded in 1 Samuel 5th chapter, it is said that the Glory departed from the Tabernacle, to return no more, for the Ark never returned to the Tabernacle built by Moses. However, when David had taken Jerusalem from the Jebusites and God had designated it as the chosen city, in which He would dwell and bless His people, then David built a new Tabernacle of Mt Zion. This new Tabernacle built by David was a type of the new Church built by Jesus Christ, for David was ever a type of Christ; and, in keeping with the same line of typology, David built the new Tabernacle and placed it on Mt Zion, not on Mt Moriah, for it was reserved for the location of the Temple built by Solomon as a type of the sanctified, Spirit-filled soul under the Holy Ghost dispensation."

The Scripture passage in Hebrews 12:18-24 becomes much more meaningful in the light of the contrasts and comparisons of these two Tabernacles.

"For ye are not come to the mount that might be touched, and that burned with fire, nor unto blackness and darkness, and tempest. And the sound of a trumpet and the voice of words . . . And so terrible was the sight, that Moses said, I exceedingly fear and quake. But ye are come unto mount Sion, and unto the city of the living God, the heavenly Jerusalem . . . And to Jesus the mediator of the new covenant . . . "

The believer, both Jew and Gentile, is not come to Mt. Sinai, the Tabernacle of Moses, but unto Mt Zion, the Tabernacle of David; not to Moses the Old Covenant mediator but to Jesus the New Covenant mediator.

The understanding of the differences between these Tabernacles becomes a key to unlock the glory and truths of the Epistle to the Hebrews.

Chapter 29

THE PRIESTHOOD OF ZADOK

No Tabernacle is complete without a ministering priesthood. The very purpose of the existence of a Tabernacle necessitates a functioning priesthood (Hebrews 8:1-6).

The Tabernacle of Moses had the Aaronic priesthood. The Tabernacle of David had the Aaronic and Levitical priesthood. The Temple of Solomon also had the priesthood. The New Testament Church must of necessity have a priesthood, and it does. This priesthood is after the order of Melchisedek. The Lord Jesus Christ is our great High Priest after the order of Melchisedek as the Book of Hebrews reveals (Hebrews 5:1-11; 7:1-28; Psalm 110).

Believers, both Jews and Gentiles are called to be kings and priests unto God and Christ after this same order. "But ye are a chosen generation, a royal priesthood, an holy nation, a peculiar people . . ." (I Peter 2:9, with Revelation 1:6; 5:9-10).

What is the purpose of Daivd's Tabernacle? The whole purpose is to be a ministering priest unto the Lord in the priestly Body of Christ. It is to be "built up a spiritual house, an holy priesthood, to offer up spiritual sacrifices, acceptable to God by Jesus Christ" (I Peter 2:5). In relation to the present subject we discover that there were two priesthoods ministering at the Tabernacle at Gibeon and Zion. Two priesthoods of the same Levitical tribe, yet each having their distinctive functions. There were those priests who ministered at the Tabernacle of Moses and there were those priests who ministered at the Tabernacle of David. But what a great contrast is seen in their respective functions. One priesthood functioned according to the law and commandment of Moses. The other company functioned according to the commandment of David (Numbers 3:1-13, with I Chronicles 16:38-40; 2 Chronicles 1:1-3).

In relation to these two Tabernacles there were two High Priests and these are especially dealt with in Scripture. These two priests were Abiathar and Zadok. Abiathar was priest at the Tabernacle of David in Zion and Zadok was priest at the Tabernacle of Moses in Gibeon until he was succeeded by Abiathar (I Chronicles 16:16, 39-40; 21:29).

From the story of these two priests particular spiritual lessons can be drawn and applied to the believers of the New Testament priesthood. Therefore we will consider the brief life stories of these two men as the Holy Spirit has given in the inspired record. We will consider the three main tests that each of them had to go through and their response to the same.

A. Abiathar the Priest.

1. Abiathar and David - The Wilderness.

Abiathar, his name interpreted as "Father of Peace" or "Father of Abundance," or "Father of a Remnant," was the tenth High Priest of Israel. He was the son of Ahimelech and the fourth High Priest in descent from Eli, of the line of Ithamar, younger son of Aaron. He was the only one of Ahimelech's sons who escaped the vengeance of Saul in the slaughter of the eighty five priests at the city of Nob (I Samuel 21:1-9; Mark 2:26; I Samuel 22:9-23). It was the mercy of the Lord that he escaped with his life.

Abiathar fled to David at Keilah in his period of rejection under King Saul's reign and David asked him to abide with him promising to be his safeguard.

As far as David was concerned it was the blessing of the Lord to have Abiathar the priest with him in these wilderness experiences.

When Abiathar escaped the slaughter at Nob he took the priestly Ephod with him. David was thus able to enquire of God through the priest and received Divine communication by Abiathar's ministry. Through this means he was able to escape Saul on several occasions

(Compare Exodus 28 with I Samuel 23:6,7-13).

King Saul had previously had Ichabod's nephew, Ahiah, the son of Ahitub, to be his priest but even then he evidenced impatience and could not wait for God to speak to him (I Samuel 14:3, 17-20, 35-37). But the anointing and the Spirit of God had departed from Saul. Apostacy had set into his heart and this culminated in the slaughter of the priests of the Lord by the hand of Doeg the Edomite and in the end Saul sought to enquire of a familiar spirit (I Samuel 28:6-7; I Chronicles 10:13-14). Hence it was God's mercy that David had a godly priest to enquire by and to receive counsel from the Lord.

In the conflict at Ziklag David enquired of God through Abiathar the priest and the Lord showed him that he would recover all that was lost in the battle (I Samuel 30:6-8). Abiathar, as High Priest, was in touch with the Lord and could minister to the King.

In due time Saul died and David came to the throne. He established the Tabernacle in Mt Zion. Abiathar, along with Zadok shared in the bringing up of the Ark into the Tabernacle of David (I Chronicles 15:11). He was also involved in the priestly courses established by David (I Chronicles 24:6; 27:34). Both of these men had the glorious privilege of being amongst David's counsellors in his kingdom. Abiathar had been a faithful and loyal priest in the sufferings of the wilderness and now he was honoured in the reigning period. "If we suffer, we shall also reign with him . . ." is the lesson applied here (2 Samuel 8:17; I Chronicles 18:16; 2 Timothy 2:12).

Abiathar proved faithful in this wilderness test, abiding with David the anointed, yet rejected, king. He recognized that Saul had lost the anointing of the Spirit of God and that the anointing was now on David. Trials, hardships, temptations, and deprivations were the order of the wilderness days. But, as usual, it would be first the sufferings, and then the glory of the kingdom would follow.

2. Abiathar and Absalom - The Rebellious Son.

After about twenty years glorious reign, evil days befell King David because of his sin. David's rebellious son, Absalom, coveted the throne of his father. He stole the hearts of the people (2 Samuel 15:1-18). King David fled from Jerusalem out into the wilderness again even as he had fled previously from King Saul.

Zadok and Abiathar, and other Levites accompanied David, bringing with them the Ark of God out of the Tabernacle of David. David asked Zadok and Abiathar to return to Jerusalem with the Ark of God and to keep in touch with him in the wilderness, letting him know what events were transpiring there (2 Samuel 15:24-30).

Hushai the Archite desired to go with David also. However, David suggested that he also go to Jerusalem with Zadok and Abiathar and watch Absalom's activities. Zadok's son, Ahimaaz, and Abiathar's son, Jonathan, would be able to act as messengers to David in the wilderness (2 Samuel 15:32-37). On several occasions these priests and their sons were able to deliver messages to David (2 Samuel 17:15, 16; 18:19-32).

In time, the usurper king, Absalom, was slain. David sent a message to Zadok and Abiathar to encourage them to encourage the elders to bring him back to his throne and his house (2 Samuel 19:11-15).

Thus Abiathar, along with Zadok, proved loyal in the test under the spirit of lawlessness and rebellion manifest in Absalom and his men.

3. Abiathar and Adonijah - The Usurper King.

There remained one further great test for Abiathar and this was to take place under another rebellious son, Adonijah. The story is recounted for us in the Book of Kings.

King David was old and stricken in years. Death was soon to come. Adonijah the son of Haggith, Absalom's brother, exalted himself to be king, seeking to gain his father's throne. He called a conference with Joab the king's commander in chief and Abiathar the High Priest. Together these men agreed to help him obtain the throne. Zadok however was not involved in this conspiracy (I Kings I:I-IO).

The prophet Nathan told the queen mother, Bathsheba of the plot and the coming usurpation of David's throne. Nathan and Bathsheba went to David and told him of the plot and how even Abiathar the priest had joined forces with Adonijah (I Kings I:II-27).

David assured Bathsheba that Solomon was the son that the Lord had ordained to take his throne and that he would assuredly be king (I Kings I:28-3I).

After this David called for Zadok the priest, Nathan the prophet, and Solomon his son. They took the horn of anointing oil out of the Tabernacle and anointed Solomon to be the new king amidst great joy and rejoicing (I Kings I:32-40).

The tragic end of this story is that Abiathar made himself worthy of death because of his identification with the rebel Adonijah. Solomon spared him from death because he had been faithful to David in all the wilderness afflictions as well as under the rebellion of Absalom. But Abiathar was disposed from his priestly office and ministry unto the Lord, thus fulfilling the prophetic word against the house of Eli, spoken years before in Shiloh (Compare I Kings 2:26, 27, 35; 4:4 with I Samuel 2:27-36).

Abiathar had been tested three times. He had proved faithful in the test of the wilderness by staying with David the anointed, yet rejected, king. He stood the tests under Saul and Jonathan. He also overcame in the test when the ursurper Absalom took the throne, when there was great internal strife and trouble. Abiathar had been true to God's anointed King.

But he failed in this third test under Adonijah. He got caught in the spirit of rebellion and the mystery of iniquity that was at work in the kingdom then. After all he had been willing to suffer with King David, after all the joys of the Tabernacle of David, he failed at the last and thus forfeited his priestly ministry.

The spiritual lessons may truly be applied to believers as New Testament priests. All believers will experience like temptations and tests. One can enjoy the order of David's Tabernacle and yet fail in the end by allowing oneself to be caught up in the mystery of lawlessness, thus forfeiting priestly ministry unto the Lord and His people.

B. Zadok the Priest.

The other priest of prominence in David's time is Zadok. We consider Zadok and the similar tests that he also experienced along with Abiathar and notice his response in these tests.

1. Zadok and David - The Throne of David.

Zadok, whose name interpreted means "Just," "Justified," or "Righteous," was the son of Ahitub, of the line of Eleazar, another of Aaron's sons (I Chronicles 6:8-I5, 53).

The first direct mention of Zadok is in 2 Samuel 8:17 where we see him joining forces with David at Hebron, as chieftain of his father's house. He was a mighty man of valour (I Chronicles 12:23-28). Thus we see that Zadok, like Abiathar, identified himself with David, God's anointed, after all the trouble that had taken place under the reign of Saul.

2. Zadok and Absalom - The Rebellious Son.

In 2 Samuel 15:24-37 we see Zadok, along with Abiathar, remaining true to David in the rebellious times of Absalom against his father. Zadok allowed his son to be a messenger to David in the wilderness, as did Abiathar also. Zadok and Abiathar together helped preserve King David's life in these troublous times. Ahimaaz, Zadok's son, however was an impatient runner and did not have the clear message (2 Samuel 17:15-16; 18:19-32).

David sent to Zadok and Abiathar, after Absalom's death, and asked them both to call the elders together to bring him back to his throne (2 Samuel 19:11).

Together these two priests shared ministry in David's reign (I Chronicles 18:16; 2 Samuel 20:25). Both shared in bringing up the Ark of God into David's Tabernacle, and both found their places in the courses of the priesthood which David established (I Chronicles 15:11; 16: 39-42; 24:3, 6, 31; 27:17). Zadok was particularly placed in ministry in the Tabernacle of Moses at Gibeon while Abiathar was at Zion's Tabernacle. Both of these priests were faithful in this test under Absalom.

3. Zadok and Adonijah - The Usurper King.

It was under the third test that the tragic separation came. As considered already, Abiathar took part with the usurpation of David's throne by Adonijah. Zadok remained true to the king. He was willing to wait for the word of the king as to who should take the throne. He was not going to be involved with the spirit of rebellion (I Kings 1:1-45).

It is at this point that Abiathar and Zadok part company. Zadok had the joy of anointing the new king, of pouring out the oil upon the man of God's choice (I Kings 1:39-40).

After Solomon took the throne, he disposed Abiathar from his high priestly ministration and replaced him with the faithful Zadok (I Kings 2:26-27, 35; 4:1-6; I Chronicles 29:22).

He had stood the three major tests with David. Abiathar and Zadok had been together with David in the wilderness under Saul's reign. They had been together with David in the rebellious times of Absalom. But now they separate in the final test under the usurper Adonijah. After all that they had been through together, failure came in the end for Abiathar, and Zadok and he parted company. Zadok was taken from the Tabernacle of Moses and ministered in the Tabernacle of David and to King Solomon.

It is because of the faithfulness of this priest that God promised He would establish the priestly line of Zadok. This is seen in the prophecies of Ezekiel in the temple of The Lord (Ezekiel 44:15-16). This is also the fulfillment of the Word of the Lord to Phinehas, the son of Eleazar, the son of Aaron in Numbers 25:6-13. The Lord said, "Wherefore say, Behold, I give unto him my covenant of peace: And he shall have it, and his seed after him, even the covenant of an everlasting priesthood; because he was zealous for his God and made atonement for the children of Israel." (Compare Numbers 25: 12, 13 with Exodus 40:15.)

This does not mean that the Aaronic priesthood was to be everlasting or eternal, as the only eternal priesthood is the order of Melchisedek (Psalm 110, and Hebrews 7). It did mean that it would be everlasting in Aaron's generations, or as long as this seed would last. The covenant of an everlasting priesthood is given to Jesus Christ and the Church. The only way anyone under the Old Covenant, or any of the faithful in the days before the cross could have an "everlasting priesthood" would have to be in and through Christ by receiving eternal life (Revelation 1:6; 5:9-10). It is in this way that these promises find their ultimate fulfillment.

The genealogy of the priestly line of Aaron shows that Abiathar came from Aaron through his son Ithamar, to Eli, upon whose house judgment was pronounced. It also shows that Zadok came from Aaron through his son Eleazar, and Phinehas, and it is this seed line that is given the covenant of an everlasting priesthood. (Refer to Genealogy of the Chart of the Aaronic Priesthood at the close of this chapter.)

Abiathar forfeited his birthright; Zadok came into the fulness of his. The one was disloyal, the other was loyal. The priestly house of Zadok becomes an everlasting priesthood in and through the everlasting priesthood of the Lord Jesus Christ.

There were a number of Zadok's in the Old Testament priesthood and it seems as if this name is used by the Lord to speak of a priesthood that is holy, true and upon which He places special blessing. Undoubtedly this is because of that which was exemplified in the life story of the first priest known by this name in the times of David (Read these Scriptures which refer to these other Zadok's: 2 Kings 15:33; I Chronicles 9:11; 2 Chronicles 27:1; 31:10; Ezra 7:2; Nehemiah 3:4, 29; 10:21; 11:11; 13:13).

C. The Priesthood of Zadok.

In concluding this chapter it will be profitable to see the privileges and blessings which the Lord bestows on the Zadok priesthood as spoken of in Ezekiel.

Ezekiel 44:9-31 speaks of two companies of priests; the priestly Levites and the priestly sons of Zadok. Both have areas of ministry given to them in priestly service, but the privileges of the Zadok house are the greater. For convenience we will note these things in outline form.

1. The Levites in Priestly Ministry - (Ezekiel 44:9-14).

This company of Levitical priests were chosen for the following:

a. To be ministers in the Sanctuary.
b. To have charge of the gates of the house of the Lord.
c. To minister to the house.
d. To offer the sacrifices for the people in the court.
e. To minister unto the people.
f. They were not to come near in the office of the priest.
g. They were not to come into the Most Holy Place, or Holiest of All.
h. They were limited because of iniquity, idolatry, uncircumcised hearts and previous abominations when God had called them to priestly service.

Thus this company of priests would serve the Lord and His house but would not be able to enter into the Holiest of All as priests because of their sins. They limited themselves in the service of God. This is in great contrast to the Zadok priesthood.

2. The Priests, the Levites, the sons of Zadok - (Ezekiel 44:15-16).

The seed of Zadok was chosen by the Lord for the following:

a. To come near unto the Lord.
b. To minister unto the Lord.

c. To stand before the Lord.

d. To offer the fat and the blood to the Lord (Representative of the highest and best in the offerings).

e. To enter the Sanctuary, the Holiest of All.

f. To come near to His Table.

g. To minister to the Lord and keep His charge.

h. All service above was because they had kept their priestly charge and did not go astray when Israel strayed from the Lord. (Read also Ezekiel 40:46; 43:19; 48:11.)

Surely there are great spiritual lessons which may be derived from these things for the believers today. All believers are called to be priests. All are called to stand before Him, to serve Him, to minister unto Him in the priestly office (I Peter 2:5-9; Revelation 1:6; 5:9-10). All are called to a life of holiness unto the Lord (I Peter 1:15-16). The New Testament epistles are calling believers unto holiness of living.

But how many believers will be like Abiathar or Zadok? How many believers will be like the Levites spoken of in Ezekiel who fail to cleanse themselves of iniquity and idolatry or other abominations (Galatians 5:19-21; I Corinthians 6:9-11). They limit themselves in priestly service. It is not that God is a respector of persons, but believers determine how far they desire to go on in the things of the Lord.

The greatest and highest service is that which is exemplified in Zadok in the times of David and spoken of in the ministry of Zadok priesthood in Ezekiel.

Some will be like Abiathar, thrust from the priesthood and the glory of the kingdom because of disloyalty, unfaithfulness and involvement in the spirit of rebellion (Galatians 5:21; I Corinthians 6:10).

Some will be like Zadok and his seed and will enjoy the blessings of an everlasting priesthood in Christ Jesus, but it will be after the order of Melchisedek. Such will finally enter within the heavenly veil and minister in the heavenly Sanctuary forever (Hebrews 6:19-20; 10:19-22; Revelation 5:9-10).

GENEOLOGY CHART OF THE ORDER OF AARON

No.	Line of Eleazar	Line of Ithamar	References
* 1.	Aaron First High Priest in Israel		Ex. 23:13; 6:20 1 Chr. 6:3-15, 49-53
Nadab - Abihu 2.	Eleazer -	Ithamar	Lev. 10:1; Num. 3:4; I Chr. 24:2
3.	Phinehas		Ex. 6:25; Ps. 105:30; Num. 25:11; Ex. 40:15
4.	Abishua		"Covenant of Everlasting Priesthood"
5.	Bukki		
6.	Uzzi	Eli	1 Sam. 1:3
7.	Zerahiah	Phinehas-Hophni	I Sam. 3:2:22,33; 4:11
8.	Meraioth	Ahitub-Ichabod	I Sam 4:19-22; 14:3
9.	Amariah	Ahimelech-Ahiah	I Sam.22:9(Ahimelech slain by Doeg for helping David) I Sam. 14:3, 18(Ahiah priest to Saul)
10.	Ahitub	Abiathar	I Sam. 22:20-23;23:6(Fled to David, yet failed in Adonijah's case)
11.	Zadok (Abiathar put out, Zadok set up as first High Priest in Solomon's Temple, judgement on house of Eli)		I Kings 2:26, 27, 35
12.	Ahimaaz		I Chr. 6:8,9
13.	Azariah		
14.	Johanan		I Chr. 3:15 (supposed Jehoida)2 Kgs. 11-12; 2 Chr. 23, 24
15.	Azariah		2 Chr. 26:17-20; I Chr.6:10-11(Zechariah)
16.	Amariah		I Chr. 6:11
17.	Ahitub		
18.	Zadok		
19.	Shallum		Neh. 11:11; I Chr. 9:11; Meshullam
20.	Hilkiah		2 Kings 22:4; 2 Chr. 24:9 with King Josiah
21.	Azariah		1 Chr. 9:10,11; 2 Chr. 31:10
22.	Seraiah		
23.	Jehozadok(Aaronic priesthood into Babylonian captivity)		2 Kings 25:18,21; Ezra 1:1; Neh. 11:11; Jer. 3:24,27; 2 Kings 25:18-21; Ezra 3:2; 5:2; Jozadak
24.	Joshua (High Priest in Return of captivity)		Ezra 3:2; 5:2; Neh. 12:26; Hag. 1:1, 12; 2:2; Zech. 3:1; 6-11
	Annas and Caiphas (Joint High High Priests in the time of Messiah-crucified him; not of Aaronic descent)		Lk. 3:2; Jn. 18:13,24; Acts 4:6, 5:17-27, 7:1, 23:4 (Last priests mentioned in Bible history)

The Lord Jesus Christ
Covenant of Everlasting
Priesthood after the
Order of Melchisedek
Ps. 110; Heb. 7; Rev. 1:6,
4:10, 20:6; Ex. 19:6;
I Pet. 2:5-10.

Temple destroyed 70 A.D.

Jewry has been desolate of priest and sacrifice ever since this time.

Thus from Aaron to the Babylon Captivity; from the Captivity to the Crucifixion of Messiah, King-Priest; and to the destruction of the Temple in Jerusalem -- such is the order of the Aaronic Priesthood!

* The names of the priests, from 1-23 are in the order according to the geneology in 1 Chronicles 6:3-15.

Chapter 30

AS THE MOUNTAINS ROUND ABOUT JERUSALEM

Isaiah the prophet, along with Micah, in looking down to the Messianic era prophecied, "And it shall come to pass in the last days, that the mountain of the Lord's house shall be established in the top of the mountains, and shall be exalted above the hills; and all nations shall flow unto it. And many people shall go and say, Come ye, and let us go up to the mountain of the Lord, to the house of the God of Jacob; and he will teach us of his ways, and we will walk in his paths; for out of Zion shall go forth the law and the word of the Lord from Jerusalem" (Isaiah 2:2-3 with Micah 4:1-2).

A consideration of this prophecy in the light of both Old Testament history and New Testament revelation shows us that the prophets were speaking of Christ and His Church.

The expression "the last days" gives us the time element of the fulfillment of this utterance. Oftentimes the prophets speak of "that day" or "the last days" and New Testament revelation shows us that these expressions refer to Messianic times beginning with Christ's first coming and consummating in His second coming (Isaiah 12:1-6; 26:1-4; 27:1-3, 13; Jeremiah 31:31-34; Daniel 2:44; Hebrews 1:1-2).

Two of the greatest utterances concerning "the last days" are those found in Joel and Isaiah. Joel foretold the fact that God would pour out His Spirit upon all flesh in the last days (Joel 2:28-32). Peter on the day of Pentecost identifies that original outpouring of the Spirit as the beginning of these "last days" (Acts 2:14-21). However, that was not the complete fulfillment of Pentecost for none of the associated signs took place then. The major sign was the outpoured Spirit upon the 120 disciples evidenced by speaking with other tongues (Acts 2:1-4). Pentecost was simply the inauguration of the last days outpouring. It is consummated in the events of the Book of Revelation. This outpouring was to continue over the dispensation of the Holy Spirit through to the coming of the Lord Jesus Christ.

The next great utterance concerning "the last days" was that of Isaiah, the greatest of the Old Testament prophets when it comes to Messianic revelation. His emphasis was upon the fact that in the "last days" the mountain of the Lord's house would be established.

Joel and Isaiah, along with Micah, list two great things together concerning these last days. These are, an outpouring of the Spirit and the house of the Lord being established. We are in the last of these last days (cf. Psalm 90:1-4 with 2 Peter 3:8). The very purpose of God pouring out His Spirit is to build His house.

The prophet Isaiah said that the Lord's house would be established in the top of the mountains. He called this the mountain of the Lord's house. A look at mountains in their geographical settings in Scripture throws much light on the interpretation of Isaiah's utterance. Mountains in Scripture take on great significance because of that which God did in them. The Hebrew mind was saturated with the concept of God at work in mountains. The Psalmist said "As the mountains are round about Jerusalem, so the Lord is round about His people from henceforth even forever" (Psalm 125:1-2).

A very rich and interesting study may be found in the topic of mountains in Scripture, both Old and New Testaments. Palestine was a land of hills and valleys. It was a land of mountains. God identified His work from time to time with certain mountains. We may think of the giving of the Law Covenant at Mt Sinai (Exodus 19). We may also think of Mt Gerizim and Mt Ebal, the Mt of Blessing and the Mt of Cursing (Joshua 8:30-35 with Deuteronomy 27:1-20). Other mountains of note are Mt Nebo, Mt Hermon, Mt Seir, and Mt Olivet. These, along with many others, could be considered.

Jerusalem and its environs was surrounded by mountains. However, there were three mountains marked out as having special significance. These three mountains were Mt Gibeon, Mt Zion, and

Mt Moriah. We ask ourselves, "Why were these mountains so important?" The reason these were so significant was because each of these had some particular habitation of God associated with them. In the Hebrew mind, the thought of "the mountain" and "the house" were vitally linked. We list these mountains and their respective typical structures in their proper order.

1. Mt Gibeon - The Tabernacle of Moses was pitched here.

2. Mt Zion - The Tabernacle of David was pitched here.

3. Mt Moriah - The Temple of Solomon was built here.

Geographically Mt Gibeon was about seven miles north of Jerusalem. Mt Zion and Mt Moriah were in closer proximity to each other in Jerusalem itself. Thus these mountains were significant because of the house of the Lord that was in them. Mt Gibeon had the Tabernacle of Moses pitched there (I Chronicles 16:29 with 2 Chronicles 1:1-5, 13). Mt Zion had the Tabernacle of David pitched there (I Kings 8:1; Psalms 48:2, 11-12; 2 Samuel 6:12-14). Mt Moriah had the Temple of Solomon built there (2 Chronicles 3:1)

Rev. J. T. Horger, in Fundamental Revelation in Dramatic Symbol (pp. 195-197, 204-207) speaks of the Tabernacle and the Temple. He writes:

> "It was about 1491 B.C. when Moses built a temporary Tabernacle at Mt Sinai, which served until he built the Tabernacle, the same year, according to the specific pattern given him by Jehovah, on Mt Sinai, where the Israelites were then camped. This Tabernacle was carried by the Israelites, through the 40 years of wilderness life, and maintained as a Holy Sanctuary whereever they worshiped, for over 350 years in the land of Canaan. And then, about 1045 B.C., David built a new Tabernacle, and pitched it on Mt Zion in Jerusalem; and went and got the Ark, which had been out of the Tabernacle which Moses built, for about 100 years, and put it in the new Tabernacle which he had built on Mt Zion. (Read together I Sam chapter 4 with I Chronicles, chapters 15 and 16). And then it was about 40 years after David installed the Ark in his new Tabernacle, that Solomon built the magnificent world-wonder Temple on Mt Moriah, also located in Jerusalem. . . . As such, St James refers to the Tabernacle built by David, and set up on Mt Zion, in the southwestern corner of Jerusalem, as a type of the Church composed of the disciples of Jesus Christ -- quoting the prophet he says, "After this I will return, and will again the Tabernacle of David" (Acts 15:16, 17).

The prophet Isaiah said that the mountain of the Lord's house would be exalted above these mountains, that His house would be established in the top of the mountains. That is to say, the Lord's house which is the Church, would be exalted above Mt Gibeon, Mt Zion, and Mt Moriah. These geographical mountains and these structures simply pointed to a spiritual house, even to Christ in His Church. That which was historical becomes typical and finds its fulfillment spiritually in the Church of New Testament times.

A mountain in Scripture is generally significant of a kingdom, whether it be the Kingdom of God, or Satan or the world systems (Read Jeremiah 51:25; Daniel 2:35, 45; Joel 2:1; Revelation 17:9; 21:10).

A house in Scripture is generally symbolic of a Church, whether true or false. The Church is God's house (Hebrews 3:6). The believers together constitute the household of God (Ephesians 2:19). The Church is a spiritual house and the believers are kings and priests to offer up spiritual sacrifices acceptable to God by Christ (I Peter 2:5-9; Hebrews 10:21; I Corinthians 3:9; Ephesians 2:20-22).

In the symbols of "the mountain" and "the house" we see the Kingdom and the Church brought together. The New Testament reveals that the Church is the instrument for the expression and demonstration of the Kingdom of God in the earth in the "last days"(Matthew 16:16-19; 24:14).

The prophecy of Isaiah becomes significant in the light of the history of the Old Testament. God had a house in a mountain. The Tabernacle of Moses in Gibeon (the revelation having been given in Mt Sinai), was once God's house, His habitation. The Tabernacle of David, in Mt Zion, was once God's habitation, His dwelling place amongst His people. The Temple of Solomon in Mt Moriah was also His house. Each of these became typical structures in these mountains and pointed to the Church in the last days in the mountain of the Kingdom of God.

Isaiah also foretold how the Lord's house would be established and exalted in these last days. In the New Testament we see God building, establishing, and exalting His house (Acts 16:5; Romans 1:11; 2 Peter 1:12; Matthew 16:18; I Peter 2:5; I Corinthians 3:16).

What then is the purpose of God establishing His house? Isaiah answers by saying that "all nations shall flow unto it" (Isaiah 2:2). This utterance surely pointed to the Gospel of Christ going into all nations. The Gospel began to be preached at Jerusalem, then Judea, then Samaria and from thence to the uttermost part of the earth (Acts 1:8; Luke 24:47-49; Matthew 28:18-20; Mark 16:15-20).

In contrast to the Old Testament "typical" houses in those mountains which were especially for one chosen nation, the New Testament revelation of the Church is for all nations to flow into. It is in God's house that all nations will be taught God's ways and paths. Here they will learn His laws, the laws of the New Covenant (Isaiah 2:2-3; Jeremiah 31:31-34; Hebrews 8).

The drawing power of the uplifted Christ is evident here in the flowing of the nations into the house of the Lord. Out of every kindred, tongue, tribe, and nation, Jews and Gentiles will flow into God's house (Revelation 5:9-10).

God is no longer concerned with material buildings and geographical mountains. He is concerned about His Church, and His Kingdom. These things in the Old Testament simply pointed to the spiritual fulfillment in the New Testament.

Thus:

The Old Testament		The New Testament
(The Former Days)		(The Last Days)
1. Tabernacle of Moses in Mt Gibeon		The Church, God's Tabernacle, God's House
2. Tabernacle of David in Mt Zion		
3. Temple of Solomon in Mt Moriah		
The natural, material, and the temporal, the typical	pointed to	The spiritual and the eternal, the reality

The following diagram helps to illustrate the truths set forth in this chapter.

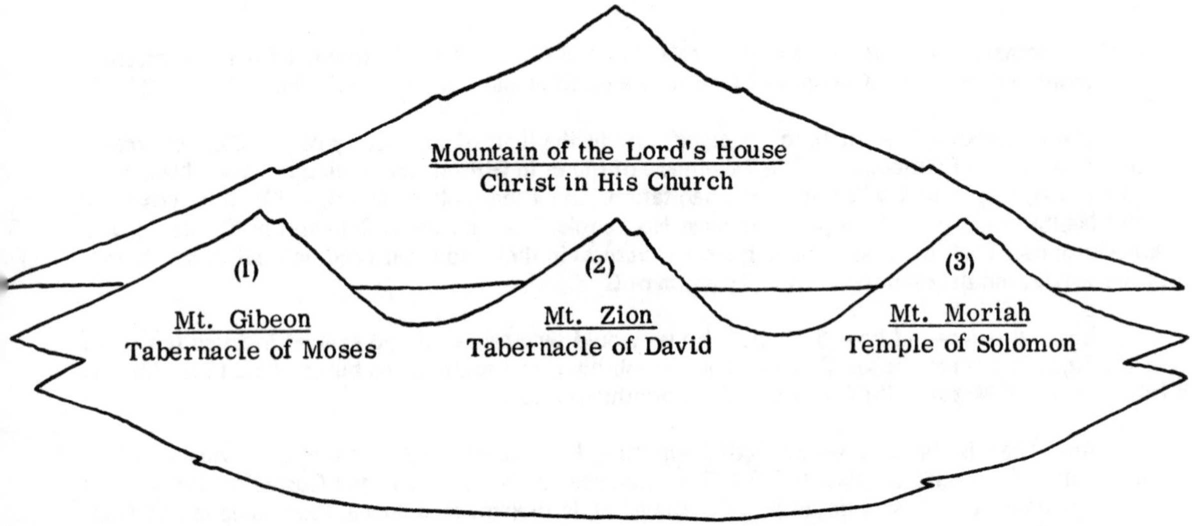

The last of the last days are upon the world. God is building His house and nations are flowing into His Church. The worship of David's Tabernacle, which was incorporated into Solomon's Temple, is being established in the true Zion, the Spiritual habitation of God which is His Church.

Chapter 31

THE ARK INTO SOLOMON'S TEMPLE

In this chapter we come to the final resting place of the Lord. This was in the Temple of Solomon. The journeyings of the Ark have been followed from its construction at Mt. Sinai through to the Tabernacle of David in Mt. Zion. The Ark of the Lord had been with Israel all through the wilderness wanderings. When Israel entered Canaan the Ark was set in the Tabernacle of Moses at Shiloh. With the corruption of the priesthood at Shiloh under Eli's period of ministration the Ark is taken from Shiloh and captured by the Philistines. After a number of months in the various cities of the Philistines, by reason of the judgments of God they were forced to return the Ark to God's people. In due time, after David had fulfilled God's due order concerning the Ark when in transit, it was brought into the Tabernacle of David in Mt. Zion. In Zion David established the order of worship around the Ark of God. The Ark had been transferred from the Tabernacle of Moses to David's Tabernacle never ever to return there. As already noticed, the Ark represented the presence and glory of God in the midst of His people.

The Tabernacle of David was in function for over thirty years in David's time and continued into the early years of Solomon's reign. The time came when the Temple was built and the Ark experienced its final journey.

It should be remembered that David not only pitched the Tabernacle in Zion under the will of God, but he also was the one who received the revelation and pattern of the Temple (1 Chronicles 28:11-21;29:1-25). Not only did David receive the Temple pattern but the order of worship which was established in his Tabernacle was incorporated into the order of Solomon's Temple. David himself could not build the Temple as he had been a man of war and had shed blood abundantly in battle. Solomon, the king of peace, would build it in the great period of Israel's rest from surrounding enemies (1 Chronicles 22:6-10).

There are several ways in which to view the Temple of Solomon, even as the Tabernacle of Moses. Each of these views have their particular facet of truth. The Temple may be considered in the following ways:

1. The Temple as a type of the Lord Jesus Christ. He is THE Temple of God (John 2:19-21).

2. The Temple as a type of the Church, the Body of Christ (1 Corinthians 3:16; 6:19; Ephesians 2:18-22).

3. The Temple as a type of the eternal Kingdom order as seen in the city of God which is called the Tabernacle of God with men (Revelation 21:3).

The New Testament writers confirm the things mentioned here. The Temple of Solomon is a complete study in itself, even as the Tabernacle of Moses and the Tabernacle of David. It is the third facet of truth which is applied here because of the consistency of interpretation of the type under consideration throughout this book.

The details of the building of the Temple of Solomon are recorded for us in the Book of Kings and Chronicles (1 Kings 5-7; 2 Chronicles 3-4).

The Temple was built of timber and stones overlaid with gold. The walls inside the Holy Place and the Holiest of All were overlaid with gold. They were also studded with all manner of precious stones and ornamented with figures of Cherubim, lions, oxen, and palm trees. Even the floor of the Temple was covered with gold. In the Holy Place there were ten Golden Candlesticks, ten Tables of Shewbread and then the Altar of Incense. All was built according to the Divine pattern given to David.

The final act on the day of dedication was the bringing up of the Ark of the Lord out of the Tabernacle of David in Mt. Zion to the Temple in Mt. Moriah.

The Scripture tells us how Solomon assembled all the elders of Israel, the heads of the tribes, and all the men of Israel to bring up the Ark of God. This took place significantly in the seventh month, in the Feast of Tabernacles (1 Kings 8:1-2; 2 Chronicles 5:1-3). The Feast of Tabernacles was the most glorious Feast of the year; greater than Passover, greater than Pentecost (Leviticus 23). These Feasts find their antitypical fulfillment in Christ and the Church also.

Solomon, the elders, and the Levites brought the Ark of God up out of David's Tabernacle and placed it in the Holiest of All in the Temple. The Holiest of All was called "The Holy Oracle." It was foursquare, being 20 X 20 X 20 cubits in cubical measurements.

As soon as the Ark of God was set in the Most Holy Place, the staves were taken out of it and placed beside the Ark. These staves made of shittim wood and overlaid with gold had been placed in the sides of the Ark under the command of the Lord to Moses and were never to be removed (Exodus 25:13-15 with 1 Kings 8:8; 2 Chronicles 5:9).

All through the journeyings of the Ark the staves were used to transport it, being carried on the shoulders of the priests. The staves were significant of the fact that the Lord was with His people who were really strangers and pilgrims in this world looking for a city whose builder and maker is God (Matthew 18:20; John 15:19; 1 Peter 2:11; 1 John 3:1; Hebrews 11:10-16; 13:14).

There was no rest or permanency in the wilderness wanderings. But when the staves were removed from the Ark it was because the journeys were ended. Rest and permanency were found in the Temple of the Lord.

Not only were the staves taken out but we are told that there was nothing in the Ark except the two Tables of the Law (1 Kings 8:9; 2 Chronicles 5:10). The Golden Pot of Manna was gone. The Budding Rod of Aaron was gone. Only God's eternal Law remained.

While the dedication service was in progress, the priests and the Levites with the trumpeters and singers were worshipping according to the order of David. For about thirty years or more this order had been in preparation. Now it was the day of dedication for the Temple. When the singers and trumpeters were one, making one sound in praise and music, the Scripture tells us that the Glory of the Lord filled the house. The priests came out of the Holiest of All and none could minister by reason of the Glory of the Lord (1 Kings 8:10-11; 2 Chronicles 5:11-14). All of this took place in the Feast of Tabernacles, the most glorious Feast in Israel.

Years before, at the dedication of the Tabernacle of Moses at Mt. Sinai, the Glory had descended upon the Ark, filling the Tabernacle with its light. No man could minister by reason of that Glory (Exodus 40:34-38). And now, years later, the Glory settles upon the Ark of God in the Temple of Solomon in Mt. Moriah.

God had indeed gone from "tent to tent, and from one tabernacle to another" (1 Chronicles 17:3-5; 2 Samuel 7:4-7). And now He has moved from the tent or Tabernacle of David into the Temple.

The tent stage also was significant of the pilgrimage character of God's people. They have lived in tents in the wilderness days. Now in Canaan houses are replacing the tents. Permanency is taking precedence over the wanderings. The journeys and travelling days are over. Peace, rest, and permanency are the things which characterize the Temple stage. No staves, no Manna, no Budding Rod; just the Law of God and the Shekinah Glory of God dwelling upon the Ark, God's throne. Having taken His people out of Egypt, the house of bondage; having travelled with them all through the wilderness; having been with them through the temptation, trials, servitudes and deliverances in Canaan, God's Glory and presence is now visibly manifest as He takes up His abode upon the blood-stained mercy seat. The priests now minister in the Temple of the Lord in their twenty four courses.

But it is here that our type completes itself. We conclude our chapter by comparing the typical truths in the Temple with that which is set forth in the City of God, the eternal habitation of the redeemed.

	The Temple of God (O.T. Type)		The City of God (N.T. Antitype)
1.	The Temple, the habitation of God	---	The City, the Tabernacle of God
2.	The Ark of God set in the Holiest of All, which was foursquare	---	The City of God is foursquare
3.	The Glory of God was the only light	---	The Glory of God is the light thereof
4.	The Presence of God in the midst of His people	---	The Presence of God and the Lamb in the midst of the redeemed
5.	The staves removed from the Ark, journeyings ended	---	The throne of God and the Lamb - journeyings are over
6.	No Manna in the Ark	---	Christ, the hidden Manna (Revelation 2:17).
7.	No fruitful Rod in the Ark	---	Christ and the Church have the Rod of God (Revelation 2:26-27)
8.	The Tables of the Law only remain in the Ark	---	The Law of God now written in the the fleshy tables of the heart of the redeemed (Jeremiah 31:31-34).
9.	Mt. Zion and Mt. Moriah vitally linked in David's Tabernacle and Solomon's Temple as God's habitation	---	The City of God seen in an exceeding great and high mountain as God's eternal habitation
10.	The walls and floor of the Temple lined with gold. Priests walk on gold floor	---	The City and streets of transparent gold, for redeemed to walk on
11.	The walls are studded with all manner of precious stones	---	The foundation walls are garnished with twelve precious stones
12.	Dedicated in the Feast of Rest and Glory; Feast of Tabernacles	---	Saints will experience eternal Rest and Glory in Tabernacle of God
13.	The Feast of the Seventh Month was called the Feast of Tabernacles	---	Revelation is a Book of Sevens, and closes with the Tabernacle of God being with men forever

14.	Rest, peace, and permanency characterize the Temple	---	Eternal rest, peace, and permanence characterize the City of God
15.	The Priests minister with sacrifices and incense to the Lord	---	The redeemed are Kings and Priests to to God and the Lamb, offering spiritual sacrifices and incense of prayer and praise eternally
16.	The Priests minister in their twenty-four courses day and night	—	The redeemed will minister day and night eternally in their courses
17.	David's order of worship with singers and musicians was incorporated into the Temple order	---	The Son of David's order of worship with singing and music will be established forever in the Tabernacle of God

These comparisons could be extended. Sufficient have been given here to show the aspect of truth typified in the Ark being taken from David's Tabernacle into the Temple as its final resting place. The City of God is the Tabernacle of God with men. It is the eternal habitation of God and the redeemed.

God has always desired to dwell with and amongst His redeemed people. The Old Testament typical dwellings show the progressive revelation of this redemptive theme.

He dwelt with man in the Garden of Eden (Genesis 3:8, 24).
He dwelt among His people Israel in the Tabernacle of Moses (Exodus 25:8, 22).
He dwelt with Israel in the Tabernacle of David (1 Chronicles 17:1-3).
He dwelt with His people in the Temple of Solomon (2 Chronicles 5).

The full revelation was in the Lord Jesus Christ, who was God's Tabernacle and Temple personified (John 1:14; 2:19-21; Colossians 1:19; 2:9). His eternal dwelling place is the City of God, the new and heavenly Jerusalem (Revelation 21-22).

> "And I John saw the holy city, new Jerusalem, coming down from God out of heaven, prepared as a bride adorned for her husband. And I heard a great voice out of heaven saying, Behold the Tabernacle of God is with men, and He will dwell with them, and they shall be His people, and God Himself will be with them, and be their God. And God shall wipe away all tears from their eyes; and there shall be no more death, neither sorrow, nor crying, neither shall there be any more pain; for the former things are passed away" (Revelation 21:2-4).

Chapter 32

THEOLOGICAL TRUTHS IN THE TABERNACLE OF DAVID

It is recognized as a principle of Biblical interpretation that God used people, offices and institutions in the Old Testament to shadow forth and typify either Christ or His church, or both.

In an earlier chapter we saw that God often got men to do typically in the Old Testament what He Himself would fulfill actually in the New Testament. This was true of the life and times of king David.

While we do not build doctrine on types, types may be used to illustrate doctrine. We note in our final chapter some of the major theological truths foreshadowed and typified in David's Tabernacle, whether it be the kingly Tabernacle or the priestly Tabernacle. Amplification of these have been covered in the text, so they are listed out only in summary form here.

1. The Davidic Covenant finds its fulfillment in the New Covenant, in David's greater Son, Jesus Christ, King of kings and Lord of lords (Matthew 1:1; 2 Samuel 17; Psalm 89; Jeremiah 33:17-26; Revelation 5:5; 22:16).

2. The throne of David pointed to the throne of Christ. Christ sat on David's throne in His resurrection and exaltation to the Father's right hand. He is ruling and reigning in His kingdom now (Acts 2; Psalm 2; Psalm 24; Psalm 72).

3. The Ark of the Covenant of the Lord, with its blood-stained mercy seat finds fulfillment in His atoning work. It is a finished work and so Christ sits at the right hand of the Father until all His enemies become His footstool (Psalm 2; Psalm 110; Hebrews 7).

4. Mt. Zion and Jerusalem pointed to the heavenly Mt. Zion and Jerusalem which is above. Zion was a political and governmental city for KING David on his throne. Zion was also an ecclesiastical and spiritual city for the PRIESTS to minister before the Ark of God under David's order. Zion had both established there. So does the heavenly Zion of which the earthly one was but a shadow.

5. David being a king also touched the office of a priest. This foreshadowed the royal priesthood, the order of Melchisedek, as fulfilled in Christ and His church. Believers are a royal priesthood of which Christ is the head (1 Peter 2:5-9; Revelation 1:6; 5:9-10; 20:4-6; Hebrews 7; Psalm 110; Genesis 14:18-20).

6. The cessation of animal sacrifices, after the dedicatory sacrifices, pointed to the dedicatory sacrifices of Christ's body and blood and the cessation of animal sacrifices after Calvary (Daniel 9:24-27; Hebrews 9-10 chapters).

7. Sacrifices of praise, joy, thanksgiving and worship became the order of David's Tabernacle, around the Ark (throne) of God (Psalm 27:5, 6; Hebrews 13:13-16; Romans 12:1-2; 1 Peter 2:5-9). David established the order of singers and musicians in that Tabernacle. Such are the sacrifices of believers in the church as they praise and worship the Lord.

8. The transfer of the Ark of the Covenant from the Tabernacle of Moses on Gibeon to the Tabernacle of David on Zion signified the transfer of the glory and presence of God from the Old Covenant to the New Covenant church. It symbolized access within the veil, into the presence of God, access within the Holiest of All (Matthew 27:51; Hebrews 6:19, 20; Hebrews 10).

9. **The Tabernacle of David would become open to the Gentiles as well as the Jews under Messianic times. So it foreshadowed the Jews and Gentiles coming into the kingdom of God, and into the New Covenant church as one body. Here they would worship together apart from ceremonials and ritualisms of the Mosaic law (Acts 10-11; Acts 15; Romans 9, 10, 11; Zechariah 2:11; Malachi 1:11; Isaiah 11:10).**

10. **The Lord said He would build again the Tabernacle of David that was fallen down. He said He would build His church. The New Covenant church is the Tabernacle of the Lord that is being built today (Matthew 16:15-19; Acts 15:15-18; Amos 9:11). All that was foreshadowed forth in the order of praise and worship, as to that in spirit and truth, finds fulfillment in the church of our Lord Jesus Christ.**

— AMEN AND AMEN —

CONCLUSION

Our study is completed. Under the outpouring of the Holy Spirit in the early Church on both Jew and Gentile, James, by a word of wisdom quoted the prophecy of Amos concerning the building of the Tabernacle of David. The whole purpose of this was for the coming in of the Gentiles. The Gentiles were not to be placed under the Law, that is, in the Tabernacle of Moses under the Old Covenant. They were to come in on the ground of grace, that is, into the Tabernacle of David which was symbolic of the New Covenant. In this Tabernacle, Jew and Gentile would become one in Christ on the ground of grace, apart from the works of the Law and ceremonials of the Law Covenant.

Our consideration of the historical setting of David's Tabernacle and the details involved therein have shown us the typical and spiritual significances foreshadowed.

David, in this experience, reached over to another dispensation – the dispensation of grace. His Tabernacle becomes a typical and symbolic representation and enactment of that which the Son of David would fulfill in New Testament times.

There are several persons in the Old Testament dispensation who were permitted by God to reach over to the New Testament dispensation and to experience the powers of another age to come. Enoch experienced the change over from mortality to immortality and was translated from earth to heaven without dying. He reached over several thousands of years and experienced that which is especially reserved for the generation alive at the second coming of Christ (Genesis 5:21-24; Hebrews 11:5; Jude 14, 15; with 1 Thessalonians 4:13-18).

Elijah also had a similar experience (2 Kings 2:9-11). As already referred to, Aaron's entrance within the veil in the Tabernacle was also a typical and prophetic foreshadowing of Christ's entrance within the veil of the heavenly Sanctuary (Hebrews 9:1-10; 6:19-20; 10:19-20). Abraham experienced the truth of justification by faith and was counted a faith righteous man (Romans 4), even though the full revelation of faith righteousness was founded upon the blood of Christ under the New Testament dispensation.

And the same is true of David and his Tabernacle. The period of time during which the events pertaining to David's Tabernacle transpired was a foreshadowing of the coming dispensation of grace. King David and the Levites in the order of worship before the Ark of God reached over into the New Testament dispensation. All pointed to the transference of the Holiest of All and entrance within the veil being made available for Jews and Gentiles under the New Covenant era.

The New Testament dispensation is the fulfillment of that Old Testament historical, typical and prophetical enactment of David's Tabernacle. God is not building a literal or material tent as David pitched for the Ark. He is building His Church, a spiritual house, a habitation of God by the Spirit (Matthew 16:18; 1 Corinthains 3:9; 1 Peter 2:5; Ephesians 2:20-22; Acts 15:16). Both Jew and Gentile together constitute the Church, Christ's house. There was only ever one Tabernacle of Moses, one Tabernacle of David and one Temple of Solomon. All of this pointed to the fact that there would only ever be one Christ and one true Church, which is His Body. This one house would be composed of Jew and Gentile, all one in Christ. Here around the true Ark, the Lord Jesus Christ Himself, Jew and Gentile, gather together for worship within the veil.

Today, that order of worship and freedom of access within the veil, lost to the hearts of God's people during the "dark ages" of Church history, is being rediscovered and all may enter in.

APPENDIX I

INTERPRETATION OF "SELAH"

The following quotation is taken from John Stainer in Music of the Bible, (pp. 82, 83), printed by Novello & Company, Ltd., London., 1879. Here he suggests some interpretation of this word Selah.

> "The Lord is known by the judgment which he executeth: the wicked is snared in the work of his own hands. Higgaion. Selah." The marginal note translates Higgaion as a "meditation." As the root of the word suggests "meditation," or "murmuring," and as it is used In Lam. iii. 62 of the murmurings of malicious enemies, the term can hardly be considered as a musical direction. But on the other hand it occurs in Ps. xcii. 3, in such an association as to render a musical reference almost necessary: - "Upon an instrument of ten strings, and upon the psaltery; upon the harp with a solemn sound," or, as the margin has it, more correctly, "upon the higgaion (solemn sound) with the harp." The Prayer-book version, it will be remembered, here reads "upon a loud instrument." It may possibly allude to a solemn and deep-toned performance on harps, which was found conducive to private meditation. Its conjunction with Selah makes this explanation the more probable.
>
> The term Selah, which occurs three times in the Book of Habakkuk, and no less than seventy-one times in the Psalms, has been variously interpreted as indicating (1) a pause; (2) repetition (like Da Capo); (3) the end of a strophe; (4) a playing with full power (fortissimo); (5) a bending of the body, an obeisance; (6) a short recurring symphony (a ritornello). Of all these the last seems the most probable. In a lecture on the subject, given by Sir F. Ouseley, a Psalm was sung into which such ritornelli on stringed instruments and trumpets were introduced at every occurrence of the word Selah. The effect was considered imposing and devotional. The fact that twenty-eight of the thirty-nine Psalms in which this word occurs have musical superscriptions seems to compel belief that it was a direction to the musical performers.*

Stainer (pp. 90-94) expresses his indebtedness to the Reverend E. Capel Cure for his especial study of the poetry and musical allusions in the Psalter, and for the clearest and most convincing account of the actual use of the Selah.

Because the book in its original printing is not generally available to the reader, Reverend E. Capel Cure's explanation is reproduced in full from Stainer's Music of the Bible.

> Baethgen and other commentators consider that Selah is an attempt on the part of Hebrew scribes to represent the Greek word Psalle (ψαλλε) meaning "play," derived from some Greek bandmaster and used as the direction for a musical interlude. I am, however, greatly indebted to the Rev. E. Capel Cure, who has made an especial study of the poetry and musical allusions of the Psalter, for the clearest and most convincing account of the actual use of the Selah. His explanation is as follows, the quotations being made from the Revised Version: - "To say that Selah - whatever its derivation - is a musical interlude throws no light on the difficult problem which such passages present as are to be found in Psalm lv., verses 7, 19: for here there seems little sense in orchestral interludes rushing in upon incomplete similes and unfinished sentences, reducing both to meaningless incoherence. Surely the introduction of music in these and similar passages cannot have been intended for idle interruption, but for a definite purpose, that is, for an illustration in sound of the words sung, in the same way as a picture would present an illustration in line and colour of the letterpress. Such a sound-picture at once delays and sustains the imagination, filling (in the first instance mentioned above) the ears and mind of the listeners with the fury and noise of the storm through which the frightened dove beats its way to a peaceful wilderness: the

longer the storm of clapping hands and beating feet lasted (imitating the roll of thunder and hiss of hail), the more the pulse of the harp arpeggios (so singularly like the beat of the dove's wing) was heard, now lost in the turmoil of these mingled means of musical description and now, as the rushing wind and rain lulled and lessened, rising with a triumphal sense of final safety, the more meaning did this intrusion of picture-music carry into the words with which at length the choir enter 'I would haste me to a shelter from the stormy wind and tempest.' So also in the 19th verse of the same Psalm, 'God shall hear and answer them': thus sing the choir; and there is no need for the poet to say more, for the instruments with an impressive eloquence indicate the horror of the answer. As in the Selah the reed-pipes wail out the familiar funeral dirge, all men know what God's answer is: and when the dirge is finished and silence reigns, the choir complete the sentence to which this significant interruption has given such subtle irony, 'God will answer . . . the men who have no changes' with the change of Death. Selah then is always a musical interlude, but not always what is known to modern critics as 'pure music.' Where it separates stanzas, it may be mere sound appealing by the beauty of its melody or combination of instruments: more often it represents what we now call 'programme music,' and is consciously and deliberately descriptive of the text which it accompanies.

"Besides the Flight and Storm motive, which we ascribe to the harps and clapping hands and feet, and which may be found very effectively employed also in Psalm lxi. after the 4th verse, 'I will take refuge in the covert of thy wings. Selah,' and besides the Death motive (probably given out on the reed-pipes) which illustrates so many Psalms with its cruel suggestiveness (Ps. lii.5; lvii.3; lix.5, 13; &c), there are two other Selahs in constant use - the Sacrifice and War Selahs - both with trumpets, though probably with different sorts of trumpets.

"It is known that the sound of trumpets accompanied the ritual of the altar, a blare of silver trumpets blowing, as it were, the sacrificial smoke heavenwards: once the victim was consumed the offertory music was silent. Here then is the explanation of the difficult words 'God is gone up with a shout, the Lord with the sound of a trumpet' (Ps. xlvii.5). The Selah preceding this verse was the sacrificial interlude of trumpets augmented with loud hallelujahs, which die away as the smoke grows thinner until, over the dying embers of the sacrifice, the Levites come in again to say that Jehovah, who had seemed to them to stoop from highest heaven to receive the gift, had returned once more to His lofty throne.

"The Selah in Psalm lxvi. 15, proves the poem to be a true service of the altar. 'I will offer bullocks with goats' is sung, and straightway, in a pause which the priests fill with their trumpets, the bullocks and goats are really offered, after which the singers resume their song.

"The War motive is found picturesquely enough in Psalm lx.4 and lxxvi.3, and less certainly in Psalm l.6. It would probably be given out on the shophar, the curved ram's horn, which had its own tremendous associations of alarm and terror (Exodus xix). In Psalm xlix, there is a striking combination of motives: between verses 13 and 14 comes the Death Selah to emphasise the awful threat 'Death shall be their shepherd,' while the words of the later verse, 15, 'He shall receive me.' find their explanation in the Sacrificial Selah, trumpets declaring the favour of God on the living sacrifice of the worshipper's self and soul.

"With what eloquent effect the Selah could be used by one who was both artist and prophet may be seen in Habakkuk's hymn (Habakkuk, Ch. 3). Nowhere else in the Old Testament is anything so like our modern libretto to be found, where obviously the words are written with conscious regard to the effect and colour of the accompanying music.

"It is a most vivid word-picture of a tropical storm, which, however, depends on the orchestra for its fullest effect. The storm motive with its mimic thunder rushes in in the first Selah (verse 3) to explain how 'God came from Teman.' Always for the Israelite the Creator was behind His creation, but here His presence is audible. The music makes its own picture of heavy thunder-clouds, which envelop Mount Teman and come sweeping upward from the western horizon. Soon, however, words are introduced to give a clear description of the path and progress of the devastating storm, the wild melody being sustained and reinforced by a restless agitato of the string accompaniment. In effective contrast to this the composer provides a double opportunity for new orchestral colour in two other Selahs, intended not merely to relieve the ear, but, as it were, to illuminate and emblazon the truths which He wished to enforce. God's power, as exhibited in the rush of wind and roll of thunder, is the measure alike of His unbroken word and His awful justice. 'The oaths to the tribes were a sure word' (verse 9) - at once the strings are hushed before a blast of trumpets, carrying with it the solemn associations of the Sacrifice and all it implied of God's covenant of protection. But if there is mercy, there is also judgment; and the terrible vision of the battle-field, where the sweeping scimitar has exposed the very bones of the severed neck, receives a thrilling intensification, from the Death Selah, which immediately follows (verse 13).

"In this interpretation of the word Selah, it will be seen that no excessive demand is made on the technique or resources of primitive performers: but - while every effect was produced by the simplest means - the instrumentalists of the Temple did for the singers what the artist does when he adds colour to the outline: in fact, so much do some of the Psalms depend upon their instrumental performance, that many of the phrases are only intelligible with the due understanding of their Selahs; while in all cases where the Selah is not a mere symphony between stanzas, the interludes deepen the glowing intensity of the words as much as Wagner's music glorifies his libretti."

APPENDIX II

DANCING

One of the more expressive forms of worship is the dance. As with other expressions of man's being, dancing may be associated with good or evil. Phil Kerr in Music in Evangelism (p. 24), states, "Dancing was originally used only in religious worship. Dancing is an expression of emotion, just as music is, and mankind employed both dancing and music in expressing the natural desire for worship." Both in Bible days and throughout history to our modern times, dancing has been associated with either good or evil in various cultures.

A. Dancing associated with good.

1. Exodus 15:20, Miriam and the women in Israel danced and sang before the Lord with timbrels after the victory of the Red Sea. It was unto the Lord, not to man or mere display. This is the first recorded dancing in the Bible. After being in bondage for several hundred years, God delivered them. They danced out of great joy before the Lord for such deliverance. The Hebrew word "mekholaw" (S.C. 4246) means "a round dance, a company of dancers." The believer has been delivered from bondage also by the blood of the true Passover Lamb, Jesus Christ. Therefore he can dance before the Lord.

2. Judges 11:34, Jephthah's daughter came out to meet her father with timbrels and dances after the victory the Lord had given in the battle against the Ammonites. The same Hebrew word (S.C. 4246) is used here as in Exodus 15:20.

3. 1 Samuel 18:6-7; 21:11; 29:5, the women of Israel sang and danced with tabrets of joy and instruments of music after David had killed the giant Philistine, Goliath of Gath. The Lord had given David a great victory. The Hebrew word is the same as the previous two Scriptures, and signifies "a round dance, a company of dancers."

4. 2 Samuel 6:14-16, David danced before the Lord at the coming up of the Ark on the day of dedication of the Tabernacle of David. The Hebrew word "karar" (S.C. 3769) means "to dance, to whirl about." Thus, David danced or whirled about vigorously before the Lord as an act of worship. Michel despised this manifestation of joy, but David said that it was done before the Lord.

5. 1 Chronicles 15:29, the account here is the same as above, and records how David danced before the Ark of the Lord. The writer here used the Hebrew word "raqad" (S.C. 7540) which means "to stamp, to spring about, wildly or for joy" and it is translated by the words dance, jump, leap and skip. Other Scripture references to this same word may be found in Psalms 114:4, 6; Psalms 29:6.

6. Jeremiah 31:(4), 12, 13, Jeremiah prophesied of the time coming in Zion when the Lord would restore the dance to young and old alike. They would rejoice before the Lord with dancing and singing. The virgin, the young and the old would have their mourning turned to joy and would dance before the Lord in Praise. The Hebrew word used here is a derivative of "chuwl" (S.C. 2342) and means "to twist or whirl in a spiral or circular manner." This Hebrew word has a vast majority of usage and has to do with extreme grief, pain, fear, shakings, and even the pangs of childbirth. The word is used to describe expressions of grief or joy. In this prophecy of Jeremiah it is indicative of great joy in the dance. Read also Deuteronomy 2:25; Micah 4:10; Psalms 10:5; 29:8, 9; Job 15:20.

7. Lamentations 5:15, no dancing in Israel was a sign of mourning. When Judah was taken to Babylonian bondage, the dance was lost. "The joy of our heart is ceased, our dance is turned into mourning." When a person is in spiritual bondage, joy and dancing are lost (S.C. 4234).

8. Psalms 30:11, David rejoiced that God had turned his mourning into dancing. The Hebrew word "chuwl" (Refer to S.C. 4246, 4234 with 2342) again tells us that David danced before the Lord in a twisting or whirling manner.

9. Psalms 149:3, we are to praise the name of the Lord in the dance.

10. Psalms 150:4, we are to praise Him with the timbrel and the dance (S.C. 4234).

11. Luke 15:25, at the return of the prodigal son to the Father's house, there was music and dancing. The elder brother refused to go in. His wrong attitude to his father and his brother robbed him of entering into the joy of the feast. The Greek word "choros" (S.C. 5525) means "a ring, or round dance ("choir"), dancing."

As God the Father is restoring the prodigal sons to His house today, music and dancing are part of the festival joy. Believers must not have the spirit or attitude of the elder brother and rob themselves of that which already belongs to them.

12. Matthew 11:17; Luke 7:32, the children used to pipe and dance in the market place. The Greek word "orcheomai" (from "orchos", S.C. 3738) means to "dance, in a row or ring, from the rank like or regular motion."

Thus, dancing was an expressive form of joy or praise or worship in the history of the nation of Israel, God's people.

B. Dancing associated with evil.

1. Exodus 32:19, Israel danced before the golden calf in idolatrous feasting and riotous music. The very nation which had danced in joy before the Lord at the Red Sea now dances before a golden calf. The dance was corrupt because of the god they worshipped and the music that was associated with it. The Hebrew word is the same as in Exodus 15:20 (S.C. 4246).

2. Judges 21:21-23, the men of Benjamin used the dances of Shiloh to take a wife for themselves because of the previous judgment which had fallen on the tribe for its sin (Refer to S.C. 2342 with 4246).

3. Job 21:7-12, the wicked use the timbrel, harp, and organ in their dancing also (S.C. 7540). The same word as used in 1 Chronicles 15:29.

4. 1 Samuel 30:16, the Amalekites were eating and drinking and dancing over the spoils of battle. The Hebrew word "chagag" (S.C. 2287) means "to move in a circle, to march in sacred procession, to observe a festival" and by implication "to be giddy." Thus, the Amalekites were having a festival, reeling to and fro in the dance and march because of their victory over David and his army.

5. Matthew 14:6; Mark 6:22, Herod's daughter danced before him. He became so infatuated with her dancing that he had the prophet John the Baptist beheaded because of his vain promise. The Greek word used is "orchemai" (S.C. 3738) and is the same word as used in Matthew 11:17 and Luke 7:32.

C. Other related expressive words.

There are other Hebrew and Greek words used in Scripture which also show an emotional or physical expression, used either for good or evil. These words are noted here.

1. Old Testament words.

a. Rejoice, Hebrew "geel" or "gool" (S.C. 1523).

This word means "a revolution," from "to spin around (under the influence of any violent emotion)," and it is translated "rejoice," and "be joyful." Refer to Psalms 2:11; 32:11; 9:14; 13:4,5; 14:7; 51:8; 53:6; 118:24; Isaiah 35:1,2; 65:18; Joel 2:21.

b. Leap, Hebrew "dah-lag" (S.C. 1801).

This word means "to spring or leap." Several examples of this are found in the following references: Zephaniah 1:9; 2 Samuel 22:30; Psalms 18:29; Isaiah 35:6; Song of Solomon 2:8.

2. New Testament words.

a. Rejoice, Greek "agalliao" (S. C. 21). From "agan" (much) and "hallomai" (to jump, leap, spring up).

It means "to jump for joy," and is translated "exult," "be exceeding glad," "with exceeding joy," "rejoice greatly" (Luke 1:14, 44, 47; 10:21; Matthew 5:12; John 5:35; 8:56; Acts 2:26, 46; 16:34; I Peter 1:6,8; Revelation 19:7).

b. Leap, Greek "skirtao" (S.C. 4640).

This word means "to jump, move, leap (for joy)," or "to skip." It is used in Luke 1:41, 44; 6:23.

c. Leaping, Greek "hallomai" (S.C. 242).

The word means "to jump, leap, spring up." (John 4:14; Acts 3:8; 14:10) The lame man went walking, and leaping and praising God, into the Temple with Peter and John.

In concluding our remarks upon the dancing in Scripture we see how this expression was related to either good or evil. All nations on earth have some form or type of dancing. Heathen dancing, as seen in Africa on their festival occasions, as well as other nations, cause the body to make various gyrations. These gyrations stimulate sensual drives. The tribal dances are accompanied with jungle music and associated with the worship of false gods. Together the music and dancing opens the way for the evil spirit to enter and take control. These dances generally end up with the most vile orgies. These heathen voodoo rites, these vulgar sensuous body movements, find their modern counterpart in the "Rock Festivals" of recent years.

Over the centuries, various forms of dancing have come and gone. The dance has been taken by Satan and corrupted. He has used the power of this expression to speak a body language that is earthly, sensual, and devilish.

The type of music affects dancing also. It is because music and dancing have become associated with sensuality and immorality that the Church, as a whole, shrinks from the very mention of the word. Especially if this is associated with worship unto the Lord.

True joy and rejoicing belongs to the redeemed people of the Lord. When these things can be done to the glory and praise of God, they are expressions of worship. If the motivation is self display, or associated with sensuous movements of the body, then it is carnal and glorifies Satan.

"Dancing in the Spirit" is not used in the Scripture but "dancing before the Lord" is a Scriptural expression. Music and dancing were generally associated with WORSHIP! If the heathen can worship false gods in the dance, and the unregenerate worship their "hero" in the dance, the believer should be able to worship the true God in the dance, whether individually or collectively. It is interesting to note that Elisha, the prophet with the double portion of the Spirit, was born in "Abel-meholah," which some Bible Dictionaries suggest means "the meadow of the dance." Apparently it was a place set aside for dancing, whether in mourning or rejoicing.

The believer may truly worship the Lord, either privately or along with other believers, in the dance. There will be times when the Spirit of the Lord will quicken and energize the believer to rejoice, to exalt, to leap, spring about, skip and jump before the Lord. There will be times when groups of believers will join together in worship and joy, as a company of dancers. It will not be by reason of evil or sensuous motivation but a desire to glorify the Lord with the whole being.

However, it is good to remember the injunction, "To every thing there is a season and a time . . . there is a time to dance . . . "(Ecclesiastes 3:4). The one responsible, especially in leadership of corporate worship, will not stereotype services but will allow the Holy Spirit to direct when such an expression of worship may be permitted. The test of all things is whether life and edification is the result in believer's lives, and whether God is glorified or not.

APPENDIX III

BIBLICAL HISTORY OF THE ARK OF THE COVENANT

Because of the importance of the Ark and the great number of references to it, the following brief outline of its history as recorded in the Scripture is given for the student to develop.

The history of the Ark of the Covenant is prophetic of the life story of Jesus Christ. It is HIS-STORY! A key thought or some New Testament Scripture is supplied to open up these areas of truth. Remembering that there are more references to this article than all the other pieces of furniture shows to us the importance of this piece to the Lord God.

As the Ark was first and foremost in Israel's history, so is Jesus Christ first and preeminent in all things before the Father and in the Church, Spiritual Israel. Colossians 1:17-19, "It pleased the Father that . . . in all things He (the Son) should have the preeminence."

The journeyings of the Ark speak of the Lord Jesus Christ in His Birth, Anointing, Life, Ministry, Death and Resurrection, Ascension and Glorification, as well as His Presence with His Church in the Wilderness walk of this earth unto the Eternal Rest and City of God.

A. The Ark at Mt Sinai.

1. Revelation and directions given by the Lord to Moses for the Ark to be made (Exodus 25:10-22).

a. Made of shittim wood. Symbolic of Christ's perfect, sinless, and incorruptible humanity (Psalms 16:10; Luke 1:35; I Peter 1:23; I John 3:5; Jeremiah 23:5; Zechariah 3:8; 6:12).

b. Overlaid within and without with gold. Symbolic of Christ's deity, The Divine nature, The Fulness of the Godhead in Him (I Timothy 3:15-16; Isaiah 7:14; John 1:14; Colossians 1:19; 2:9).

Wood and gold = two natures in the one Person of Christ.
Deity and humanity together making the new creation.

c. The crown of gold round it. Jesus crowned with glory and honor (Hebrews 2:9; Revelation 19:11-21).

d. The four rings of gold in the four corners thereof. The worldwide ministry of Christ to His people (Acts 1:8; Mark 16:15-20).

e. The staves. To keep the Ark balanced. A balanced presentation of the Gospel of Christ (Psalms 85:10).

f. The Mercy Seat and Cherubim (Hebrews 9:1-5; Romans 3:20-27). Christ our bloodstained mercy seat before the Father God. The Two Cherubim in absolute union with the mercy seat are symbolic of that union in the Eternal Godhead, as Father, Son, and Holy Spirit. One piece of gold fashioned into a triunity!

g. The contents of the Ark: the Law, the Manna, the Budding Rod. Symbolic of the Father's Law, the Son our Heavenly Manna, and the Fruitfulness of the Spirit.
Fulness of the Godhead (Hebrews 9:1-5; Exodus 16; Numbers 17; Exodus 19-20).

h. **Its measurements were 2½ cubits long, by 1½ cubits wide, by 1½ cubits high. Symbolic of the Divine standard in God and for all who come to His throne.**

2. **The position of the Ark in the Holiest of All, or Most Holy Place (Exodus 26:34; 40:3).**

3. **Made by Bezaleel according to the pattern given to Moses in the Mount (Exodus 35:12; 37:1-9; cf. Hebrews 10:5-7; Galatians 4:4). So was the humanity of Christ.**

4. **Brought to Moses for inspection when finished (Exodus 39:33-35).**

5. **Anointed with the holy oil (Exodus 30:26; 40:9; cf. Acts 10:38; Isaiah 61:1-3). So was Jesus our Ark anointed (Leviticus 8:10; Luke 4:18).**

6. **The only Meeting place between the Lord and Moses, the Mediator of the Old Covenant (Numbers 7:89; Exodus 25:22; cf. I Timothy 2:5-6). Christ Jesus is the only Mediator between God and Man under the New Covenant.**

7. **The Ark sprinkled with blood on the Day of Atonement once a year. (Leviticus 16:1-2, 14; cf. Hebrews 6:18-20; 10:19-20; John 14:1,6. So Christ was once and for all offered for our sins. Boldness to enter in by the blood of Jesus into the Holiest of All.**

8. **The Ark in the charge of the Kohathites, to be carried on their shoulders (Numbers 3: 27-32).**

9. **The Ark covered in the journey through the Wilderness (Numbers 4:5-6).**

The Covering Veil	**-**	**symbolic of the body of flesh - The Son.**
Cloth of Blue	**-**	**symbolic of the Holy Spirit.**
Badger's skins	**-**	**symbolic of God the Father, over all.**
		No human eye saw the Ark in transit.

10. **The Ark took the <u>central</u> position in the March, when the Cloud moved and the trumpet blew for the journeys of Israel (Numbers 4:13-28; 10: [21], 14-28).**

11. **The Ark was also placed "<u>in the midst</u>" of the Camp when Israel was encamped (Numbers 2:17; cf. Matthew 18:20). Christ in the midst of His people.**

12. **The Ark had various names expressing its glory and ministry.**

The Ark of the Testimony (Exodus 25:22).
The Ark of the Covenant of the Lord (Numbers 10:33).
The Ark of the Lord God (I Kings 2:26).
The Ark of the Lord, the Lord of all the earth (Joshua 3:13).
The Ark of God (I Samuel 3:3).
The Holy Ark (2 Chronicles 35:3).
The Ark of Thy Strength (Psalms 132:8).
The Ark of the Covenant of God (Judges 20:27).
The Ark of the Covenant (Joshua 3:6).
The Ark of the Lord (Joshua 4:11).
The Ark of God the God of Israel (I Samuel 5:7).
The Ark of Shittim Wood (Exodus 25:10).

So Christ has many names, each of which show forth His ministry and glory in the Church. Each have their portion of truth.

B. <u>The Ark in the Wilderness.</u>

1. The Ark's first journey from Mt Sinai leading the way to the Promised Land, seeking Rest for Israel, was three days journey (Numbers 10:33-36; Psalms 68:1-19; cf. Matthew 11: 28-30; 12:38-40). Christ brings us into Rest through the three days and three nights of Calvary.

2. Israel is defeated without the Ark of the Lord in battle (Numbers 14:44). So will the Church be without His Presence.

3. The Rod of Aaron comes alive and is fruitful before the Ark of the Lord. It is placed in the Ark as a witness and attestation of Aaron's anointed priesthood before God and Israel (Numbers 17:10; Hebrews 9:4). Christ is God's anointed and appointed High Priest (Hebrews 4:14; Psalms 110:1-4).

4. The Ark seems to have gone up with the "Holy Instruments" in the battle against Midian (Numbers 31:6). Victory with the Ark there.

5. The Book of the Law-Covenant is placed in the side of the Ark (Deuteronomy 31:9-26; cf. Hebrews 10:5-7). Christ alone kept the Law in His heart.

C. <u>The Ark in the Promised Land.</u>

1. The Ark opens up the River Jordan for the new generation to enter into Canaan, even as the Rod had opened up the Red Sea for the previous generation to enter into the Wilderness. Ark goes 2000 cubits ahead of the people (Joshua 3-4). So Christ has gone 2000 years ahead of the Church, conquering the waters of death. The Church follows Him.

2. Jericho falls after the seven Priests with the seven Trumpets compass the city seven times on the seventh day, with the Ark of the Covenant (Joshua 6; cf. Revelation 8:1-14; 11: 15, 19). Prophetic of End of the Age and Book of Revelation, unto the Second Coming of Christ.

3. Defeat in Ai through the sin of Achan. Joshua falls before the Ark as to sin being dealt with (Joshua 7). No victory while sin there.

4. The Ark is positioned between Mt Ebel, the Mt of Cursing, and Mt Gerizim, the Mt of Blessing. The Blessings and Cursings of the Law are uttered by the Levites with six Tribes of Israel on each mount (Joshua 8:30-35; cf. Matthew 25:31-41). Blessed or Cursed at Christ's coming.

5. Historical Places and Events of the Ark in Canaan Land.

a. Ark at Gilgal when land divided (Joshua 9:6; 10:7-43).

b. Ark at Shiloh (Joshua 18:1-2).

c. Ark at Shechem (Joshua 24:1-28).

d. Ark at Shiloh again (Judges 20:18, 26, 27; 21:2, 12, 19; I Samuel 1:1-6; 3:3).

e. Ark in captivity to the Philistines (Psalms 78:60, 71; Jeremiah 7:8-14). Ark taken out of Shiloh to battle at Aphek and Ebenezer (I Samuel 5:1).

- Ark at Ashdod, in House of Dagon (I Samuel 5:1-7).
  Dagon falls before the Ark (cf. John 18:3-6).
- Ark at Gath (I Samuel 5:8-9).

- Ark at Ekron (I Samuel 5:10-12). Plagues, Death.
  Ark in the hands of the Gentiles.

f. Ark at Bethshemesh. Returned on New Cart with a Trespass Offering by the Philistines. Men of Bethshemesh slain for looking into the Ark. Death on 50,070 (Psalms 132; I Samuel 6:19-20).

g. Ark at Kirjath-jearim for twenty years (I Samuel 6:21; I Samuel 7:1-2).

h. Ark possibly at Gibeah for a short time under Saul (I Samuel 14:16-18).

i. Ark back at Kirjath-jearim, or Baale of Judah (2 Samuel 6). David fetches the Ark on a new cart.

j. Ark at the House of Obed-edom. Uzzah is smitten for touching the Ark when the oxen stumbled. Ark taken into Obed-edom's house for three months (2 Samuel 6:1-11; I Chronicles 13:11-14). God may let the Philistines use the new cart, but not His own people who must find the "due order."

k. Ark taken into Tabernacle of David at Zion, Jerusalem. David prepares a place for the Ark. A Tent or Tabernacle. Ark taken on Priest's shoulders from House of Obed-edom into David's Tabernacle (2 Samuel 6:12-23; 11:11; I Chronicles 15:1-29; 16:1-3). Order of worship set up. Typical of New Testament Church Order and Worship, and the transference of the Glory of God from the Mosaic Economy to the New Testament Church.

> NB: Tabernacle of Moses and its order was at Mt Gibeon and remained there until the time of the Temple (I Chronicles 16:38; 21:29; I Kings 3:4-15; 2 Chronicles 1:1-13; I Kings 8:4).
>
> Tabernacle of David also in function at Mt Zion. Ark never ever returned to the Tabernacle of Moses again.

l. The Ark taken out of Tabernacle of David and placed in the Temple of Solomon, in the Holy Oracle. Staves taken out. Ark placed under the great wings of the Two Great Olive Cherubim, in the Feast of the Seventh Month, Feast of Tabernacles (I Kings 6: 23-30; 2 Chronicles 3:1-13; I Kings 8). David was not permitted to build the Temple, but he did receive the Pattern for Solomon to build (I Chronicles 17:1; 2 Samuel 7:2). (2 Chronicles 35:1-3-The Ark must have been taken out of the Temple during a period of apostacy, but under Josiah it is placed in the Temple again.)

In Solomon's Temple, when the Ark is placed in the Oracle there was

- no Manna in the Ark
- no Rod that Budded in the Ark
- no Staves in the Ark
- only the two Tables of the Law

(I Kings 8:9; 2 Chronicles 5:9-10; cf. Revelation 2:17; 1:6). Signifies that the believer has been made a Priest to God, and partaken of the Hidden Manna, and has come to the Divine Standard of Righteousness in Christ. The earth journeyings of the Church are over. Note the "gold floor" in Solomon's Temple (cf. Revelation 21 and 22).

m. Final mention of the Ark in the Old Testament (Jeremiah 3:16-17). Not to be remembered or come to mind, or sought after. Once the Temple was destroyed, the Ark has never been seen since.

n. The one and only reference to the Ark in the New Testament (Revelation 11:19). The True Ark seen in Heaven. The Lord Jesus Christ is the Ark of God personified.

So the Lord Jesus journeys with His pilgrim Church, and all through her history until we all come into the Eternal City of God, the Rest of God, New and Heavenly Jerusalem (Revelation 21:1-3). Then shall be ultimately fulfilled all that was typified.

"THE TABERNACLE OF GOD SHALL BE WITH MEN. . . ."

"The Lord God and the Lamb are the Light and Glory therein. . . ."

OVERVIEW OF COVENANTS, SANCTUARIES, PRIESTHOOD, KINGSHIP

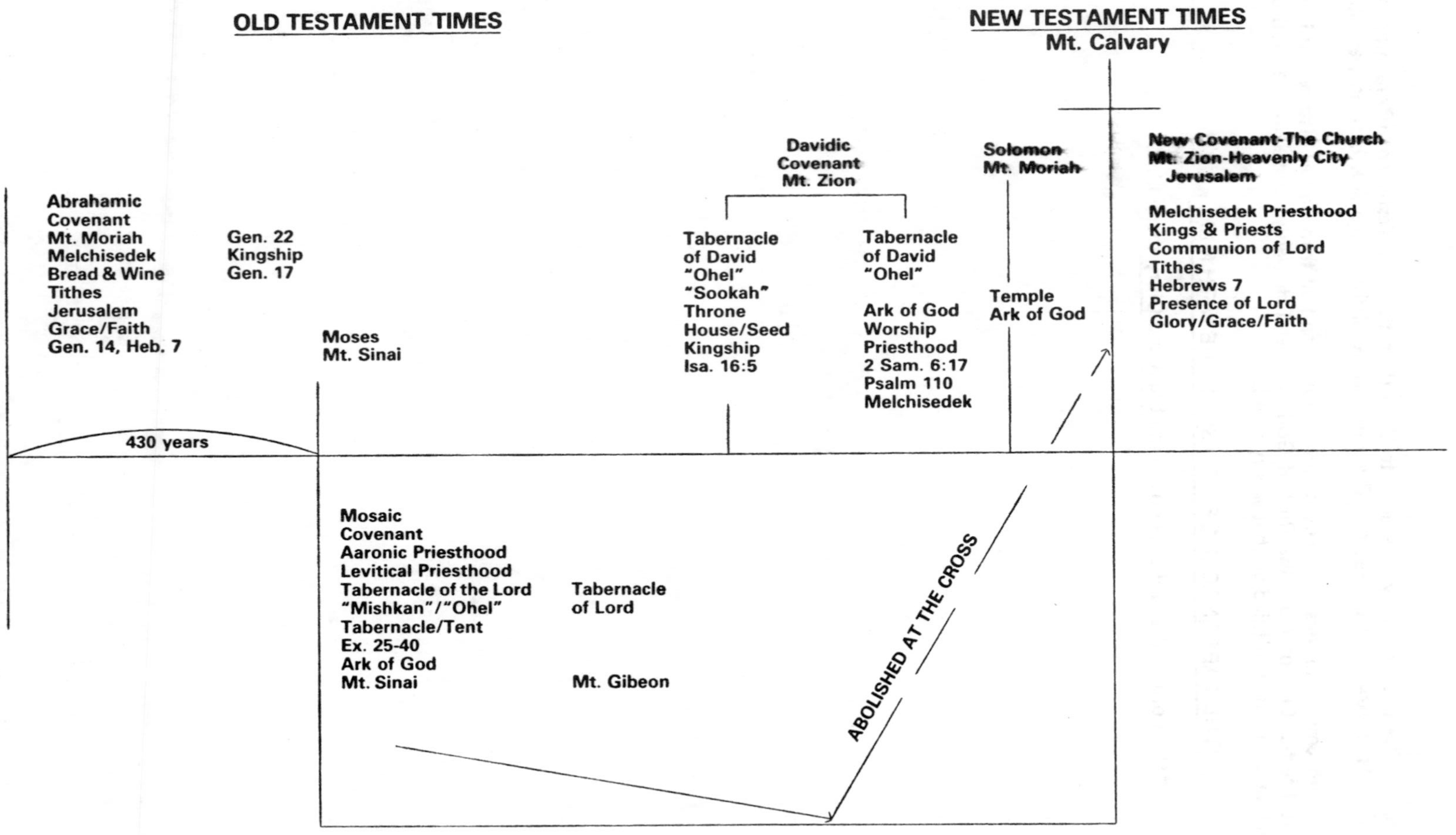

OLD TESTAMENT TIMES
NEW TESTAMENT TIMES
Mt. Calvary
Abrahamic
Covenant
Mt. Moriah
Melchisedek
Bread & Wine
Tithes
Jerusalem
Grace/Faith
Gen. 14, Heb. 7
Gen. 22
Kingship
Gen. 17
430 years
Moses
Mt. Sinai
Davidic
Covenant
Mt. Zion
Tabernacle
of David
"Ohel"
"Sookah"
Throne
House/Seed
Kingship
Isa. 16:5
Tabernacle
of David
"Ohel"
Ark of God
Worship
Priesthood
2 Sam. 6:17
Psalm 110
Melchisedek
Solomon
Mt. Moriah
Temple
Ark of God
New Covenant-The Church
Mt. Zion-Heavenly City
Jerusalem
Melchisedek Priesthood
Kings & Priests
Communion of Lord
Tithes
Hebrews 7
Presence of Lord
Glory/Grace/Faith
Mosaic
Covenant
Aaronic Priesthood
Levitical Priesthood
Tabernacle of the Lord
"Mishkan"/"Ohel"
Tabernacle/Tent
Ex. 25-40
Ark of God
Mt. Sinai
Tabernacle
of Lord
Mt. Gibeon
ABOLISHED AT THE CROSS

Kevin J. Conner

BIBLIOGRAPHY

1. Appleby, David P., History of Church Music, Moody Press, Chicago, 1965. (Used by permission.)

2. Clarke, Adam, A Commentary and Critical Notes on The Holy Bible, New York, Abingdon-Cokesbury Press.

3. Fausett, A.R., Fausett's Bible Dictionary, Grand Rapids, Michigan, Zondervan Publishing House, 1963.

4. Hart, Lowell, Satan's Music Exposed. Huntington Valley, Pennsylvania. Salem Kirban, 1980.

5. Henry, Matthew, Commentary on the Whole Bible, New York, Fleming H. Revell Company, Written, 1712, Published 1935.

6. Horger, Rev. J.T., Fundamental Revelation in Dramatic Symbol, Hondo, Texas.

7. Jamieson, Fausett & Brown, Commentary on the Whole Bible, Grand Rapids, Michigan, Zondervan Publishing House.

8. Kerr, Phil, Music in Evangelism, Grand Rapids, Michigan, Zondervan Publishing House, 1962.

9. Larson, Bob, Rock and the Church, Carol Stream, Illinois, Creation House, 1971.

10. Larson, Bob, The Day Music Died, Carol Stream, Illinois, Creation House, 1972.

11. Larson, Bob, Hippies-Hindus and Rock and Roll, McCook, Nebraska, 1969.

12. Larson, Bob, Rock & Roll, The Devil's Diversion, McCook, Nebraska, 1967.

13. Larson, Bob. Rock, Wheaton, Illinois, Tyndale House Publishers, Inc., 1980.

14. Lawhead, Steve. Rock Revisited, Downers Grove, Illinois, Intervarsity Press.

15. Mauro, Philip, The Hope of Israel, Swengel, Pennsylvania, Reiner Publications, 1970.

16. Miller, Madeleign S. & J. Lane, Encyclopedia of Bible Life, New York and London, Harper & Brothers Publishers, 1944.

17. Pamphilus, Eusebius, Eusebius' Ecclesiastical History, Grand Rapids, Michigan, Baker Book House, 1974.

18. Peters, Dan and Steve, Why Knock Rock?, Minneapolis, Minnesota, Bethany House Publishers, 1984.

19. Spence, H.D.M., Exell, Joseph S., Deane, W. J., et al., The Pulpit Commentary, New York and Toronto, Funk & Wagnalls Company.

20. Stainer, John, The Music of the Bible, London, Novello & Co., Ltd., 1879.

21. Stainer, John, The Music of the Bible, Revised edition by Francis Galpin, D A Capo Press, New York, 1970.

22. Stevenson, Robert M., Patterns of Protestant Church Music, Duke University Press, England, 1953.

23. Strong, James, Strong's Exhaustive Concordance, New Jersey, Madison, 1890.

24. Truscott, Graham, The Power of His Presence, Burbank, California, World Map Press (First Printing, Poona, India, 1969).

25. Unger, Merrill F., Unger's Bible Dictionary, Chicago, Moody Press, 1972.

26. Wolfendale, James, The Preacher's Homiletical Commentary, New York, Funk & Wagnalls Company, 1892.

27. The New Englishman's Hebrew and Chaldee Concordance, Wilmington, Delaware, Associated Publishers & Authors, 1975.

DUPLICATED NOTES

28. Living Word Bible College, Music History FA374, 115 W. Newmark, Monterey Park, California, 1975.

29. Shiloh Bible College, David's Tabernacle, Rev. Violet Kiteley, 3521 - 38th Avenue, Oakland, California, 1974.

Other Resources Available by Kevin Conner

Kevin J. Conner

Church in the New Testament
The Book of Acts
Interpreting the Book of Revelation
Interpreting the Symbols & Types
Feasts of Israel
Foundations of Christian Doctrine
The Tabernacle of Moses
The Tabernacle of David
The Temple of Solomon

Kevin J. Conner & Ken Malmin

The Covenants
Interpreting the Scriptures
New Testament Survey
Old Testament Survey

JOURNEY OF TRANSFORMATION

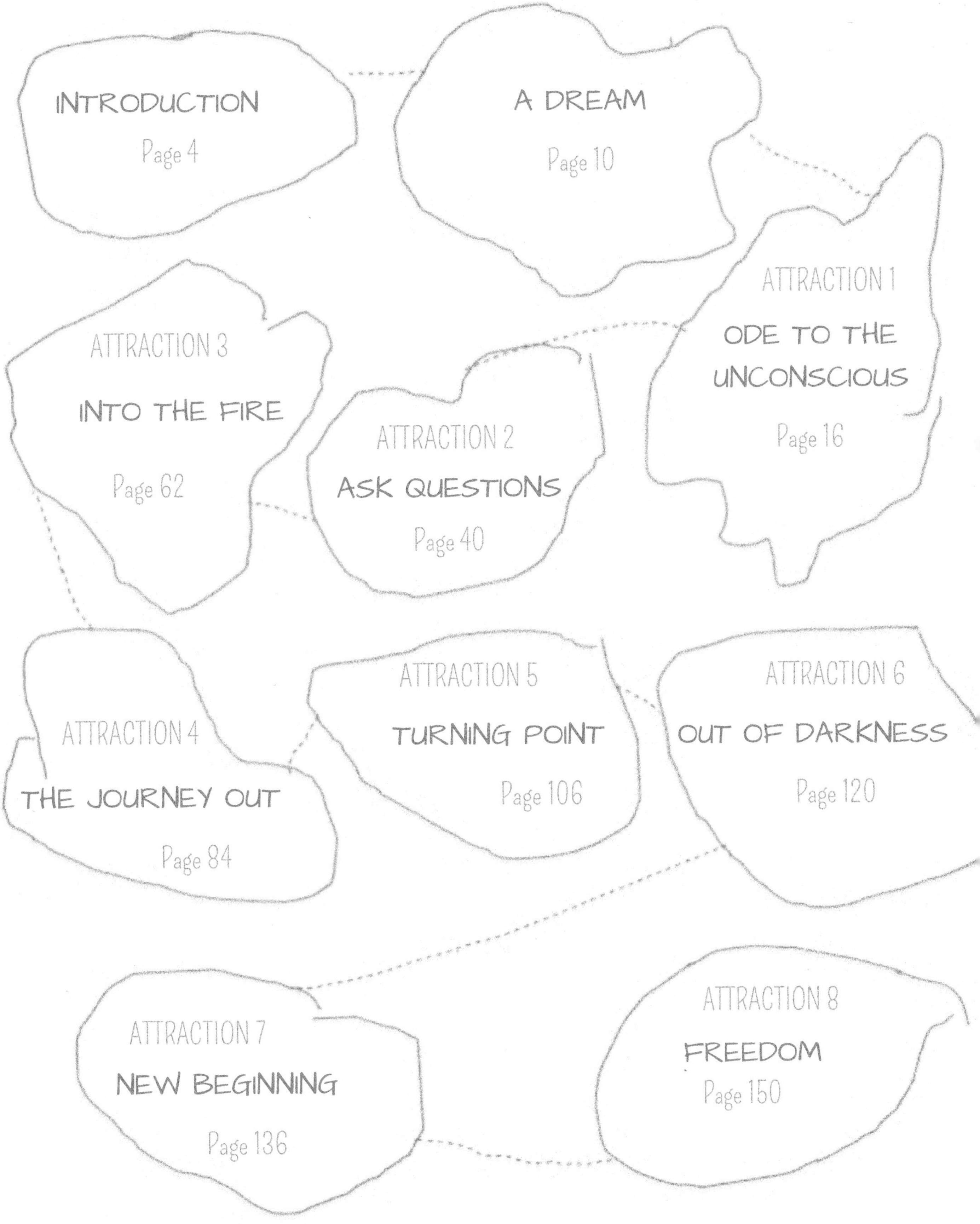
INTRODUCTION
Page 4
A DREAM
Page 10
ATTRACTION 1
ODE TO THE UNCONSCIOUS
Page 16
ATTRACTION 2
ASK QUESTIONS
Page 40
ATTRACTION 3
INTO THE FIRE
Page 62
ATTRACTION 4
THE JOURNEY OUT
Page 84
ATTRACTION 5
TURNING POINT
Page 106
ATTRACTION 6
OUT OF DARKNESS
Page 120
ATTRACTION 7
NEW BEGINNING
Page 136
ATTRACTION 8
FREEDOM
Page 150

HOW TO USE

BREAKING INTO BRILLIANCE

Dip in – until you're ready to dive in. Do what pleases you. Sift through pages, see images and gather what catches you. Engage. Start slowly.
And at some point you may want to start at the beginning and work your way through.

One particular image may lead you to a dream that has been buried. Or a particular event lying dormant might work its way up to your consciousness.

Record thoughts, feelings, questions, fears. Use drawings – paper and pencil, paints, crayons, photos and found objects. They can all be a part of your entry.

You are a creative being. You create every day, all day. You have always done so and will continue to do so. Why not make it conscious? Work with your spirit, strengthen it and sharpen it.

This kind of journey is never easy. It takes patience, perseverance and courage. Try not to judge. Play. Pour it out. I wish you a time of adventure, tuning and turning your eyes inward to self-discovery.

Creativity -
the act of creating - is an
intrinsic gift. It is our genius.

ATOMS ARE NOT THINGS

"We all have the habit of thinking that everything around us is already a thing existing without my input, without my choice. You have to banish that kind of thinking.

Instead, you really have to recognize that even the material world around us, the chairs, the tables, the rooms, the carpet, time included, all of these are nothing but possible movements of Consciousness. And I'm choosing, moment to moment, out of those movements, to bring my actual experience into manifestation.

This is the only radical thinking that you need to do. But it is so radical--so difficult – because we tend to believe that the world is already out there, independent of our experience.

It is not. Quantum physics is so clear about this. Heisenberg himself, co-discoverer of quantum physics, said, 'Atoms are not things, they're only tendencies.'

So instead of thinking of things, you have to think of possibilities. They're all possibilities of Consciousness."

- Dr. Amit Goswami, Ph.D.

(as cited in Robert Scheinfeld, Busting Loose from the Business Game (Wiley, 2009, p. 59))

A DREAM

I WOKE FROM A POWERFUL DREAM infused with an astonishing sense of the sacred. This dream, spurred by the visit from an old friend, revealed that desires from an earlier time remained unfulfilled. Here is the dream:

I am standing with a man, in front of a line of monks dressed in brown robes with clocks for faces. Behind the monks is a room – a wall of glass, framed in brown wood, with crossed boards supporting the frames. Deep into this room is a standing clock, visible through the panes of glass. There is a great depth and stillness.

The man wants sex. The choice is clear: be with the man or own myself. I join the line of monks. I am last in line, without a robe or a clock face. I then move to a high white room with a window at the top left. Light is streaming into the room.

A boy is sitting at a simple white kitchen table. He is saying "No." I have to stay in this room until he says "Yes."

I wake up thinking: It's time. The clock is ticking. It's time to say "Yes," time to change. The images are powerful and the dream, upon awakening, informs every moment.

Many years later, I recognized the true importance of this dream, and I began to check in on the boy. I did this by returning again and again to my dreamscape.

During many of my check-ins the “No” was loud. And then the walls of the white room began to collapse, then the table was gone. And then finally, the boy was outside, standing in a no man’s land. The change was daunting. The boy stood in place, frozen by his freedom. What now?

Where to go? How to go? He walked in circles. The ground under him was parched and cracked, his old ideas and fears cracking up.

A red bike appeared and he rode the cracked, parched land. Children were following, including one special girl. He rode and rode and the expanse was endless.

I ask myself, why is he a boy? Why am I a boy? Where is my girl? How can I integrate my male and female side?

He was truly breathing, wild with joy at the freedom and beauty. His speed was now nearly outside of time. I recognized my male side, my power, needed to grow up and learn to be strong in the world.

My girl needed to believe in her partner, her boy, to come through, to meet her creativity and especially her spirit and integrity. She needed the boy to grow up, be dependable and trustworthy. They needed to marry so I could find my balance.

Suddenly, he's at an important university, near the Mediterranean. He's thoughtful, sincere, a sense of purpose is in his face. He graduates this great university and is at a desk writing. Above him, in his room, golden balls of possibility dance.

Not knowing where his writing and teaching are going to take him, he is moving in an unknown country. He will reveal this to me as he is becoming a sweet, brave, strong, sensitive male, someone to hold me in his male power. He is my partner in flight, to be the soaring bird, I see, I am.

"Create the Life You Want No Matter What it Takes."

..where are you
living now?

I. ODE TO THE

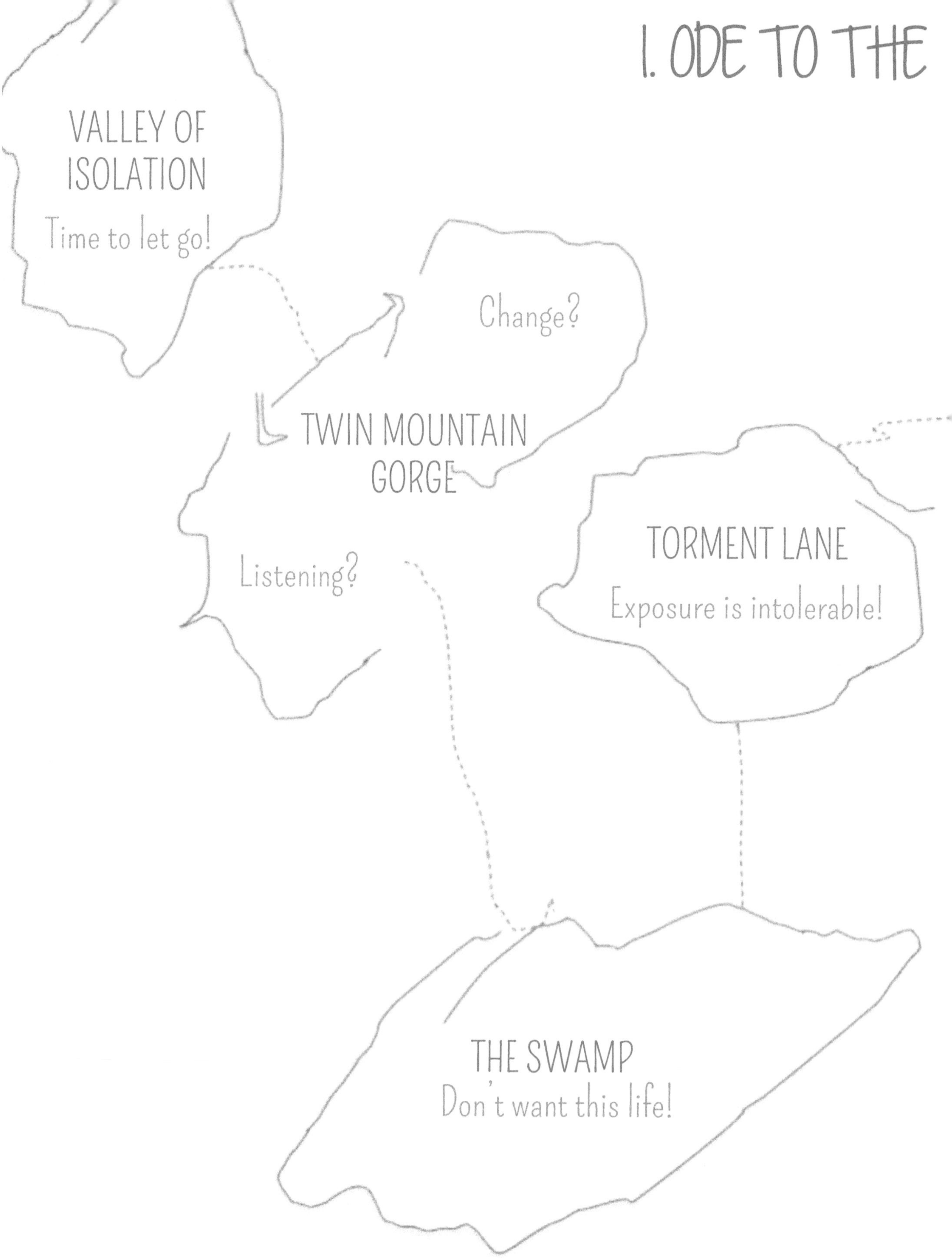
VALLEY OF ISOLATION
Time to let go!
Change?
TWIN MOUNTAIN GORGE
Listening?
TORMENT LANE
Exposure is intolerable!
THE SWAMP
Don't want this life!

UNCONSCIOUS

LAKE OF HOPE
Healing place
CAVE ROAD
Thoughts create reality
CHANGE LANES
Transformation
Breath; courage
THE OASIS
Study a cat
OCEAN'S GIFT
A new voice
STORY ROAD
Make a film

WELCOME...

TO THE LAND OF THE UNCONSCIOUS...

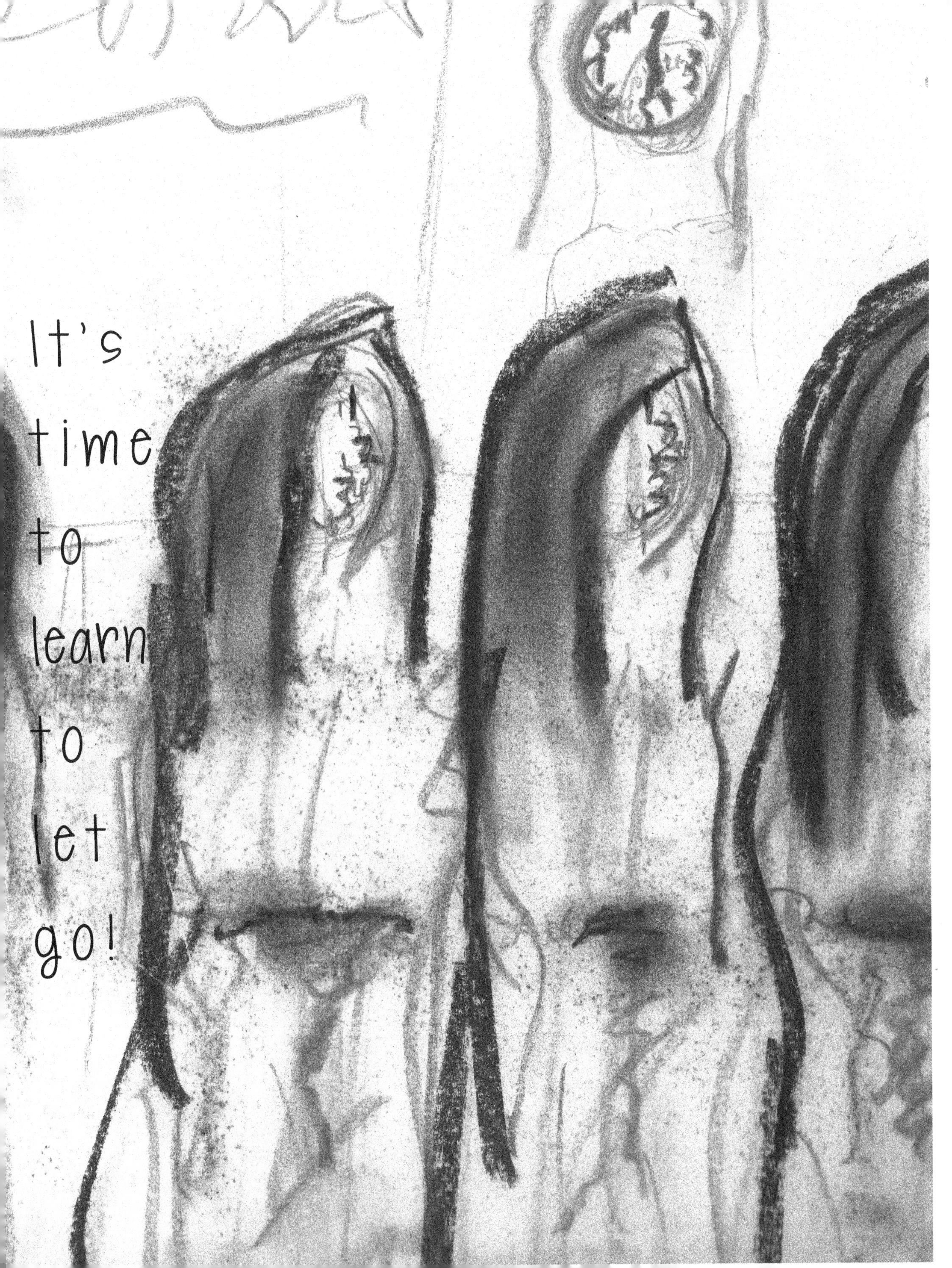
It's time to learn to let go!

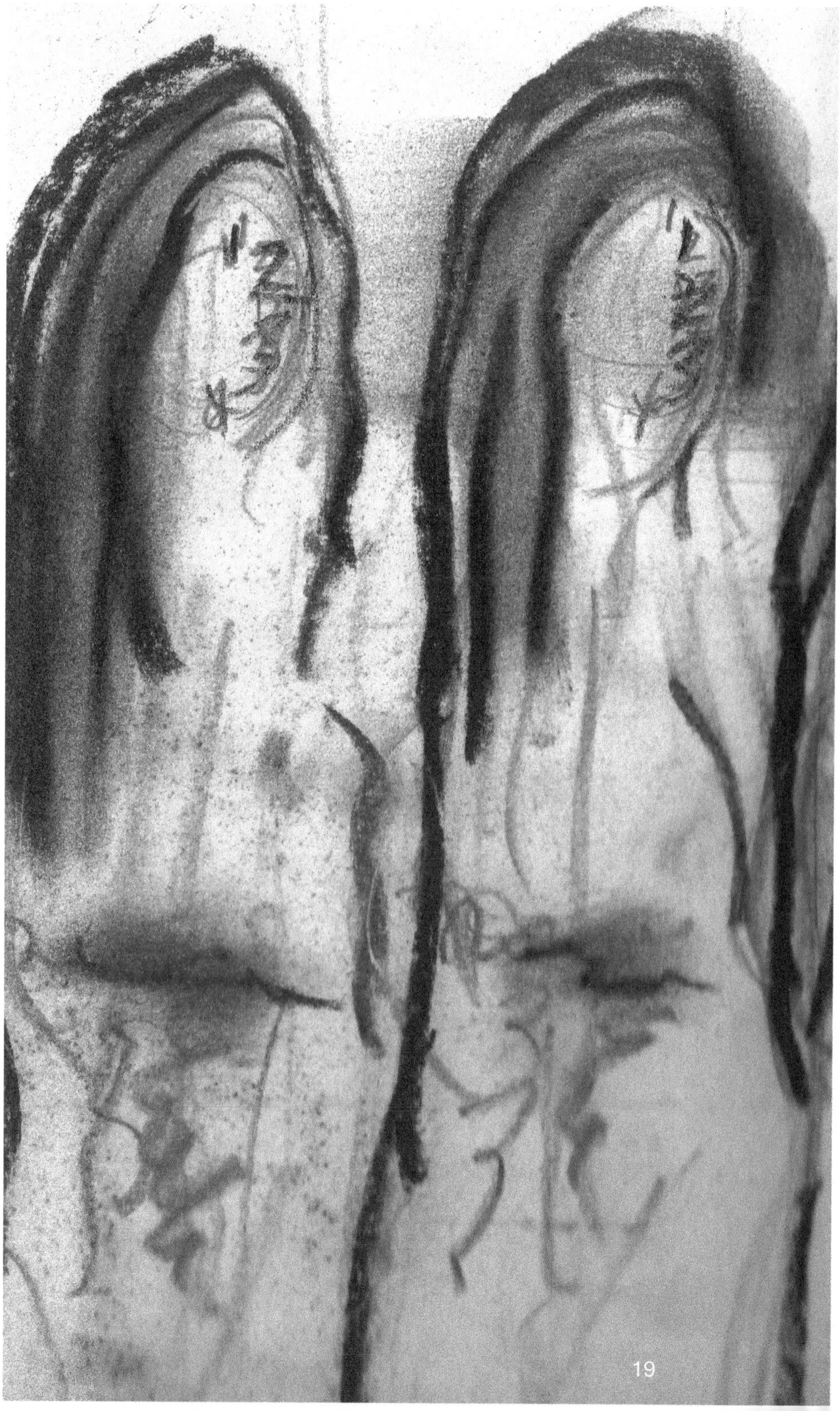

It's
time

It's not my FAULT!

I like to drink!

I like sex!

I like food!

I like cigarettes!

I like drugs!

I like spending!

AND ANYWAY, I DON'T WANT TO HEAR IT!!

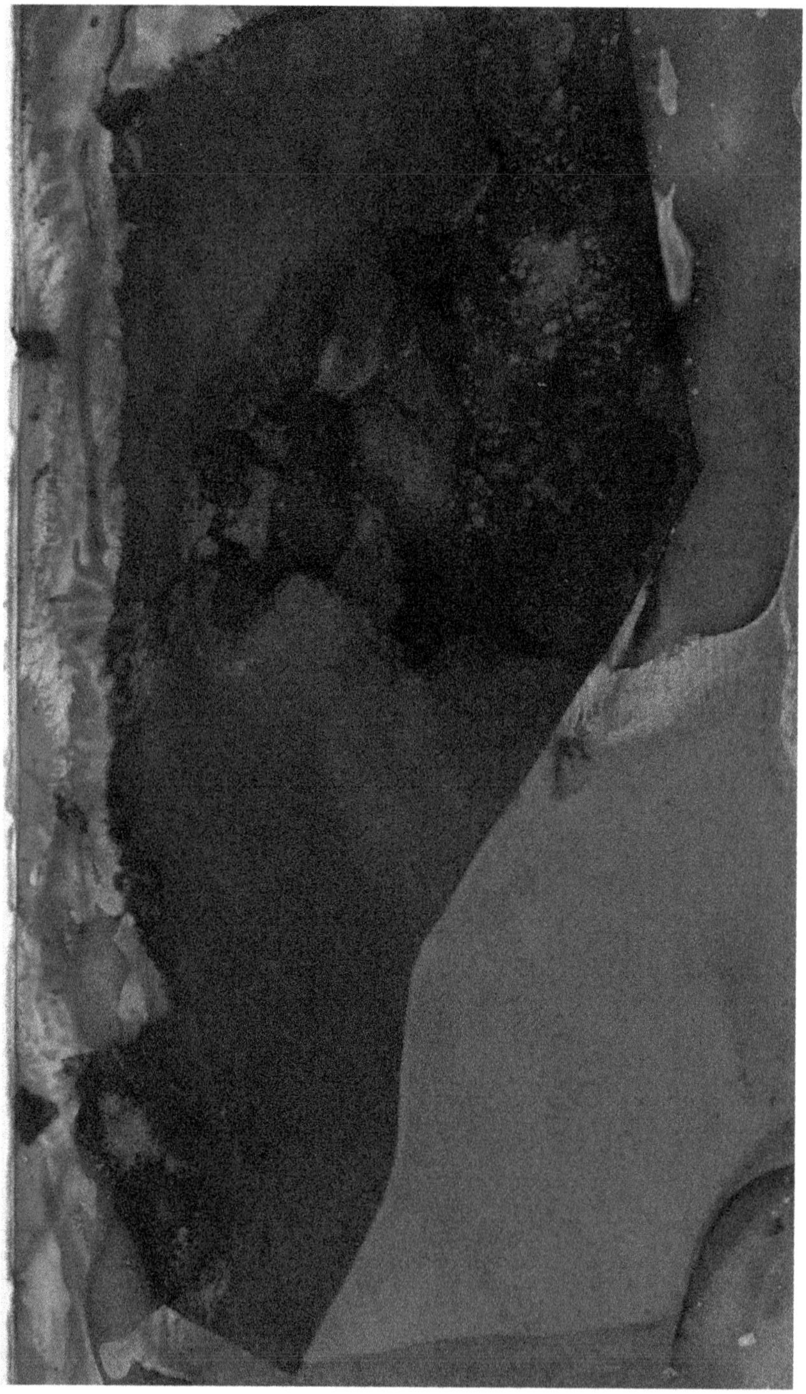

I'LL
NEVER
CHANGE!!

AND I
DON'T
WANT
TO!!!

Sex + Drugs + Rock + Roll
This is not the life I want.

The pain is strong
in unconsciousness
and the familiarity
of the pain is strong.

The fear of trusting our
feelings with ourselves
or with others encases
us in the comfort of bad
thoughts. They protect
us. Feeling our
vulnerability is awful.
Exposing our
vulnerability
is intolerable.

We will die of embarrassment - helpless, young and at the mercy of everyone that might "see." We hear that we can have anything we want but we don't believe it. We know we will never believe it, because the words are empty, a salve for our doubt and pain. Now we live in the doubt and pain and punishment.

I can't be visible.

Here is the dilemma:

IT'S ALWAYS THE WRONG GUY ---

Him again!

***!!^^##**&

HOW do we make better choices?

We make better choices by changing our thoughts. And we can choose our thoughts.

Quantum physics tells us that:

Our

thoughts

create

our

reality.

So be careful what you think about.

THERE WAS A MOMENT with a shaman when I saw myself in two separate parts. One was glowing, clear, joyous, childlike. The other was darker, watchful, worried. I was given an opportunity: change the fearful beliefs, and claim my beauty.

As a child, our core nature constantly gets interrupted with hurt, fear and anger. If unexpressed, these feelings find a dark, contorted home deep in our body. Yet our consciousness is always communicating to us through this pain in our body and our psyche, begging us for awareness and clearing.

So how DO we change our beliefs? We change our beliefs by looking at the stories we tell ourselves about who we are, and looking at the fallacies that are deep within the stories. We have to acknowledge the hurt. When we acknowledge the hurt, we can change the story.

The wound is the place of healing. And when the wound has healed, the true self emerges. Deep body work is necessary to access and cleanse the wound. Breathing deeply into the contorted places unlocks the information and allows the body to speak its truth. And when the body speaks, it will create the new story.

rock
shell

BREATHING CAN CHANGE YOUR LIFE

Breathing makes you more courageous

Breathing is the royal road to the unconscious, the subconscious, and the imagination: to stories that need to be shifted, the griefs, the terrors, the shame that longs to be cleansed.

You will find new ideas about yourself, you will experience a shift in your paradigm and begin to integrate this new vision.

The "breath of life" is a part of every physical practice and many spiritual practices.

BEGIN WITH THIS . . .

Touch Your Breath

Can you relax your spine? Lying down on the floor, mentally scan your spine slowly with the intention to relax it. Can you scan the body? Begin at your toes and sense what you are holding onto and let it go.

Direct Your Breath

Can you widen your back into the floor? Use your breath to sink in and expand your muscles.

Ground Yourself

Can you settle your thoughts? Breathe in relaxation and strength. Breathe out fatigue and anxiety. Can you do the roll down? Standing up, with your legs shoulder width apart, begin to roll your head and shoulders down toward the ground. Relax your neck, soften your knees. Spread your toes till they look something like a starfish. It's time to think about a Yoga class.

Put away the alcohol, chocolate & all other delicious, malicious addictions.

TRY STUDYING A CAT

Watch the moves she'll make. As a cat jumps off a high perch to low ground, isn't there a wave of breath, and isn't it beautiful?

Practice breathing like a cat, with that wave of breath. Breathe in and breathe out.

Breathe out stress.
Breathe in love.

Breathe out anger.
Breathe in wonder.

Breathe out fear.
Breathe in awe.

New thoughts and feelings can be very slippery. They are easy to forget if you don't write them down. And writing it down helps create the changes in you.

Sometimes when I read my journal, I am surprised at what I had to say and what I had been feeling. And it was wonderful to remember the new ideas.

STILL BREATHING?

Are you aware of your breathing . . .

with children?
with animals?
in lovemaking?
in difficult moments?

ODE TO TRANSFORMATION

I would like to be a cat
independent and mysterious.
Oh, to be held in high honor
like the cat in ancient lands.

I would like to be a rabbit
creating new life
quick, sensitive,
a creature of the moon.
Oh to follow her into magical realms.

I would love to be a snake
and shed my skin
bringing rebirth
to swallow my tail and dream of eternity.

Inspired by Ted Andrews. Animal-Speak. (St. Paul: Llewellyn Publications, 1997), 258-259, 303-30, 361.

GROUNDHOG DAY

A film that seems to be a comedy, drenched in magical realism. A very unhappy man, living in unconsciousness, finds himself waking to exactly the same day, every day.

He tries to end his days by ending his life over and over. Each unsuccessful attempt is funnier and more extravagant than the last.

And finally, he begins to give in. He grows more with each day. He sees and seizes the moment. He loves.

Are you making conscious choices in how you live your life every day?

THE POWER OF FILM

If you could make a movie that could influence millions of people, what kind of story would you tell? How would it begin and how would it end? What would be its message? What would be the pivotal moment in the film?

Film has great influence, the power to change the world. As the new consciousness and the sacred female energy strengthens, new stories will follow.

This moon energy will open us to an inner life of unimaginable beauty, a new sensibility, and a deepening of our truer self. Will your film come along?

HEARING A NEW VOICE

Have you ever heard a "voice" really clearly? Like someone in your head is talking, but it's not your thoughts? The first time I heard a voice, it was as if someone was speaking through me, to me. The moment was simple and powerful. I was very still, filled with immense relief.

At the far edge of Long Island, I am being led to the water by a dog named Bella Lisa. It was late at night, very dark and all I heard was the sound of the water. The voice said: "*You're going to be fine. It will take some time.*"

2. ASK

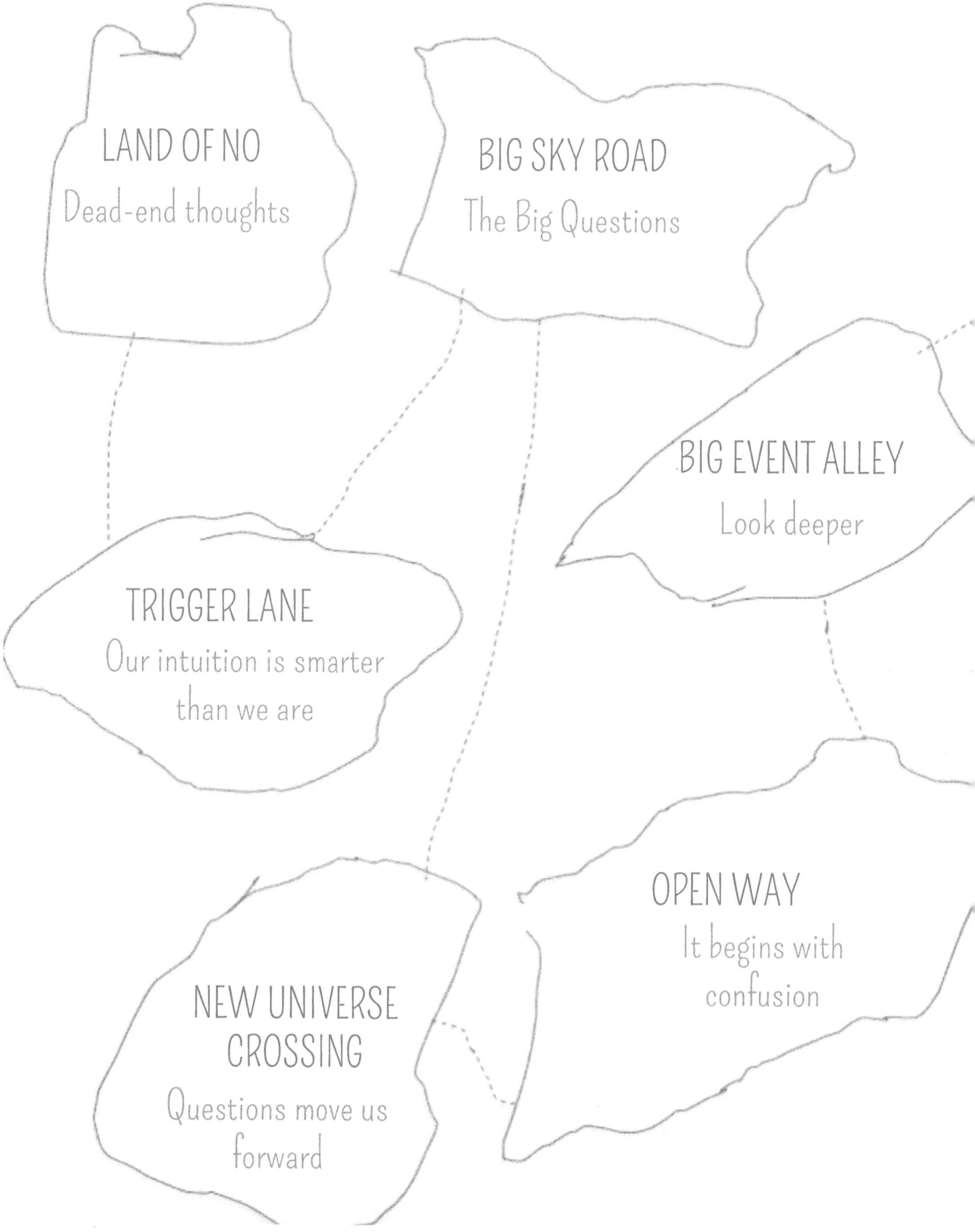
LAND OF NO
Dead-end thoughts
BIG SKY ROAD
The Big Questions
BIG EVENT ALLEY
Look deeper
TRIGGER LANE
Our intuition is smarter than we are
OPEN WAY
It begins with confusion
NEW UNIVERSE CROSSING
Questions move us forward

QUESTIONS

BREATH OF LIFE STREET
Talking to the breath...
RIVER'S BEGINNING
Drop the baggage
PORT OF REMARKABLE ENCOUNTERS
"Antwone Fisher" film
SEA CLIFF SHELTER
Forces of change

IT'S TIME

TO ASK QUESTIONS...

I had to sit with him in this room until he said "Yes."

WHAT TRIGGERS QUESTIONING?

Don't you think our intuition and unconscious are smarter than we are? And that when the time is right, the unconscious gives up information and answers?

And don't we know that things change in order to teach us something?

What creates an opening?

YOUR SPIRIT IS CALLING YOU

to look, to question . . .

A Car Accident

Have you ever had a car accident? Did you ask why?

A Divorce

Is your heart broken and your family broken apart? Did you ask why?

A Nervous Breakdown

Are you vulnerable and frightened? Are depression, anger and creativity all yelling for your attention? Did you ask why?

A Child is Born

Are your priorities changing with the changes of your body? Are you totally absorbed in this new life? Who are you now? Why **this** child?

Before

You have the accident

Before

You have the child you can't take care of

Before

You blame your boss and you're fired

Before

You sabotage your marriage

Before

You drink yourself into oblivion

Before

You lose yourself in sex

Why am I here?

What am I really supposed to do?

Why is it so hard?

Why is it scary?

Who is GOD?

What is GOD?

WHO AM I???

MOOOORE QUESTIONS!!

What does it feel like at

What now?
We Stay

Or we can open

the edge of the universe?

can ignore it.
dull.

it up and ask.

And when I began asking questions,

I

felt

worse

before

I

felt

better.

Everything is opening, so messy and uncertain, angry and fuzzy.

Confusion.

INHALE FOR STRENGTH, EXHALE FOR RELAXATION

Breathing is blissful.

We cannot breathe without our diaphragm, a huge dome shaped muscle beneath the ribs. We can feel, when breathing in, that our diaphragm tightens and moves downward. And we can feel more room in our chest cavity and our lungs expanding. The muscles between the ribs help this expansion by pulling the rib cage up and out. If I really concentrate I can feel that all this is happening at the same time!

The diaphragm is a magical creature. It brings me breath and the breath brings me feelings.

I turn my eyes inward and I look into my diaphragm. I question it. Is it happy, anxious, constricted? What's in there?

The diaphragm can reveal new information. Contact your diaphragm. Lie on your back and bring your knees to your chest. Breeethe against your knees. Then with your knees released and your legs extended, massage your diaphragm. Do this for a full minute and a half. Then just let go. Write whatever thoughts, feelings or images come to you.

"Diaphragm in Respiratory System." Innerbody.com. HowToMedia, Inc., n.d. Web. 18 Dec 2015. http://www.innerbody.com/image_chest1/musc82.html#full-description

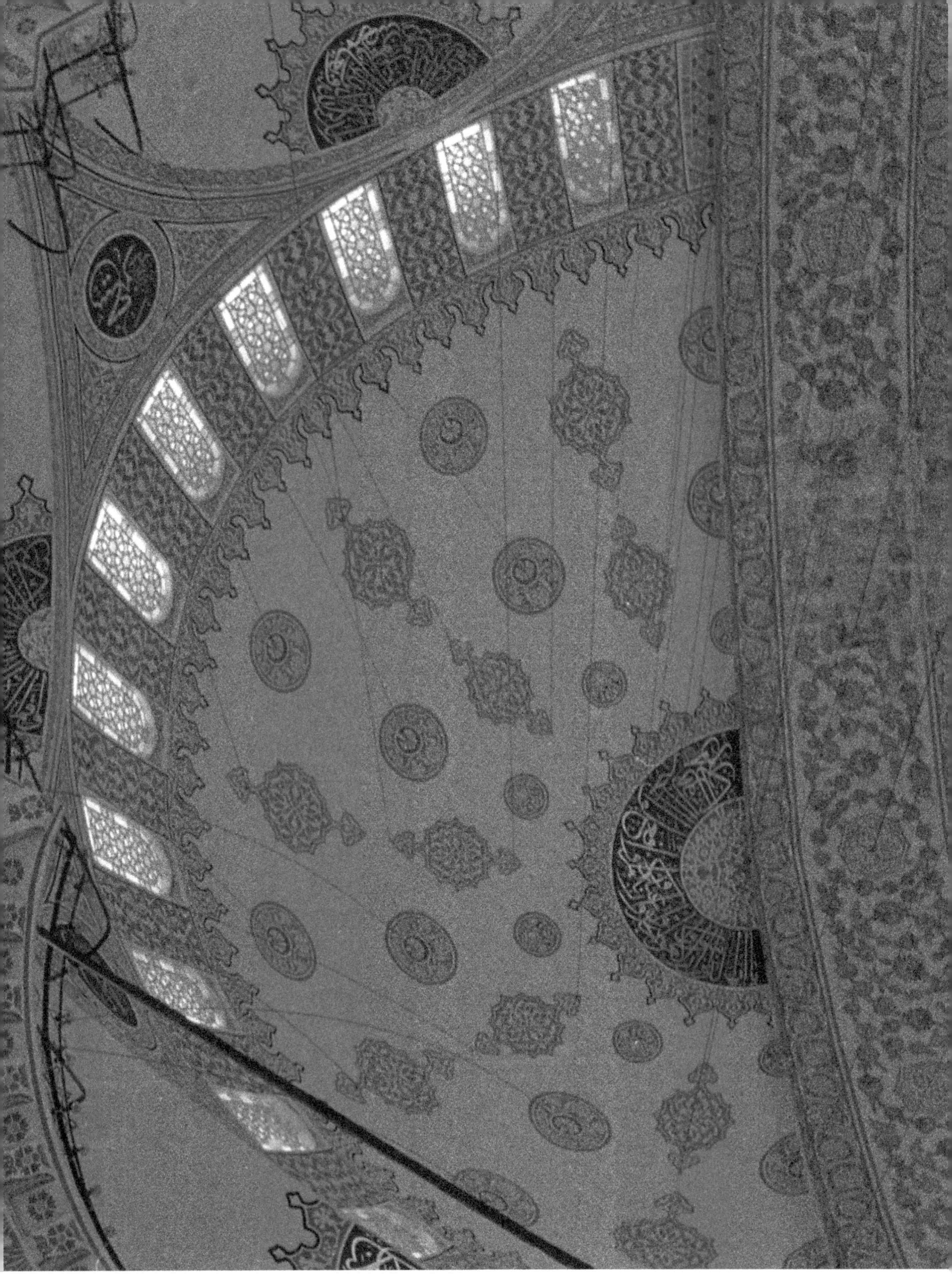

TAKE TIME TO JUST BREATHE

I talk to my breath as if it were a living creature. I ask it questions. Where isn't it going and why isn't it going there? Is it trying to hide something – something I should know about? After all, breath is the royal road to the imagination, the unconscious and the sub-conscious!

Jaw and Tongue

I love to yawn, and to massage my jaw and chin. And to do the "Lion Pose", dropping my tongue out of my mouth, which stretches my tongue and makes me feel free. But the best is moving the back of my tongue around like a cow chewing its cud. I can feel my voice growing.

Asking Yourself Questions

Sitting quietly with yourself is not always easy! Try to concentrate on your breath. Take a few minutes. Breathe in and out on the count of five until a deep relaxation happens. Can you feel the power of concentration?

This can be tricky: begin to think about a question you have. Allow this question to float up easily, without judgment or worry. Or simply ask yourself, "What isn't working for me?" Write in your notebook what you encounter.

MEDITATION

SOMETIMES I ASK BREATH to bring me answers on a wave. In that way it becomes a meditation. Things that have plagued me, things I don't want to hear are revealed. Hearing like this on the crest of a wave smoothes my rough edges, and then the truth is a great relief.

ANTWONE FISHER, born in jail, is unwanted and abandoned by both parents. Finally he removes himself from the physical and sexual abuse of a foster home. Some time later, a day after his closest friend is shot, in desperation, he joins the Navy. Again and again, his world explodes. He studies, writes poetry, learns languages, and stays sober and off of drugs.

However, Antwone's violent episodes with shipmates brings him to the care of a naval psychiatrist. It is Antoine's nature that truly saves his life – a sensitive, complex, extraordinary nature. The choices he did not make under the repeated assaults saved his life.

Somehow, somewhere, he was always listening to the voice beyond the terror.

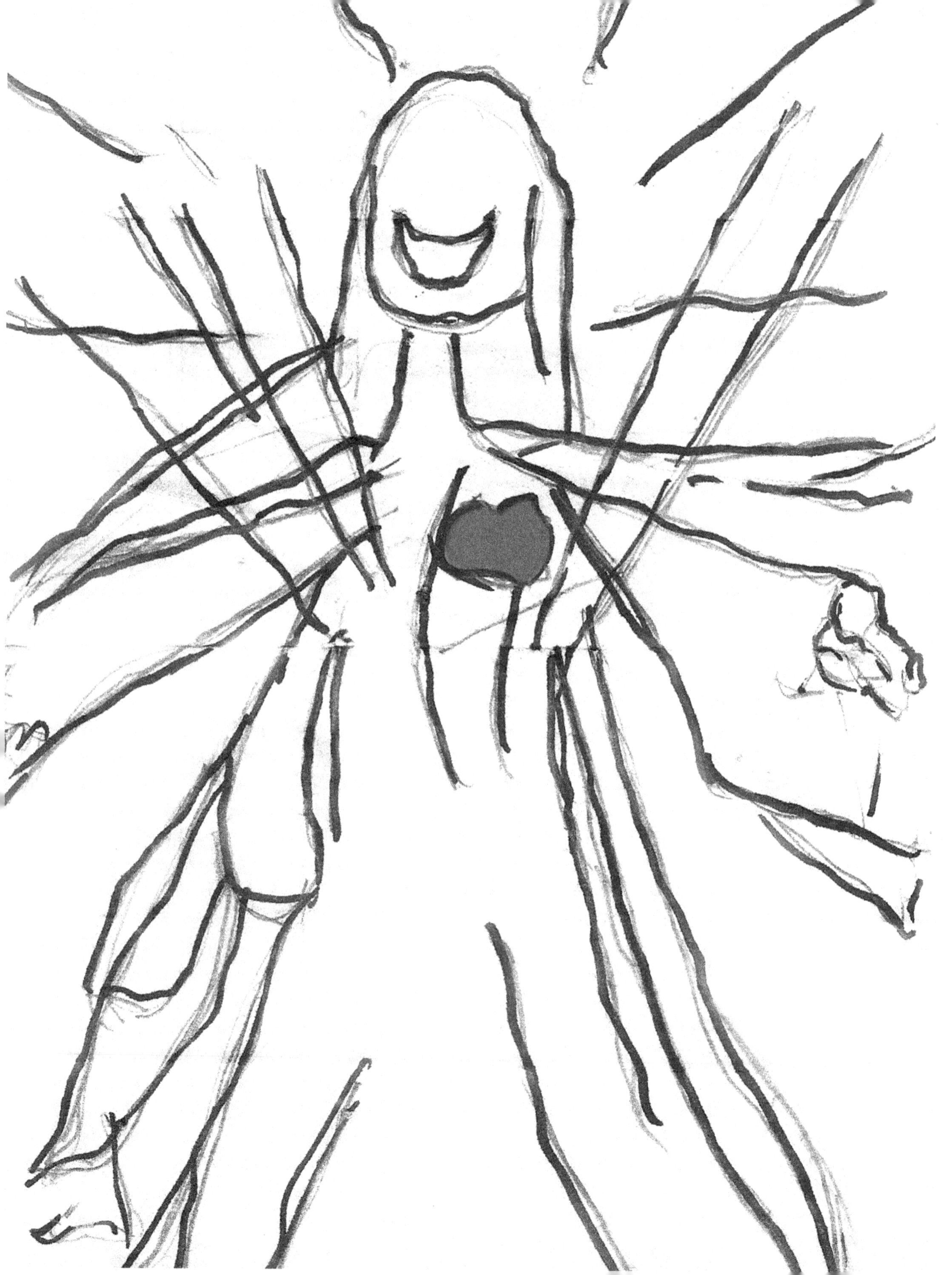

WHO would I be...

...without all this

baggage?

SHE IS STANDING with her back to the edge of the cliff. Magnetic forces from the volcano are at work here, forces of change.

3. Into

PARK OF INNER CITY HELL
Stunned!
DIRTY VALLEY
The lower depths
SALT MINE HILLS
Persistance
SEA'S END
Through the storm
BLACK QUARRY
Shame's beginning

the Fire

SLIPPERY SLOPES
Edge of the cliff
RIVER OF LIFE
New thoughts
DARK CLOUDS LIFTING
Say it out
TWISTED ROAD
Confrontations
SACRED TREE PLACE
Dead skin drops off

STEP INTO

THE FIRE . . .

Stunned

What do we hide in the Shadows?

What are we a slave to?

Who is the witch in us? What is the darkness in us? What is the chaos in us?

The spider

(Meta Segmentata)

is in her
web
+
the male

waiting.

I will ease my PAIN. I OWN YOU!
I AM IN CONTROL!

WHAT IS STANDING BETWEEN ME & ME?

When we get lost, what are we really doing? What are we afraid to hear? We hate ourselves. We believe the lies. We are bad. We ate the apple. God banished us from heaven. We are alone. Out there, all those billions of planets and galaxies and stars have nothing to do with me.

Why do we have bad thoughts? Why doesn't our mother seem to love us? She certainly doesn't want us to grow up and leave her, because then she will be alone, and of course, she never really grew up. Why is it we have parents who are really adolescents?

How do we break the chain of lies and fear and anger? How is it we left ourselves? How do we learn to love ourselves? Everyone tells us this is what we must do. Don't you get sick of hearing it when you can't do it?

TAKING MY CHILDHOOD

He punctured my trust and my beauty. My skin got tighter, created a rubbery shell, as I squeezed myself down into myself. The self – smothered in a veil of uncertainty down in a tiny but palpable space in my body, mostly settled between the shoulder blades and deep in the chest – was screaming "I better be quiet, I will be killed."

For years, there was not much movement. Her fear and loneliness and my anger protected us well. Finally, on the day of alchemy, I asked, "Who would I be – she be – without the anger, without the protection? What is propping up all this fear?" Shaking off the dust and debris began to remind her that I was in charge now.

It took some time convincing her that I was now taking care of her. "He said that too, so why should I believe you?" she asks.

Begin the dialogue for whatever reason. She will respond.

HOW DO WE CHANGE OUR THOUGHTS?

We stop. We listen. We get brave. Maybe we find a teacher. “I don’t want to believe all that bad stuff!”

And the teacher will hold your words and your desires and your spirit until you find yourself moved, maybe to tears.

The poison is released. A door opens, your “seams” open. You hear words that are strange and unsettling, embarrassing even, unprotected.

DEPRESSION

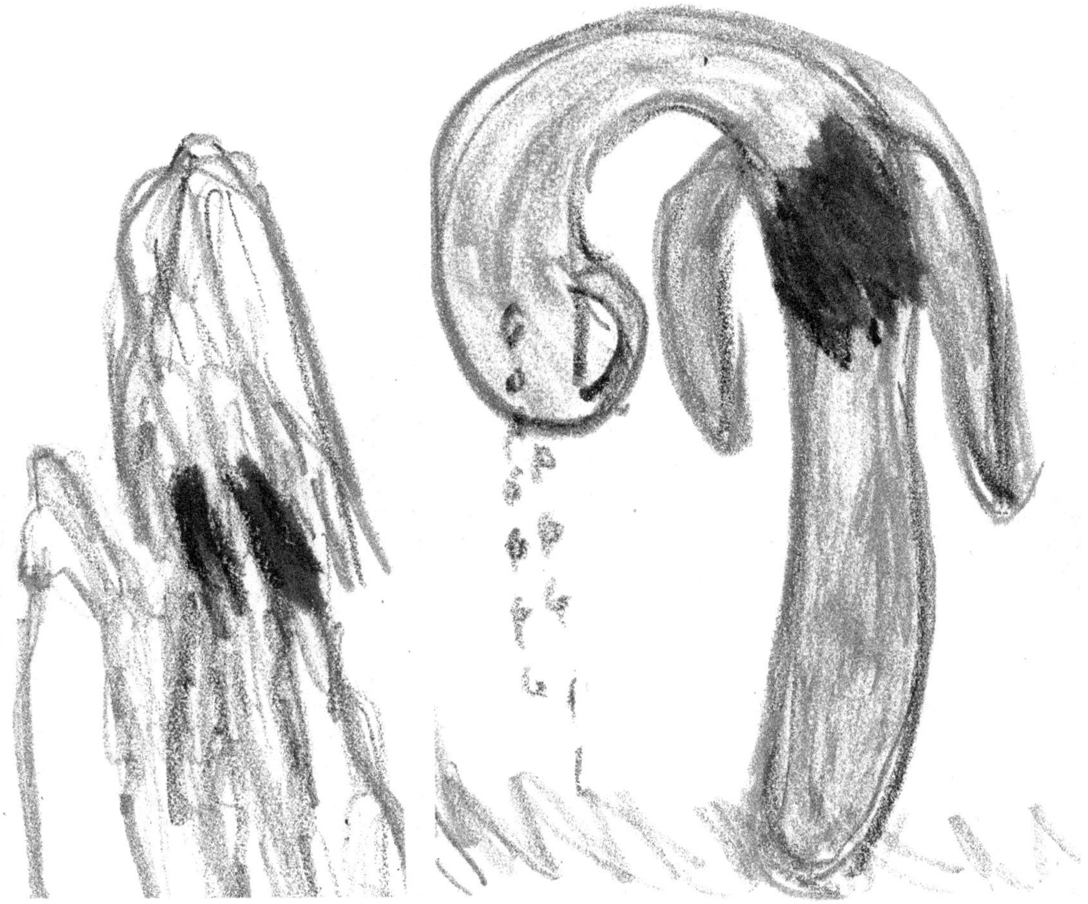

New thoughts arise from a new heart.

HOW DO WE MOVE THROUGH THE RESISTANCE?

THE ACHING DULLNESS of fear. What pathways, what colors, what sounds, what words? The itchiness is always near. I can't stand this! I can't stay in it. Scratching. I am sure there must be bugs in the house. Maybe a rat? Who can stop this? What can stop this?

Opening to what I want, moving out, releasing stuff that holds me back, bringing myself to another place in myself, face-to-face. A new me could now stare down the demon voices. Well . . . let's do it tomorrow.

Then, it gets really slippery. Trips to the refrigerator, to the bed and another nap, forgetful, anxious or angry, no sex, too much sex, procrastination, nightmares and big dreams.

I am very tricky in building my escape hatches. And some funny things happen, like walking in circles and even getting dizzy.

These are the crawlings of fear.

I ASK MY GUIDES for help: the animals, the angels. I ask for who I may become. Not being able to stay in the old shape, I want to change the shape. Stuck.

Listen: what are you hearing when you cry? Listen: what are you hearing when you talk? Listen: what are you hearing when you breathe? Listen: what are you hearing when you write?

The “seams” are opening and it is a high-wire act. In any second, if anyone mentions their animal is sick or a friend is divorcing, the tears fall. Change. Frightening, unnerving, catching a cold time, yet alive, curious. Hold the space for change. Stay in the question.

The old skin is withering. Breathe. Feel the change. Feel the new shape. The new skin, now a bit more elastic, creating new cells, rearranging the old ones.

I dreamt I jumped off a cliff. Did you hurt yourself?

...NO!

RIVER OF YOUR LIFE

What if you could see your entire life in a flash in front of your eyes? What if you could walk the "river of your life?" Would you allow the feelings and the questions to come up?

I let them come up in an empty white space. I walk the space, an empty white room, I walk and walk breathing until something else happens . . . the fullness of the space, a breathtaking sense of stillness and weight.

I can look, I can see. I can get
answers. I can just walk into my
life. I can find a space that
gives me room to breathe.
An empty space, nothing
on the walls or floors,
no smells, no sounds,
a chair and only room
to expand.

I am two and half years old. I am in my crib. My father is in front of me and he is saying goodbye, I watch his back turned to me as he walks out of the door. I know I will never see him again.

I am 6 years old. I spend the morning with the flowers in the garden. I am blissful in the morning light. I hide so I can watch the birds come to flowers. My mother keeps calling me away and it's making me angry.

Breathing.

I am 10 years old. 16 years old. 30. 35. 37. 40. 45. 47.

What am I learning?

IN THE PRESENT MOMENT

Breathe up the conflict

Conflict can grab us like an animal that won't let go, fogging our mind and our body, consuming us. Breathing fills us with courage. Inhalation gives strength, exhalation brings relaxation.

Breathing can evoke the dark underbelly, the dark thoughts. It's the part of us that we struggle with, suppress or judge. Breathe up internal conflict and let yourself talk to it.

Why am I making so many bad choices?

Questioning opens the door to change. At my table stunned, I am in deep recognition. I have a terrible relationship with myself. I am angry. I am to blame. I am carrying lifetimes of fury and disbelief.

Want to try something even harder?

Try telling your best friend something you have never told anyone, something that you are not proud of, something that in the past deeply hurt you, or something that deeply affected you. Release judgment, let go, feel and observe. Remember, Carl Jung told us that we get the light by looking into the darkness.

If all of this is not even thinkable, do a little tap dance while you sing:

"Resistance, Resistance, Resistance."

RACHEL GETTING MARRIED

In this film, Kym, a recovering addict, home from 9 months of rehab, is a bridesmaid at her sister Rachel's wedding. Before the wedding, in the heightened reality of new families coming together, Kym is struggling with God and forgiveness and self. She was responsible for the death of her younger brother years before.

Kym's relentless needs, fierce determination and dis-ease, brings a mirror to the family's dysfunction – all the pieces of denial, protection and blame. And through the crashes of tempers, cars and a fist, Rachel is getting married, in extraordinary joy, deep love, beauty and a sea of music.

Kym returns to the clinic. She has bigger eyes now or she is more grounded. She's seen her father's emotional confusion, her mother's selfishness and cruelty, and her sister Rachel's love – who always, even in anger and jealousy, always gathers Kym up into her very wide arms.

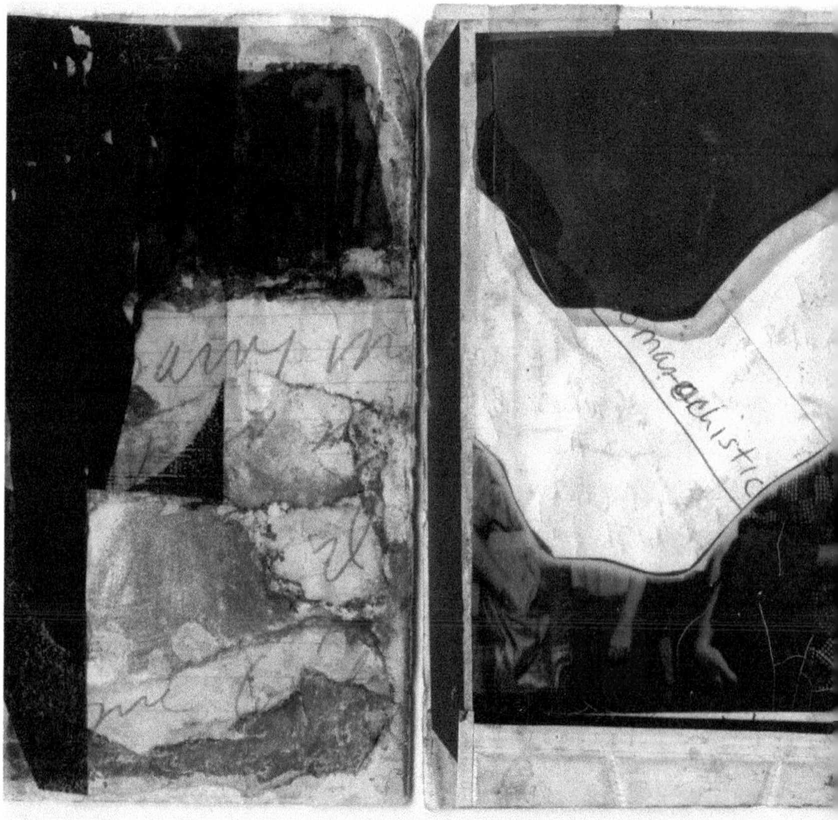

CONVERSATIONS WE DON'T WANT TO HAVE

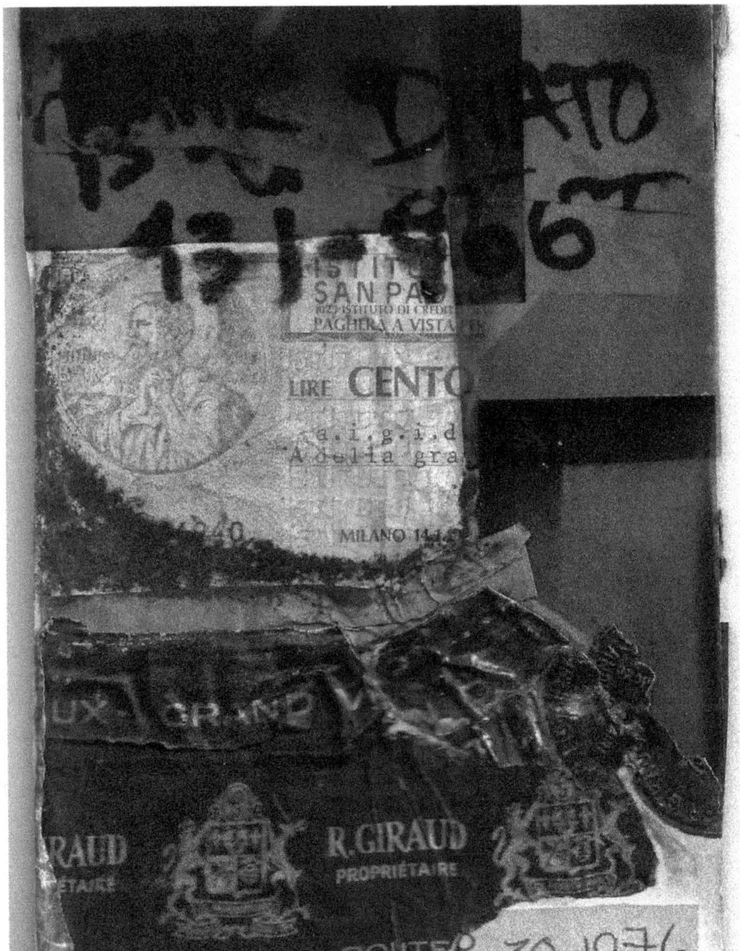

I always want to say things that never get said. I want to look at the yuck that is steaming and streaming in me. I want the gunk in my head and my belly to get cleared out. It's time to talk.

It's scary, this gathering your self back to yourself. Sometimes, I do it through sweaty hands, heart fast and my voice wobbly. I say things out loud that are unsayable, even unspeakable, maybe ineffable, waiting for a barrage, a dark cloud of closed ears or worse.

Sometimes, happily, I am greeted with kisses or thank you's or "yes, this is good!" The creaky doors, the heavy habits, the torture has been shifted. The molecules in the room have changed.

Leaves
drop . . .
the dead skin
drops off,
the dead
pieces,
the pieces that
held us
hostage.

4. The Journey

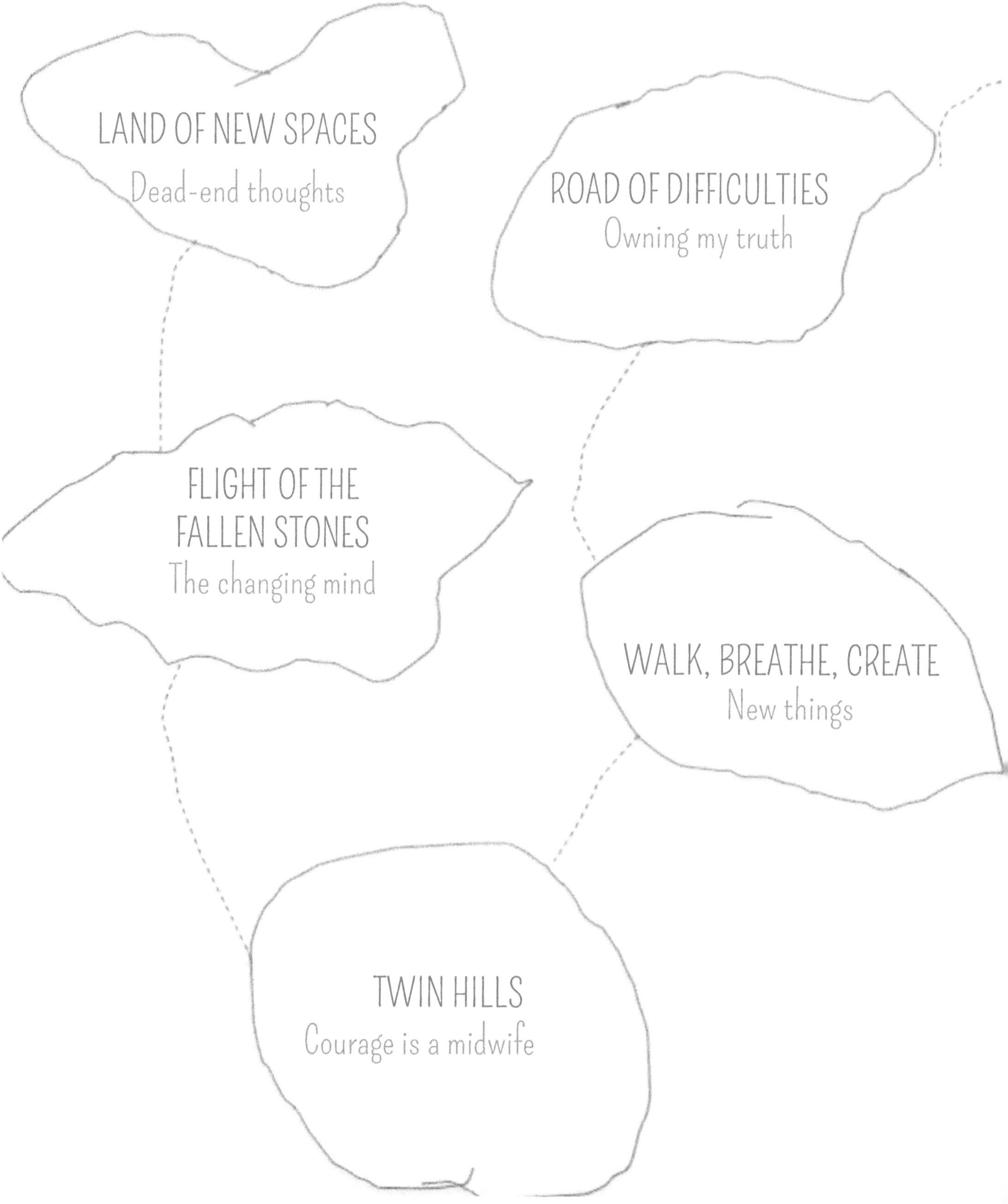
LAND OF NEW SPACES
Dead-end thoughts
ROAD OF DIFFICULTIES
Owning my truth
FLIGHT OF THE FALLEN STONES
The changing mind
WALK, BREATHE, CREATE
New things
TWIN HILLS
Courage is a midwife

Out

OWNERSHIP MOUNTAIN
Bring me higher
CAVE OF ANIMAL VIZUALIZATIONS
Your true nature
ANIMAL GUIDE PEAK
Awaken your intuition
HORSE TALK AVENUE
Out of the shadows

GO . . .

JOURNEY OUT

The space

has opened up.

But how do I get from

“no”

to “yes?”

EVER HEARD THESE?

"You're not good enough… you don't deserve anything… it's your fault I'm not getting what I want… don't you dare try to leave me … someone should put you in your place."

EVER DONE THESE?

Said "yes" when you mean "no" and then punish the other person because you can't say "no?"

Given in, in order to appease because you're afraid of confrontation?

Held out the carrot and then pulled it back at the last moment? Punished someone for telling the truth? Betrayed a loved one in order to protect yourself?

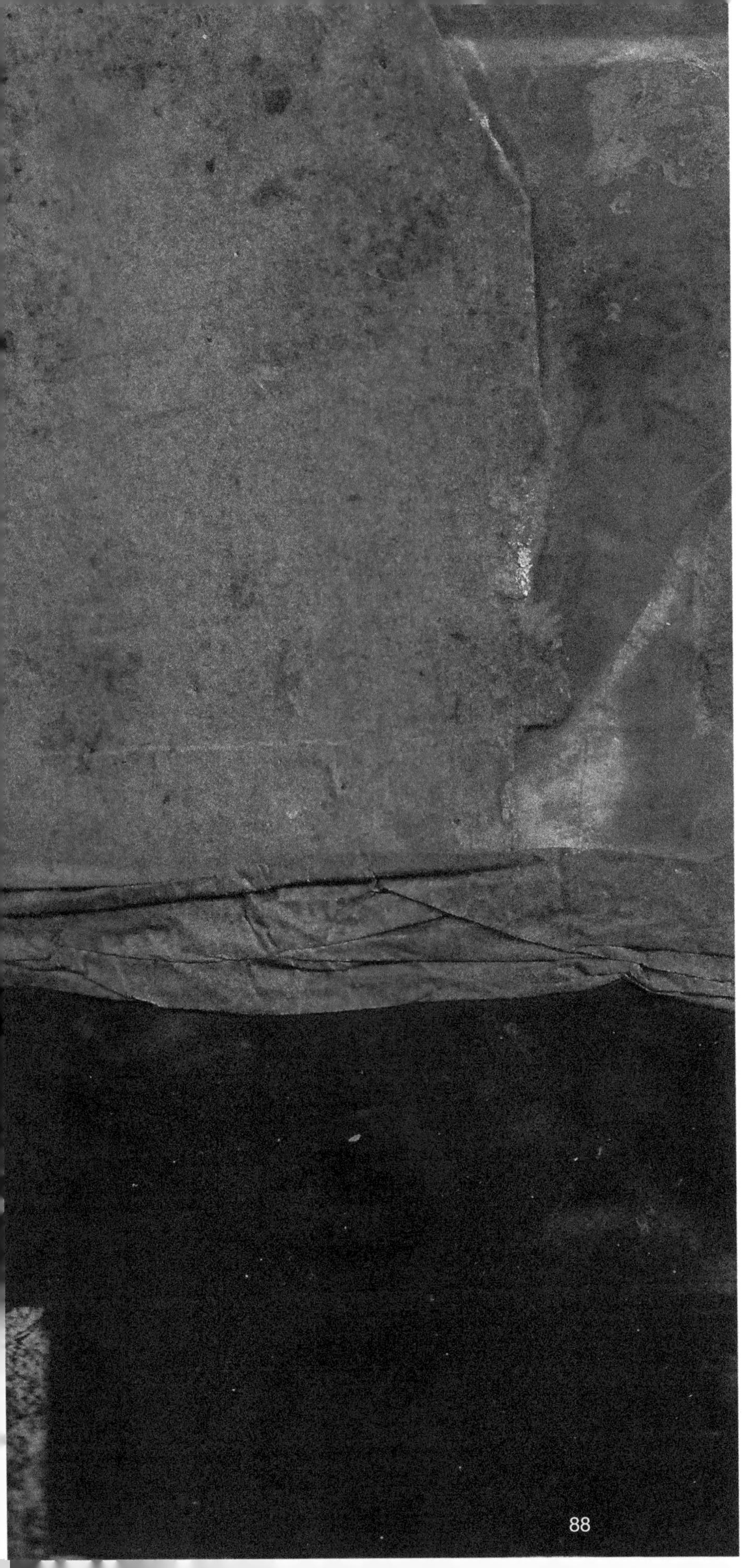

To
Own
My
Truth
Is
Very
Scary.

COURAGE & POWER

Isn't courage a word that we reserve for the brave feats of soldiers, athletes and fire fighters? Maybe it takes as much courage to acknowledge the small, private, painful, vulnerable pieces of our lives.

Do you ever wonder how much of yourself is simply running on automatic? Do you feel foggy at moments that demand you stand and be heard? Is it really hard to say 'no' ?

Do you trust yourself? Do you hit a home run one day and strike out the next? If the walls are coming down, isn't it the time to start talking? To someone, anyone!

Own your power, own yourself
and heal your broken heart.

WALK, BREATHE, CREATE

1. Plan a Walk

Plan a walk as a meditation. Walk a walk that you walk, and stay inside that walk. Smell the breeze, listen to the sounds, and feel the space of the outdoors.

2. Breathe Slowly

Breath slowly, very slowly, allow the questions to arise with the breathe . . . Why do I feel so bad, so anxious or scared, angry, impatient? Can you feel the relief of slowing everything down? Just let the questions arise.

When did I first start to encase myself in the lie about myself? When do I first remember believing their lies about themselves and the world?

3. Create a Collage

Create a collage from stuff you might throw away, things you find on your walk, notes and torn envelopes. If you give your imagination some breathing space and let it kick in, you will be amazed at what will surface!

Gather petals and stones and beads and magazine clippings and stuff you have encountered during your day. Fabric, plastics, twigs and feathers, anything that will help tell your story.

Isn't it interesting how I've told stories to myself and maybe have written the end of the stories before I have even begun to live.

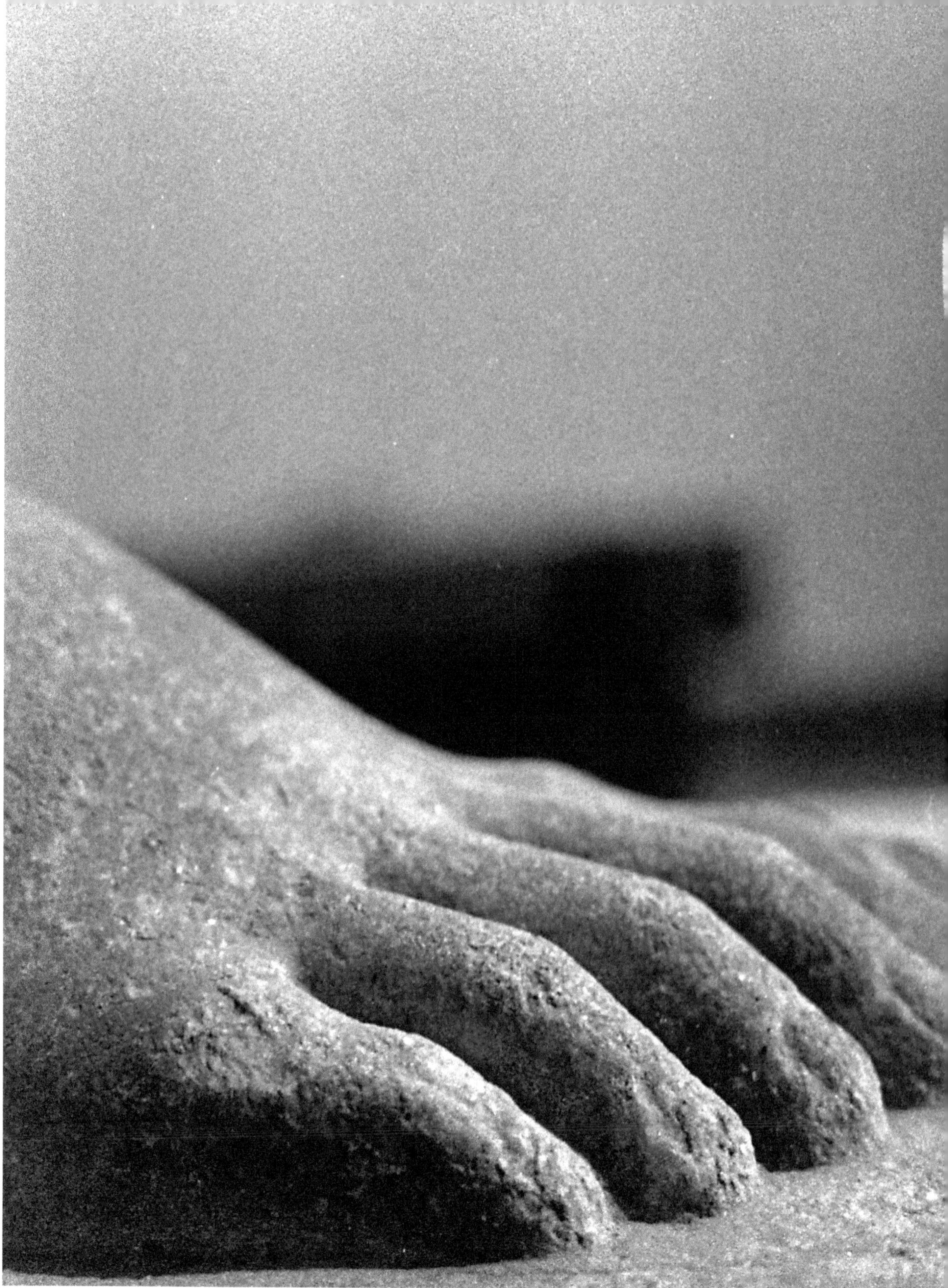

COURAGE TO OWN YOUR POWER

In the ancient – and some think mythological – land of Mu, the greeting upon meeting one another was "Espavo": "Thank you for taking your power."

I look at my life, society, choices, friends, boyfriends, education and work. I see me ripening. I create a new past. I walk the earth as the Master I am becoming. I choose to believe that I and every one of us will know this path. This is what we are doing here. How badly do I want freedom? What would happen if I moved so far from my old habits that my old life would be as a shadow?

A friend faced his drinking habit high in the Andes on a vision quest with shamans. The mountain brought him higher and higher, calling for change.

Is my mountain calling me?

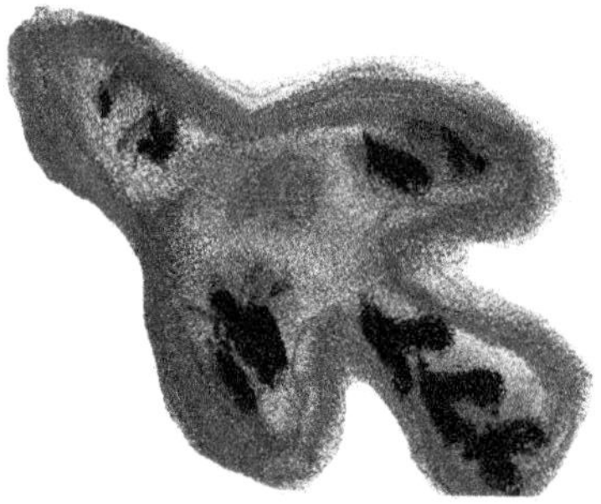

ANIMAL GUIDES

Pay special attention when a creature shows up in your life. When an animal or any creature comes into our lives – a spider, a mouse – even for a short visit, they open our imagination and our senses. They help keep the child alive and they help keep magic alive.

Intuition in animals is the stuff of legends. Does the animal you live with sense when you are coming home? Does she help you in some unexpected way? Animals have been known to save our lives.

Animal nature, animal sounds, animal appetites, animal exercises for actors. We know animals have a symbolic power over us because they mesmerize us. What animal do you gravitate towards? Do you show the qualities of a leopard, or fox, or blue jay?

Maybe these qualities point you in the direction of your animal guides. Follow your intuition and investigate the animals that are special to you. Look to them, study them and ask them for answers. Your animal totems are here to walk your life with you.

The shamans of all indigenous people know this and they dress as animals to bridge the worlds, gathering sacred information.

Certainly a surprise can be waiting for you as your guides appear, maybe at the edge of a small lake. I didn't expect a deer, a bird and a rabbit, but was filled with ecstasy when they appeared. I knew I had gathered a new piece of myself.

Recently a huge cobra has begun to take up residence behind me. Transformation.

ANIMAL VISUALIZATION

Lie down, resting comfortably on the floor with palms facing up. Visualize yourself walking out of your room and bring yourself to a beach. It is a hot day, the sun is high, the sky and the water are blue.

The air is clear and you are feeling like a part of nature. Taking your shoes and socks off, begin to walk along the water's edge feeling the "lap lap" as your feet move in the water. Take off your clothes and notice the sweetness of the air. As you continue to walk, you will see way in the distance a grove of palm trees. You come nearer and nearer to the grove, and walking through it, you enter a rain forest.

The oxygen is deep and strong and it clears you immediately. The forest is alive with palm trees and ferns and vines, and tropical flowers and birds, and other creatures big and small. This forest is deeply sensuous, rainy, lush and vibrant.

Your senses are stimulated. As you walk down the path, a waterfall sprays you, cleansing you. The forest is aware of you, and in fact, it has been waiting for you. Here you are protected and embraced. Way in the distance you see a clearing and as you come upon the clearing, you notice a dwelling.

It is your particular dwelling, one that resonates with your spirit. It may be an igloo or a hut or a Mediterranean mansion, a colonial house or a southwestern-style ranch. It is your home. And on the lawn, or the clearing around the house, is a creature. It may be animal or reptile or bird. It knows you and it has been waiting for you. It has much compassion for you.

You may talk with your creature.

ASK YOUR CREATURE its name. Why am I seeing this creature? What does my creature mean to me? What qualities do I need to learn from my creature? What special instructions does my creature wish to give me? You may experience answers telepathically, that is, you may just sense the answer or you may hear an answer or your creature may point or touch a part of your body.

You thank your creature by bowing deeply. Knowing you may return at any time, you begin to walk out of the rain forest.

You pick up something from the floor of the forest to remind you of your journey. It can be anything, something of the forest or not. It can be a jewel or an object that is precious to you. You will see it and feel it. As you are walking back down the path you are sprayed again by the waterfall.

As you come to the edge of the forest and onto the sandy beach, you notice that the sun is going down.

The sunset is magnificent and increases your sense of beauty and peace. You come back to the edge of the water and you find your clothes and dress yourself. You find your shoes and socks and put them on. You walk back through the door to your room and you come back to your body, stretching your arms and your legs and wiggling your fingers.

Allow yourself to enjoy the quietude and peace and solidness you may be feeling.

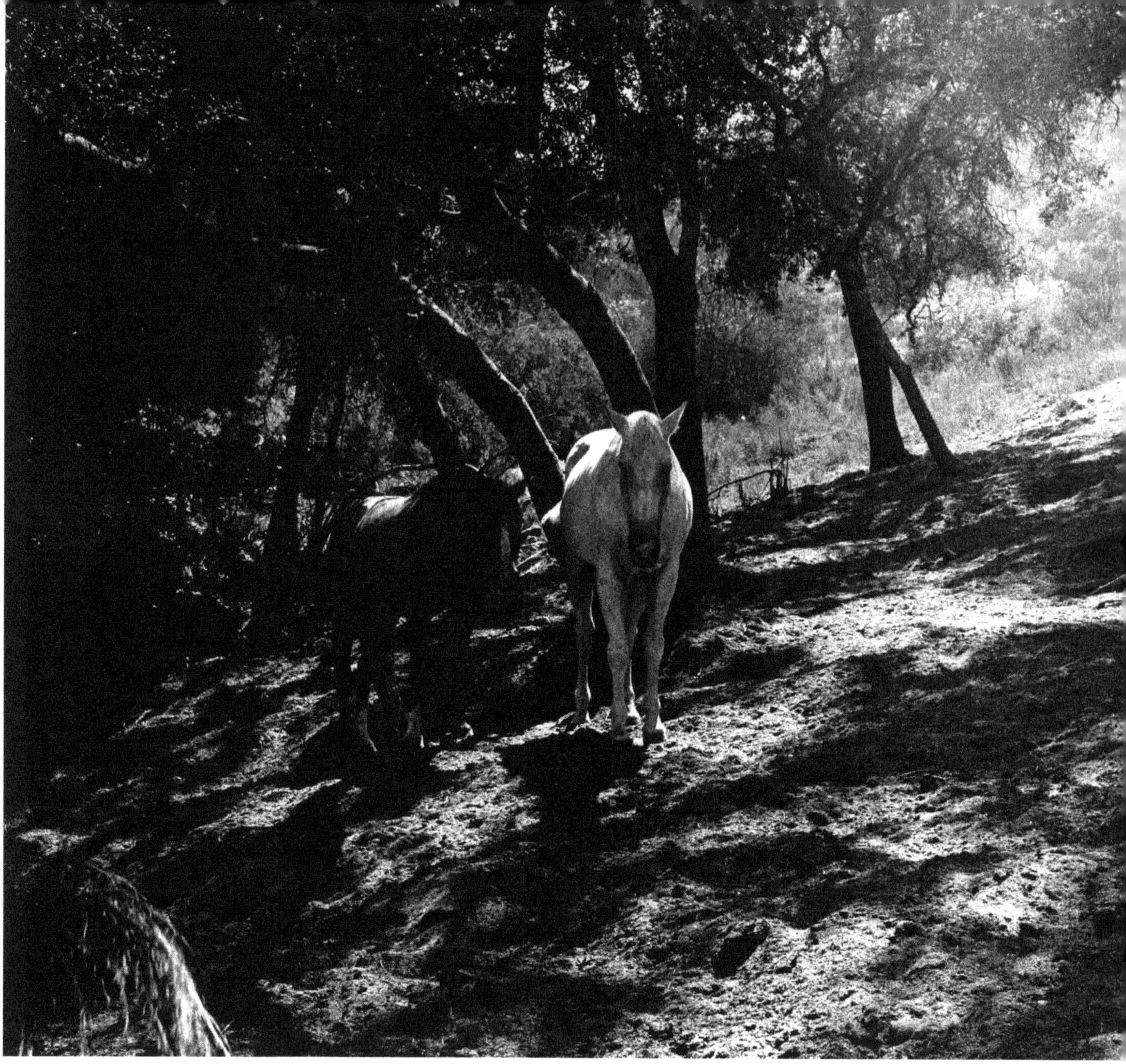

We believe that the courage we need to change will send us hiding under the bed. We believe that taking our power will hurt others.

Let your courage bring you out of the shadows.

5. TURNING POINT,

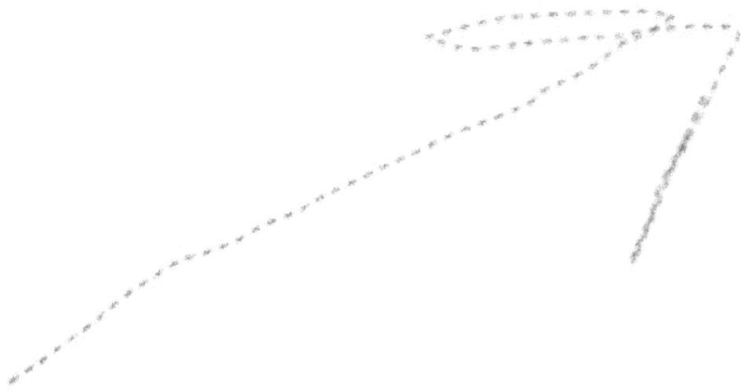

NEW UNIVERSE

TURNING POINT. . .

TIPPING POINT

Ecstasy

CHANGE IN ALL ITS FORMS

Rain to water to steam to ice. Have you ever looked in the mirror until your face is no longer your face? What does your face become if it is no longer your face? We all know change. These moments can be revelatory and thrilling or they can be difficult and frightening. What do we learn at these moments? What happens to who we are?

Is there a moment in the wedding that foreshadows a moment in the marriage? Are these moments the same and yet profoundly different? What happens to us when we call for change? When is the moment when we have gone too far, or not far enough? Who do we become? What happens when we confront a death of any kind? Does something in us die to hold a new sense of self?

Journey

Love

Union

Conflict

A dream
unfulfilled

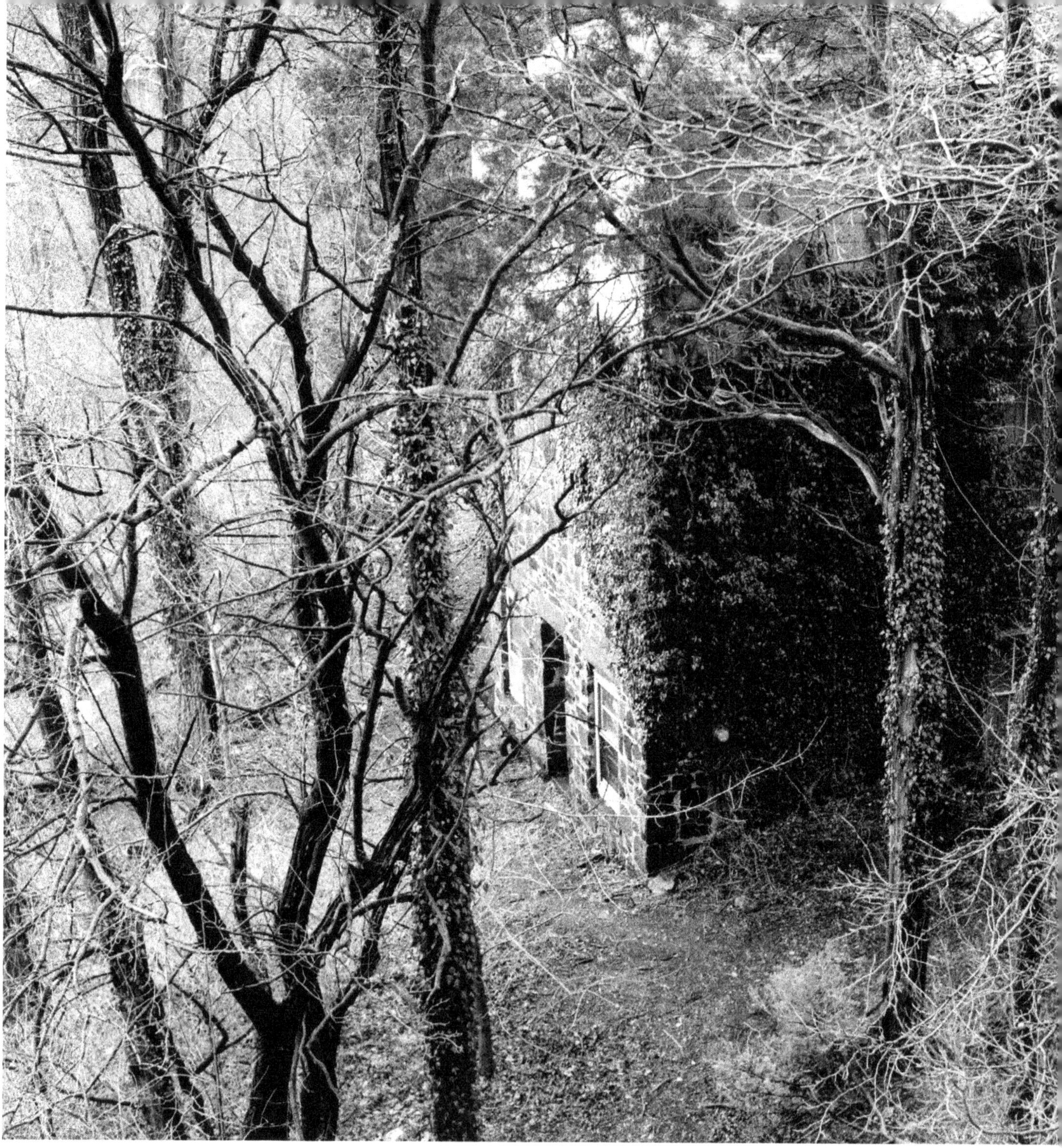

Interior life

Learning....

I FOR
MYSE
love
CO

GIVE
LF
I love
love me
PLETELY

6. Out of the

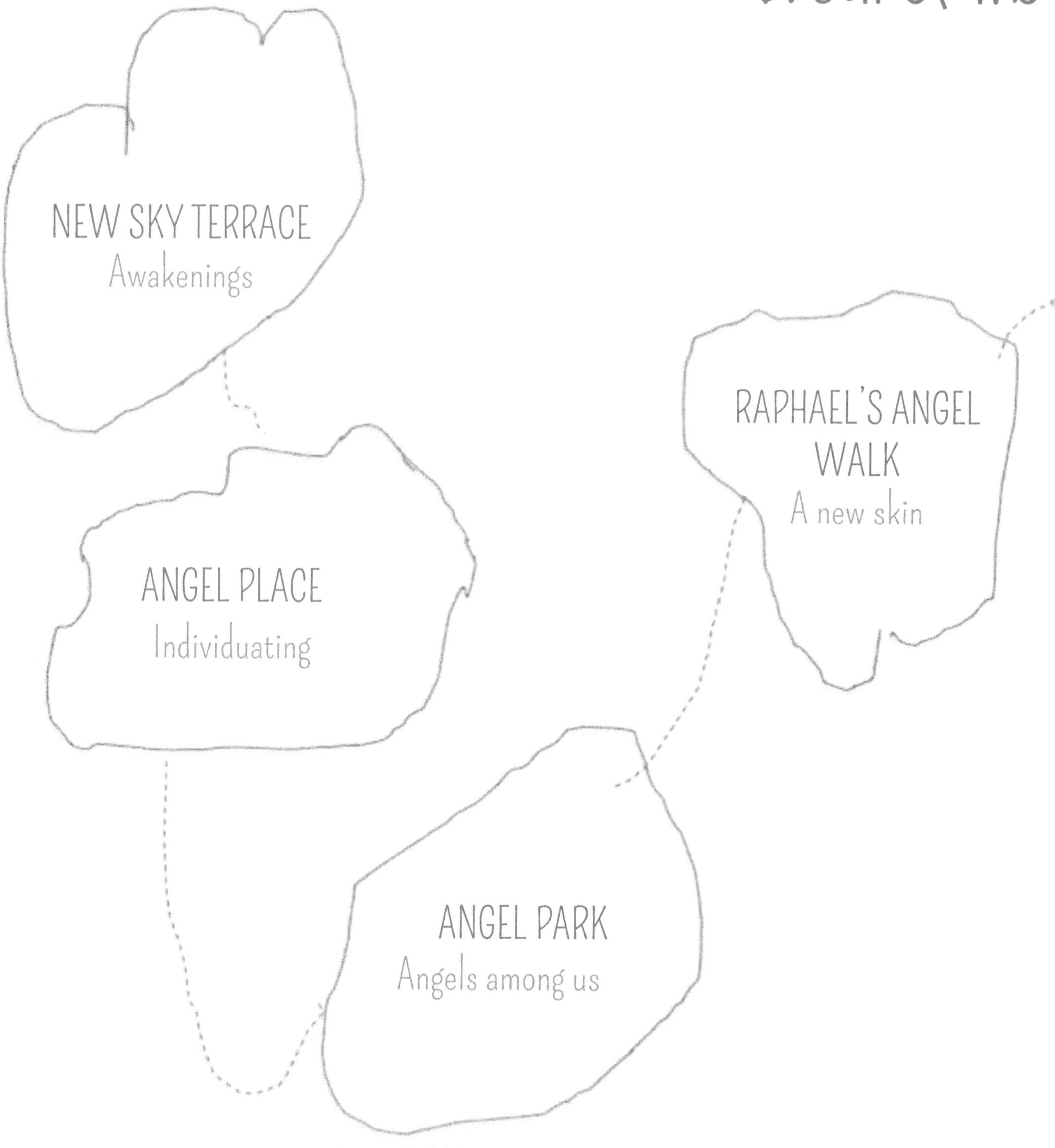
NEW SKY TERRACE
Awakenings
ANGEL PLACE
Individuating
RAPHAEL'S ANGEL WALK
A new skin
ANGEL PARK
Angels among us

Darkness

GABRIELLE'S OVERLOOK
Voice is a fingerprint
JEWEL DREAM WALK
Beauty's gift
SEA OF MIRACLES
Creating belief: "The Notebook" film

COME...

...OUT OF DARKNESS

vol
sea
door
terrace

AN ANGEL APPEARS

Yea! In comes the angel. A healing angel comes to me. I call him Max.

He is a 12' 2" tall angel in a tuxedo with a huge wingspan. I release fear and the belief that there is a crack in my subconscious.

I release "I am bad." I release punishment. Max brings me a sense of sweetness.

WHO IS YOUR ANGEL??

Who taught us that we weren't angels, that we were not good enough for God? Who are these people?

WHO WOULD I BE IF

I were completely aligned with the universe?

See, this is how we get locked in: Seeing my godmother, I felt my aloneness and my mother's isolation. My mother's profound emotional removal was deeply palpable. She had to remove herself in order to survive. I hated it, yet it was so familiar. In this moment with my godmother – my charismatic, earthy, ambitious, present godmother – I missed my mother terribly.

I release...my mother's helplessness.

I release...my mother's fear of abandonment.

I release...my mother's sadness and hysteria.

I release...my mother's pain.

I release...my mother's anger and hate.

EXTRAORDINARY ACCOMPLISHMENTS

At the edge of the summit of Mt. Everest, some climbers want to go home. Hundreds of feet in front of them is the end of their journey. They can see it – after the misery of freezing cold, sleet, fear and unbearable exertion – they want to turn back. The freedom is unbearable. Maybe confronting this freedom is why they make such a climb.

What is your wall???

Who is your angel?

TRYING ON A NEW SKIN

My angel Max gave me a glimpse of a golden, deep perspective. But can I hold it and accept it?

I will become an angel of Raphael's, as in the painted altarpiece "Madonna and Child Enthroned with Saints." I will learn to hold Max's grace through acting. I am good at this . . . I will go into a heightened state and give birth to an angel! I will hold this being inside me. The world is suddenly brighter, sharper. Colors are different.

But I get frightened and almost have to leave the Museum. I think I had better start with another genius, one not quite so angelic. A Rembrandt self-portrait. Here was a power I could play with. Raphael's angel is so pure, so exquisite. Rembrandt's genius is here on the earth. He mixes heaven up with earth. He makes his own miracles. Has anyone ever been so honest in self-portrait?

To completely embody Rembrandt, I will need the clothes he is wearing in his portrait. That might send me to a costume rental shop or a thrift store.

I must create the environment of the portrait. A part of the painting is not clear. It has very dark shadowing, chiaroscuro.

I must arrange things to give me the feeling that I see in the portrait.

I want to imagine what Rembrandt is thinking and doing the five minutes before he sits for the portrait. I write a scenario. Is this his home? Where is Saskia, his wife? Did he just get some difficult news? Does he have any physical pain? What is really in his face??

There is a depth of feeling in his face, an honesty. His spirit is palpable and so is his pain and his confusion. WHO IS HE? What does he know that I need to learn? He is after all, a Master's Master. Why am I drawn to him?

PUT YOUR VOICE INTO THE WORLD

Is your voice lush and mellifluous, full of resonance and eloquence? Go to your favorite literature, a poem or a story. Read very, very slowly, savoring each word. Elongate your vowels as if you are singing. You may feel a vibration in your body. Vowels carry the music and the emotion. This takes PRACTICE. Stretch yourself and what you know. Then, read the same piece in your day to day voice. Different?

Now, read and exaggggggerate consonants. Finish your final consonants. Yes, this might feel very strange and uncomfortable. You might feel a new strength in your body. Consonants carry the meaning and the articulation. PRACTICE.

Now, balance the vowels and the consonants. Balance the female and the male energy. This is training – this deliberate elongation and exaggeration. Just keep this up and eventually your use of language will be stronger and more eloquent and more courageous.

Breathe. Go to the river or the sea or the ocean, a park, a mountain, a meadow. Say your name over and over and over until there is a deep satisfaction, a fulfillment, until you hear your name with new ears. Yes, I am.

AND NOW... MORE BREATHING

Yoga & Ujjayi breath. Victorious breath – ocean breath – wind breath.

The Yogis believe that breath, that is, prana or life force, is a bridge between the physical and the energetic worlds. They also believe that Ujjayi breath can give us access to boundless energy.

I am enthralled by the idea that my breath can sound like the ocean. By inhaling with a closed mouth and breathing out through my nose, while constricting my throat, I create Ujjayi breath. It may sound like the wind, or the ocean and feel similar to a whisper. Yes, I can connect to a deeper sense of self.

The sound of blowing wind in my throat is something I am never prepared for! And then comes the real gift, the calming of the nervous system. Ujjayi breath, one more blissful encounter with the body!

Steiner, Robert, et al. "Ujjayi Pranayama—the victorious breath." International Infopage for Ashtanga Yoga. http://www.ashtangayoga.info/ashtangayoga/basics/breathing-ujjayi/ (accessed December 18, 2015); The Chopra Center for Wellbeing. "Ujjayi Breath." Chopra.com. http://www.chopra.com/ujjayi-breath (accessed December 28, 2015).

A DREAM OF JEWELS

Walking on a private beach on a hot clear day, walking and walking, it becomes important to take off my shoes in order to feel the water against my ankles. This beach doesn't seem to be in a country I know. The beauty and sweetness of the air is a soothing breath. Walking and taking off my clothes, the freedom seems to be a part of nature.

Then, there is a big, old fashioned trunk in the water, way out. The trunk is the strongest image in the dream and it's magnetic. Swimming out to it and already inside it, I find it's filled with my favorite gems and jewelry. They take my breath away. As I roll over the jewels, they feel like a second skin.

At the bottom of the trunk is a note. I open it and my heart fills with happiness. The note says: "you are coming home". Waking up brings a feeling of deep security, covered as I am with jewels. I am jewels. We are jewels.

THE NOTEBOOK

The heart of this film – the magic of love – holds us as the miracle of love holds this couple together. He builds a house for her not knowing if she is returning. Much later, when her memory is gone, his belief creates another miracle. He reads to her from a novel she had written years before, a memoir of their young life and of their trial by fire. She's lucid when they choose to die together, simply by willing it. What seems like a fairy tale is pointing to the new reality:

"See it, believe it, create it."

AT THE SEA OF GALILEE

I was free when thinking about the idea of being able to walk on water. If you believe with every cell of your body that you can do it, you will do it.

7. A New

QUARRY OF GRACE
Gathering newness
FOREVER LANE
Keeping on
CLIFFS OF GRATITUDE
Create your feelings
BEACH ROAD
Heaven on Earth

Beginning

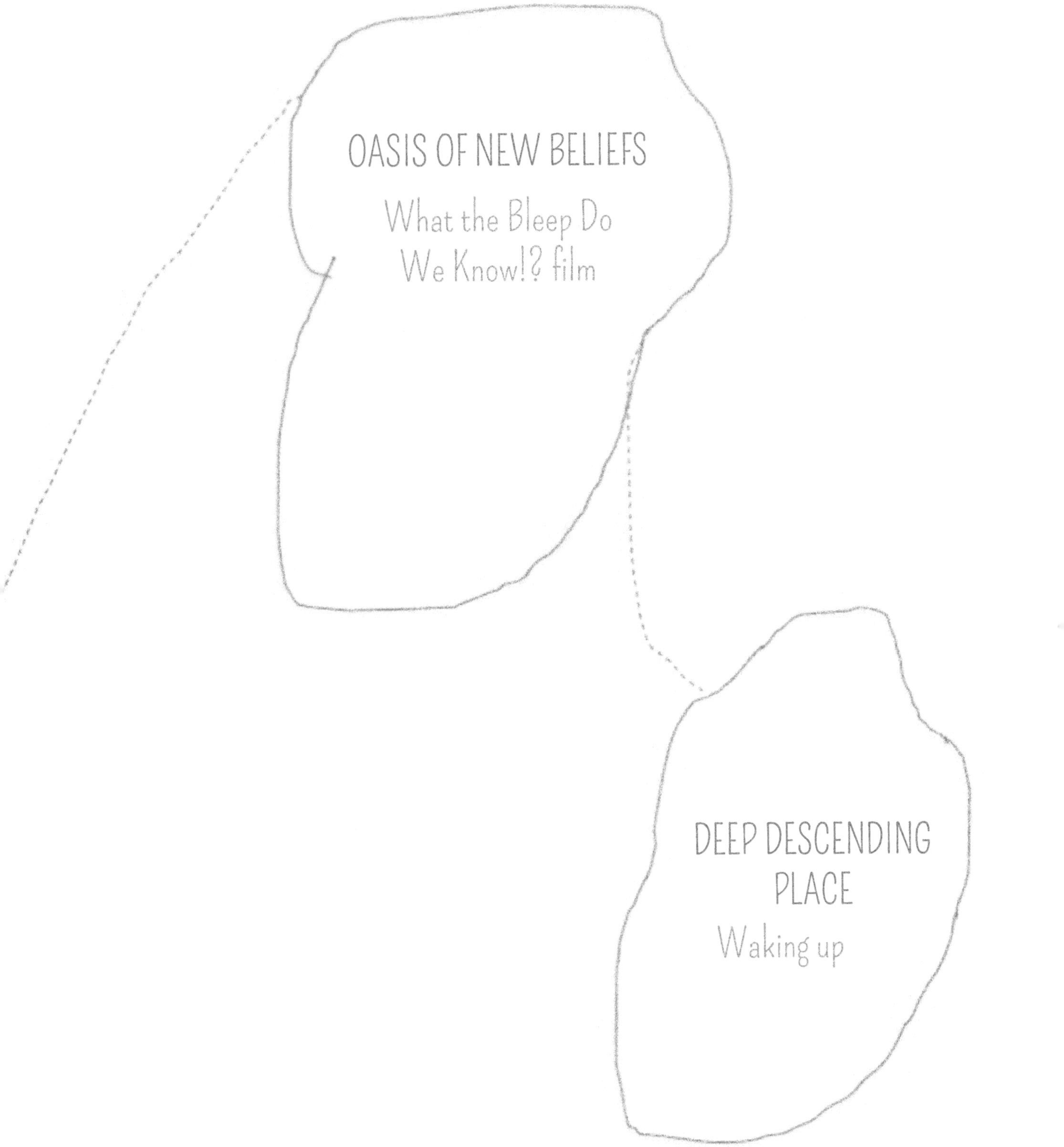
OASIS OF NEW BELIEFS
What the Bleep Do We Know!? film
DEEP DESCENDING PLACE
Waking up

OWN A NEW BEGINNING

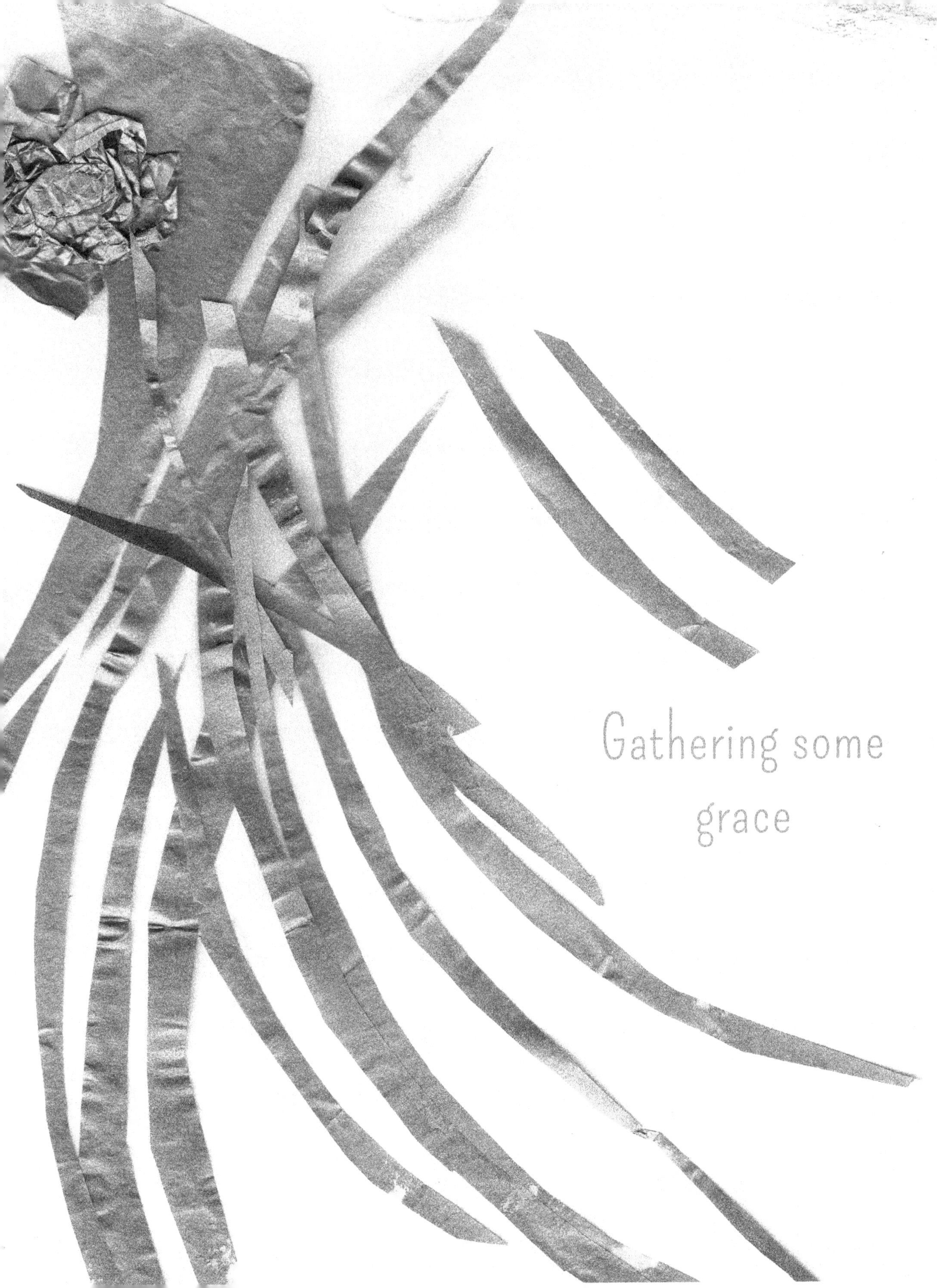

Gathering some grace

WHY DO I KEEP

beginning a new beginning?

Because when I lose myself and fall into the fear of the everyday, I remember the body is a reminder of something greater.

Why do I keep on beginning a new beginning? Because when I stop breathing and believing, I remember the chakra system, the 7 wheels of energy that exist inside our body, reaching from earth to God.

Why do I keep on beginning a new beginning? Because I remember that the world is framed in sacred geometry; that all these shapes, spirals, circles and triangles are universal, connecting us to all things everywhere, including the billions of planets in the billions of galaxies.

Why do I keep on beginning a new beginning? Because when I cannot stop crying, I remember beauty. I remember da Vinci, van Gogh and Shakespeare who in a dream said to me: "You are harder on your actors than I ever was." I remember humor, screwball comedies, laughter and Buster Keaton's face. I remember poetry and dancing and the sublime Einstein and Chaplin.

You can't want to die if you think you may never again hear Chopin or Mozart or Mingus.

BECAUSE I AM in the lineage of the Greek priest, Thespis, who was the first to step out of the line of priests to sing a dithyramb solo.

BECAUSE I WANT to know what is buried at the foot of the Sphinx and because I can call upon anyone: da Vinci, Archangel Gabriele, Athena, Jesus, Saint Germaine, Emily Dickenson, the goddess Venus to come to me and teach me. Because when I forget who I am, I cry, I scream and I yell at God that I don't want to be here, that I want to go "home", that I want the sweetness of heaven.

BECAUSE I REMEMBER that we can have heaven on earth if we wish – but only if we get out of the way and allow who we really are to be here with us IN PEACE.

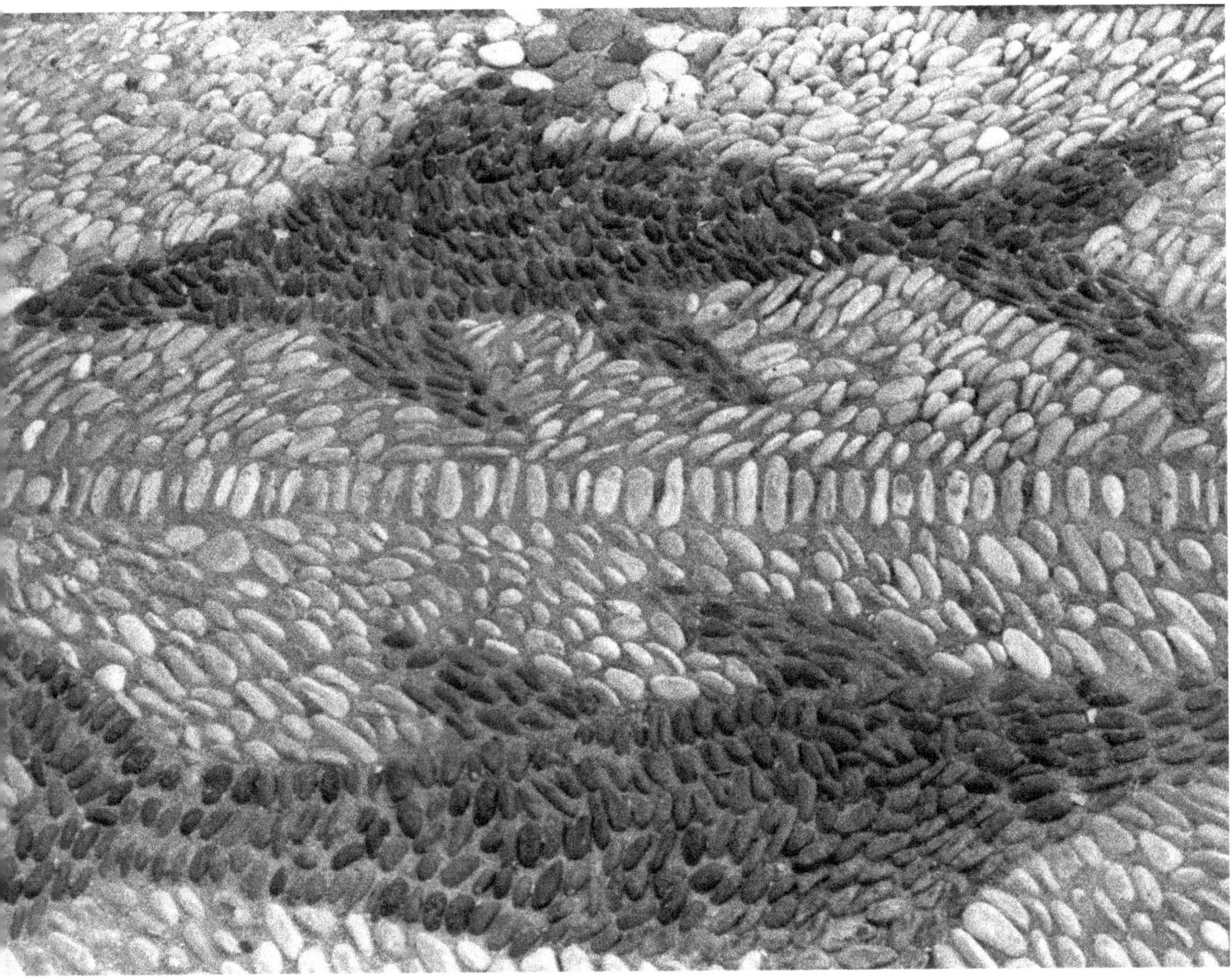

WHEN HAVE YOU . . .

. . . transcended your conflict? Playing, creating, making love, running, dancing, being with children? Is it at the ocean . . . in the mountains . . . in the air?

When in fear, in deep conflict, out of touch with my own authority, I tested myself with a question, "How can I get out of this darkness?" I walked the beach asking for peace and clarity from the ocean. The most sacred space on earth is where the water meets the land. Slowly the place beyond the sky was visible again.

Creative beings create their feelings, not just experience them.

The Masters know this.

APPRECIATION

I appreciate the love that is with me; the teachers and healers. I am grateful I am moving into belief.

I appreciate beauty and my gifts; this voice and what it has brought me, the depth and humor and passion of my being. I appreciate the messages received from dreams and the ability to move in and out of many worlds.

I appreciate health and healing, friends, children, guides and the light of animals.

I appreciate the sanctuary of stories, films, literature, poetry, jewels, flowers, colors, music, art, design, spirit, the Divine.

I appreciate the protection and abundance of my home across the ocean in the Mediterranean, the lava hills, the watery caldera carved by ancient volcanos and the inner stillness of Santorini. I appreciate the changes that are happening in me, around me, and in the world.

When
the
spine is
strong
it feels
like a
heart.

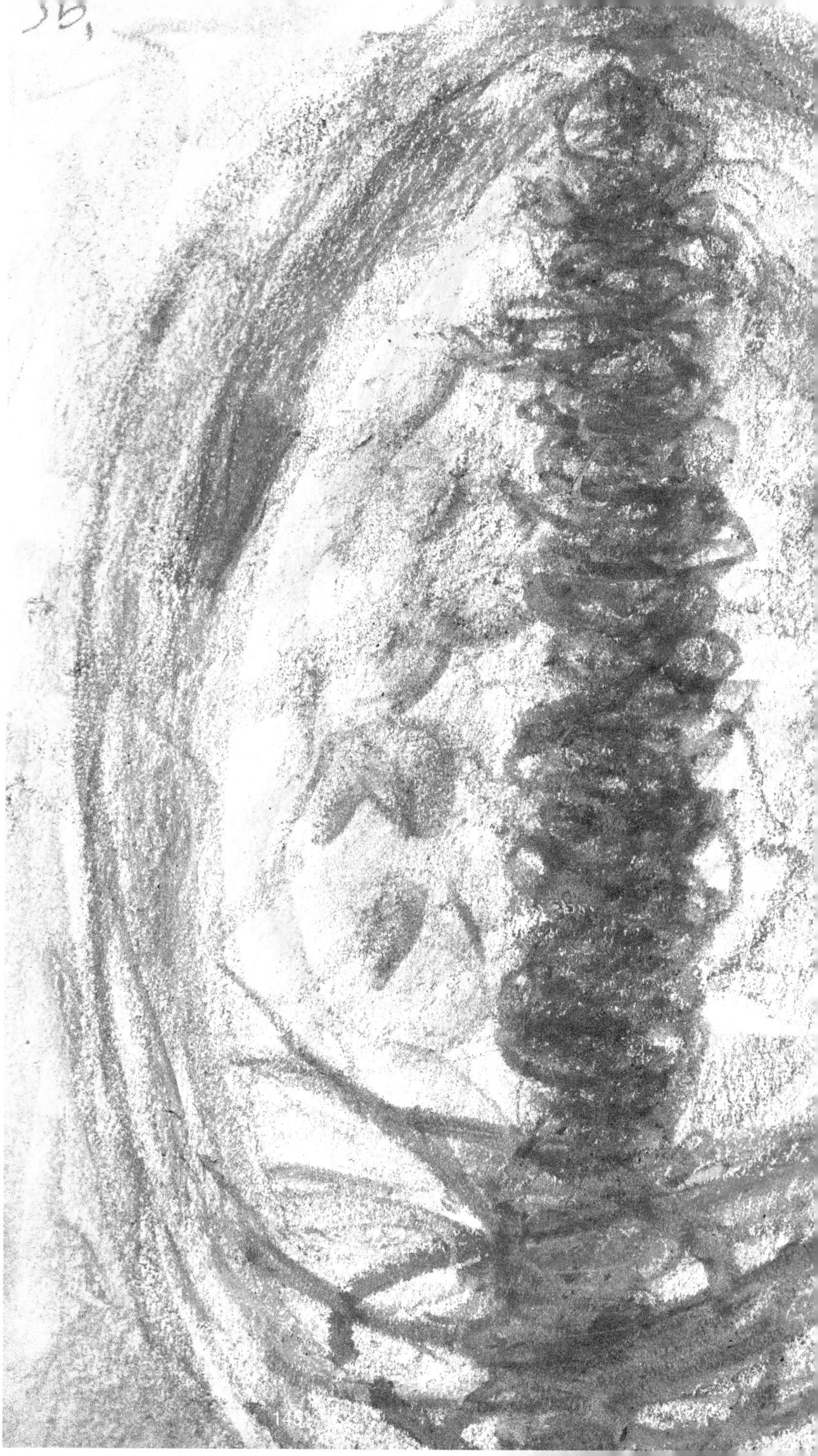

WHAT THE BLEEP DO WE KNOW!?

In this film, the nature of who we are and the nature of reality is told in an unusual mix of story, animation, interviews and an expanded sense of time and place. The film creates this structure to fulfil its vision of a multi-dimensional Universe and consciousness. Our heroine, a photographer, is plagued with anger, anxiety, and lack of self-awareness. Extraordinary events, dreams and coincidences shake her foundation and wake her to a multi-dimensional existence.

Scientists and healers comment throughout the story, as psychedelic visuals splash forth the internal workings of our cells and synapses. Our senses are assaulted and help us recognise the vastness of what we live in.

Running late, at a subway platform, our photographer encounters a mini installation about the power that thoughts have on water. She then encounters a whiz kid in his private basketball court in an alternate reality. This whiz demonstrates how nothing comes into focus until we bring it into focus. Later, in a dream, a shaman standing in full regalia of feathers and tattoos pokes our photographer's third eye, her psychic center. Finally, in a film theatre, we watch our heroine see the she that is she in other dimensions and another times.

We are mesmerized watching quantum physics in action.

I wake

up

hearing

"give."

My

left brain

is in white

light.

8.

FREEDOM'S GARDEN WALK
Golden sun
FREEDOM'S HILLS
To a new world
FREEDOM'S PROMISE END
Becoming a Master
FREEDOM LANE
Choices matter
DEEP WATERS OF FREEDOM'S PATH
Song of our senses
FREEDOM'S ESSENCE LAKE
Who are you really?

Freedom

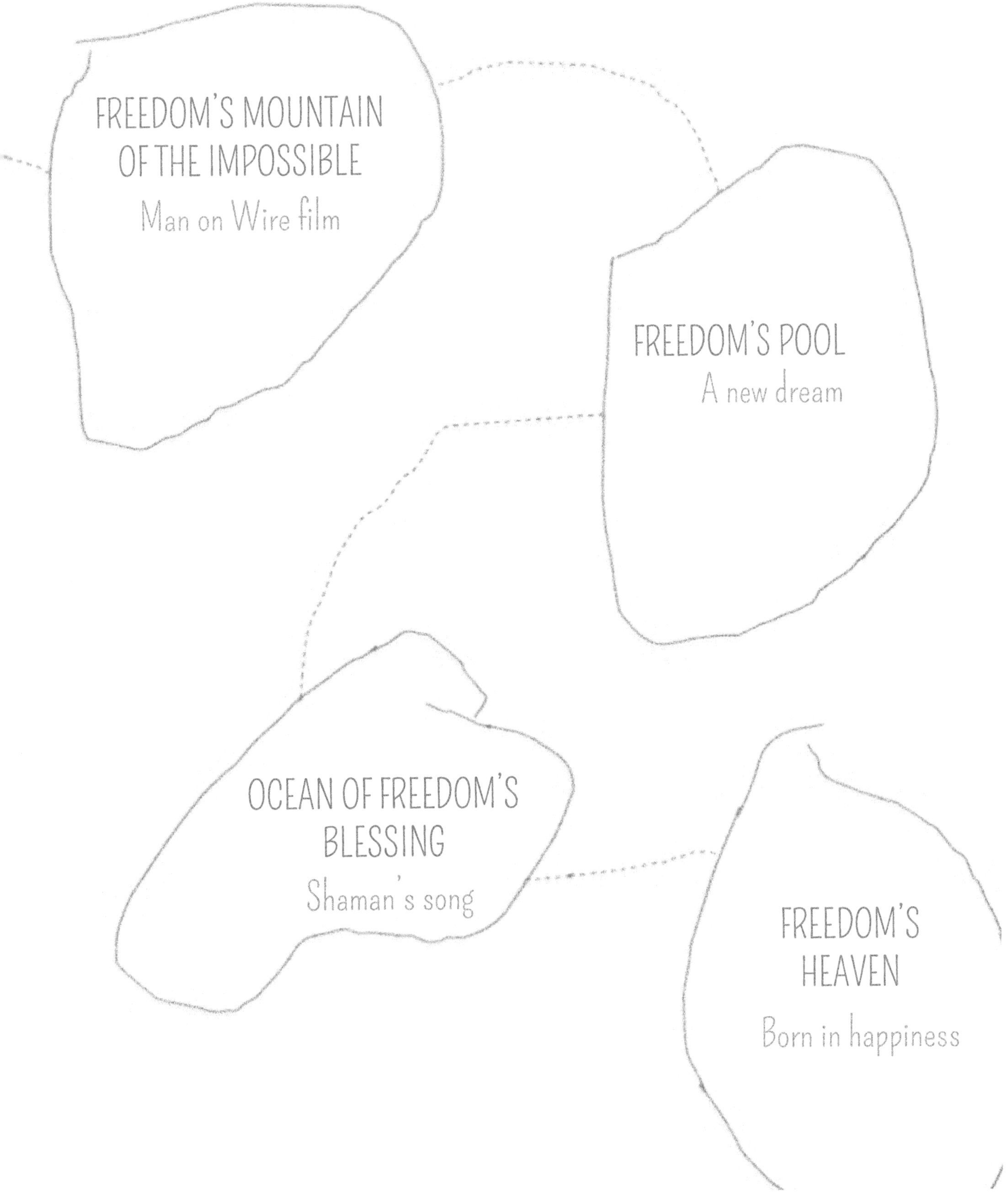
FREEDOM'S MOUNTAIN OF THE IMPOSSIBLE
Man on Wire film
FREEDOM'S POOL
A new dream
OCEAN OF FREEDOM'S BLESSING
Shaman's song
FREEDOM'S HEAVEN
Born in happiness

CREATE

FREEDOM

F
O
R

A

N
E
W

W
O
R
L
D

walk

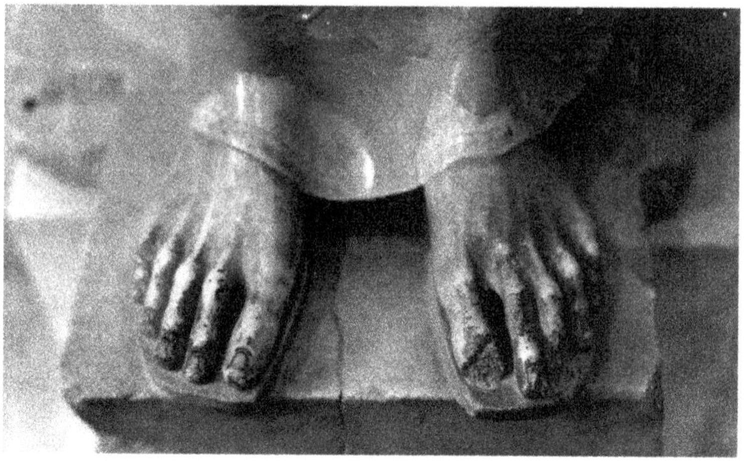

to the

starting block

FREEDOM MANTRAS

If you leap the Universe is there to catch you

The Dark is necessary to see the Light

Become the Goddess/God you came here to be

Give the Goddess a chance

The Universe is bursting with creativity

Who would we be if we heard Womankind all day

The portal to the Aquarian Age has opened

Gratitude changes everything

MEDITATION

What is my genius?
"I am here to realize and grow my perfect self
through show and tell."

HEIGHTENING YOUR SENSES

Tasting the perfect coffee and holding the pleasure of that perfect day in my mouth. I can dance. I mean really dance. I have the legs, but mostly I have the rhythm, I have the grace, its perfect, my timing is perfect. And the work and exhaustion is worth it. I am beyond spent and in perfection.

To Smell brought a moment when another realm opened to an olfactory hallucination, a smell so sweet seeped in. The memory of heaven, intoxicating, almost dizzy.

Seeing new things presented in front of my eyes, and I feel 10,000 new connections in my brain. I feel the jump in my body when beauty startles my eyes and my synapses and everything else falls away. Love floods through me.

Touching her, I feel the silk of her cat paws. Freedom escapes from her as we run, tripping over the dead leaves. Falling over her, I almost bury her. I am with the night and I am safe, finally.

Hearing the ocean over and over hypnotizes me. Bringing with it a stillness that comes with the release of all the words—the words that weigh me down, burn and scrape. Thankfully, everything dissolves in the sound of the ocean, and into peace.

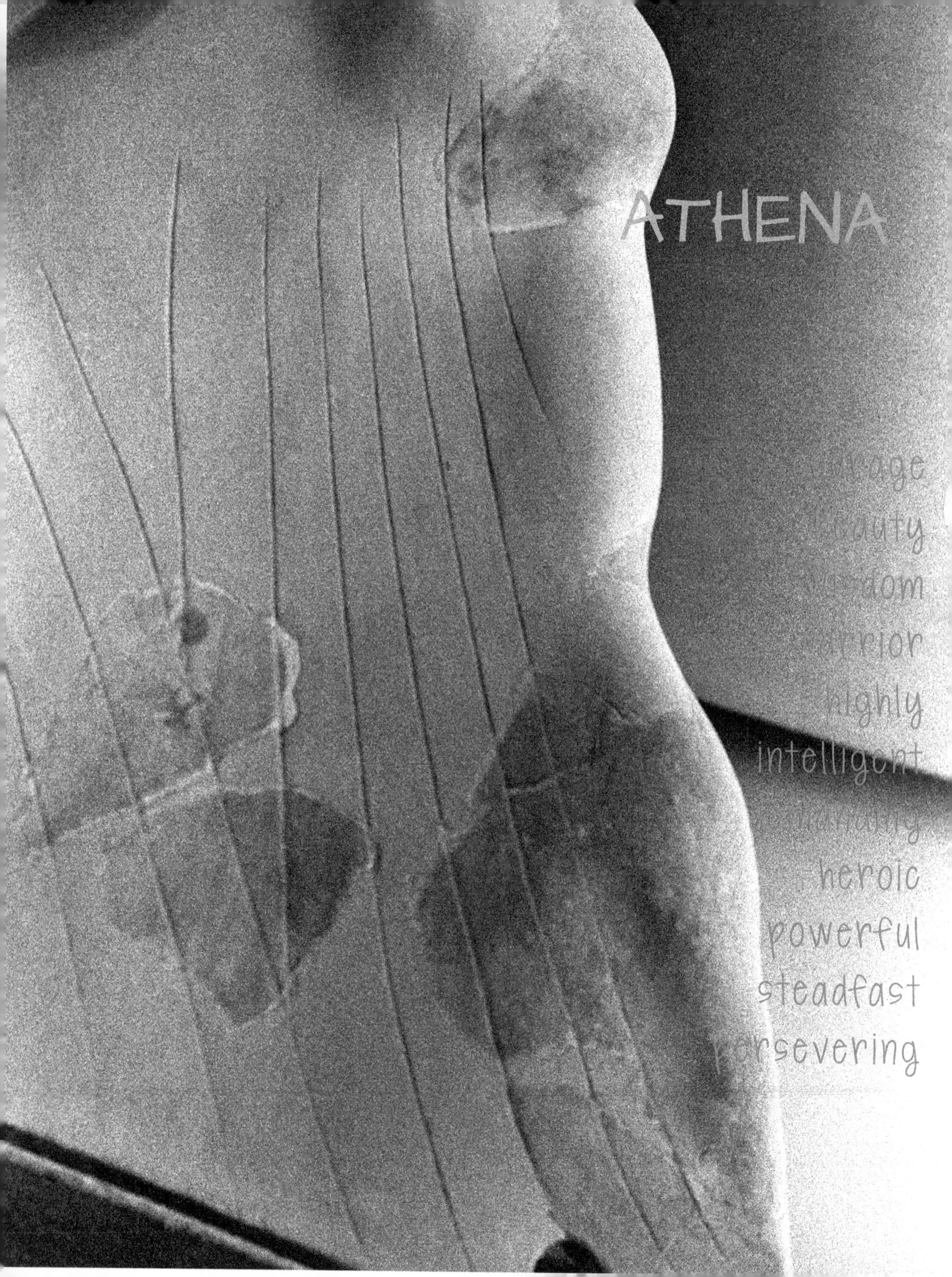
ATHENA
highly
intelligent
heroic
powerful
steadfast

COSTUME YOUR ESSENCE

Who are you really?

Write a personal monologue about an event in which you showed up fully, a time when you were displaying your Essence.

Shop the thrift store, the attic of your grandmother or her closet, or any eccentric place that calls to you. Create the perfect costume for your Essence.

Write words which describe your Essence, describe the genius that is you. Maybe a mythological figure or a character from a story or from history symbolizes your Essence. Perform in full costume in front of a dear friend.

QUANTUM PHYSICS AND

Quantum physics is investigating the world at the subatomic level. At this level, thoughts become matter. Quantum physics is proving what all religions and all indigenous tribes have known. We and nature and the Universe are all one. With our thoughts and our intent we are all creating everything.

Our choices matter and have an effect beyond our lives and beyond the earth. Our consciousness creates our reality. The world, cannot exist without our input. We help bring the world into reality.

THE NATURE OF REALITY

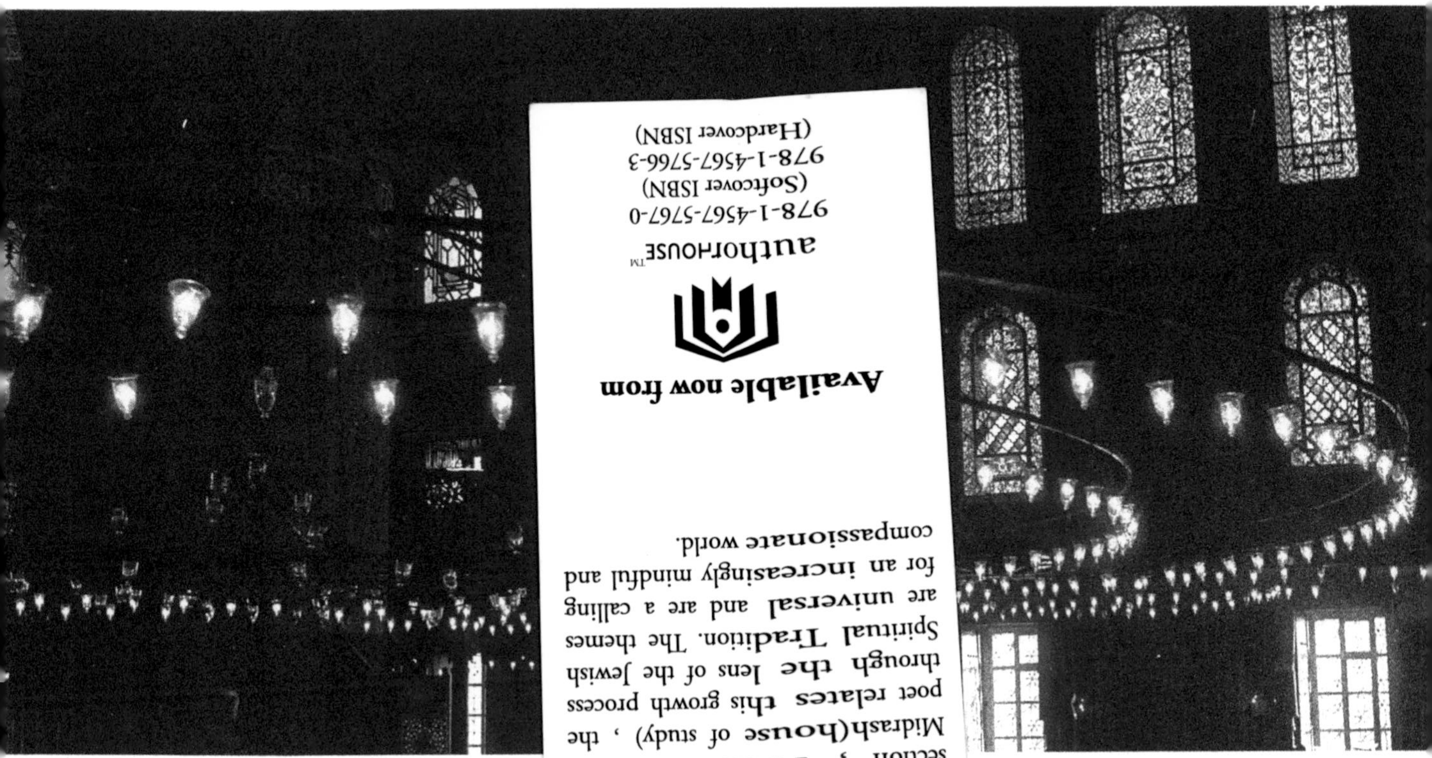

Some believe that we ... lives learning how to become an av... has become fully conscious, understan... e beauty and the love that is at the ... is all.

Consciousness is cre... the billions of planets and galaxies. ... , all the time. We can change ourse... and our relationship to all-that ... learn who we really are and that is ...

I WANT TO BE A MASTER

I am always working to make sense of being here, who we are and how we get to be a Master – those skilled practitioners who know the secrets of creation and manifestation, and who have learned to live in their truth.

We are being taught a new paradigm that we have an energy that seems unfathomable. The billions of cells in our brain, mirror the billions of stars in the Universe. Just splitting one atom gave us the atom bomb and we are this multitude of atoms. How can we understand that kind of power? How can we understand a world without end? We have to expand how we perceive, not just how we think. I revel in this expansion. I want to know what the Masters know, and I want to rest in eternity, as I am walking the earth. I don't want to die to learn this.

The artists are unseen lovers, awakening us to us. They carry secrets. They can put us right inside the connection to ourselves. Artists are a different kind of priest. And for now, I'll take that. And this is why the poets, in particular, call me.

POETS MAKE AN ATTEMPT to discover the heart of existence, naming things that are unnamable. We can read the words and hear the words. Even when the words don't seem to make much sense, the meaning between the words calls us to our intuition and leads us inward helping us move to those deeper recesses in our psyche and soul. And maybe this is heaven.

O sages standing in God's holy fire
As in the gold mosaic of a wall,
Come from the holy fire, perne in a gyre,
And be the singing-masters of my soul.

Consume my heart away; sick with desire
And fastened to a dying animal
It knows not what it is; and gather me
Into the artifice of eternity.

- William Butler Yeats

Yeats, W.B. "Sailing to Byzantium." In The Collected Poems of W.B. Yeats, edited by Anne Yeats, (New York: Scribner Paperback Poetry, 1989), 193.

MAN ON WIRE

Aerialist Phillippe Petit

Aerialist Philippe Petit walked 104 stories above ground in an uncanny deed – he, his feet and a wire. This took a year of planning, and a lifetime of dreaming and preparing, to complete an early morning astonishment.

Who is this? Striding between heaven and earth, Philippe Petit had an unusual amount of otherworldliness that morning. And of course, he was arrested! He refused the old model and created his own - he dreamt it and he knew he could.

He believed it in every cell of his body. This is clear in his face and his body and his concentration as we watched him claim his dream in front of our eyes.

A NEW DREAM

I find myself standing in front of an infinity pool, near a high wall. Large crossed black wires are burning brightly at the base of the wall. In front of the wall, a black crow is standing, very still. I could reach out and touch this gorgeous bird of mystery and magic and I want to pick it up, however, I am afraid. I come very close to it. Waiting for me, it never moves.

As I throw water from a small bottle into the pool, I hear my friends laughing at me gently, “So much poetry in her head.” I am agreeing and laughing along with them while getting a big pitcher of water to throw in the pool. I am adding to infinity. I am expanding. In this dream, the sense of space is huge, like a vast art installation. It is clear in this dream that I can have my life as big as the ocean. It is clear in this realm that the secret magic of creation is calling – the messengers of creativity, magic and spiritual strength are calling. The walls are here to scale, and the fire of creativity is always burning. We can have it all – all of us, all the time.

I wake up with a deep sense of beauty.

The crow is calling us to the magic of creation.

My friends are telling me...

A SHAMAN'S SONG

In beauty I walk. In beauty before me I walk.
In beauty behind me I walk. In beauty above me I walk.
In beauty all around me I walk. It is finished in beauty.
It is finished in beauty. It is finished in beauty.

THE TAO TE CHING

Seeing into darkness is clarity.
Knowing how to yield is strength.
Use your own light
and return to the light.
This is called practicing eternity.

Lao-tzu, Tao Te Ching, trans. Stephen Mitchell (New York: HarperCollins Publishers, 1988), 52.

"Beauty is truth, truth beauty,—that is all"

Keats, John. "Ode on a Grecian Urn." In The Oxford Anthology of English Poetry, edited by John Wain, (Oxford: Oxford University Press, 1986), 268-69.

THE BIRTH OF NAAMA

"I want her to be born in happiness." Her voice was different on the phone that day. She was tired so I didn't catch it at first. But emotion was always our strongpoint and I was expanding. My seams were opening.

"I want her to be born in happiness." I remember wondering how Dana knew such an idea . . . to be born in happiness. Astonishing. Revolutionary.

And I remember that day on the phone that I wasn't saying much and that my breathing had changed. It was as if I was hearing about the beginning of the world, the creation of the Universe. It was as if I was surrounded by the beginning of everything, and of time. There it was: a sense of eternity.

I didn't want to leave that space, I didn't want to stop being in this creation, I wanted to live in it. I sat stunned, wondering . . . who is this woman, my dearest friend, who knows it is time for us to learn the lessons of happiness.

She was calling for this in me and calling for this in all of us.

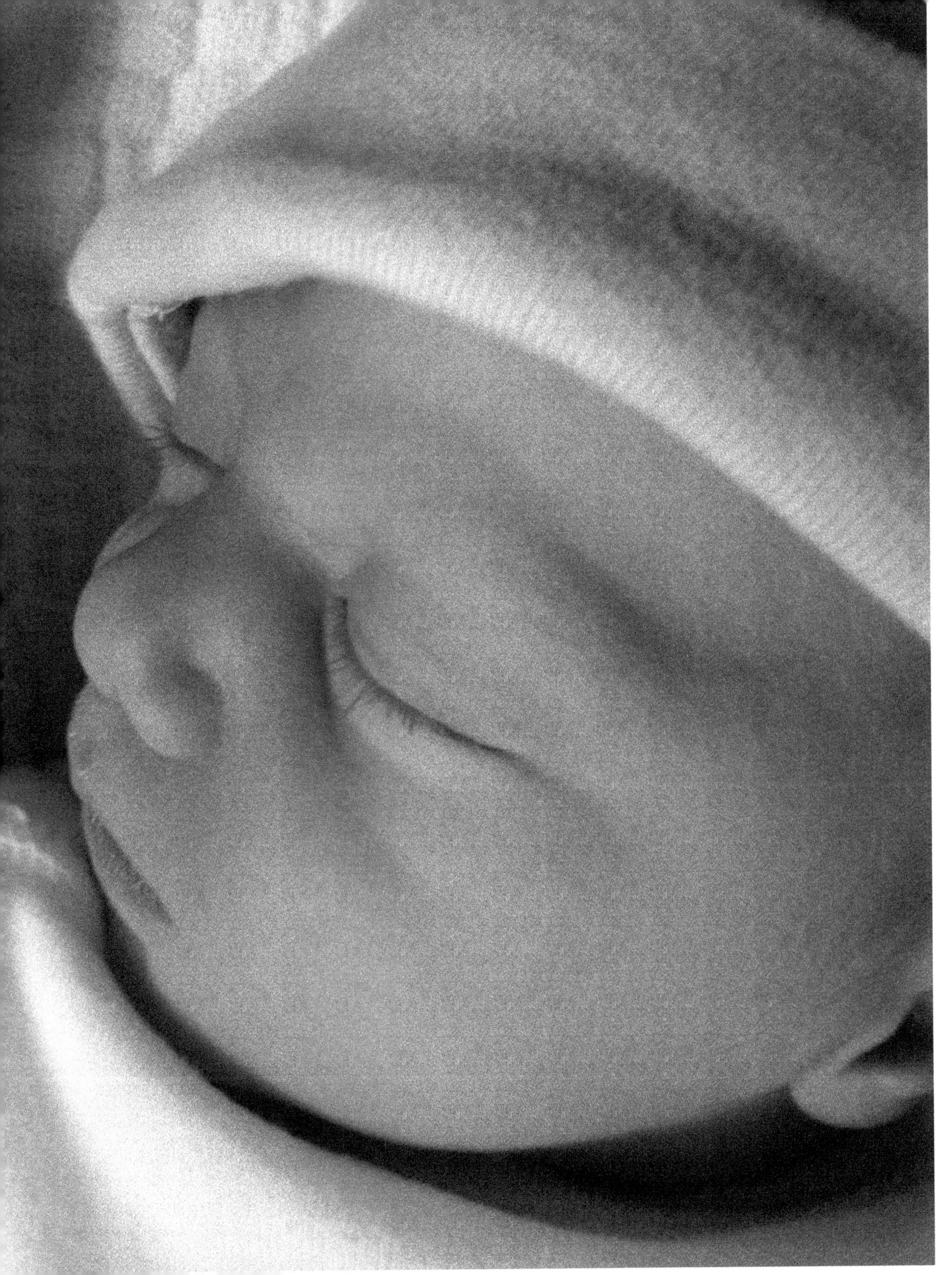

IN GRATITUDE

Breaking into Brilliance has had mid wives and whiz kids. Dana Parness dreamt this book into being and then lent me her magic. This book would not be the book it is, without the many parts Kelly Caldwell played in helping structure the entire work. As my project manager and creative consultant, Kelly lent me her exquisite attention, belief, beauty and her light. Blake Hackler for being there at the beginning and naming the 'attractions'.

Editors Rosemary Ahern and Diane O'Connell brought structure and clarity. Author and editor, Susan Lander, brought more beauty with her unerring eye and ear and a heartfelt Foreword. Jim Kennelly and Lotas Productions, for exquisite recording, editing and sound effects and the heart, ears and weight of your powerful support. Sadhna Sharma, my animator, a gentle spirit with big eyes for more beauty. Stephen Mitchell Brown, how did you ever put together the technology that has made this possible?

Lisa Prado for the refining of the title. Dolores Cotton, Leni Wolfenson and Smudge Studio for technical support, Diana Lab for original prints and Dominick Pietrzak for video. Lauren Lo Guidice, Tom Burke, Kevin Urban, Gary S. Duff and ErinYasgar for dragging me kicking and screaming into social media.

THANK YOU TO MY friends, healers, teachers, students and clients who have supported my alchemy, growth and art --- especially Fred Tumas, Jamie and Gary Brant, Choan Kim, Therese Tucker, Kalliope Koutelos, Jeannie Whyte, John Germain Leto, Carol Reynolds, Jeannette LoVetri.

And thank you to the many friends, students and collogues who have peeked at many versions of this and lent me their belief and their excitement.
Dedication is to my students who keep staying true to their heart and to the students I have yet to meet. To all the children, Sara, Jane, Elia, Naama, Romey, Celeste, Yasho, Maddie and Tristan.

In memory of my parents, Helen Kramer Singer, Lester E. Singer: please work with Breaking into Brilliance wherever you are. It will make our next earthly meeting so much easier.

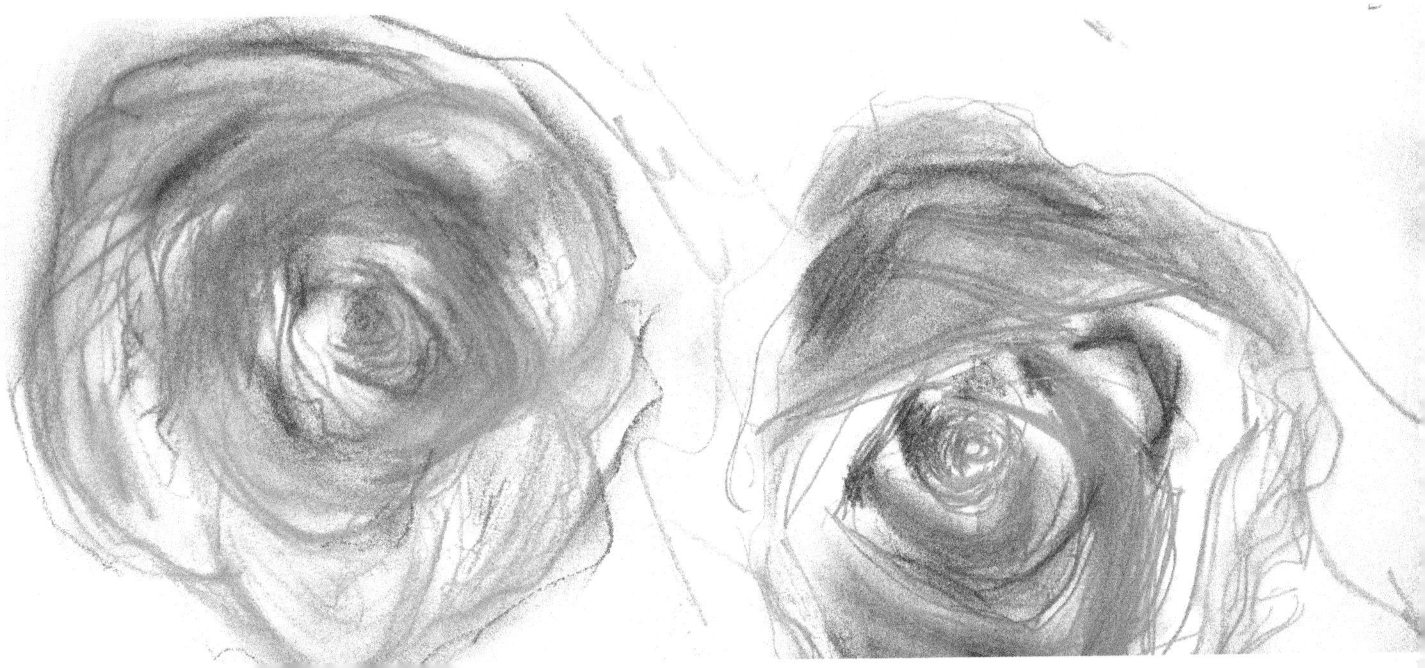

A NOTE FROM LYNN

I started my own process too fast. Under the influence of drugs I moved into chaos, in touch with unseen worlds. My third eye was open. I could see (psychically). I was in hell, suicidal. In the center of this storm, I claimed my heart‘s desire – the long suppressed desire to be on stage.

Many years and all kinds of alternate healing techniques were needed to integrate my body, mind and spirit. I sought a clairvoyant and a shaman. My task was huge and my resistance was strong.

A pivotal moment came at the ocean, when I heard a voice outside my own thoughts: “You’re going to be fine. It’s going to take some time."

In this new paradigm time is speeding up, and we can ask for things with greater ease. And with greater ease, we can find the endless, timeless being that we are.

THIS BOOK IS DEDICATED to all of my teachers and students who have brought me to this beginning, seeking, changing, transforming . . . and to the transformation in our world that is happening before our eyes.

Anyone who changes anything important in their lives always finds many demons on their journey. The process of change is not easy, but remember you are not alone.

I want a revolution – a revolution in our thoughts, in how we feel about ourselves, in how we embrace ourselves, our love, our power, our beauty and our peace in the universe.

It is a most extraordinary time to be alive.

Love, Light, Peace,

Lynn

ABOUT THE AUTHOR

Lynn Singer was born with a special voice and an ear for spoken language.

For over thirty years, she has helped people find their voice. She taught acting, speech and voice at Yale, NYU, The New School, Circle in the Square, The Actors and Directors Lab, the Gene Frankel Theater and at the T. Schreiber Studio in New York City. She works with a wide range of clients, from Tony, Emmy, Golden Globe, Pulitzer Prize and Fulbright winners, to Fortune 500 companies and top business and management executives.

Lynn has led training seminars at companies like Merrill Lynch Corporation and J. Walter Thompson. She has coached professional individuals (Goldman Sachs, Lehmann Bros, Deutsche Bank, Direct Energy, Inc., etc.) for business presentation and sales, and she has led workshops in New York, California, Florida, Japan and Spain for actors and business executives.

A well-known voice of radio and television commercials Lynn has appeared in Off-Broadway theater, on television and film. She holds a degree in English Literature from San Francisco State College and has completed post-graduate work in theater.

Reflecting on her experience teaching acting, voice and diction (which she still offers through her long established LS Voiceworks practice), Lynn recognized the path to her student's sustained success was in awakening their creative consciousness.

In her new book, Breaking into Brilliance, Lynn documents her own awakening while simultaneously guiding others through theirs. Lynn, now, also offers group, and private sessions for people who are interested in breaking into their brilliance. For more information, go to www.breakingintobrilliance.com.

BREAKING INTO BRILLIANCE

Awakening Creative Consciousnes

For many of her students, Lynn's legacy practice of voice coaching is the first step to unlocking their brilliance.....

> 'Lynn was the first person to illuminate for me the idea of training the voice to be a powerful and versatile instrument of character.'
>
> - Edward Norton, actor, filmmaker, activist

For more information or to work with Lynn directly, go to www.lynn-singer.com.

CPSIA information can be obtained
at www.ICGtesting.com
Printed in the USA
FSHW01n0933030518
47751FS

9 781389 698866